T0407770

STUDIES IN MEDIEVAL AND RENAISSANCE MUSIC 25

Composers in the Middle Ages

Studies in Medieval and Renaissance Music

ISSN 1479-9294

General Editors
Tess Knighton
Helen Deeming
Jared C. Hartt

This series aims to provide a forum for the best scholarship in early music; deliberately broad in scope, it welcomes proposals on any aspect of music, musical life, and composers during the period up to 1600, and particularly encourages work that places music in an historical and social context. Both new research and major re-assessments of central topics are encouraged.

Proposals or enquiries may be sent directly to the editor or the publisher at the addresses given below; all submissions will receive careful, informed consideration.

Professor Tess Knighton, Tknighton@icrea.cat

Professor Jared C. Hartt, Jared.hartt@oberlin.edu

Boydell & Brewer, PO Box 9, Woodbridge, Suffolk IP12 3DF,
editorial@boydell.co.uk

Previously published titles in the series are listed at the back of this volume.

Composers in the Middle Ages

Edited by

Anne-Zoé Rillon-Marne and Gaël Saint-Cricq

THE BOYDELL PRESS

First published 2024
The Boydell Press, Woodbridge

ISBN 978 1 83765 035 4

The Boydell Press is an imprint of Boydell & Brewer Ltd
PO Box 9, Woodbridge, Suffolk IP12 3DF, UK
and of Boydell & Brewer Inc.
668 Mt Hope Avenue, Rochester, NY 14620–2731, USA
website: www.boydellandbrewer.com

A CIP catalogue record for this title is available
from the British Library

The publisher has no responsibility for the continued existence or accuracy of URLs for
external or third-party internet websites referred to in this book, and does not guarantee
that any content on such websites is, or will remain, accurate or appropriate

Contents

Illustrations

Figures

Facere, Componere, Invenire: Reassembling the Composer in the Long Thirteenth Century, *Mark Everist*

W. de Wicumbe as a Composer of Alleluya Rondelli, *Karen Desmond*

The editors, contributors, and publisher are grateful to all the institutions and persons listed for permission to reproduce the materials in which they hold copyright.
Every effort has been made to trace the copyright holders; apologies are offered for
any omission, and the publisher will be pleased to add any necessary acknowledgement in subsequent editions.

Musical Examples

Tables

Contributors

Margaret Bent, Emeritus Fellow at All Souls College, Oxford

Catherine A. Bradley, Associate Professor in Early Music at the University of Cambridge and Fellow of St John's College

Charles E. Brewer, Professor of Musicology at Florida State University

Karen Desmond, Professor of Music at Maynooth University

Brianne Dolce, Educational Policy Advisor at Leiden University

Estelle Doudet, Professor of Literature at the Université de Lausanne

Mark Everist, Professor of Music at the University of Southampton

Manon Louviot, Post-doctoral researcher at the University of Oslo

Henry Parkes, Associate Professor of Music at the University of Nottingham

Yolanda Plumley, Professor of Historic Musicology, emeritus, at the University of Exeter

Anne-Zoé Rillon-Marne, Associate Professor of Musicology at the Université catholique de l'Ouest (Angers)

Gaël Saint-Cricq, Professor of Musicology at the Université Lumière Lyon 2

Alison Stones, Professor Emerita of History of Art and Architecture at the University of Pittsburgh

Anna Zayaruznaya, Associate Professor of Music at Yale University

Acknowledgements

We are very grateful to the various colleagues and friends who have helped us lavishly throughout this long-term project around the medieval composer, from the conference *Composer(s) in the Middle Ages* held at the Université de Rouen in May 2019 to the final stages of the making of this volume.

We are thankful to Eglal Doss-Quinby, Catherine A. Bradley, and Jared C. Hartt for their help in preparing the project. We are enormously grateful for the generous scientific and/or linguistic assistance and advice of Antonio Sordillo, Maï Le Gallic, Mark Everist, Yolanda Plumley, William McKenzie, Mary Channen Caldwell, the anonymous reviewers of the project and the book, and of the various colleagues who helped the contributors shape their chapters. We are thankful to Caroline Palmer and Laura Bennetts for their unstinting editorial support and to the general editors of the book series in which this volume appears, Tess Knighton and Helen Deeming.

Our deepest gratitude naturally goes to the contributors to this book: may they be thanked for their trust and patience and for the many exchanges that have continually nourished this volume.

Finally, our grateful and friendly thoughts go to Nigel Wilkins, our first guide around the world of medieval music.

Abbreviations

Cited Manuscripts

Aachen, Stadtbibl., Beis E14	Aachen, Stadtbibliothek, MS Beis E14
Albi, Méd. Amalric 26	Albi, Médiathèque Pierre-Amalric, MS 26 (*olim* 9)
Aosta, Sem. mag. 15	Aosta, Seminario maggiore, MS 15
Apt, Trésor 16bis	Apt, Musée Trésor de la Cathédrale Sainte-Anne, 16, Ms. 16bis
Arras, MM 290	Arras, Médiathèque municipale, Ms. 290
Arras, MM 316	Arras, Médiathèque municipale, Ms. 316
Arras, MM 424	Arras, Médiathèque municipale, Ms. 424
Arras, MM 1088	Arras, Médiathèque municipale, Ms. 1088
Bamberg, Staatsbibl., Lit.1	Bamberg, Staatsbibliothek, Msc. Lit. 1
Bamberg, Staatsbibl., Lit. 115	Bamberg, Staatsbibliothek, Msc. Lit. 115 (*olim* Ed.IV.06)
Bern, Burgerbibl., A 35	Bern, Burgerbibliothek, Cod. A 35
Besançon, BM, I, 716	Besançon, Bibliothèque municipale, Ms. I, 716
Bologna, Q.15	Bologna, Museo Internazionale e Biblioteca della Musica di Bologna, MS Q.15
Bologna, Q.16	Bologna, Museo Internazionale e Biblioteca della Musica di Bologna, MS Q.16
Boulogne-sur-Mer, BM 117	Boulogne-sur-Mer, Bibliothèque municipale des Annonciades, Ms. 117

Brussels, KBR 4	Brussels, Bibliothèque royale de Belgique, Ms. 4
Brussels, KBR 79	Brussels, Bibliothèque royale de Belgique, Ms. 79
Brussels, KBR 118	Brussels, Bibliothèque royale de Belgique, Ms. 118
Brussels, KBR 456–57	Brussels, Bibliothèque royale de Belgique, Ms. 456–57
Brussels, KBR 4783	Brussels, Bibliothèque royale de Belgique, Ms. 4783
Brussels, KBR 13076–77	Brussels, Bibliothèque royale de Belgique, Ms. 13076–77
Brussels, KBR 19606	Brussels, Bibliothèque royale de Belgique, Ms. 19606
Brussels, KBR 21532–5	Brussels, Bibliothèque royale de Belgique, Ms. 21532–5
Brussels, KBR IV 119	Brussels, Bibliothèque royale de Belgique, Ms. IV 119
Brussels, KBR IV 453	Brussels, Bibliothèque royale de Belgique, Ms. IV 453
Budapest, OSK, MNy 79	Budapest, Országos Széchényi-Könyvtár, MNy 79
Burgos, Las Huelgas, s/n	Burgos, Monasterio de las Huelgas, s/n
Cambrai, Le Labo 133	Cambrai, Le Labo, Ms. 133
Cambrai, Le Labo, B 1328	Cambrai, Le Labo, Ms. B 1328
Cambridge, CCC 410	Cambridge, Corpus Christi College, MS 410
Cambridge, Fitzwilliam 192	Cambridge, Fitzwilliam Museum, MS 192
Cambridge, Fitzwilliam 368	Cambridge, Fitzwilliam Museum, MS 368
Cambridge, GCC 408/414	Cambridge, Gonville and Caius College, Ms. 408/414
Cambridge, Jesus College, QB1	Cambridge, Jesus College, MS QB1
Cambridge, TCL, R.3.20	Cambridge, Trinity College Library, MS R.3.20

Carpentras, Bibl. inguimbertine 411	Carpentras, Bibliothèque inguimbertine, Ms. 411
Chantilly, Bibl. Château 564	Chantilly, Bibliothèque et Archives du Château, Ms. 564
Chicago, Newberry Lib., Case 54.1	Chicago, Newberry Library, Case MS 54.1
Codex Calixtinus	Santiago de Compostela, Archivo-Biblioteca de la Catedral, Codex Calixtinus
Cologny, Bodmer 127	Cologny, Fondation Martin Bodmer, Cod. Bodmer 127
Copenhagen, DKB 291, 8°	Copenhagen, Det Kongelige Bibliotek, MS Thott 291, 8°
Copenhagen, DKB 1810 4°	Copenhagen, Det Kongelige Bibliotek, 1810 4°
Darmstadt, ULB 397	Darmstadt, Universitäts- und Landesbibliothek, Hs. 397
Dendermonde, SPP, Cod. 9	Dendermonde, Sint-Pieters- en Paulusabdij, MS Cod. 9
Dijon, BM 517	Dijon, Bibliothèque municipale, Ms. 517
Douai, Bibl. Desbordes-Valmore 1105/3 fragment 74.4/1	Douai, Bibliothèque Marceline Desbordes-Valmore, MS 1105/3 fragment 74.4/1
Douai, BM 340	Douai, Bibliothèque municipale, Ms. 340
Évreux, BM 2	Évreux, Bibliothèque-Médiathèque, MS 2
Évreux, BM 39	Évreux, Bibliothèque-Médiathèque, MS 39
Florence, Arch. di San Lorenzo 2211	Florence, Archivio del Capitolo di San Lorenzo, MS 2211
Florence, BML, Ashburnham 115	Florence, Biblioteca Medicea Laurenziana, Ashburnham 115
Florence, BML, Ashburnham 116	Florence, Biblioteca Medicea Laurenziana, Ashburnham 116

Florence, BML, Mediceo Palatino 87	Florence, Biblioteca Medicea Laurenziana, Cod. Mediceo Palatino 87
Florence, BML, Plut. 29.1	Florence, Biblioteca Medicea Laurenziana, Pluteus 29.1
Florence, Bnc, Panciatichiano 26	Florence, Biblioteca nazionale centrale, MS Panciatichiano 26
Gent, Univ. 233	Gent, Universiteitsbibliotheek, MS 233
Graz, Univ. 409	Graz, Universitätsbibliothek, Hs. 409
Heidelberg, Univ., Germ. 848	Heidelberg, Universitätsbibliothek, Cod. Pal. Germ. 848
Ivrea, Bibl. cap. 115	Ivrea, Biblioteca capitolare, MS. CXV (115)
Karlsruhe, BLB, Cod. Aug. perg. 36	Karlsruhe, Badische Landesbibliothek, Cod. Aug. perg. 36
Karlsruhe, BLB, Cod. Aug. perg. 60	Karlsruhe, Badische Landesbibliothek, Cod. Aug. perg. 60
Karlsruhe, BLB, Cod. Licht. 82, flyleaf	Karlsruhe, Badische Landesbibliothek, Codex Lichtenthal 82, flyleaf
Kortrijk, Stadsbibl., Goethals-Vercruysse 135	Kortrijk, Stadsbibliotheek, Fonds Goethals-Vercruysse, MS 135
Leuven, Alamire Foundation 1	Leuven, Alamire Foundation, MS 1
Lille, MM 366	Lille, Médiathèque municipale Jean Lévy, Ms. 366
London, BL, Add. 17302	London, British Library, Additional MS 17302
London, BL, Add. 29987	London, British Library, Additional MS 29987
London, BL, Add. 36881	London, British Library, Additional MS 36881
London, BL, Add. 54180	London, British Library, Additional MS 54180
London, BL, Add. 57950	London, British Library, Additional MS 57950
London, BL, Cotton Claudius B VI	London, British Library, MS Cotton Claudius B VI

London, BL, Cotton Claudius C IX	London, British Library, MS Cotton Claudius C IX
London, BL, Egerton 274	London, British Library, Egerton MS 274
London, BL, Harley 978	London, British Library, Harley MS 978
London, BL, Lansdowne 763	London, British Library, Lansdowne MS 763
London, Westminster 21	London, Westminster Abbey, Chapter House, MS 21
Lucca, Arch. di Stato 184	Lucca, Archivio di Stato, MS 184
Machaut Vg	Kansas City, private collection of James E. and Elizabeth J. Ferrel (Machaut manuscript)
Madrid, BNE 20486	Madrid, Biblioteca Nacional de España, Mss/20486
Modena, Bibl. Est., α.M.5.24	Modena, Biblioteca Estense, MS α.M.5.24
Montecassino, BA, Cod. 318	Montecassino, Biblioteca dell'Abbazia, Cod. 318
Montpellier, BIU, H 196	Montpellier, Bibliothèque interuniversitaire, Section Médecine, H 196
Monza, S. Giovanni, Cod. 88	Monza, Tesoro della Basilica S. Giovanni, Cod. 88
Munich, BSB, Cgm 716	Munich, Bayerische Staatsbibliothek, Cgm 716
Munich, BSB, Clm 4660/4660a	Munich, Bayerische Staatsbibliothek, Clm 4660/4660a
Munich, BSB, Clm 14094	Munich, Bayerische Staatsbibliothek, Clm 14094
Munich, BSB, Clm 14274	Munich, Bayerische Staatsbibliothek, Clm 14274
Münster, ULB 382	Münster, Universitäts- und Landesbibliothek, Hs. 382
Namur, MA 104	Namur, Musée Archéologique, ms. 104

New Haven, Beinecke 91	New Haven, Yale University Library, Beinecke MS 91
New York, Morgan, G.24	New York, Morgan Library & Museum, MS G.24
Ostiglia, Bibl. mus. Greggiati, s.s.	Ostiglia, Biblioteca musicale Greggiati, s.s.
Oxford, Bod. Lib., Add. 44	Oxford, Bodleian Library, MS. Additional 44
Oxford, Bod. Lib., Bodl. 125	Oxford, Bodleian Library, MS. Bodley 125
Oxford, Bod. Lib., Bodl. 264	Oxford, Bodleian Library, MS. Bodley 264
Oxford, Bod. Lib., Bodl. 717	Oxford, Bodleian Library, MS. Bodley 717
Oxford, Bod. Lib., Canon. Class. Lat. 112	Oxford, Bodleian Library, MS. Canon. Class. Lat. 112
Oxford, Bod. Lib., Canon. Misc. 213	Oxford, Bodleian Library, MS. Canon. Misc. 213
Oxford, Bod. Lib., Lat. liturg. b.19	Oxford, Bodleian Library, MS. Lat. liturg. b.19
Oxford, Bod. Lib., Rawl. C.400*	Oxford, Bodleian Library, MS. Rawlinson C.400*
Oxford, Bod. Lib., Rawl. C.510	Oxford, Bodleian Library, MS. Rawlinson C.510
Oxford, New College 3–6	Oxford, New College, MS 3–6
Oxford, New College 362	Oxford, New College, MS 362
Paris, Arsenal 5059	Paris, Bibliothèque de l'Arsenal, MS 5059
Paris, Arsenal 5218	Paris, Bibliothèque de l'Arsenal, MS 5218
Paris, BnF, fr. 122	Paris, Bibliothèque nationale de France, fonds français 122
Paris, BnF, fr. 146	Paris, Bibliothèque nationale de France, fonds français 146
Paris, BnF, fr. 160	Paris, Bibliothèque nationale de France, fonds français 160

Paris, BnF, fr. 819–820	Paris, Bibliothèque nationale de France, fonds français 819–820
Paris, BnF, fr. 844	Paris, Bibliothèque nationale de France, fonds français 844
Paris, BnF, fr. 1433	Paris, Bibliothèque nationale de France, fonds français 1433
Paris, BnF, fr. 1584	Paris, Bibliothèque nationale de France, fonds français 1584
Paris, BnF, fr. 1586	Paris, Bibliothèque nationale de France, fonds français 1586
Paris, BnF, fr. 1591	Paris, Bibliothèque nationale de France, fonds français 1591
Paris, BnF, fr. 1597	Paris, Bibliothèque nationale de France, fonds français 1597
Paris, BnF, fr. 1635	Paris, Bibliothèque nationale de France, fonds français 1635
Paris, BnF, fr. 8541	Paris, Bibliothèque nationale de France, fonds français 8541
Paris, BnF, fr. 12476	Paris, Bibliothèque nationale de France, fonds français 12476
Paris, BnF, fr. 12615	Paris, Bibliothèque nationale de France, fonds français 12615
Paris, BnF, fr. 12786	Paris, Bibliothèque nationale de France, fonds français 12786
Paris, BnF, fr. 15123	Paris, Bibliothèque nationale de France, fonds français 15123
Paris, BnF, fr. 20050	Paris, Bibliothèque nationale de France, fonds français 20050
Paris, BnF, fr. 24332	Paris, Bibliothèque nationale de France, fonds français 24332
Paris, BnF, fr. 24333	Paris, Bibliothèque nationale de France, fonds français 24333
Paris, BnF, fr. 24341	Paris, Bibliothèque nationale de France, fonds français 24341
Paris, BnF, fr. 25547	Paris, Bibliothèque nationale de France, fonds français 25547

Paris, BnF, fr. 25566	Paris, Bibliothèque nationale de France, fonds français 25566
Paris, BnF, it. 568	Paris, Bibliothèque nationale de France, fonds italien 568
Paris, BnF, lat. 1023	Paris, Bibliothèque nationale de France, fonds latin 1023
Paris, BnF, lat. 2415	Paris, Bibliothèque nationale de France, fonds latin 2415
Paris, BnF, lat. 3639	Paris, Bibliothèque nationale de France, fonds latin 3639
Paris, BnF, lat. 4880	Paris, Bibliothèque nationale de France, fonds latin 4880
Paris, BnF, lat. 5268	Paris, Bibliothèque nationale de France, fonds latin 5268
Paris, BnF, lat. 10972	Paris, Bibliothèque nationale de France, fonds latin 10972
Paris, BnF, lat. 11935	Paris, Bibliothèque nationale de France, fonds latin 11935
Paris, BnF, lat. 13575	Paris, Bibliothèque nationale de France, fonds latin 13575
Paris, BnF, lat. 15128	Paris, Bibliothèque nationale de France, fonds latin 15128
Paris, BnF, lat. 15139	Paris, Bibliothèque nationale de France, fonds latin 15139
Paris, BnF, lat. 15163	Paris, Bibliothèque nationale de France, fonds latin 15163
Paris, BnF, lat. 17737	Paris, Bibliothèque nationale de France, fonds latin 17737
Paris, BnF, mus. Rés. Vmc 57	Paris, Bibliothèque nationale de France, Département de la musique, Rés. Vmc ms. 57
Paris, BnF, n.a.f. 1051	Paris, Bibliothèque nationale de France, nouvelles acquisitions françaises 1051
Paris, BnF, n.a.f. 1261	Paris, Bibliothèque nationale de France, nouvelles acquisitions françaises 1261
Paris, BnF, n.a.f. 1445	Paris, Bibliothèque nationale de France, nouvelles acquisitions françaises 1445

Paris, BnF, n.a.f. 1789	Paris, Bibliothèque nationale de France, nouvelles acquisitions françaises 1789
Paris, BnF, n.a.f. 6221	Paris, Bibliothèque nationale de France, nouvelles acquisitions françaises 6221
Paris, BnF, n.a.f. 6514	Paris, Bibliothèque nationale de France, nouvelles acquisitions françaises 6514
Paris, BnF, n.a.f. 13521	Paris, Bibliothèque nationale de France, nouvelles acquisitions françaises 13521
Paris, BnF, n.a.f. 23190	Paris, Bibliothèque nationale de France, nouvelles acquisitions françaises 23190
Paris, BnF, n.a.l. 3126	Paris, Bibliothèque nationale de France, nouvelles acquisitions latines 3126
Paris, BnF, Rothschild 2973	Paris, Bibliothèque nationale de France, Rothschild 2973 (979a)
Paris, Bibl. Mazarine 1002	Paris, Bibliothèque Mazarine, MS 1002 (942)
Paris, Bibl. Sainte-Geneviève 98	Paris, Bibliothèque Sainte-Geneviève, Ms. 98
Périgueux, MAAP, B. 1721	Périgueux, Musée d'Art et d'Archéologie du Périgord, inv. B. 1721
Perugia, Bibl. com. Aug. 3065	Perugia, Biblioteca comunale Augusta, MS 3065
Philadelphia, FLP, Lewis E 39	Philadelphia, Free Library of Philadelphia, Lewis E 39
Philadelphia, Univ. of Pennsylvania, Codex 902	Philadelphia, University of Pennsylvania, Rare Book & Manuscript Library, Ms. Codex 902
Prague, Národní knihovna XII D 8a	Prague, Národní knihovna České republiky, rkp. XII D 8a
Princeton, UL, Garrett 119, frag. A	Princeton, University Library, Garrett MS. 119, fragment A
Rome, Bibl. Casanatense 2856	Rome, Biblioteca Casanatense, MS 2856
Rouen, BM 364	Rouen, Bibliothèque municipale, Ms. 364 (*olim* O.68)

Rouen, BM 666	Rouen, Bibliothèque municipale, Ms. 666 (*olim* A 506)
Rouen, BM 1050	Rouen, Bibliothèque municipale, Ms. 1050
Saint-Omer, BA 112	Saint-Omer, Bibliothèque d'agglomération, Ms. 112
Siena, Arch. di Stato, Framm. Mus. busta n.1, ins. n. 11	Siena, Archivio di Stato, Frammenti Musicali busta n. 1, ins. n. 11 (*olim* 207, *olim* 326–327)
St Gallen, Stiftsbibl., Cod. Sang. 339	St Gallen, Stiftsbibliothek, Cod. Sang. 339
St Gallen, Stiftsbibl., Cod. Sang. 390–391	St Gallen, Stiftsbibliothek, Cod. Sang. 390–391
Seville, Bibl. Col. 5-2-25	Seville, Biblioteca Colombina, MS 5-2-25
Strasbourg, BM 222 C.22	Strasbourg, Bibliothèque municipale, MS 222 C.22 (destroyed 1871)
Tournai, Bibl. ville 101	Tournai, Bibliothèque de la ville, Ms. 101
Tours, BM 558	Tours, Bibliothèque municipale, Ms. 558
Trent, Cast. Buonconsiglio 1379 [92]	Trent, Castello del Buonconsiglio, Monumenti e Collezioni Provinciali, MS 1379 [92]
Trier, Stadtbibl. 261-1140 2°	Trier, Stadtbibliothek Hs. 261-1140 2°
Troyes, MGT 1148	Troyes, Médiathèque du Grand Troyes, Ms. 1148
Troyes, MGT 1471	Troyes, Médiathèque du Grand Troyes, Ms. 1471
Turin, Bnu, E.V.20	Turin, Biblioteca nazionale universitaria, MS E.V.20
Turin, Bnu, J.II.9	Turin, Biblioteca nazionale universitaria, MS J.II.9
Turin, BR, varia 42	Turin, Biblioteca Reale, MS varia 42
Vatican, BAV, Chigi C.VIII.234	Vatican, Biblioteca Apostolica Vaticana, MS Chigi C.VIII.234
Vatican, BAV, Reg. lat. 1490	Vatican, Biblioteca Apostolica Vaticana, Reg. lat. 1490

Vatican, BAV, Rossi 215	Vatican, Biblioteca Apostolica Vaticana, MS Rossi 215
Vercelli, Bibl. Agnesiana 11	Vercelli, Biblioteca Agnesiana, MS 11
Vorau, BAC 23 (Frag. 118D)	Vorau, Bibliothek des Augustiner Chorherrenstifts, 23 (Fragment 118D)
Warsaw, Bibl. Narodowa III. 8054	Warsaw, Biblioteka Narodowa, MS III. 8054
Warsaw, Bibl. Narodowa, Lat. F. I. 378	Warsaw, Biblioteka Narodowa, MS Lat. F. I. 378 (lost, extant photographs in Poznań)
Washington, LoC, De Ricci 127	Washington, Library of Congress, De Ricci 127
Washington, LoC, M2.1 C6 1400 Case	Washington, Library of Congress, MS M2.1 C6 1400 Case
Washington, LoC, M2.1 L25 Case	Washington, Library of Congress, MS M2.1 L25 Case
Wellesley, WCSC, P858	Wellesley, Wellesley College Special Collections, P858
Wiesbaden, HLB 2	Wiesbaden, Hochschul- und Landesbibliothek RheinMain, Hs. 2
Wolfenbüttel, HAB, Cod. Guelf. 9 Blankenburg	Wolfenbüttel, Herzog-August-Bibliothek, Cod. Guelf. 9 Blankenburg
Wolfenbüttel, HAB, Cod. Guelf. 287 Extrav.	Wolfenbüttel, Herzog-August-Bibliothek, Cod. Guelf. 287 Extrav.
Wolfenbüttel, HAB, Cod. Guelf. 334 Gud. lat.	Wolfenbüttel, Herzog-August-Bibliothek, Cod. Guelf. 334 Gud. lat.
Wolfenbüttel, HAB, Cod. Guelf. 628 Helmst.	Wolfenbüttel, Herzog-August-Bibliothek, Cod. Guelf. 628 Helmst.
Wolfenbüttel, HAB, Cod. Guelf. 1099 Helmst.	Wolfenbüttel, Herzog-August-Bibliothek, Cod. Guelf. 1099 Helmst.
Worcester, CL, Add. 68, frag. xxxv	Worcester, Cathedral Library, Add. 68, frag. xxxv
Worcester, CL, Add. 68, frag. xxviii	Worcester, Cathedral Library, Add. 68, frag. xxviii

Other Abbreviations

ACA	Archivo de la Corona de Aragón
AdN	Lille, Archives départementales du Nord
AdPC	Arras, Archives départementales du Pas-de-Calais
AGH	Archief van de Graven van Holland
AH	Analecta Hymnica
BAC	Barcelona, Archivo de la Catedral
BnF	Bibliothèque nationale de France
CAO	Corpus Antiphonalium Officii
CNRTL	Centre National de Ressources Textuelles et Lexicales (https://www.cnrtl.fr/)
CS	Edmond de Coussemaker, *Scriptorum de musica medii aevi.*
DIAMM	Digital Image Archive of Medieval Music (https://www.diamm.ac.uk)
GR	Gent Rijkarchief
IRHT	Institut de Recherche et d'Histoire des Textes
L	Long
MGH	Monumenta Germaniae Historica
PAn	Paris, Archives nationales
PL	Patrologia Latina
RS	Song text as catalogued in Spanke 1955
USTC	Universal Short Title Catalogue (https://www.ustc.ac.uk/)
WF	Worcester Fragments as catalogued in Dittmer 1957

Introduction: From Composer to Composers[1]

Gaël Saint-Cricq, with Anne-Zoé Rillon-Marne

The Great Medieval Composer

The Canon of the 'Great Composer'

In the influential *Oxford Companion to Music*, written by Percy Scholes in 1938 and republished a dozen times before being replaced only in 1983, fourteen plates comprising a series of portraits of 'great masters', from Bach to Elgar, via Schumann and Wagner, provide a guide to reading the hundreds of articles in the volume.[2] These portraits, specially designed for the book, are signed by the artist Oswald Barrett who, Scholes tells us in his preface, wanted to 'penetrate to the mind of the character represented and express his personality'.[3] The first of these portraits, the frontispiece of the opus, is that of Beethoven: in a tense, concentrated pose, the solitary composer stares into the distance with an unearthly, tormented, bluish gaze, illuminating a head that is slightly oversized in relation to the body. This oil portrait and the gallery of 'great masters' that it inaugurates perfectly encapsulate the canon of the 'great composer' as it culminated in the nineteenth and twentieth centuries, in which the history of music is embodied by exceptional individuals, and the creative act conceived as the culmination of the mental and psychological process of a remarkable and inspired personality. The article 'composition' in the same dictionary is a case in point.[4] Composition is described as the fruit of the composer's 'inspiration', itself defined as a 'thing given … a strong and definite mood, which possesses [the composers] and which they thereupon, under a feeling of compulsion, proceed to express in music', and to which composers give form through their 'inventiveness'. But it is the notion of originality that unquestionably prevails in the creative process of the composer outlined by the article; this is measured both by 'a strong expression of personality allied to a high degree of craftmanship' and by an 'actual novelty in melody, harmony, form, orchestration, etc.'. Many examples of innovations considered important in the history of

---

[1] This text was translated from French by Mark Everist and benefited from revisions and rewarding comments by Yolanda Plumley. The editors are profoundly grateful for their very generous assistance and friendly support. They are also deeply thankful to Mary Channen Caldwell for her careful proofreading of the final version of this text.

[2] Scholes rev. Ward (ed.) 1970. The dictionary, written entirely by Scholes, was reprinted ten times between 1938 and 1970, the last two times with slight revisions. It was replaced by the *New Oxford Companion to Music* edited by Denis Arnold in 1983.

[3] Scholes rev. Ward (ed.) 1970, p. xiii.

[4] Scholes rev. Ward (ed.) 1970, pp. 218–27.

music are listed by Scholes: the new recitative style of Caccini and Peri, Field and his invention of the piano nocturne, Wagner and his leitmotif, Debussy and impressionist music, and so on. In this long list of feats by which the great composer personifies a style, a genre, a technique, or a current, the Middle Ages of course struggle to find their place. Nonetheless, the era is mentioned in the examples of the 'first man to employ Organum' and 'Dunstable … in his introduction of new contrapuntal devices'. There is only one other implicit mention of the Middle Ages when, in his introduction, Scholes immediately excludes from the scope of his article – and therefore from the field of composition as he understands it – most of the output of earlier periods, since, he asserts, 'musical composition [was] entirely melodic and probably [was] far more instinctive than reasoned'.

Although medieval music is largely excluded from the field of composition in Scholes's article and volume (only polyphonists such as Adam de la Halle, Perotinus, and Guillaume de Machaut are honoured with entries), the post-Enlightenment canon of great composers was, on the other hand, to have a decisive influence on, and repercussions for, the way that histories of music approached the medieval period and its composers throughout the nineteenth and a significant part of the twentieth centuries. But the construction of the figure of the great composer was not exclusive to this period. It began to take shape at the end of the Middle Ages, through authors' manuscripts or collections (sometimes arranged in such a way as to offer a narrative of the composer's work), through biographical self-allusions in the texts of the works themselves or by means of musical or textual (self-)quotations, laments, (self-)representations in iconography, or even authors' signatures printed in the works themselves.[5] The Renaissance continued to scaffold the persona of the great author, by fabricating mythical figures and forging a historical narrative into which were woven genealogies of great composers, some of whom personified a style or a period.[6] But at the very moment, in the nineteenth century, when a historical science of music emerged and large sections of medieval musical repertoires were discovered, it was naturally the post-Enlightenment canon of the great composer and the notion of individual creation that guided the approach to composers of the Middle Ages, in a discourse that remained influential throughout most of the twentieth century.

5   On the well-known case of Adam de la Halle's construction of authority through authorial manuscript, biographical self-allusion, or self-citation, see the various contributions in Saltzstein (ed.) 2019, especially Haines 2019. See Leach 2011, chap. 3, on Machaut's construction of the authorial figure. On various means of constructing the authority and *persona* of the composer in the Middle Ages, see the chapters by Louviot and Bradley in this volume.

6   On the tendency to draw up lists and genealogies of composers in the Renaissance and to insert them into a narrative of styles, see the contributions by Parkes and Bent in this volume as well as Wegman 1996. A well-known example of the 'mythologisation' of composers is that of Josquin Des Prez, through the numerous laments on his death or his incarnation of the *Ars perfecta* in Heinrich Glarean's *Dodekachordon*.

The Medieval 'Great Composer' in the Nineteenth and Twentieth Centuries

The crucible of the great medieval composer naturally began with a search, in the manner of Barrett's illustrations scattered throughout Scholes's dictionary, for a gallery of composers capable of ordering and personifying the history of medieval music. The first portrait to hang there was probably that of Adam de la Halle by the hands of François-Joseph Fétis and Edmond de Coussemaker in the nineteenth century.[7] At a time when only a few meagre examples of medieval polyphony were in circulation – all that was essentially known of the musical Middle Ages was the 'primitive'[8] monodic repertoire of plainchant and the chansons of the trouvères[9] – the rediscovery of the manuscript Paris, BnF, fr. 25566 enabled Fétis in 1827 to bring to light an important polyphonic corpus and also to assign it to a real composer: Adam de la Halle.[10] The discovery of Adam's polyphonic work was experienced, with some relief, as the discovery of the origin – hitherto elusive – of the contemporary 'harmonic' language legible to Fétis or Coussemaker, and from then on, Adam became a crucial figure in the history of music: he was the missing link between the first organa and the polyphony of the fifteenth century; through the versatility of his work, he also represented a bridge between the monody of the trouvères and polyphonic composition. The first composer to 'combine the talents … of melodist and dechanteur',[11] 'musician-melodist and harmonist',[12] Adam's entry into the pleiad of great composers was assured by Coussemaker. Enthroned as the first trouvère to compose polyphonically and identified as one of the authors of the motets in the Montpellier, BIU, H 196,[13] Adam, finally, was the first medieval composer to receive a complete musical and literary edition in his own name in 1872, with critical notes and a vast introduction in which the great author's topics emerge to evoke his creative activity ('imagination', 'full and complete freedom', 'multiple, elegant and fertile genius').[14] Clearly, for both Coussemaker and Fétis, Adam's entry ticket into the pantheon of great composers was validated by his polyphonic music; and the need to be a polyphonist in order to be admitted to the rank of composer would remain implicit in the musicography of the twentieth century – as Scholes's essay illustrates. Faced with the paucity of attributions, composer names, and information on composers in medieval sources, musicographers and musicologists obviously encountered

---

[7]   For an excellent account of the recuperation of Adam's polyphonic works in the nineteenth century, see Haines 2004, pp. 165–78.

[8]   In the words of Coussemaker 1865, p. vi.

[9]   See Haines 2004, chaps. 2 and 3, on the transmission and the study of the trouvère song from the sixteenth to the eighteenth century.

[10] Fétis 1827.

[11] Fétis 1837, p. cxciii.

[12] Coussemaker (ed.) 1872, p. vi.

[13] Coussemaker 1852, pp. 70–71; Coussemaker 1865, pp. 193–95.

[14] Coussemaker (ed.) 1872. The introduction appears at pp. xiii–lxxiv.

the challenge of linking further works (and especially polyphonic ones) to specific names: the historiographic construction of certain great figures, the propensity for rash attributions, and until the twentieth century, the tendency to inflate composers' works with uncertain or questionable attributions thus constituted means of satisfying the greed for names and works in the canon of the great composer.[15]

The musicographic discourse surrounding Adam de la Halle in the nineteenth century undoubtedly marks the beginning of the inclusion of medieval musicians in the canon of the post-Enlightenment composer, a narrative powered by several springs and cogs. The first step in the discourse of the great medieval composers includes a narrative of the history of music in the Middle Ages, read through the lens of the remarkable achievements and influence of some musicians. For Hugo Riemann, Adam's works 'are of capital importance for the musical history of his time',[16] while Friedrich Ludwig suspects Adam's motets are 'nothing less than the most important works of his time'[17] and Friedrich Gennrich suggests Adam 'indicated directions to be taken in periods following'.[18] In this way, the most important medieval figures were seen as emblematic of a given repertoire or style and thereby the embodiment of a particular period of musical development.[19] Beyond the medieval period, such composers become part of a teleological account of the history of music 'from its origins to the present day', embodying 'musical progress'. Thus, Adam de la Halle's first 'harmony' was also described, right up until the twentieth century, as the starting point of a historical continuum leading to modern music: suspected by Coussemaker of having 'given harmony a certain impetus', Adam's polyphonic rondeaux were recounted in 1942 by Jacques Chailley as crucial advances whose 'compositional freedom … was to be lost in the following centuries until

---

[15] An example of misleading attributions is that of seventeen polyphonic pieces in Montpellier, BIU, H 196, which are attributed to thirteen names of 'trouvères harmonistes' in Coussemaker 1965 (pp. 180–208) on the basis of loose criteria (concordances, style, references contained in the texts, etc.). Other examples of misleading attributions are dealt with in Brewers's chapter in this volume on the *Planctus ante nescia*. An example of the tendency to inflate the works of composers by putative attributions are the fifteen or so clausulae attributed to Perotinus in Husmann (ed.) 1940, Waite 1961, Sanders 1967, and Thurston (ed.) 1970, in addition to the works already attributed to him by Anonymous IV. For the case of Petrus de Cruce, see the contributions by Everist and Bradley in this volume; for the musicological attributions to Philippe de Vitry, see the chapter by Zayaruznaya. A discussion of the historiographic construction of Gregory the Great's role in the composition of plainchant is in Henry Parkes's contribution to this volume.

[16] Riemann 1884, p. 8.

[17] Ludwig quoted in Gennrich 1949–51, p. 78.

[18] Gennrich (ed.) 1962, p. 4.

[19] Thus, the organa and clausulae of *Ars antiqua* polyphony and their innovations are entirely personified by Perotinus and Leoninus, among others in the introduction to Friedrich Ludwig's *Repertorium* (Ludwig (1910) 1978, vol. 1/1, pp. 1–6) and even more so by Théodore Gérold, who does not hesitate to attribute the *Magnus Liber Organi* to Leoninus in a dauntless shortcut (Gérold 1936, pp. 326–27). For historiographic reflections on the attachment of the *Ars nova* rhythmic system to the figure of Philippe de Vitry, see the chapter by Zayaruznaya in this volume.

these very last years'.[20] In this type of account, the great composers are singled out for their 'genius' and their role as 'precursors'[21] and are willingly invested with the most miraculous inventions. Perotinus, for example, was 'probably the first composer ever to write in as many as four parts', to have developed 'devices such as imitation, exchange of parts (*Stimmtausch*)'[22] and to have practically single-handedly invented the organum clausulae and the motet.[23] Adam de la Halle, too, is unambiguously referred to as a 'precursor of modern tonality' through his work as a composer of chansons.[24]

Such a discourse is naturally combined with discussion of the masterpiece, an indispensable attribute of the great composer since it is precisely this magnum opus that consolidates the composer's innovations and establishes his influence. It was thus 'with the *Messe* that Guillaume de Machaut rose to the rank of a truly great master',[25] and its status as a masterpiece no doubt goes some way to explaining the luxuriant proliferation of editions of this mass in the late 1940s and 1950s and typically hyperbolic discourses in their commentaries.[26] Indeed, the work is praised for its 'harmonic daring', the 'richness of its rhythmic combinations' and the use of 'genuine themes', which make it a 'work of synthesis intended by the master at the height of his talent';[27] it constitutes the 'most exceptional monument of the musical Middle Ages'[28] and the 'best-known of all mediaeval polyphonic works',[29] both crucial 'to the history of musical development' and to the narrative of a national musical history, as 'one of the monuments of French music'.[30]

As this last quotation reflects, another key feature of the discourse of the medieval 'great composer' is its inclusion in nationalist narratives in which the composer becomes a monument to a country, culture, language, or people. This discourse is first and foremost applied within the confines of medieval music. An example is *Les primitifs de la musique française* (The primitives of French music), published by Amédée Gastoué in 1922 in the collection 'Les musiciens célèbres' (Famous musicians), which is both symptomatic of the writing of a history of medieval music 'by characters' and of its inclusion in a narrative of medieval French music.[31] This type of narrative is conducive to the establishment of genealogies such as the one proposed by Armand Machabey in his biography of Machaut: 'following the path from

---

[20] Chailley 1942 (ed.), p. vi.

[21] Riemann 1884, p. 8 and Gennrich (ed.) 1962 (Vorwort), both about Adam de la Halle.

[22] Thurston (ed.) 1970, p. 1.

[23] Gérold 1936, p. 327; Gennrich (ed.) 1955, pp. vii–viii.

[24] Coussemaker (ed.) 1872, pp. lx–lxii.

[25] Gastoué 1922, p. 63.

[26] With no fewer than six editions in eight years: Chailley (ed.) 1948; Machabey (ed.) 1948; De Van (ed.) 1949; Besseler (ed.) 1954; Hübsch (ed.) 1953; Schrade (ed.) 1956, pp. 37–64.

[27] Chailley (ed.) 1948, pp. v–vii.

[28] Machabey 1955, vol. 2, p. 113.

[29] De Van (ed.) 1949, p. ii.

[30] Chailley (ed.) 1948, p. viii.

[31] Gastoué 1922.

Perotinus to the Rémois is not a task devoid of interest; it involves following step by step the evolution of French music in all its elements over one hundred and fifty years'.[32] Moreover, these lines of descent take place on a wider scale in the history of music: in the words of Chailley, Adam de la Halle is considered a direct precursor of Ravel and Debussy in a continuum that presents no less than the national narrative of a French style.[33] The narrative can occasionally be regional rather than national: Coussemaker and Chailley contextualise Adam's polyphonic and monodic work not only in the narrative of the 'great' history of music but also in the patrimonial narrative of the trouvères of northern France where, as Coussemaker asserts, his compositions 'became popular and are still sung today'.[34]

An important iron in the forge of the great medieval composer is recognition through the publication of editions of his works. Following in the footsteps of critical publishing in the field of musicology in general, with the Bach-Gesellschaft from 1850 onwards followed by the various *opera omnia* editions published by Breitkopf & Härtel, several medieval composers received the honour of a critical edition or author's anthology[35] and sometimes even several, as did Adam de la Halle in the four volumes of works devoted to him between 1872 and 1967.[36] More subtly, aside from *opera omnia* and anthologies of named composers, the importance attached to the notion of composer can determine the structure of an edition, even when attributions are lacking. For example, in an anthology of motets supposed to be representative of the genre, Gennrich makes a point of structuring his edition into two parts, first 'unattributed works' and then 'attributed works', even though the second section contains eight works and the first, forty-five.[37] In this type of historical anthology of medieval music, the importance of the composer and the attribution can also influence the choice of works selected.[38]

A final aspect contributing to the shaping of the great medieval composer lies in the celebration and canonisation of these figures in tributes in later musical compositions or in arrangement of their works for various ensembles and different levels of musical practice. The example of Perotinus and Leoninus is instructive in this respect.[39] Several compositions for organ from the 1970s pay tribute to them, including music for the Office,[40] and it is for this same instrument that three arrange-

---

[32] Machabey 1955, vol. 1, p. 161.

[33] Chailley (ed.) 1942, p. vi.

[34] Coussemaker (ed.) 1872, p. ix. See also Chailley (ed.) 1942, p. iv.

[35] In addition to Coussemaker's edition of Adam de la Halle, there is the complete edition of Adam of Saint Victor's sequences (Misset and Aubry (eds.) 1900) and Ludwig's complete edition of Machaut's works (Ludwig (ed.), 1926–29).

[36] Coussemaker (ed.) 1872; Chailley (ed.) 1942; Gennrich (ed.) 1962; Wilkins (ed.) 1967.

[37] Gennrich (ed.) 1966.

[38] Of the forty or so medieval pieces selected in Schering's florilegium (Schering (ed.) 1931), no fewer than twenty-five are attributed works.

[39] For the example of Machaut, see the exhaustive list of tributes and arrangements of his works in Earp 1995, pp. 69–72.

[40] Berthier 1970; Brandmüller 1979; Migot 1979. A tribute is also paid to Leoninus in a piece for two male voices from Charles Koechlin's *Quinze Motets de style archaïque*, composed

ments of Perotinus's work were made. The *Alleluya V Nativitas gloriose*, in fact, is the subject of three successive arrangements for organ: in 1939, then in 1957 published by the Schola Cantorum; and finally in 1942 in the collection 'Anthologie des Maîtres classiques de l'orgue' (An anthology of the great masters for organ), where Perotinus rubs shoulders with Bach and Buxtehude. In two of these arrangements, Perotinus is referred to – ambiguously enough – as the 'organist' of Notre Dame of Paris, completing a narrative in which, through tributes and adaptations, Perotinus is co-opted into both the canon of liturgical music and the pantheon of organ masters.[41] Leoninus also found his way into the heritage of the popular repertoire of amateur choral practice through a transcription for male choir published in 1983 by the Fédération musicale populaire (Popular Musical Federation), in the collection 'L'art musical populaire' (Popular art of music), where Leoninus's adaptation appears alongside those of various traditional and folk songs.[42]

Rethinking the Medieval Composer

The Limits of the Traditional Approach

The traditional composer-based approach to music history remains powerful in current university and conservatoire teaching, and important medieval music figures naturally remain influential in scholarly accounts of medieval music.[43] Nevertheless, it is now clear that despite any critical overhang, the application of the post-Enlightenment composer canon to the Middle Ages collides with the more collaborative realities of medieval composition and, quite simply, the evidence of sources and documentation.

Indeed, the difficulty of attaching names to works – especially before 1400 and particularly in the polyphonic repertoire – is the first stumbling block to the traditional approach. The vast majority of musical output is relegated to the category of 'anonymity', a terminology whose privative nature (that which has no name) clearly indicates the extent to which the absence of ascriptions is experienced as a lack. Indeed, the importance traditionally attributed to the 'birth of individualism' as a mark of humanist thought did nothing to soften the tension between the Middle Ages plunged into the obscurity of anonymity and a Renaissance bringing its creative individuals to the firmament.[44] Thus, ascriptions are extremely rare in music collections before 1400 and are limited to repertoires for which the process of attribution is an integral part of the literary game, as in the songs of the troubadours

---

in 1950 (op. 225).

[41] Gastoué 1939 (ed. and arr.); Dupré (ed. and arr.) 1942; Valois (ed. and arr.) 1957.

[42] Philippot (ed. and arr.) 1983.

[43] The five volumes of musicological studies devoted to Machaut over the last thirty years (Earp 1995; Robertson 2002; Leach 2011; McGrady and Bain (eds.) 2012; Earp and Hartt (eds.) 2021) or the three recent volumes devoted to Hildegard of Bingen (Bain 2015; Bain (ed.) 2021; Meconi 2018), in addition to the numerous editions on Machaut and Hildegard published in this and other fields over the last twenty years, are proof of this.

[44] For a critical approach to the notion of the individual in historiography, see Schmitt 1989 (2001); Iogna-Prat 2005.

and trouvères, or to rare sources in which ascriptions guarantee the legitimacy of the collection, as is the case in the Codex Calixtinus. With regards to polyphony, Margaret Bent shows in this volume that only a few exceptional corpora are named within the broader anonymous crowd (Adam de la Halle, Guillaume de Machaut, Jehan de l'Escurel, and Philip the Chancellor), while attributions based on external documentation (treatises, poems, and other texts) or authors' signatures embedded in the works themselves are found in only a handful of pieces. But beyond the difficulty of matching extant works to specific names, the truth is that we possess scant composers' names at all: at least before the fourteenth century, treatises lack reflective historical approaches to composers and composition. Moreover, the lives of composers – their education, their socio-economic condition, or their geographical and institutional trajectories – are undocumented, thereby preventing the full understanding needed to underpin our historiographic reconstructions.

However, the notion of 'composer' is not unknown in medieval texts: the texts refer to the creator of music in numerous ways, including with the noun *compositor*, although the use of this word is not limited to music.[45] The term *compositor*, according to the few usages found in Latin musical theory texts, refers to the authority of the person who shaped the melody,[46] or who knew the rules of music better, or as well as the singers.[47] This person was able to exercise a will that guaranteed the authenticity of his production: Johannes de Grocheo used the expression *voluntatem compositoris* on several occasions, considering the figure of the composer as an indeterminate but nonetheless decisive entity.

The idea of novelty associated with creation of music did not appear until the fourteenth century onwards. This can be explained by the medieval concept of authority, which was based on respect for ancient texts and in particular the Scriptures (and in the musical context, the liturgical repertoire)[48] and also on the productive etymology of the *auctor* as developer, continuer, and commentator.[49] This is how John of Afflighem (Johannes Cotto) describes the legitimacy of the creation of new songs in the Church by the composers who preceded him: 'Verum quia non solum praefati sacri cantus officiales in Sancta Ecclesia modulati sunt, sed et alii quidam non longe ante nostra tempora cantuum compositores extitere, quid nos quoque cantum vetet contexere non video' (It is true that not only the aforesaid official sacred songs were composed in the holy Church but also that some other composers of songs existed not far before our times; I do not see what forbids us to compose a song).[50] The verbs describing the act of creation here refer to *modulatio* (Johannes uses the term 'modulator' several times, referring to the figure of the composer) or to assemblage

---

[45] Bourgain 2001, pp. 364–65.

[46] Hucbald, *De harmonica institutione*, PL 132. 921.

[47] According to Frutolf of Michelberg: Vivell (ed.) 1919, p. 181.

[48] See Minnis 1988, who shows how the emergence of the notion of authority was progressive during the medieval period and hinged on the search for the authorship of biblical texts, aiming to distinguish the human contribution from the inspired Word.

[49] See the fundamental lexical study in Chenu 1927.

[50] Smits van Waesberghe (ed.) 1950, p. 117.

(*contexere*). But the use of the term 'compositor', which was rare in Afflighem's time, albeit in a plural and deliberately indeterminate form (*alli quidam compositores*), is here clearly associated with the introduction of a certain novelty into the tradition. Although in the fifteenth century innovation would become consubstantial with the definition of the composer ('Compositor est alicujus novi cantus editor' [The composer is the author of any new song], Tinctoris would assert[51]), this was rarely formulated in the Middle Ages, at least until it appeared in the writings of the fourteenth-century *Ars nova* theorists.

Another stumbling block to the traditional musicological approach to the composer of the medieval period lies in the glaring discrepancy between the concept of the composer as it is conceived today (a specialised task carried out by a particular individual and resulting in a definitive work) and the creative realities of the Middle Ages, which were far more complex, fluid, and collaborative. As shown in the chapters by Estelle Doudet, Mark Everist, and Yolanda Plumley, a gap exists between the contemporary fixity of attribution and the notion of authorship, on the one hand, and the collaborative realities of medieval creation, on the other hand – those that link a musical author and a textual author, a composer and a 'recomposer'. In the same vein, the notion of a fixed work – long anchored in the concept of authority – is ill-suited to the plasticity of medieval works, as confirmed by (re-)compositional processes such as contrafactum, centonization, and the addition or substitution of voices in polyphony, all of which offer possibilities for recomposing, adapting, or recycling versions of pre-existing pieces. In this respect, it is symptomatic and somewhat paradoxical to note how, in the trouvère chanson corpus, the addition, substitution, or subtraction of stanzas, or the existence of alternative melodies for the same poem dilute our notion of their authority and identity as composers, even though this repertoire is rich in ascriptions.

Circumventing the many pitfalls of the 'composer' concept as applied to medieval music, recent musicological scholarship has largely bypassed the question of the composer, approaching the creative act in alternative ways, especially by focussing on compositional processes. For example, whether the arts of memory, orality, and improvisational practices can best account for the act of composition,[52] or rather approaches inspired by recent literary criticism such as transtextuality, hypertextuality, or intertextuality,[53] these perspectives have often relegated the question of 'compositional actors' (to use the words borrowed from Bruno Latour in Everist's chapter) to the background, in favour of disembodied compositional models, imagined as abstract processes that shaped and reshaped works. In this way, the question of composers has been largely avoided and even silenced – and the term

---

[51] Johannes Tinctoris, *Diffinitorium musicae* in Coussemaker (ed.) (1864–76) 1963, vol. 4, p. 179.

[52] A good example of this approach can be found in Busse Berger 2005 and Gross 2007.

[53] Studies according to the intertextual perspective forged by Julia Kristeva or Michaël Riffaterre are very numerous in medieval musicology; various examples can be found in the contributions in Plumley, Di Bacco, and Jossa (eds.) 2011. For an example of a hypertextual approach, according to a concept developed by Gérard Genette, see Saint-Cricq 2019.

'composer' often politely dismissed in favour of the less connotative 'author' – in favour of an approach to the creative act based on questions that are adjacent to, though consubstantial with, the question of the composer.

New Approaches

Although it is now easy to see that the modern notion of the composer is unsuited to medieval musical conceptions and repertoires, formulating the ways in which the medieval composer can be brought back to centre stage, rethought, and theorised remains a complex and still-new undertaking. This is precisely the ambition of this book, which brings together new and innovative perspectives that make the notion of the composer useful and fruitful once again as a way of exploring the musical practices and repertoires of the Middle Ages. Among the many avenues for reflection that run through the various chapters, a few that recur between chapters can be highlighted here.

An appropriate starting point for rethinking the medieval composer is undoubtedly to study the medieval terms then used to designate the creative act and its creators. In the wake of relatively recent terminological studies relating to the plainchant repertoire,[54] many chapters in this book extend the investigation into how composers were referred to and highlight the lexicological luxuriance that surrounded the act of composition. Admittedly, this abundance is linked to the length of the medieval period and the multiplicity of repertoires, but it also bears witness to the variety of tasks and skills involved in the creative act. Three main layers of terminology can broadly be discerned in musical and literary fields. First, the Latin *facere, invenire, componere, profere* (chapters by Everist, Brewer, Doudet, Bent, Plumley) or the French *trouver, faire, controuver, composer, disposer* (Doudet, Bradley) refer to actions as close as possible to the creative act itself. Second, the Latin words *compilare, ordinare, neumizare, editare, scribere, imponere, excipiere, notare* (Parkes, Desmond, Bent) seem to modulate the idea of creation by highlighting the tasks associated with it, which sometimes seem to merge with it. Finally, the French *radouber, habiller, corriger* (Doudet) or the Latin *emendare, corrigere, centonisare* (Parkes, Desmond) seem to be linked to the tasks of recomposition. This network of tasks is matched by a multiplicity of terms to designate the creators: *compositor, musicus, cantor, discantor, rimator, poetus* (Bent, Doudet) and in French, *trovere* (Dolce), *compositeur, faiseur, translateur, imitateur, composeur, inventif*, and so forth (Doudet). This lexicological wealth not only testifies to the multiplicity of skills involved in creation and the variety of players that it required, but it certainly attests, too, to the fluidity of roles in the creative chain – as suggested, for musical composition, by the tendency to use the term 'singer' to designate the composer (Bent).

The variety and fluidity of skills, roles, and players lead several chapters (Parkes, Stones, Desmond, Plumley, and particularly Doudet and Everist) to approach medieval composition as a 'writing workshop', to use the notion by Bernard Cerquiglini, who in 1989 invited us to abandon the fixity of the medieval work in favour of a creative process conceived as a continuous labour.[55] In this workshop, collaboration,

---

54   Kelly 2006; Page 2010, pp. 383–441.

55   Cerquiglini 1989, p. 57; on this, see the chapter by Doudet in this volume.

on the one hand, is simultaneous or synchronic: it can bring together, for example, the author of a piece of music with the author of a text (Everist, Plumley, Bent) or a composer with a minstrel (Plumley); in the field of dramatic performance, it can link the different creative agents of a performance: author of the story, writer of dialogue, versifier, set designer, and so forth (Doudet). On the other hand, collaboration can be successive or diachronic, as suggested above by the medieval terms of recomposition: the long-term development of a repertoire emanating from various strata of authority (Parkes); the adaptation or recomposition of works according to the occasions, forces, and expectations of communities (Doudet); the notational avatars of copies of a work (Everist); the replacement and citation of pre-existing works (Everist). These medieval modes of recomposition are well known in both musicological and literary studies, and some were even the subject of formulations and metaphors in the Middle Ages.[56] However, the contributions in this book take this recent approach in a new direction by conceiving of the workshop and its collaborations not primarily in terms of compositional processes but above all in terms of a network of actors and skills. These chapters indeed reveal how the composition of a medieval work involved a sometimes-dizzying array of agents (poets, composers, performers, copyists, decorators, dramatists, compilers, commissioners, audience, etc.), analyse the direct and indirect relationships and interactions between these different authorities, and finally demonstrate the fundamentally interdisciplinary nature of the skills involved in creating musical works.

Naturally, one of the difficulties for modern scholarship is to negotiate the relationship between, on the one hand, the network of actors that may have presided over the existence of a work and, on the other hand, the seeming unequivocality of ascriptions, attributions, and signatures – when they exist in the sources or in the documentation. The chapters in this collection, in turn, offer a synthetic reflection on the equivocal nature and paradoxes of this relationship (Bent), raise the problem of unique ascriptions in collaborative works, possibly from a workshop (Stones), address the case of double and/or contradictory ascriptions (Plumley, Bent), and question the meaning of a unique ascription for musical pieces that also involved the composition of a text (Everist, Plumley, Bent). Attributions are also examined in Manon Louviot's chapter, which looks at authors' names woven in the fabric of the work itself rather than in the unstable paratext: Louviot shows that these signatures were part of a building process that contributed to the construction and legitimisation of the figure of the composer at the end of the Middle Ages. This chapter, as well as those, from other perspectives, by Henry Parkes, Charles E. Brewer, and Catherine A. Bradley, provide valuable insights into the medieval construction of authority.

---

[56] For example, the metaphor of a fabric made up of several pieces or of different dyes, used respectively by Gottchalk of Limburg to refer to one of his sequences (see the chapter by Parkes), and by Jean Renart in connection with the lyrical interpolations that adorn his *Roman de la rose ou de Guillaume de Dole* (Lecoy (ed.), 1979, lines 1–15). We might also mention the botanical metaphor of the *ente* in the case of motets *entés*, a term used in several medieval sources of thirteenth-century motets, whose mode of composition consists of grafting pre-existing material onto newly composed material (Butterfield 2003, 69–72), and likewise the ballade *entée* mentioned by Machaut and illustrated by ballades composed (with and without music) in the fourteenth century (see Plumley 2013).

A corollary perspective to that of the composing workshop is to approach composers not from the traditional individual angle but as members of cultural, social, and economic groups sharing the same creative and performative practices, whose compositions are the products of these associations. Considering communities of creators – whether ecclesiastical, confraternity-based, or professional – offers an alternative perspective to that of the individual composer, which makes it possible to extract the composer from a narrow understanding. Rather than freezing composition in a specialised act and placing the author in a watertight category, the composer can be approached in relation to all the musicians and creators of a given community in which the roles of authors, singers, instrumentalists, or poets are fluid and interdependent. Several chapters embrace this perspective, suggesting that the authorship of a work or a collection can be seen not only as the product of a particular author but also as the fruit of the practices of a monastic community (Desmond) or a confraternity (Dolce), the realisation of the work of a workshop (Stones), or the result of collaborations fostered by international socio-professional networks (Plumley). Brianne Dolce's and Yolanda Plumley's contributions also offer a glimpse of the benefits of the prosopographical method in this collective approach to medieval composers.[57] They show just how much our understanding of medieval authorship benefits from considering composers not only from the perspective of their output and its manuscript transmissions but by measuring the influence of their social, economic, and professional environments, their networks and institutional mobility, on their creative and compositional practices.

Finally, the question of style, a notion integral to the post-Enlightenment canon of the composer insofar as it is associated with the individuality of the creator, is revisited in various chapters of this book. In art history, style is firstly a notion that makes it possible to erase the simplistic alternative between attribution and anonymity, as Everist's chapter reminds us: the terms 'workshop of', 'school of', or 'style of' are well known in art history and had a fairly short-lived echo in musicology in the second half of the twentieth century,[58] although it persists with the term 'School of Notre Dame', sometimes still used to refer to Parisian polyphony of the thirteenth century. But style is also a traditional analytical tool for confirming ascription, evaluating attribution, and uncovering the authorship of a given work.[59] The notion of style is addressed in Everist's chapter, which points out the limits, in medieval music, of its application as an alternative to individual attributions – many works ascribed to the same author in the sources show no stylistic unity. Anna Zayaruznaya, for her part, warns of the dangers of subordinating musical styles to the lives and careers

---

[57] A method called for in the field of musicology in Fassler 2018.

[58] Several anonymous Parisian polyphonic pieces are attributed to 'Notre-Dame de Paris' in Husmann (ed.) 1955. In Davison and Apel (eds.) 1947, the pieces are in turn signed 'School of Compostela', 'School of St. Martial', 'School of Notre-Dame', 'In Perotinus style', 'School of Worcester', or 'Period of Petrus de Cruce'. See also the attributions 'School of Vitry' and 'Follower of Vitry' in Leech-Wilkinson 1982–83 in Everist's chapter.

[59] See the chapters by Bradley and Zayaruznaya, respectively, for the musicological attributions to Petrus de Cruce and Philippe de Vitry on the grounds of the style of the pieces.

of particular composers and vice versa. In the chapters by Stones, Brewer, and Desmond, style is seized on as a resource for the evaluation of authorship: while the first shows by example how it remains a traditionally powerful tool in art history, the other two demonstrate that when combined with other indicators (codicological, palaeographic analysis, transmission of sources, external documentation), it remains an efficient agent in the evaluation of putative attributions. In Bradley's chapter, style even appears to be one of the stratagems used in the staging and construction of the composer in the late Middle Ages, consciously wielded c. 1300 by an author or a group of creators (a 'circle' in the author's terminology) to distinguish themselves from an earlier famous composer, with the underlying – and modern – idea of musical evolution and 'progress'.

These different perspectives and reflections are presented in the twelve chapters of this volume, the first to be devoted entirely to the idea of the medieval composer. The composers are approached both in terms of a reflection on the definition and validity of the notion of composer for the medieval period and as a study of individuals and groups active in the creative processes surrounding music. Chapters alternate between synthetic reflections and case studies. Two of the contributions transpose these reflections into fields related to musicology: a contribution on the history of art (Stones) and another on the history of late-medieval theatre (Doudet) show the nuances, but especially the commonalities, between these creative fields and music around this issue of medieval *auctorialité*. The twelve contributions deal with the question of composers throughout the different phases of the Middle Ages, from the seventh century to the early Renaissance, in different geographical areas of western Europe (northern and southern France, England, the Iberian Peninsula, Italy), in different contexts (ecclesiastical and clerical communities, confraternities, princely and royal courts, lay workshops), and across a wide range of corpora (plainchant, Latin song and polyphonic conductus, liturgical polyphony, the motet from the thirteenth to the fifteenth centuries, trouvère song, *Ars nova* and *Ars subtilior* polyphonic song, drama, illuminated Gothic manuscripts). Lastly, the different contributions provide an insight into the wealth of methods, tools, and documents needed to investigate composers in the Middle Ages: musical and literary stylistic analysis, codicological and palaeographic analysis, studies of various sources and archival documents (correspondence, obituaries, legal documents, chronicles, manuscripts and fragments), treatises, as well as iconographic, epigraphic, and prosopographical studies.

The first part of the book, 'Historiographic Critique', comprises three chapters devoted to historiographic reflections on the musicological application of the notion of the composer in the Middle Ages, on the re-examination of traditional attributions, and on the construction of authority in the Middle Ages. Henry Parkes devotes his chapter to a fundamental historiographic cog in the machine of medieval musical authority: the myth that Pope Gregory the Great was the inspired composer of Franco-Roman plainchant, an account that makes it possible to assign an unequivocal source to a repertoire with obscure and complex origins. Reversing the usual critical perspective on this well-known myth, Parkes asks whether medieval people ever believed in this 'Gregorian' narrative, and whether this myth might not itself be a myth. Looking at the documents and texts from the seventh to the fifteenth century that describe the creation of the repertoire, Parkes shows that its development is described as an eminently collaborative process, explained as a layering of various creative authorities, and attributed to different constellations of authors depending on the various segments of the corpus. In the medieval accounts of this long-running cumulative workshop, Gregory is thus associated with other illustrious contributors, between whom different genealogical relationships and different modes of collaboration are proposed – text/music, psalm/song, theory/practice, and so forth. As it emerges, the medieval figure of Gregory seems to have functioned only as a synecdoche for the creative plurality of plainchant.

In Charles E. Brewer's chapter, historiographic questions are addressed within Latin devotional song of the twelfth century, with a case study of one of the most widely and durably transmitted pieces in this repertoire, the *Planctus ante nescia*. Brewer dismantles the historiographic mechanism by which this work, anonymous in sources, was consecutively attributed to Bernard of Clairvaux, Godefroi de Breteuil, Bonaventure, and above all, Godefroy of Saint Victor. Brewer investigates medieval documents, the provenance, and dating of the song's sources and employs comparative stylistic analysis to demonstrate the implausibility of these attributions. From an examination of two medieval documents that mention the *Planctus* as well as a parallel with the writings of Hildegard of Bingen, Brewer concludes that the question of the composer was in fact far less important to contemporaries of the *Planctus* than the notions of inspiration and revelation in accounting for the creative process of sacred song. In this way, the chapter argues for a renewed awareness of these concepts of medieval creation, our understanding of which has been distorted by the all-out search for 'great names' to attach to 'great works' in post-Enlightenment historiography.

Anna Zayaruznaya closes this first section with a wide-ranging historiographic reflection on the way in which we relate the history of music to the history of individuals. For Zayaruznaya, the highly compressed dates of activity attributed by historiography to Petrus de Cruce and Philippe de Vitry are no more than a convenient means of drawing up a comfortable teleological account of the evolution from post-Franconian notation to the *Ars nova* in which Petrus functions as a brief moment of transition and Philippe as a young and ephemeral innovator. Relying in turn on existing documentation, a re-reading of the treatises and the works themselves, Zayaruznaya credits Petrus and Philippe with a much more persistent activity and influence than is traditionally acknowledged. Instead of a narrative in which Petrus and his Petronian system would make way for Philippe and his *Ars nova*, she envisages a more complex reality in which the notational practices of the two composers converge for a time around *Ars vetus* notation. By proposing this continuity between two systems and two careers usually considered successive, Zayaruznaya invites us to challenge the historiographic tendency to attach musical systems and styles to individuals and conversely to reflect on the way in which our understanding of composers' lives and careers has consequences for the chronologies and narratives we construct.

The second part of this volume, 'Ascriptions, Attributions, Signatures', is devoted to an overview and typology of medieval attribution and to a reflection on the meanings, ambiguities, and paradoxes that lurk beneath existing attributions. Margaret Bent takes up the nagging question of the virtual absence of ascriptions of polyphonic works in musical sources up to around 1400, which she considers paradoxical given the importance of authority throughout the Middle Ages and in view of other fields that are better provided for in this respect (monodic song, poetry, literature, visual arts). Her chapter offers an exhaustive overview and typology of the traces of authorship in polyphonic works from the thirteenth to the fifteenth centuries: ascriptions in the headings of the works, attributions in various types of external writings (poems, romances, treatises, archival documents), and authors' self-signatures in the texts of the pieces. Bent notes, through the many examples she cites, that composers are rarely identified as such in works and documents but rather are referred to as musicians and above all singers, reflecting a fluidity of terms and roles around musical creation in the Middle Ages that modern conceptions of the composer find difficult to accommodate. Although many composers' names are probably hidden among the singers, instrumentalists, and theorists mentioned in texts of the works and in documents, a major challenge we face remains, in the virtual absence of attributions before the fifteenth century, the ability to link these names to specific works.

Alison Stones extends the question of authorship into the field of art history by examining the significance of authors' signatures and attributions in the realms of manuscript decoration and copying in the thirteenth and fourteenth centuries. Stones proposes three case studies focussing on the artists Philippe de Troyes, Master Honoré, and Pierart dou Thielt, whose names are associated with one or more decorated manuscripts, through signatures in colophons or attributions in external documents. These different cases highlight the ambiguity of these signatures, ascriptions, and attributions and in so doing question the reality of the artistic work around manuscripts c. 1300: the names given may conceal a division of tasks in the chain of creative skills, hide a collaboration or the collective work of a workshop, or, on the contrary, testify to a concentration of tasks in the hands of a single notator-decorator. These studies give rise to a reflection on the value of stylistic study as a criterion of attribution in art history, in the absence, as in the case of music, of abundant signatures and given our difficulty in associating names gleaned from external documentation with particular manuscripts.

The third part, 'Medieval Constructions of Authority and of the Authorial Persona', is devoted to the staging of authority and the composer in medieval musical works, demonstrating how medieval practices contributed to the modern construction of the composer, through quotations, references, and self-representation. Manon Louviot reflects on a composer's ciphered signature inscribed in a four-voice Marian motet from the fourteenth century, *Ferre solet/Ana theos de gracia*. In the upper voices of this sophisticated work, a first acrostic gives the name of the composer, Frater Johannes Vavassoris, a second acrostic presents the year of composition (1374), while a telestich forms the first words of the Marian prayer *Ave Maria*, the melody of which serves as the tenor of the motet. Through a survey of cases of encrypted authorial signatures in musical and literary works of the fourteenth century, Louviot highlights the various functions of the performance of identity in *Ferre solet*: for Vavassoris, it is as much a question of asserting his authorship and inscribing it indelibly in the work itself as, by subtly staging the page and notation and engaging the reader's participation, demonstrating his virtuosity and thus legitimising his status as a composer. Lastly, Louviot shows that the originality of this otherwise well-known procedure lies in the relationship that develops between the composer's signature and the devotional telestich addressed to the Virgin, which sketches the self-portrait of a composer participating in the prayer of Marian devotion conveyed by his motet.

Adam de la Halle's self-promotion as a 'great author' is well known in medieval studies. However, Catherine A. Bradley shows in her chapter that whereas his songs and refrains were indeed lastingly transmitted or quoted in later works, his motets seem to have been less revered around 1300 by a younger generation of polyphonists linked to Petrus de Cruce. Bradley shows how two motets, one attributed to Petrus and the other anonymous but comparable in style, make particularly original use of quotations from fragments of Adam de la Halle's motets. The sophisticated staging of these quotations and allusions is intended to convey Adam's musical and literary idioms as outdated, in contrast to the new literary, rhythmic, and declamatory style of the two Petronian motets in which they are embedded. This refined interplay of quotations and references betrays the ambiguity and fragility of Adam's status as a composer of motets: while he serves as a yardstick against which these young composers measure themselves, the negative connotations surrounding the quotations from the Artesian author erode his status as a model, and he is now overtaken by the proponents of an innovative style.

The fourth part of the book, 'The Composing Workshop', follows on from recent critical reflections on medieval authorship, which envisage works not as the creation of a particular individual but as the emanation of a collective process, through a compositional workshop that is both simultaneous and successive. The two chapters in this section focus on the actors in this compositional workshop. Estelle Doudet's chapter investigates the composition of dramatic performances in the late Middle Ages and early Renaissance, which she approaches as a collective 'writing workshop', not just from a textual perspective but also from social, economic, and legal viewpoints. A lexical examination shows how the growing wealth of terminology surrounding the creation of drama in the late Middle Ages reflects the plethora of roles and skills in the creative process of plays. This variety of roles is tangible in the textual mobility of dramatic texts, whose plasticity – arrangements, montage, seriality, reduction – presupposes the successive interventions of a cumulative authorship. Authorship was also collaborative, and Doudet gives various examples of the interactions between the various players in the creative chain – from composer to actors, via commissioners, proofreaders, and the communities themselves – within which the socio-economic negotiations between the different authorial positions could prove tense. Finally, Doudet looks at authorship from a legal angle, showing how dramatic composers managed to escape punishment from the authorities by conveniently dissolving their responsibility in the collective authorship of their works, thus playing on the complexity of medieval *auctorialité*.

Mark Everist's chapter takes us to another composing workshop, that of polyphonic music in the long thirteenth century. With a view to theorising the act of composition and the compositional actor in the Middle Ages, Everist draws on the heuristic value of the terms *facere, componere,* and *invenire,* which were used in turn to refer to the act of composition in treatises on *musica mensurabilis* in the thirteenth century. This multiplicity of terms reveals the diversity of tasks and players involved in creation, and it is by reassembling this jigsaw of skills and agents that Everist proposes to understand the compositional act and actor. By way of example, he unfolds the sprawling intertextual network around the variable-voice conductus *Naturas Deus regulis,* which involves two other conducti, different strata of texts including a Latin miracle, a responsory, and a polyphonic Benedicamus Domino. Highlighting the multiplicity of compositional interventions, creative skills, and actors implicated in the building-up of this network over dozens of years and numerous existing and lost witnesses, Everist shows the profoundly multidisciplinary and collaborative nature of medieval creation for which only a broad and therefore medieval acceptance of composition and of the composer can account.

The book closes with a part on 'Composers as Communities', approaching composers not from the angle of isolated creators but from the perspective that these authors and their works were the fruits of the social, cultural, and economic communities and networks of creators to which they belonged. Karen Desmond's chapter sets the scene for a reflection on the authorship of twelve polyphonic alleluias within the community of Reading Abbey in thirteenth-century England. These pieces are part of a corpus usually attributed to W. de Wicumbe, precentor at Reading Abbey, based on a list of works linked to, and probably copied by, him. Desmond presents an exhaustive analysis of these twelve complex polyphonic pieces, today divided across different fragments, to determine whether their stylistic characteristics allow them to be associated with a single composer. Desmond highlights the specific features of these alleluias, notably the addition of freely composed sections (preludes, interludes, and postludes) and the use of rondellus and voice exchange in the preludes, which distinguishes them from other insular polyphonies of the thirteenth and fourteenth centuries. Moreover, united by the presence of a principal copyist and singled out by the virtual absence of concordances in other sources, these polyphonic works thus appear to be linked to compositional and performative practices specific to the Reading Abbey community. The collection of twelve pieces seems in part to comprise a compilation of works emanating from this community and of the personal creations of its precentor.

Brianne Dolce's contribution takes the form of an investigation into the cultural, social, and creative practices of the trouvères. Against the historiographic inclination to reduce them to composers of vernacular music and poetry, Dolce argues for a broader understanding of the socio-cultural activities of this group of individuals associated with the creation of vernacular song. To this end, Dolce adopts a prosopographical perspective, excavating from the obituary of the Confraternity of Jongleurs and Bourgeois in Arras the biographical data of thirty-nine names involved in the creation and performance of song. Dolce shows the impact of the economic activities of these individuals on their cultural practices and brings to light the ecclesiastical functions of many of them and their involvement in the liturgical musical life of Arras. In this way, the study highlights the versatility and diversity of the activities of the trouvères of Arras and reveals the many bridges and connections between fields of musical and literary creation that are usually considered to be watertight.

Yolanda Plumley's chapter closes the part and the volume with a plunge into the heart of the professional and courtly networks of the musicians of the *Ars subtilior*. Plumley investigates the possibility of collaboration around the creation of songs, taking the ballade *Puis que je sui fumeux* as a case in point. This work, whose text relates an obvious proximity to certain poems by Eustache Deschamps and his *cercle* of the *fumeux*, is apparently ascribed jointly by the same hand to Jehan Simon de Hasprois and Jaquet de Noyon in the Chantilly codex. Plumley investigates the mechanisms and contexts that may have resulted in a piece marked at once by the imprint of a Parisian poet, a minstrel linked to the southern courts of Europe and a church musician attached to the papal court of Avignon. Using unpublished as well as published archival documents from the court of Aragon and elsewhere, she traces Jaquet's career through his employment and travels to various European courts. This journey shows the astonishing mobility of musicians whose careers took strategic advantage of the geopolitical game played by courts. It also attests to the existence of truly international professional networks within which poets, musicians, and composers of all kinds continually crossed paths, enabling exchanges conducive to collaborations such as the one suggested by *Puis que je sui fumeux*.

The title of this opening essay, 'From Composer to Composers', aims to capture the dynamics of this collection. It first indicates how the different chapters approach the medieval composer both as a notion and as a study of individuals active in the music of the Middle Ages. But above all, this title teases out a path that, from the historiographic critiques of the canon of the great composer in the first chapters to the notions of 'workshop' and 'communities' emerging in the final sections of the volume, invites the reader and future scholarship to conceive of the medieval composer in the plural and to rethink the medieval creative act in its collective, collaborative, and interdisciplinary dimensions.

PART I

HISTORIOGRAPHIC CRITIQUE

1

Gregory and Friends: Plural Authorities in the History of Romano-Frankish Chant

Henry Parkes

In the famous iconography, it is a private scene. Pope Gregory sits alone, behind a curtain, as the Holy Spirit in the form of a dove reveals to him a musical repertory for use in church. In the story's original early eighth-century telling – which concerns Gregory's homilies on Ezekiel and was only adapted to the topic of Romano-Frankish chant in the tenth century – the pope's moment of divine intimacy is inadvertently witnessed by a member of his household, who is then instructed to keep quiet about the matter until after his death.[1] In the grand scheme of Christian history, the injunction to keep silent is nothing but a stage whisper: a chance to project the pope's humility, and thus his sanctity, and to forestall any challenges to the contrary. But the solitude of the scene also dramatises a vital elision of person ('Gregorian') and tradition ('chant') that has remained in currency for well over a thousand years. Whatever we may make of the association, no one can deny the story's historical utility. In the face of a thousands-strong repertory of liturgical compositions from across the medieval West, of murky origins, hard to enumerate and historically even harder to capture in writing, it affords an origin narrative that is focussed and memorable, centred on an illustrious church father whose historical coordinates (Rome, c. 600 CE) are as well known as any.

This chapter is not concerned with the question of whether Gregory was the historical 'composer' of his eponymous chant tradition so much as with the question of whether anyone in the Middle Ages really saw it that way. Superficially, the case seems to be very strong. What Pope Leo IV referred to as 'Gregorian songs' (*Gregoriana carmina*) and John the Deacon as 'Gregorian chants' (*Gregorianis cantibus*), both in the ninth century, was consolidated north of the Alps in the eleventh century with the now-familiar formulation 'Gregorianus cantus', found in the work of William of Hirsau (a theorist), John of Worcester (a chronicler), and countless others thereafter.[2] Continental chant books of the eighth and ninth centuries were

---

[1] Colgrave (ed. and trans.) (1968) 1985, pp. 121–23 (chap. 26). For a sense of how this narrative developed in a musical context, see Hucke 1955 and Hiley 1993, pp. 503–13. For another reference to the 'Gregorian scene' in the Harker antiphoner (St Gallen, Stiftsbibl., Cod. Sang. 390–391), see the chapter by Brewer in this volume.

[2] Ninth-century sources quoted from Hucke 1955, 264. The eleventh-century sources mentioned are Harbinson (ed.) 1975, pp. 44, 54; McGurk (ed. and trans.) 1998, pp. 38–39.

famously prefaced with the 'Gregorius praesul' poem, possibly of Anglo-Saxon authorship, in which readers learned that the pope had 'put together this little book of musical art' (*composuit hunc libellum musicae artis*).[3] Pronouns advertised similar responsibilities when Egbert of York (d. 766) referred to Gregory and 'his antiphoner' (*suo antiphonario*); the English authors of the tenth-century *Regularis concordia* likewise chose to respect what 'he himself ordained in the antiphoner' (*quam ipse antiphonario dictavit*).[4] By the eleventh century, the word *auctor* was also in circulation. Whereas Otloh of Saint Emmeram (William of Hirsau's teacher) claimed that Gregory was 'the first author of the antiphoner' (*auctorem primum antiphonarii*), the contemporary theorist Aribo considered him to be 'the author of almost all ecclesiastical chant' (*totius paene ecclesiastici cantus auctorem*).[5]

Although these are all positive endorsements, the papal association was often the stronger for being qualified or couched in the negative. John the Deacon led this particular charge in the ninth century, with a rebuke of the Frankish singers who had carelessly lost sight of Gregory's bequest.[6] That version of events was also channelled by non-Romans, including the fourteenth-century monk Guy of Saint Denis, who chided the *oltremontani* who had corrupted the 'sweetness of modulation instituted by Pope Gregory himself' (*modulationis dulcedinem ab ipso papa gregorio institutam*).[7] The twelfth-century liturgist Jean Beleth conceded the reality of 'not truly Gregorian' material at the head of the office antiphoner, before declaring unashamedly that 'the rest are Gregory's'.[8] The Cistercians instigated a major chant reform on the premise that only verifiably Gregorian material would do,[9] whilst Guido of Arezzo unveiled his staff notation in the early eleventh century with a quip about needing to distinguish Gregory's antiphoner from those which, for the sake of argument, he attributed to men named Leo and Albert.[10]

From these various narratives it would seem a fair inference that Gregory was indeed considered by medieval audiences to have been some kind of 'author' or 'composer', who had achieved for Romano-Frankish chant what he had already accomplished in writing his homilies on Ezekiel and other literary works. In Helmut Hucke's view, Gregory began to gain his wider reputation as a musical *Urheber* in the tenth century.[11] James McKinnon considered the legend of authorship to be

---

3   Hucke 1955; Stäblein 1968, pp. 537–61; McKinnon 2001. On the English connection see Page 2010, pp. 272–74.

4   Egbert of York, PL 89. 441 (chap. 16); Symons (ed. and trans.) 1953, p. 49.

5   Otloh is quoted in Jeffery 1984, 164; McCarthy (ed.) 2015, pp. 48–49 (chap. 66).

6   John the Deacon, PL 75. 90–91 (II.7).

7   Mews et al. (eds and trans.) 2017, pp. 72–73.

8   Douteil (ed.) 1976, vol. 2, pp. 106–7 (chap. 58): 'Istud tamen non est Gregorianum, id est a Gregorio compositum.... Cetera sunt Gregorii'.

9   Waddell 1970, pp. 193–207.

10 Guido, *Prologus in antiphonarium*, in Pesce (ed. and trans.) 1999, pp. 412–13. Guido's contemporary Adémar de Chabannes also used the genitive when he described 'antiphonarios sancti Gregorii': see Grier 2003, p. 47.

11 Hucke 1955, p. 264.

'complete' in the years around 1000, when Gregory was depicted dictating chants to a music scribe in the celebrated frontispiece of the Hartker Antiphoner.[12] However, such interpretations need be handled with care for two very important reasons. First, they give relatively little attention to the complicated lexicon of medieval chant authorship, explored in recent decades by both Thomas Kelly and Christopher Page, in which creative achievements were ambiguously framed and the meanings of words potentially quite different from those of their modern cognates.[13] For that reason, my own translations in this chapter are deliberately cautious, with the all-important verb *compono* understood only in its most neutral sense of 'putting together'. Second, these interpretations disregard, or at least minimise, a medieval discourse on musical authority that was almost as diverse as the commentaries, poems, and illustrations in which it appeared.

Indeed, it appears that much of the medieval discussion of Gregory and chant was concerned with making sense of the very relationship under consideration, attempting to distinguish that which could be considered a product of papal intervention from that which could not. Half a century after the Hartker Antiphoner illustration, Bern of Reichenau would try to untangle a thorny musical issue by suggesting that Gregory's contribution to the liturgy was as the 'orderer' (*ordinator*) of the antiphoner and sacramentary, 'whoever had composed those or those chants' (*quicumque has vel has cantilenas composuisset*).[14] Two centuries later, the liturgist William Durand of Mende would likewise report, with almost legalistic caution, that 'the order of the chants … is believed to have been fully arranged by Blessed Gregory', before continuing, '[together] with the many others who came before and after him who composed prayers, antiphons, and responsories'.[15] (Thibodeau's translation interpolates the relative pronoun 'who', but the original verb ending indicates that these contributing 'composers' were unambiguously plural.) Circumscribing Gregory's responsibility in a different way, Sigebert of Gembloux claimed in his eleventh-century chronicle that the pope's achievement was to have 'centonized and profitably compiled' (*centonizavit et utiliter compilavit*) the antiphoner.[16] In a clear echo of John the Deacon's 'centonate antiphoner' (*antiphonarium centonem*), Sigebert's first verb suggests the fashioning of libretti out of scripture;[17] his second potentially takes us even further in that direction, since in classical usage *compilo* bore the connotation of stealing or plagiarising. In

---

[12] McKinnon 2000, p. 98.

[13] Kelly 2006; Page 2010, pp. 383–441. For other surveys of the medieval terminology related to composition and composers, see also the introduction to this volume, the chapters by Bent, Bradley, Everist, Desmond, and Dolce, as well as Doudet's chapter on drama.

[14] Bern, *De quibusdam rebus*, in Parkes (ed.) 2019, p. 66 (chap. 1; see also commentary on p. 171).

[15] 'Ordinem cantilene … creditur beatus Gregorius plenaria ordinatione distribuisse, cum multi et ante et post eum orationes, antiphonas et responsoria composuerunt' (Davril and Thibodeau (eds.) 1995–2000, vol. 2, p. 49 (V.2.65); translation from Thibodeau (ed. and trans.) 2015, pp. 115–16).

[16] Sigebert of Gembloux, PL 160. 111 (year 592).

[17] John the Deacon, PL 75. 90 (II.6).

other accounts, Gregory had responsibilities that were specifically musical. A text ascribed to a certain John the Priest, now surviving in a single manuscript from eleventh-century Montecassino, declared that Pope Gregory had 'disposed and neumatized' (*disposuit atque neumatizavit*) the antiphoner, the latter verb referring either to the act of adding melody or to the notation itself,[18] and a gloss on Guido's *Regulae rhythmicae* reported that Gregory had 'set notes upon the antiphoner and upon the gradual' (*instituit notas super antiphonarium et super graduale*).[19]

As the ensuing discussion will show, it was actually very common for Romano-Frankish chant to be presented as a collaborative or otherwise open-ended endeavour. Gregory is almost always present in these narratives, but so too are those on whose work he purportedly built, or those who in turn augmented the pope's achievements. My chapter is structured around four such constellations of authority. In each case, the common theme is the possibility that the repertory is 'Gregorian' in some respects but not others, its authorship defined not in absolute terms but through a perceived layering of creative responsibilities. It is worth saying that this is essentially what we already know of the raw musical materials, with their regional variations and layers both chronological and compositional, not to mention evidence of hundreds of named medieval contributors.[20] It also corresponds to a medieval understanding of literary authorship, articulated by the thirteenth-century scholar Bonaventure in his commentary on Peter Lombard's *Sentences* in which the 'author' (*auctor*) is defined as the person who brings their own ideas together with those of others.[21] (Among many possible etymologies is the verb *augeo*, with past participle *auctus*, meaning 'to increase or augment'.) Yet we tend not to credit our musical witnesses with such nuances or varieties of understanding. Our post-medieval perspective undoubtedly clouds the picture; but because of the interpretative value it holds for historians today, so too does the tale of Gregory's secret encounter with the Holy Spirit. Whether or not such an event took place in Rome in the years around 600, the notion of a medieval 'myth' or 'legend' of divinely inspired composition, propagated from above and embraced by those beneath, remains one of the most efficient explanations we have for the successful acceptance and long-term canonicity of Romano-Frankish chant in western Europe from the eighth century onwards.[22] My thesis is that the 'myth' is itself a myth, or at least a marked outlier in a medieval discourse that was far less certain and far from unanimous, about what 'authorship' in Catholic chant practices really meant.

---

[18] Montecassino, BA, Cod. 318, partially transcribed in Gerbert 1774, vol. 2, pp. 2–3 n. b.

[19] Smits van Waesberghe and Vetter (eds.) 1985, p. 103 n. 68.

[20] Surveys of these contributors are offered in Kelly 2006 and Page 2010, pp. 429–41.

[21] Minnis 1988, pp. 94–95.

[22] The narrative is so often retold that it is impossible to nominate a single representative example, but for a widely disseminated version of these events, see Taruskin 2010, pp. 36–39.

Gregory, Ambrose, Ignatius

Among the earliest documents to associate Pope Gregory with any form of Western chant tradition is the text now known as *Ordo Romanus XIX*, which probably originated in the seventh century but survives only in a Frankish copy of the late eighth century.[23] After several lines about monastic mealtimes, the narrative diverts to consider a list of monks and popes who contributed to the 'holy pattern' (*sanctam normam*) of the Roman church. In keeping with later medieval legend, Gregory is accorded the honour of working 'with the inspiration of the Holy Spirit' (*afflatu sancto spiritu*), and in conformity with the idea that he was the orderer of chant, not its begetter, the text considers him to have 'nobly appointed the chant for the annual cycle' (*cantum anni circoli nobili ededit*) in Rome.[24] But far from being the solitary figure of musical responsibility, he is listed as the sixth in a sequence of ten authorities who had all apparently done the same.

As a solitary text, it could be written off as an anomaly, for no subsequent account would ever discuss so many venerable papal figures – among them Leo, Gelasius, and Boniface – in connection with Roman chant. Yet it was a common strategy for medieval authors to seek liturgical precedents in the early church. With the aid of the papal biographies contained in the early medieval *Liber pontificalis*, several ninth-century commentators set about extracting cumulative narratives of Christian liturgical history,[25] out of which there coalesced an understanding that Gregory's other eponymous liturgical collection, the sacramentary, was built on a foundation laid by previous popes, above all Gelasius but sometimes also Leo.[26] Commentators looking for an equivalent pre-history of liturgical chant ascribed particular importance to Ignatius of Antioch and Ambrose of Milan. Ignatius had reached Latin readers via a story in the sixth-century *Historia tripartita* of Cassiodorus and Epiphanius, itself drawing on a story from the Greek historian Socrates Scholasticus in which a vision of angels singing antiphons had caused him to introduce the genre to the church of Antioch, whence to all corners of Christendom.[27] Although the West could not boast such an early story, it did have Paulinus of Milan's *Vita sancti Ambrosii*, of the early fifth century, in which Ambrose was revealed to have introduced 'antiphons, hymns, and vigils' to the church of Milan.[28] Both stories were assimilated into ninth-century histories: the

---

[23] Andrieu (ed.) 1931–61, vol. 3, pp. 223–24; on the dating, see Mews 2011, 139.

[24] Andrieu (ed.) 1931–61, vol. 3, p. 224.

[25] Duchesne (ed.) (1886–92), 1955–57. See, for instance, Boretius and Krause (eds.) 1897, pp. 496–503 (chap. 23).

[26] See, for example, John the Deacon, PL 75. 94 (II.17). Other examples include the ninth-century 'Hucusque' preface to the Gregorian sacramentary, the dual portrait of Gregory and Gelasius in the copy of the Fulda Sacramentary, now Bamberg, Staatsbibl., Lit. 1, fol. 12v, and the eleventh-century *Micrologus* of Bernold of Constance in which Leo, Gelasius, and Gregory often appear as a group.

[27] Jacob (ed.) 1952, p. 596 (X.9).

[28] 'Hoc in tempore primum antiphonae, hymni, ac vigiliae in ecclesia Mediolanensi celebrari coeperunt' (Paulinus of Milan, PL 14. 31).

music theorist Aurelian of Réôme mentioned the pair as precedents for chanting practices in the Latin church,[29] as did the liturgist Walahfrid Strabo.[30] Towards the end of the tenth century, a copy of the tonary (a list of Romano-Frankish chants ordered by melodic type) by Regino of Prüm was introduced with a précis of the story about Ignatius.[31] That juxtaposition comes into particular focus when we recognise that Regino's musical selection was overwhelmingly weighted towards antiphons and antiphonal chants.

With these famous precedents it was historically but a small step for later authors to imagine that Ignatius, Ambrose, and Gregory, previously individual figures of anecdote, had belonged to a coherent musical lineage. In a music theory treatise composed around 1100, John of Afflighem presented a tightened-up version of events:

> The first use of music in the Roman church was made by St Ignatius the Martyr and also by St Ambrose, bishop of Milan. After them the most blessed Pope Gregory composed chant with the assistance and at the dictation, it is said, of the Holy Ghost, and he gave the Roman church the chant by which the Divine Service is celebrated throughout the year.[32]

Gregory is the only one being given explicit authorial responsibility, yet already we can see some movement. Both Ignatius and Ambrose seem to be aligned to the 'Roman church', despite the fact that one was Syrian, the other bishop of a church that presided over its own distinctly non-Roman rite. A few sentences later, John's guard slips even further when he situates contemporary chant compositions in a long tradition that stretches back to 'the aforementioned holy men of chant' (*praefati sacri cantus officiales*).[33] All of a sudden, Gregory is not standing alone.

In later medieval writings, these three characters became more fully entangled. The twelfth-century liturgist Jean Beleth presented a paraphrase of the sixth-century *Historia tripartita* story in which he attributed to Ignatius the institution of a (musical?) connection between psalmody and antiphonal chants, something not known to have been regulated in the West before the tonaries of the ninth century.[34] The same anachronism later reared its head in the Ignatius chapter of

---

[29] Gushee (ed.) 1975, p. 129 (chap. 20).

[30] Boretius and Krause (eds.) 1897, p. 505 (chap. 26).

[31] LeRoux 1965, p. 299.

[32] 'Primum autem a Sancto Ignatio martyre nec non et a beato Ambrosio Mediolanensium antistite usus musicae in Romana ecclesia haberi coepit. Post hos beatissimus Papa Gregorius Spiritu Sancto ei, ut fertur, assidente et dictante cantum modulatus est, cantumque Romanae Ecclesiae, quo per anni circulum Divinum celebratur officium, dedit' (Smits van Waesberghe (ed.) 1950, p. 115 (chap. 17); translation from Babb (trans.) and Palisca (ed.) 1978, p. 136).

[33] Smits van Waesberghe (ed.) 1950, p. 116; note that *sacri* can also agree with *cantus*.

[34] 'Instituit antiphonas in ecclesia cantari et psalmos secundum antiphonas centonizari' (He ordained that antiphons be sung in church and psalms centonized according to the antiphons) (Douteil (ed.) 1976, vol. 2, p. 106 (chap. 58)). The musical connotation is afforded by alternate manuscript readings for *centonizare* that include *intonizare*

Jacobus de Voragine's influential thirteenth-century *Legenda aurea*.[35] A century later, as part of a muddled attempt to explain Boethius's music theory, the author of the *Speculum musicae* named Ambrose, Gregory, and Ignatius as three precedents for Boethius in the field of Roman liturgical chant.[36] In so doing, not only did he reverse the now-accepted chronology according to which Gregory was born a decade or more *after* Boethius died; he also imagined fallaciously that these figures had left behind 'liturgical chants' (*cantus*) of the sort that could 'hardly have escaped Boethius' notice', this individual supposedly being 'a truly catholic man'.[37] By the time of Franchino Gaffurio in the sixteenth century, the authorities in Christian 'monophonic song' (*monodicam ... modulationem*) could be seen to comprise Ignatius, Ambrose, and Gregory as well as Basil, Hilary, and the aforementioned Pope Gelasius.[38] In all of these accounts, whether explicitly or implicitly, present-day chanting was seen to have emerged from a continuum of activity in the early church.

Another way to reconcile Gregory's creativity with these other historical layers was to imagine chant composition as a two-step process, comprising first the creation of a given genre or practice and then its realisation in the form of a repertory. First attested in the twelfth century, this strategy became the norm for the various Mass genres whose histories had already been foreshadowed without mention of Gregory, in the *Liber pontificalis*, and which thus needed some retrospective explanation. In a fine article on the developing medieval narratives about introit psalmody, Peter Jeffery identified this behaviour in the work of the theologian Honorius of Autun, whose economical account of the genre foreshortens two centuries of Roman history: 'Pope Celestine decreed that psalms be sung at the introit of the Mass, from which Pope Gregory afterward composed antiphons for singing at the introit of the Mass'.[39] Around the same time as Honorius, Sigebert of Gembloux offered an expanded version of the same story, attributing to Pope Celestine the singing of psalmody at the introit, gradual, offertory, and communion, before crediting Pope Gregory with their compilation in the antiphoner.[40] A decade or two later, Rupert of Deutz repeated Sigebert's account

('intone'?) and *accentuari vel centonizari* ('accentuate or centonize'?); Patrologia Latina has the verb *tonizari*.

[35] Ryan (ed. and trans.) 2012, p. 141 (chap. 36).

[36] Bragard (ed.) 1955–73, vol. 6, p. 310 (VI.113).

[37] 'Et cantus illi minime Boethio latuerunt qui fuit vir vere catholicus' (Bragard (ed.) 1955–73, vol. 6, p. 310).

[38] 'Inde ipse Aretinus Guido ecclesiasticum cantum diatonice descripsit: sed ante eum sacri Pontifices Ignatius, Basilius, Hylarius, Ambrosius, Gelasius, Gregorius Monodicam ipsam modulationem sacris ac divinis obsecrationibus ascripserant' (Gaffurio 1520, fol. Avr).

[39] 'Caelestinus itaque papa psalmos ad introitum missae cantari instituit. De quibus Gregorius papa postea antiphonas ad introitum missae modulando composuit' (Honorius of Autun, PL 172. 572 (I.87); translation from Jeffery 1984, p. 151).

[40] Sigebert, PL 160. 78 (year 426) and 111 (592).

in even terser form, adding an attribution of the tract genre to Pope Gelasius.[41] Honorius also attributed to Gregory both the composition and the introduction of the offertory chant, whilst flipping responsibilities for the gradual and alleluia, somewhat bizarrely, such that Gregory 'instituted' (*instituit*) genres that Ambrose (long since dead) had already composed or 'arranged' (*composuit*).[42] A generation earlier, Bonizo of Sutri likewise credited Gregory with instituting the gradual, alleluia, and offertory, as well as all the other Romano-Frankish propers (here, the introit is not considered to be the work of Celestine) and several key components of the Mass liturgy at large.[43] Watered-down versions of these narratives would later reach even larger audiences, first by means of Sicard of Cremona's *Mitrale*, a liturgical handbook composed around 1200 and thence into the highly influential thirteenth-century writings of Voragine and Durandus, both previously mentioned.[44] Thus was amplified Sicard's claim that 'Ambrose, Gelasius, and Gregory composed the graduals, tracts, and the alleluia and instituted them to be sung at Mass', with Durandus appending the observation that 'many other doctors of the church' had added materials too.[45]

Gregory, David, Jerome

Jeffery's work makes clear that Pope Celestine's entanglement with Romano-Frankish chant only began in the ninth century, when Carolingian authors began to misconstrue a line from the *Liber pontificalis* as referring to their own native Frankish tradition, rather than that of fifth-century Rome.[46] Specifically, Celestine's purported introduction of psalm singing before the Mass was read as a foreshadowing of the Romano-Frankish introit and thus by extension (in the view of Sigebert, among others), the larger repertory of Frankish liturgical chant. However, as we have seen, it was not until the turn of the twelfth century that Gregory and Celestine became explicitly linked. In the meantime, the common factor of the psalms had apparently encouraged a comparable association between Gregory and the biblical figure of David, who for medieval audiences was synonymous with the authorship of the psalter.

---

[41] Haacke (ed.) 1967, pp. 50–52 (II.21: 'Quomodo vel a quibus missae officium ordinatum sit'). If we trust the Patrologia Latina edition, Sigebert had already attributed to Gelasius the composition of 'tractatus': Sigebert of Gembloux, PL 160. 92 (year 487).

[42] Honorius, PL 172. 573 (I.88). A sentence later, the verb *composuit* is applied to Notker Balbulus, who is widely known for having written poetry to adorn the liturgical sequence.

[43] Bonizo, *Libellus de sacramentis*, in Berschin 1972, p. 156.

[44] Sarbak and Weinrich (eds.) 2008, pp. 129–52 (III.2–3); Ryan (ed. and trans.) 2012, p. 763–64 (chap. 181); Davril and Thibodeau (eds.) 1995–2000, vol. 2, p. 15 (V.II.4).

[45] 'Gradualia, tractus et Alleluia Ambrosius et Gregorius et Gelasius composuerunt et ad missam cantari statuerunt' in Sarbak and Weinrich (eds.) 2008, p. 148 (III.3). 'Plerique quoque alii doctores Ecclesie aliqua alia superaddidisse noscuntur' in Davril and Thibodeau (eds.) 1995–2000, vol. 2, p. 15 (V.1.II.4).

[46] Jeffery 1984, pp. 147–50.

This relationship between Gregory and David was not always spelled out, yet for seasoned liturgical performers there was surely no need. In the liturgies of Mass and Office, the chant books and psalter were inextricably connected, not only in the act of performing, via the liturgical interdependence of antiphonal chants and their psalms, but also textually since a majority of Romano-Frankish chants were themselves psalmic.[47] This relationship was embodied in the very design of the books that transmitted the repertory. The Mass antiphoner (or Gradual) normally began with the words *Ad te levavi*, introducing an introit that was verbally identical to the incipit of Vulgate Psalm 122. In English practice, the relationship was embedded materially, for the book was itself sometimes known as the 'Adtelevavi'.[48] Elsewhere, wherever a chant book was prefaced with the poem 'Gregorius praesul', the psalmic opening of the introit 'Ad te levavi' was thus encountered directly after a text trumpeting Gregory's own compositional achievements. In certain north Italian books, the effect was even more pronounced. The eighth-century Lucca fragments have an extended 'Gregorius praesul' text that, having introduced Gregory's 'little book of musical art', exhorts the reader to sing 'hymns and psalms and responsories appropriate to each feast'.[49] And in a scattering of chant books from tenth-century Italy, 'Ad te levavi' was troped such that the introit's psalmic opening was presented as having been uttered by the mouth of the divinely inspired Gregory.[50] On the basis that the Romano-Frankish repertory includes sequences of psalmic chants ordered according to their scriptural number, it is possible that singers perceived a further elision between the authorities of Gregory and David in the overall disposition of the repertory.[51]

[47] For an introduction to this relationship, see Dyer 2012, pp. 675–77; for more detailed treatment, see Dyer 1984.

[48] Gneuss 1985, pp. 103–4.

[49] Stäblein 1968, p. 543: 'hymnos ac psalmos et responsoria festis congrua pronamus subter testudine templi'.

[50] 'Sanctissimus namque Gregorius, dum preces funderet ad dominum ut musicum donum ei in carminibus daret, tunc descendit spiritus sanctus super eum in specie columbae et illustravit cor eius, et sic demum exorsus est canere ita dicendo: Ad te levavi' (As the most holy Gregory poured prayers to the Lord that He might give him a musical gift in songs, then the Holy Spirit came upon him in the form of a dove and enlightened his heart, and so he began to sing, saying thus: *Ad te levavi*) (Stäblein 1968, pp. 559–61; Planchart (ed.) 1994, vol. 1, pp. 8–9).

[51] Hiley 1993, pp. 109, 117.

A uniquely visual expression of this dualism survives on the pair of ivories that once enclosed the ninth-century 'purple' cantatorium of Monza Cathedral, one of the earliest and most sumptuous compilations of Romano-Frankish chant.[52] On the front of the volume, the reader encountered a carving of a figure identified as 'Sanctus Gregorius' and on the rear a carving of 'David rex' (see Figure 1.1). Although these images originated in the context of a sixth-century consular diptych, there is no question that they were adapted for musical purposes, for above the head of Gregory, someone later carved in the opening lines of the 'Gregorius praesul' poem.[53] With this framing comes a wealth of interesting connotations. From a theological standpoint, the poet-musician David can be seen as an Old Testament prefiguration of Gregory, thereby creating a much longer ancestry for Romano-Frankish chant practices. We can also see the pairing in distinctly liturgical terms because the function of the cantatorium was to transmit the psalm-heavy genres of gradual, alleluia, and tract. Psalmic in content, these chants were simultaneously psalmic in their delivery insofar as they were designated for soloists, thus affording striking parallels between the act of liturgical performance and the iconographic tradition of David the solo singer. It was also by means of this solo performance that the cantatorium fulfilled its function as a liturgical object at Mass, when according to Roman custom it was held aloft by a soloist at the ambo steps, not to be read but to be *seen*.[54] Thus in the Monza cantatorium, the audible dialogue between David's words and Gregory's musical settings at Mass was ingeniously and (it seems) deliberately shadowed by the visual dialogue between 'David rex' and 'Sanctus Gregorius' as they appeared on the open binding.

The fact that no comparable example survives may be attributed to the relatively short life of the cantatorium concept as well as the inevitable tendency for ivories to become detached from their original surroundings. Yet the singularity of the Monza Cantatorium may also reflect the reality that David was not strictly representative of the Romano-Frankish tradition at large. Although psalm-heavy, this repertory was characterised by a much greater breadth of scriptural and indeed non-scriptural borrowing.[55] That wider sense of textual patrimony was acknowledged in two twelfth-century antiphoners – one from a French Carthusian house, the other from the Hirsau foundation of Zwiefalten – in which medieval scribes independently annotated each successive composition with the name of the corresponding book of the Bible.[56] The first example can be explained in terms of the

---

[52] The cantatorium is Monza, S. Giovanni, Cod. 88; the ivories are held in the Monza Cathedral museum.

[53] For an excellent introduction to the reuse of ivories, see Wittekind 2008. I thank Nicole Pulichene for sharing this reference with me.

[54] Amalar, *Liber officialis*, III.16: 'Cantor, sine aliqua necessitate legendi, tenet tabulas in manibus' (Hanssens (ed.) 1948–50, vol. 2, p. 303).

[55] The borrowings are surveyed in Marbach 1907.

[56] London, BL, Add. 17302; Karlsruhe, BLB, Cod. Aug. perg. 60. A plate of the former was printed in Hiley 1993, p. 432; the latter may be seen in Figure 1.2 and online at https://nbn-resolving.org/urn:nbn:de:bsz:31-39404/fragment/page=1253174.

Figure 1.1. Ivory diptych, perhaps of the sixth century, later adapted to depict Gregory and David. Museum and Treasury of Monza Cathedral (credit: Mondadori Portfolio/ Electa/Sergio Anelli).

Carthusian mission to purify chant of its human artifice, which is to say, to max-imise the biblical content and to minimise the poetic reworkings that others had attributed to Gregory.[57] But the intention seems to have been quite different in the contemporary Zwiefalten book, whose large historiated initial *A* on the first open-ing (Figure 1.2) places musical and scriptural authorities in tension. In the lower half of the image is an instantly recognisable portrait of Pope Gregory, who writes down the chant text 'Aspiciens a longe' with the assistance of a bird speaking in his ear. (The initial *A* belongs to the same chant, which begins concurrently.) But he is not alone. In the upper half of the image are two scenes from scripture. Within the initial is the bearded figure of Isaiah, identifiable from a banner proclaiming that a virgin shall conceive (Isaiah 7:14) and sitting astride the tendrils of what appears to be a Jesse tree. Above the initial are the figures of Gabriel and Mary, acting out the annunciation that Isaiah's words have foretold, with banners proclaiming their exchange (Luke 1:28, 1:38). Announcing the beginning of this substantial anti-phoner, therefore, is an image that presents Gregory not only as an originator of the chant tradition but also as someone working in dialogue with the Old and New Testaments. Further to this point is the short marginal note to the left of the initial in which the author surmises that the text of 'Aspiciens a longe' is a mixture (or *cento*) of Isaiah and Matthew's Gospel. Twice on one page, therefore, the reader is reminded of the repertory's creative layers.

The patristic figure most intimately connected with the Bible was of course Saint Jerome, the translator of the Latin scriptures, whose name was also closely associated with the medieval lectionary practices that drew on those texts.[58] He was also invoked occasionally in connection with the textual dimension of Romano-Frankish chant, implicitly as a counterpart to the work of Gregory. In a memorable description of his own compositional activity, the eleventh-century monk Gottschalk of Limburg likened one of his sequences to a piece of cloth that had been woven from Jerome's 'words' (*verba*) and Gregory's 'melodies' (*neumas*).[59] He was not strictly speaking of a Romano-Frankish chant, yet as Michael McGrade has shown, Gottschalk had bor-rowed material from that very corpus, reusing portions of melody from an alleluia and text from an offertory, alongside a host of further scriptural passages.[60] It thus seems likely that Gottschalk's conceptual Jerome-Gregory division was as much a nod to his Romano-Frankish models as it was a comment on his own composition. Also from the eleventh century, in a slightly different permutation of authorities, the Reichenau abbot Bern wrote an essay considering how Romano-Frankish chants relate to the scriptural authority of Saint Jerome; Gregory is conspicuously absent, save for one allusion to him as the authority responsible for liturgical ordering.[61]

---

[57] Šter 2014.

[58] Frere 1934, p. 59.

[59] Quoted in McGrade 1996, pp. 369–70.

[60] McGrade 1996, pp. 384–95.

[61] Bern of Reichenau, *De varia psalmorum*, in Parkes (ed.) 2019, pp. 107–49; discussed in Parkes 2017, pp. 35–36.

Figure 1.2. Karlsruhe, Badische Landesbibliothek, Cod. Aug. perg. 60, fol. Iv. Opening initial from the twelfth-century Zwiefalten Antiphoner.

Gregory, Boethius, Guido

The fact that Bern was relatively tight-lipped about Gregory in the context of Romano-Frankish chant is not so unusual, in fact, when judged against his fellow music theorists. As David Hiley has previously observed, Western music theory seems not to have had much need to involve Gregory until a light scattering of references around the turn of the first millennium.[62] The pope's absence to this point does not necessarily warrant comment, for in a discipline that dealt in numbers, categories, and ratios, there was no formal place for anecdotes about a pope learning melodies from a dove or notating an antiphoner, except as colourful asides. In these texts, it was much more useful to hear from ancient Greek theorists, or from Boethius, or his Carolingian inheritors. However, the interesting point is that Gregory *did* ultimately become co-opted as a medieval theoretical authority and that in this role he served as one authority among many.

Initially, it appears that Gregory's function was simply to denote a musical precedent established from practice rather than theory. Symptomatic is the eleventh-century *Libellus tonarius*, whose anonymous author, well aware that this pope had never written *about* the art of music (*de arte*), referred instead to the modal norms that Gregory and his disciples had communicated *from* their art (*ex arte*) – that is, through surviving chant compositions.[63] This individual had probably read Guido of Arezzo, who in his *Micrologus* had remarked on Gregory's particular affinity for the tritus (*fa*) within the modality of chant and had twice invoked him in his *Regulae rhythmicae* to defend against modern melodic deviations.[64] There is no way of knowing what specific understandings of Gregory lie behind these comments, but in the context of each text, the purpose is clearly rhetorical, using the pope's authority to paper over the underlying gaps in a theoretical argument.[65]

However, within decades, Gregory was being presented as if a meaningful contributor to the construction of chant theory itself. In his late eleventh-century *De musica*, the German theorist Aribo devoted a chapter to the claim 'that St. Gregory has perceived the two-fold operation of the same modes' (*quod sanctus Gregorius eiusdem modi duplicem perspexerit operationem*), which is to say, the division of four modal finals into authentic and plagal.[66] On its own, the comment can be read in the same way as our previous examples: as a covert way of asserting 'this is what I believe to be correct'. (At stake was the identity of the eighth mode, or plagal tetrardus, whose *D–d* octave species rendered it liable to be conflated with the first mode.[67]) But Aribo did so with reference not only to Gregory, as mentioned in the

---

[62] Hiley 2006, p. 130.

[63] Sowa 1935, p. 86.

[64] Smits van Waesberghe (ed.) 1955, pp. 207–8 (chap. 18); Smits van Waesberghe and Vetter (eds.) 1985, pp. 103, 115.

[65] Jerome's authority is invoked similarly by Bern of Reichenau, as discussed in Parkes 2017, pp. 35–36.

[66] McCarthy (ed.) 2015, pp. 48–49 (chap. 66).

[67] Cohen 2002, pp. 337–38.

chapter title of his treatise, but also to Ambrose. It is hard to know precisely what he meant by this, yet, as Hiley has noted, the association between these two church fathers and Western modality would go on to have an exceptionally long life, up to and including early editions of Grove's *Dictionary of Music and Musicians*.[68] To cite but one prominent example, Charles Burney declared in his *General History of Music* (1782) that 'all writers on these subjects agree in saying that St Ambrose only used the four authentic modes, and that the four plagal were added afterwards by St Gregory'.[69] Along the way, one anonymous medieval author even managed to conflate the story with the aforementioned narratives about Ignatius. In the so-called Berkeley Manuscript, a French music theory collection of the fourteenth century, Gregory is said to have derived his eight modes from Ambrose's five, which were themselves based on Ignatius' three.[70]

No less interestingly, the Berkeley Manuscript author placed these details within a longer narrative of monochord division that ends with Guido and stretches back, via Gregory, Ambrose, and Ignatius, to the great Pythagoras.[71] This lineage is a curious mix of theorists and ecclesiastical figureheads, but in juxtaposing Gregory and Guido specifically, it travels a relatively well-worn path. A Middle Irish poem dated to the early twelfth century features the characters of Grigair and Gamut, the one identified as an early forerunner of Pope Gregory, the other implicitly a personification of Guido's extended chant scale.[72] Although the poem is set in the time of Christ, its early stanzas dramatise the interactions between Gregory's melodies and Guido's solmisation syllables, here charmingly personified as Gregory's pupils. What we learn is precisely what musically literate individuals were coming to learn from the eleventh century onwards, in an age of staff notation, solmisation, and practically oriented music theory: the concept of melody in church music (here represented as Gregory) was increasingly hard to separate from its visual and theoretical expression (here Guido). This dualism of sound and measurement helps to explain a sequence of images from a south German compilation of the twelfth century that begins with images of Gregory (with the dove), Pythagoras (with his hammers), and Guido (pictured opposite a monochord),[73] as well as a fascinating thirteenth-century drawing that juxtaposes the figures of Gregory and Euclid.[74] And it certainly explains Johannes de Garlandia's declaration that chant was first 'edited' (*edita*) under Gregory and then 'corrected, put together, and ordained' (*correcta, composita, et ordinati*) by Guido.[75] Interestingly, at least two fourteenth-century theorists added Jerome to this group, thereby creating a three-pronged authority for chant that, in the absence of further explanation, appears to have divided responsibilities

[68] Hiley 1993, p. 511; Rockstro 1879–90, pp. 340–43.

[69] Mercer (ed.) 1957, vol. 1, p. 417.

[70] Ellsworth (ed. and trans.) 1984, pp. 220–23.

[71] Ellsworth (ed. and trans.) 1984, pp. 212–27.

[72] Ó Cuív 1992.

[73] Wolfenbüttel, HAB, Cod. Guelf. 334 Gud. lat., fols. 1r–4v.

[74] Dyer 2019, pp. 8–10.

[75] Garlandia (attrib.), *Introductio musicae planae*, in Meyer (ed.) 1998, p. 64.

between text, melody, and notational expression.[76] In a fifteenth-century Carthusian tract, the author went further, attributing the institution of *musica plana* to 'blessed Gregory, Jerome, and Guido the Benedictine monk, Ambrose and other doctors of the holy church' (*quam quidem musicam planam beatus Gregorius, Iheronimus et Guido monachus ordinis beati Benedicti, Ambrosius et alii doctores sancte ecclesie ad laudem Dei instituerunt*).[77]

In that last example, Guido is very much the odd one out, as a lowly theorist in the company of esteemed doctors of the late antique church. However, in later medieval sources, it was equally possible for Gregory to be the anomaly, drawn from among the church fathers into the role of honorary music theorist. Illustrative examples include the aforementioned Carthusian author who was unsure whether Guido or Gregory had invented the musical scale,[78] the thirteenth-century cleric who in Joseph Dyer's reading had named Gregory as 'first inventor of all eight tones' (*primus inventor omnium octo tonorum*),[79] and the fifteenth-century commentator who distinguished between Guido's solmisation syllables and Gregory's letter notation.[80] In a prominent but slightly more cryptic formulation, Franco of Cologne began his mid thirteenth-century *Ars cantus mensurabilis* with a word about the three 'philosophers' who had treated plainchant: Boethius in theory, Guido in practice, and above all, Gregory 'de tropis ecclesiasticis'.[81]

Gregory et al.

In some of these latter examples, all from the upper range of our chronology, we can see hints that the intellectual crosshairs are moving. As Gregory's name is joined by a wash of other names, the specifics of his putative achievements are diluted. In the fourteenth and fifteenth centuries, references to Gregory and music become especially salient in the context of long lists that point far beyond the chant repertory at hand. Consider the motetus voice of the celebrated fourteenth-century motet *Sub Arturo/Fons* in which the pope rubs shoulders with the biblical musician Tubal, the ancient Greek Pythagoras, as well as Boethius, Guido, Franco, and the motet's possible author Johannes Alanus.[82] Or consider the contemporaneous metrum *Pitagoras reperit*, transmitted within the central European tradition of teachings associated with the theorist Johannes Hollandrinus, which places Gregory and Ambrose alongside Jubal and Tubal, Pythagoras, Guido, and the twelfth-century theorist John of

---

[76] Petrus dictus Palma ociosa, *Compendium de discantu mensurabili*, in Wolf 1914, p. 507; Sweeney and Gilles (eds.) 1971, p. 31.

[77] Anon., *Practica musicae*, prologue in Lebedev (ed.) 2000, p. 57.

[78] Lebedev (ed.) 2000, pp. 63–64 (chap. 6).

[79] Dyer 2019, pp. 9–11.

[80] Bartolomé Ramos de Pareia, *Musica practica* (1482), excerpted and translated in Treitler (ed.) 1998, vol. 3, pp. 134–35.

[81] Reaney and Gilles (eds.) 1974, p. 23. This text was later quoted by Jerome of Moravia.

[82] For more on *Sub Arturo/Fons*, see Bent's chapter in this volume, which also supplies other lists of musicians included in late-medieval works.

Afflighem.[83] Many fifteenth-century authors would go on to construct even longer musical genealogies. Adam of Fulda's list of 'discoverers of the art' (*artis inventores*) places Gregory somewhere in the middle, just after Boethius and before Isidore of Seville, Guido, Odo of Arezzo, Bern of Reichenau, Jehan des Murs, and the composers Guillaume Du Fay and Antoine Busnois.[84] In Johannes Tinctoris's *Proportionale musices*, the reader encounters an even more impressive showing of late antique or early medieval figures (Gregory, Ambrose, Hilary, Boethius, Martianus Capella) followed a little later by a who's who of recent and contemporary composing greats (John Dunstaple, Guillaume Du Fay, Gilles Binchois, Johannes Ockeghem, Antoine Busnois, Johannes Regis, Firminus Caron).[85]

What matters to these authors is not the specific patrimony of Romano-Frankish chant so much as the cumulative achievements of the 'great men' who discovered the art of music. It should be stressed that this is not a new category of discourse, for narratives on the invention of music can be traced back to Isidore in the sixth century and subsequently appear in Aurelian of Réôme and the *Speculum musicae*, among others.[86] But Gregory is most certainly a new inductee. On one level, the presence of multiple authority figures in these latter lists, many of them connected to Latin monophony, underlines the central theme of this chapter – that the pope rarely stood alone. But on another level, it is possible to see how Gregory's arrival in this venerable pantheon is actually hastening the end of an older medieval narrative of collaborative or iterative authorship. There are two ways in which musicians' lists point in this direction. The first is the implied equivalence. Placed into the company of musical innovators both ancient and modern, Gregory's persona is stripped of its former nuance. All of the various chant-specific achievements that used to be discussed by medieval authors are here of little consequence; in their place is a generically musical identity that sits somewhere on an undifferentiated continuum between Boethius and Busnois. The second is the teleology. Read forwards, the lists present Gregory and other doctors of the church as foundational figures in a Western craft of composition, begetting through their innovations a lineage of great 'composers' in a newer, more modern sense.[87] Read backwards, the list encourages the fifteenth-century reader to project the achievements of a modern-day Ockeghem or Regis onto the biography of a sixth-century pope. Suddenly, there is real potential, as never before, for the Romano-Frankish tradition and its figurehead to be united under the modern concepts of 'composer' and 'work'.

If we accept that Gregory's identity was crystallising in this way for early modern audiences, it should perhaps give us pause to reflect on the authorship narratives we tell today. As we have seen, James McKinnon saw the year 1000 as a threshold

---

[83] For a concise overview of its transmission within the *Traditio Hollandrinus*, see Meyer 2016, p. 77.

[84] Gerbert 1784, vol. 3, p. 341 (chap. 7).

[85] Seay (ed.) 1975–78, vol. 2a, p. 10 (prologue).

[86] Isidore of Seville, PL 82. 163 (chap. 16); Gushee (ed.) 1975, pp. 61–64 (chap. 2); Bragard (ed.) 1955–73, vol. 1, pp. 25–27 (I.6).

[87] On this newer sense, see Wegman 1996.

in medieval understandings of Gregory, as a formerly unsettled, hybridised tradition of liturgical singing eventually began to be treasured as an authoritative musical singularity for which the pope had ultimately been responsible. There is no question that medieval singers did widely credit Gregory with having contributed to the Romano-Frankish chant tradition, as far back as *Ordo Romanus XIX* in the seventh or eighth century, though always in different ways and to very different extents. Nor is there any question that the pope's authoritative status within the church gave considerable heft to the chant books that bore his name. But for the greater part of the Middle Ages, I find no strong evidence of a belief in Gregory's creative monopoly or in his purported identity as the 'divinely inspired composer' of Romano-Frankish chant. So far as the surviving discourse reveals, people freely discussed the repertory in relation to authors and creators plural, both of text and of music, whether medieval contemporaries or distant church fathers, and they did so without much sense of contradiction. And to the extent that Gregory was indeed synonymous with this musical tradition, I suggest that this was little more than synecdoche: a figure of partial responsibility standing in for the whole. That medieval audiences might occasionally have misinterpreted this message is of course quite possible, though I suspect that this is far easier for modern audiences, who inherit from Renaissance thought a rather two-dimensional view of what Gregory was considered to have achieved. As Elizabeth Eisenstein put it sagely, reflecting on the intellectual transformations wrought by the printing press in the fifteenth century, 'many problems about assigning proper credit to scribal "authors" may result from misguided efforts to apply print-made concepts where they do not pertain'.[88] The medieval sources surveyed here reveal a rich and diverting plurality of stories about Romano-Frankish chant and the *auctores* who augmented it. We should be wary of the possibility that a famous iconography and a decontextualised papal adjective have conditioned us to see it otherwise.

---

[88] Eisenstein 1983, p. 85.

2

Inspiration versus Attribution:
The Voice of the *Planctus ante nescia*

Charles E. Brewer

Planctus ante nescia was one of the most well-known twelfth-century songs during the late Middle Ages and early modern period, completely or partially preserved in nine musical sources and sixteen text manuscripts.[1] It was also influential: its adaptations can be found in middle-high German, Icelandic, Norwegian, and Hungarian, and the melody was used for contrafacta in Norman French and Middle English.[2] It is perhaps one of the most published medieval Latin poems and a subject of critical study since the late nineteenth century. Appendix 1 provides the most recent consensus concerning the twenty-five manuscript sources that include this song.[3] It seems that its popularity persisted up to the beginnings of the Council of Trent, as shown by Ulysse Chevalier's list of the printings of the *Planctus* in liturgical books (mostly from the early sixteenth century[4]), and that the last printing of part of the

---

[1] *Planctus ante nescia* will be hereafter referred to as *Planctus*, and general references to the genre will use the lower case, *planctus*. The sources for the *Planctus* and their abbreviations are listed in Appendix 1. The *Planctus* is 'L 79' in Anderson 1972–75, pp. 213–14, which includes a relatively complete bibliographic listing. See also Schumann and Bischoff (eds.) 1970, pp. 129–34; Yearley 1983 (the *Planctus* is discussed in vol. 1, pp. 3, 5–8, 11–12, 15, 78, 111–12, 154–55; vol. 2, pp. 42, 384–87 (text and translation); vol. 3, pp. 176–95 (transcriptions)); Yearley 1981, p. 25. Earlier editions of the melody are cited in Brewer 2012, p. 72, with the addition of Stevens 1986, pp. 131–35.

[2] Concerning German influences of the *Planctus*, see Schönbach 1874; Hennig 1992; Mehler 1997. For Scandinavian versions, see Schottmann 2013, p. 270 (Islandic prose translation) and Bekker-Nielsen 1968, pp. 35–36. The Hungarian lament (Budapest, OSK, MNy 79, fol. 134v) is discussed in Vizkelety 1985, 1986a, 1986b; Dobszay 1988, pp. 17–19 (hypothetical transcription). Concerning the Anglo-Norman and Middle English contrafacta, see Page 1976, pp. 73–74 (facsimile of fols. 160v–161r at 83). These are edited in Dobson and Harrison (eds.) 1979, pp. 110–16 (emended text and critical notes), pp. 229–37 (music, with editorial accompaniment added), and pp. 296–97 (critical notes on the music); Deeming (ed.) 2013, pp. 135–37 (transcriptions and translations). They are discussed in relation to other English contrafacta in Deeming 2015b.

[3] Appendix 1 corrects the source lists in Schumann and Bischoff (eds.) 1970, pp. 131–32; Yearley 1983, vol. 2, p. 42; and Brewer 2012, p. 72, in light of more recent contributions. These sources will be hereafter referenced by Appendix 1 and number in the text.

[4] Chevalier 1889–1920, vol. 2, p. 317 (#14950). The edition of the *Planctus* in Kehrein (ed.) 1873, pp. 177–78, is taken from the *Missale ad sacrosancte Romane ecclesie usum* (Paris, 1520), on fol. 63v ('Commune Sanctorum').

text is perhaps in János Kájoni's *Cantionale catholicum* from eighteenth-century Hungary.[5] Within the earlier studies, as will be seen, there has been an overemphasis on establishing an attribution which has also affected many later literary and musical conclusions about the *Planctus*. A re-evaluation of the actual medieval evidence is necessary to refocus discussions on what was deemed significant about the *Planctus* in the twelfth and thirteenth centuries. When it is then placed in the context of similar works from this period, the question of authorship or attribution fades and that of medieval discussions of inspiration become more significant.

The False Trails

In the earliest manuscript sources, there are no ascriptions to the *Planctus*. The first false trail, ascribing the work to Bernard of Clairvaux, is in a fifteenth-century manuscript (Appendix 1:25): 'Incipit Planctus virginis Marie Bernardi abbatis' (Incipit of the lament of Virgin Mary by Abbot Bernard).[6] The second trail began in 1722 when Casimir Oudin, a French Premonstratensian monk and bibliographer, listed the 'Planctus Beatæ Mariæ Virginis' among the works of 'Godefridus Sancti Victoris Parisiensis Supprior' on the basis of a Victorine manuscript (Appendix 1:5) and an earlier Saint Victor chronicle.[7] Oudin's attribution was repeated in 1820 in the *Histoire littéraire de la France*, the probable source for many later authors.[8] Neither Édélestand Du Méril's publication of a shorten text nor Franz Joseph Mone in his study of early German drama attributed the *Planctus* to any specific author, but through a misreading of Mone's edition, some later authors designated Bonaventure as the author of the *Planctus*.[9]

The *Planctus* was published in 1895 by Guido Maria Dreves with an attribution to 'Gottfried, Supprior von St Viktor'.[10] Ten years later, Dreves published the first edition

---

5   Kájoni (1676) 1719, p. 160.

6   Schumann and Bischoff (eds.) 1970, p. 132.

7   Oudin 1722, col.1566–68; col.1568: 'And so the Historiographer recounts in a manuscript from Saint Victor Paris, p. 102 of his history: "Other little works are also possessed from him made with the same rhythmic verses, as, for example, a song to the God-bearing Virgin, a lament of the Blessed Virgin Mary, and a proclamation about Saint Augustine, bishop and doctor of the church, and also thirty-one sermons on various solemnities of the year retained among us, all of which manuscripts our library preserves"'. For an edition of the third poem mentioned by the 'Historiographer', see Damon 1960. The 'Canticum ad Deiparam Virginem' – that is, *Unius numinis* – will be discussed later.

8   [Brial] 1820, p. 85: 'Oudin, on the basis of the annalist of Saint Victor, tells us that Godefroy had also composed a song in honour of the Blessed Virgin and a lament in the style of the *Stabat* [*Mater*]. These two pieces do not exist in the manuscripts of Saint Victor held by the royal library'. The statement about manuscript sources was clearly incorrect.

9   Du Méril 1843, p. 176 and Mone 1852, pp. 359–66. On p. 362, Mone wrote before his edition of the *Planctus*, 'As the introduction shows, this lengthy poem belongs to the entombment of Christ. In other manuscripts it is attributed to Bonaventure (d. 1274)'. Mone's reference is not to the *Planctus* but the *Horæ de compassione BWV*, which Mone titled 'Horæ de planctu beatæ virginis, quas composuit papa Johannes XXII' on p. 361. The Bonaventure attributions are found in Wilken 1872, p. 76, and in Schönbach 1874, p. 5, quoting Wilken.

10 Dreves (ed.) 1895, pp. 156–58, based only on Appendix 1:11 and 1:20; the statement of attribution on p. 158 is without any source reference but is most likely based on that

of a song ascribed to Godefroy in the fifteenth-century Paris, BnF, lat. 15163 (Appendix 1:24), *Unius numinis* (fols. 227r–229r), a poetic expansion of the Magnificat, and transcribed the headnote placed above the work in the source: 'Canticum beatae virginis et matris Iesu Christi, studio Godefridi, subprioris Sancti Victoris extensum' (Song of the Blessed Virgin and Mother of Jesus Christ, extended by the zeal of Godefroy, the subprior of Saint Victor).[11] This source also includes the *Planctus* as an anonymous work, but presumably because it is copied right after *Unius numinis*, Clemens Blume misrepresented in 1909 that both the *Planctus* and *Unius numinis* were ascribed to Godefroy in the source – Blume was, however, unaware of the connection of the source Appendix 1:5 to Saint Victor, though it had been used to edit *Unius numinis*.[12] Adding even more confusion, Blume was following Antoine Charma's 1868 edition of the *Fons philosophie* in linking the name of Godefroi de Breteuil, the subprior of Sainte-Barbe-en-Auge, with other works by Godefroy of Saint Victor.[13] The attributions by Dreves and Blume to Godefroi were frequently repeated and has continued in publications, mostly crediting Godefroi de Breteuil as the author of the song.[14] The situation changed with Philippe Delhaye's edition of Godefroy of Saint Victor's *Microcosmos*, which clarified the distinction between Godefroi de Breteuil and Godefroy of Saint Victor, and most later editions have followed his research.[15]

In the recent scholarly discussions of the *Planctus*, there is little consensus concerning its dating: Janthia Yearley suggested the later twelfth century,[16] while Peter Dronke proposed the 1140s based on the evidence that the *Planctus* is cited in a twelfth-century letter from the Abbey of Bec.[17] Even though he suggested that the piece is 'probably by Godefrey of Saint-Victor',[18] Dronke at the same time expressed reservations concerning this traditional attribution:

---

published in *Histoire littéraire de la France*.

[11] Dreves (ed.) 1905, pp. 137–39, based on Appendix 1:24 and 1:5; the headnote was published on p. 139.

[12] Dreves and Blume (eds.) 1909: see the editions of *Unius numinis* (vol. 1, pp. 282–83) and *Planctus ante nescia* (vol. 1, pp. 283–84). At p. 281, Blume quotes the passage from the *Histoire littéraire de la France* cited above and adds a correction: 'The latter statement is incorrect. Both pieces can be found in the Codex Parisinensis 15163 from Saint Victor and are there expressly referred to as works "Godefridi, supprioris Sancti Victoris"'.

[13] Charma (ed.) 1868, pp. 16–19 (biography of Godefroi de Breteuil). On p. 13, the letters to Lyra (to be examined below) are briefly mentioned, and Oudin's attributions of *Unius numinis* and the *Planctus* are repeated on p. 14.

[14] Manitius 1931, pp. 777–79: 'As for poems, he [Godefroi de Breteuil] wrote a *Preconium metricum divi Augustini* in 127 rhythmic stanzas (each with four rhymed thirteen syllable lines), then a *Canticum beatae Mariae virginis* and a *Planctus beatae Mariae virginis* with musical notes'.

[15] Delhaye 1951, pp. 13–19. Recent discussions of the Victorine sources are in Delhaye 1951, pp. 251–59; Szövérffy (ed.) 1965, pp. 148–49; Schumann and Bischoff (eds.) 1970, p. 131; Gasparri 1982, 1985; Fassler 1993, pp. 334–38; Dobson and Harrison (eds.) 1979, p. 117.

[16] Yearley 1983, vol. 1, p. 3. Later, in Table 3B (pp. 72–73), she gives the date as '>1190'.

[17] Dronke 1992, p. 458 (revision of an article first published in 1988). The nature of this citation and the controversial issues related to dating this letter will be discussed below.

[18] Dronke 1992, pp. 463–64.

The *planctus*, which is cited already as the work of *quidam* in a mid-twelfth-century letter, is included in the early thirteenth-century corpus of Godefrey's works in the manuscript Paris, Bibl. Mazarine 1002 [Appendix 1:5]. My slight remaining hesitation about the authorship is connected with the generally accepted date of Godefrey's birth, ca. 1125–30. If this is correct, he must have been extremely young when he composed *Planctus ante nescia*, whereas its extraordinary verbal artistry suggests to me a poet at the summit of his powers.[19]

Dronke's suggested chronology has been cited in more recent studies.[20] In contrast, Jan Ziolkowski has suggested a much later dating for the *Planctus*: 'between 1173 and 1182', most likely based on the traditional dating of Godefroy of Saint Victor's *Fons philosophie* (before 1176) and a date of 1178 recorded in the margins of source Appendix 1:5.[21]

There are reasons to doubt the received attribution to Godefroy of Saint Victor when the *Planctus* is compared to his acknowledged song, *Unius numinis*, given the very different styles of their texts and melodies.[22] Additionally, the dating and provenance of the surviving sources (listed in Appendix 1) do not indicate a strong Victorine provenance as only three manuscripts have Augustinian associations: the two from Saint Victor (Appendix 1:5 and 1:24, the second being quite late) and one possibly from the Abbey of Wigmore in Wales (Appendix 1:13). Finally, there is also no clear reason to attribute an anonymous song (the *Planctus*) written by a different scribe to the known author of the previous song written in his own hand (*Unius numinis*), a case of 'guilt by association', especially when it is copied along with other anonymous works, such as the Marian chant Alleluya *V* Virga Iesse floruit. Together with the textual and musical differences between the *Planctus* and the single acknowledged song by Godefroy, it seems improbable that the latter was the composer of the *Planctus*. As the Abbey of Saint Victor was becoming more interested in Marian compositions during the later twelfth century, as noted by Margot Fassler, the *Planctus* may have come to Godefroy's attention, though its use apparently never caught on there.[23]

Contemporary Documents

Two sources contain the only medieval references to the *Planctus*. Dronke based his discussion of the attribution and dating on a series of seventeen letters from the Abbey of Bec in Normandy, the first of which was addressed 'ad Priorem de Lira' (to the prior of Lyra), in Paris, BnF, lat. 13575, fol. 44r. Barthélemy Hauréau believed they were written between 1130 and c. 1150, which influenced Dronke's suggestion of an early date for the

---

[19] Dronke 1992, p. 464.

[20] See, for example, Boynton 2004, p. 332.

[21] Ziolkowski 2004, p. 135. The dating of the *Fons philosophie* is discussed in Michaud-Quantin (ed.) 1956, p. 22, and Gasparri 1982. Appendix 1:5 is discussed in Gasparri 1982, 46–49.

[22] See Brewer 2012 for further details. These same differences exist between the *Planctus* and the sequence for Saint Victor, *Ecce dies triumphalis*, that Fassler suggests might have been written by Godefroy of Saint Victor (Fassler 1993, pp. 337–38).

[23] Fassler 1993, pp. 321–34.

Planctus.[24] However, based on the more recent controversial speculations that some of these letters were written by Alan of Lille, they also have been dated to 1167–70.[25]

In the sixth letter, a letter of admonition, the entire stanza 13b of the *Planctus* is given as an example, clearly highlighting that the unique quality of the *Planctus* was recognised:

> Cast your thoughts upon Christ. Hide yourself 'in the hollow places of the wall, in the clefts of the rock' [Cant. 2:14], concerning which the Apostle speaks: 'and the rock was Christ' [I Cor. 10:4]. Look upon the image of Christ crucified, and in that [image] consider how little you should render to your Lord 'for all the things which he rendered to you' [Ps. 115:12]. Look to the piercing of the hands and feet, the cut through the side, and regard more attentively how mercifully, embracing his loved ones, he would have extended [his] hands. Whence someone exceedingly elegantly says: [13b] 'Throw yourselves into his embrace / while he hangs on the cross. / He waits for the embrace / of those who love him, / with arms outstretched'.[26]

If the earlier dating of these letters is correct, letter six is most likely the first document referring to the existence of the *Planctus*, predating any of the other musical or textual sources, and, as Dronke pointed out, it becomes less likely that Godefroy was the author. In any case, in this near contemporary letter from the same likely region as the lyric, Normandy, the author of the *Planctus* is only noted as 'quidam' (someone). And even if the later dating of the letters is correct, thus indicating that the *Planctus* was written before 1167–70, Godefroy is still an unlikely candidate on account of the Benedictine provenance of the letters.

Palémon Glorieux noted that this quotation from the *Planctus* appeared in the manuscript Paris, BnF, lat. 13575 also within the seventh sermon on the *Pater noster* (fols. 36r–41v), which is based on the seventh petition, 'Sed libera nos a malo':

> Here! Here! Our Lord, Jesus Christ, likewise most manifestly declares the good fortune of love, while to embrace the beloved, in the manner of a rapturous lover, he reveals externally extended hands. Whence someone exceedingly elegantly

---

[24] Hauréau 1890–93, vol. 2, p. 240; extracts from the letters are on pp. 237–39. The complete set of letters with a brief commentary is edited in Leclercq (ed.) 1953, and in Hudry (ed.) 2003.

[25] See Glorieux 1972, and Hudry (ed.) 2003, pp. 13–15. For a brief summary of the difficulties with this hypothesis, see Lena Wahlgren-Smith's (2006) review of Hudry's edition and the more extensive criticism in Rossi 2009 and Rossi 2017, which propose as a possible author Henry, a monk from the Bec Abbey, later abbot of Préaux. Letter 6 is edited in Hudry (ed.) 2003, pp. 106–12.

[26] 'Allide cogitatus tuos ad Christum. Absconde te "in caverna maceriae, in foraminibus petrae" de qua dicit apostolus: "Petra autem erat Christus". Respice ad imaginem crucifixi Christi, et in ea diligenter perpende quam modico retribuas Domino tuo pro omnibus quae retribuit tibi. Attende ad manuum et pedum transfixionem, lateris perforationem, et quam misericorditer amatoribus suis amplectandis manus habeat extensas attentius intuere. Unde quidam satis eleganter dicit: "In amplexus ruite / Dum pendet in stipite; / Mutuis amplexibus / Se parat amantibus, / Brachiis protensis"' (Paris, BnF, lat. 13575, fols. 48r–49r, at fol. 48v; Leclercq (ed.) 1953, p. 159, and Hudry (ed.) 2003, p. 110). Hudry in this quotation incorrectly reads 'dixit' for the manuscript 'dicit', as printed by Leclercq. According to Hauréau 1890–93, vol. 4, p. 330, 'Godefroy, sub-prior of Saint Victor, was a very mediocre writer; he is nevertheless well known'.

says: 'Throw yourselves into his embrace / while he hangs on the cross. / He waits for the embrace / of those who love him, / with arms outstretched'.[27]

Sara Lipton, in her examination of how crucifixes were visualised in the later Middle Ages, found that the earliest example she discovered of this imagined embrace was in a commentary on Matthew by the Benedictine Rupert of Deutz, written in 1127.[28] Although not conclusive, Rupert's vivid commentary would suggest that the anonymous letters and sermons in Paris, BnF, lat. 13575 and their evocation of this dramatic topos of the divine embrace with the quotation from the *Planctus* were also from the earlier twelfth century.

The second medieval reference to the song is found in an anonymous prologue to the *Planctus* (see Appendix 2), found in a thirteenth-century manuscript from the Benedictine Fleury Abbey at Saint-Benoît-sur-Loire (Appendix 1:14), which provides a contemporary view of the inspiration for the work.[29] The *Planctus* and its prologue are copied in the midst of a collection of lyrics for songs from the twelfth century also found in manuscripts such as the Aquitanian *versaria* or the so-called Later Cambridge Songbook, including a few that have been attributed to Gautier of Châtillon.[30] As Yearley pointed out, whether it represents the actual story or not, the prologue confirms its importance as a devotional lyric.[31]

Even though there are not any explicit dramatic implications, the time at which the vision of the Virgin Mary appears in the prologue – after the office of Matins, when the other monks have been sent off to bed and before Lauds – resonates with another description for a paraliturgical performance of a *planctus* found in a thirteenth-century service book from the Benedictine Abbey in Toulouse ('in ecclesia B[eate] M[arie] Deaurate Tolos[atii]'), which took place after Matins on Maundy Thursday:

> The Office of Matins begins at a better hour due to the solemnity of the day (Feria V, on the Lord's Supper) and for the sake of the multitude of the people and also

---

[27] 'Hic! Hic! Dominus noster Ihesu Christe secundum amoris etiam manifestissime declaravit, dum more amantis amantem amplecti gestientis, manus in cute protensas exhibet. Unde quidam satis eleganter dicit: "In amplexus ruite / Dum pendet in stipite; / Mutuis amplexibus / Se parat amantibus, / Brachiis protensis"' (Paris, BnF, lat. 13575, fol. 37v).

[28] Though the *Planctus* is not cited in Lipton 2005, it offers further support for her study.

[29] The anonymous prologue from Paris, BnF, lat. 4880, fol. 83v, is edited in Delhaye 1951, pp. 253–55. See Appendix 2 for a full emended text and translation. This prologue and the complete *Planctus* was translated among the miracle stories added to the Old Norse-Icelandic *Mariu Saga*, edited in Unger (ed.) 1871, pp. 890–93. See also the summary of the Old Norse in Bekker-Nielsen 1968, pp. 35–36. Given the evidence for a Benedictine provenance of the *Planctus*, it is unlikely that the passage in the *Mariu Saga* represents any Victorine influence.

[30] This collection was edited by Wilmart 1937, pp. 341–65. See also the short critical discussion of Wilmart's attribution of some songs in this source to Gautier of Châtillon in Traill (ed. and trans.) 2013, pp. xxvi–xxvii. A fuller examination of the musical implications of this manuscript collection is in preparation.

[31] Yearley 1983, vol. 1, p. 76.

for the sake of the *planctus* of the Blessed Virgin Mary, which is said after Matins by two little boys, and they ought to be monks, if they can be found suitable to this. However, conversely, [suitable boys] can be found from the seculars for this, if there are deficiencies among the monks. And all the candles are extinguished after Matins, namely after the *Kyrie eleyson* that is said before the altar with the verses, except one candle, which remains lit until the end of the *planctus*. This is a sign that on this day all faith will remain in only the Virgin Mary, because all the disciples had erred or doubted afterwards, more and less, except for the Virgin Mary. Thus the *planctus* is said in the pulpit of the preacher, and the aforementioned pulpit ought to be covered and encircled with white curtains completely, because saying or singing the above-mentioned *planctus* [the two boys] should not be able to be seen by the people, nor should they see the people, so that they would be able to sing more securely without fear, because they might strongly tremble in seeing the people.[32]

There was probably a double reason for the singers to be hidden from sight: the dramatic effect of the covering would have been to create the illusion of an unseen heavenly voice, and the practical effect was to avoid stage fright. That one of the extant musical sources for the *Planctus* is from Albi (Appendix 1:4) might suggest that the *planctus* mentioned at Toulouse was also the *Planctus ante nescia*, and the fact that it was from a Benedictine abbey links this description with the other confirmed Benedictine sources for the *Planctus*, such as the three manuscripts from Normandy (Appendix 1:1, 2 and 3) and the letters from Bec. Both the prologue and the Toulouse rubric place the *Planctus* during the ceremonies of Holy Week following Matins; in Toulouse on Maundy Thursday and in the prologue presumably on Good Friday. Finally, both of these documents also describe an extra-liturgical context for a *planctus*.

One other aspect of the prologue should be considered since it was apparently important to its author that the Virgin Mary appears to 'a man, religious and advanced in age'. If both the questionable attribution to Godefroy of Saint Victor and that the monk of the prologue was an older man are admitted as evidence for dating, it would place the creation of the *Planctus* in the later part of the twelfth century. However, even if we accept the recent theory that some of the letters from the Abbey of Bec with their citation of the *Planctus* were written by Alan of Lille in 1167–70, Godefroy

---

[32] 'Officium Matutinorum incipitur hora meliori propter solempnitatem diei (feria v in Coena Domini) et propter gentium multitudinem et etiam propter Planctum Beatissimae Virginis Mariae, quae dicitur a duobus puerulis post Matutinum, et debent esse monachi, si possunt reperiri, ad hoc apti, sin autem dicetur a secularibus ad hoc fundati, monachisque deficientibus. Et omnes candelae extinguntur post Matutinum, scilicet post *Kyrie eleyson* quod dicitur super altare cum versibus, excepta una candela quae remanet accensa usque Planctus finiatur; ad denotandum quod in ista die tota fides remanserit in sola Virgine Maria, quia omnes discipuli erraverunt seu dubitaverunt secundum magis et minus, excepta Virgine Maria. Ita Planctus dicitur in cathedra predicatorii, et debet esse coperta et circumcincta de cortinis albis praedicta cathedra ad finem, quod dicentes sive cantantes praedictum Planctum non possint videri a gentibus, nec ipsi videant gentes, ut securius possint cantare sine timore, quia forte videndo gentes turbarentur' (Young 1933, vol. 1, p. 698, quoting from Du Cange 1883–87, vol. 6, p. 353, who did not cite a specific source for this quotation).

of Saint Victor, based on Delhaye's proposed biography, would have been between thirty-seven and forty-five years old. In terms of twelfth-century life spans, this may not have been considered 'old age'.[33] If Khan-al-Din's interpretation of the medieval evidence is correct, someone would need to be older than fifty to be perceived as 'old' and perhaps about sixty to be considered as 'in his old age'.[34] Again, if this were applied to Godefroy, it would place the creation of the *Planctus* between about 1175 and 1180 or even 1185–90, again beyond the latest theoretical dates suggested for the letters, before which the *Planctus* was already in existence. When combined with the sixth letter from Bec, the prologue begins to provide parameters for reassessing attributions, and again Godefroy of Saint Victor seems a very unlikely candidate.

Abelard, Heloise, and the Six *Planctus*

The closest parallels to the *Planctus* are the six *planctus* attributed to Peter Abelard, traditionally dated between the 1130s and before 1146, and there might be a temptation to suggest that he or Heloise were the author of the *Planctus*.[35] Although the six *planctus* are described as being written for Heloise, there is no clear evidence for this.[36] Like the *Planctus*, Abelard's laments are also based on amplifications of biblical stories, though his choices were only from the Old Testament. Both also find dramatic and evocative ways through word choice and rhetoric to imbue their lyrics with intense personal emotion. Regarding form, the *Planctus* and Abelard's lyrics are both built on the intricate metrical structures of the *lai*-like sequence as opposed to the more regular patterns of the so-called Victorine repertoire.[37] Again like the *Planctus*, the consensus is that Abelard's *planctus* were not liturgical.[38] Only his *Planctus David super Saul et Ionatha* was included in a liturgical manuscript, the Nevers Troper-Proser, though there it was copied in the context of three other *lai*-like compositions also mentioned in the Paraclete Old-French Ordinary.[39]

---

33   Khan-ad-Din 2003 indicates that 'perception of expected life span, not statistics, defines "old age", so people in medieval England did not consider those under 50 years as "old" and would not have been surprised by "elderly" colleagues living into their 60s'.

34   On the perceptions of 'old age' in the Middle Ages, see also Zayaruznaya's chapter in this volume.

35   An overview of previous scholarship is in Ruys 2014, pp. 61–90. Although other pieces in a similar style have been attributed to either Abelard or Heloise, these are still quite controversial and will not be examined here; see, for example, Dronke and Orlandi 2005, pp. 123–46.

36   Ruys 2014, pp. 65–66 mentions that the six *planctus* 'differ from Abelard's other writings to and for Heloise in that they appear to be pure gift', and on the later page, 'I would argue, however, that the *planctus* were primarily sent to Heloise as a personal offering, as part of Abelard's turn again toward the familial'.

37   The six *planctus* are closely examined in Buckley 2003 and Weinrich 1969, with a focus on the *Planctus David super Saul et Ionatha*. This point is also discussed in Iversen 2009, p. 239.

38   See Ruys 2014, p. 66, for further sources.

39   For an overview of the earlier scholarship on this source, Paris, BnF, n.a.l. 3126, in addition to Iversen 2009, see Colette 2009. See also the subtle reading of this *planctus* in Kearney 2014.

Prominent among the musical similarities between the *Planctus* and Abelard's *Planctus David super Saul et Ionatha* are the sharing of the tetradus mode and a similar melodic ductus with a clear centre on G (see Example 2.1).[40] There are, however, differences, as in this example: where the melody from the *Planctus David* has a clear *AAB* form, the *Planctus* varies the two opening phrases with different cadential pitches.

There are also significant differences in the metrical form of these two works. Compared to the *Planctus*, Abelard's *Planctus David* is more regular, with longer lines of generally seven or eight syllables, and lacks the frequent use of internal rhymes and short melodic phrases of the Marian lament.[41] As noted by Stevens, the *Planctus David* also lacks the internal melodic repetitions found in the *Planctus* and other Latin *lais*.[42] A closer comparison to the *Planctus* might be with Abelard's unusual *Planctus virginum* which is much less symmetrical with many shorter lines and more frequent rhymes.[43] I believe that any similarities do not outweigh the differences, also including the limited circulation of the works attributed to Abelard or Heloise compared to the wide distribution of the *Planctus*. It is unlikely that either were the creators of the *Planctus*.

There is, however, a conceptual parallel between Abelard's attitude towards lamentation and the anonymous prologue to the *Planctus*. Ruys has pointed out that Abelard frequently associated lamentation with women.[44] This is evident in his Sermon 32 on the martyrdom of Saint Stephen:

> We read that in those vicious mobs who led the Lord to be crucified there were not missing among them the piety of lamenting women. Thus the evangelist recollects the same saying: 'And there followed him a great multitude of people, and of women, who bewailed and lamented him' (Luke 23:27). However, turning to the women, Jesus said: 'Daughters of Jerusalem, weep not over me' (Luke 23:28). If, therefore, a natural affection of piety, which greatly belongs to your sex, moved to tears of compassion the unbelieving women and the wives of both these same men and their followers, you should not ignore what you must owe to your Stephen.[45]

---

[40] Example 2.1(a) is from Paris, BnF, n.a.l. 3126, fol. 88v; see also Weinrich 1969, part 2, 468. Example 2.1(b) is from Rouen, BM 666, fol. 94v.

[41] Compare the form charts in Buckley 2003, pp. 50 and 58.

[42] Stevens 1986, p. 129.

[43] See Buckley 2003, pp. 51–59.

[44] Ruys 2014, p. 63. There is an excellent examination of lamentation and female song in Haines 2010a, pp. 34–50.

[45] 'Legimus in illis sceleratis turbis quae ad crucifigendum ducebant Dominum, non defuisse illi lugentium pietatem feminarum. Sicut idem meminit evangelista dicens: "Sequebatur autem eum multitudo populi et mulierum quae plangebant et lamentabantur eum". Conversus autem ad illas Iesus dixit: "Filiæ Jerusalem, nolite flere super me", etc. Si ergo infideles feminas, et ipsorum et persequentium uxores naturalis affectus pietatis qui maxime vestro sexui inest ad compassionis lacrymas commovit, quid vestro debeatis Stephano non ignoratis' (Peter Abelard, PL178. 580D). This is also briefly discussed in Ruys 2014, p. 63. In the final line, I translate 'ignoretis' instead of 'ignoratis'.

Example 2.1. Comparison of the first stanza of Abelard's *Dolorum solatium* (a) with the first stanza of the *Planctus ante nescia* (b).

In the same way, Abelard advised Heloise to lament Christ's Passion in his fifth letter and added a liturgical reference to a Holy Saturday antiphon:

> Suffer with him who willingly suffered for your salvation and grieve for him who was crucified for you. In your thoughts stand always beside his tomb and mourn and weep with his faithful women of whom it is written, as I have said before: 'The women sitting by his tomb in tears lamented the Lord'.[46]

[46] 'Patienti sponte pro redemptione tua compatere, et super crucifixo pro te compungere. Sepulcro eius mente semper assiste, et cum fidelibus feminis lamentare et luge. De quibus etiam ut iam supra memini scriptum est: "Mulieres sedentes ad monumentum lamentabantur flentes Dominum"' (text from Muckle 1953, p. 91; translation from

These and similar texts indicate that Abelard believed women had a special ability to respond to tragic events through their own lamentations that was lacking not only in himself but also other men. Although his *Planctus Dine filie Jacob* and *Planctus virginum Israel super filia Iepte Galadite* both include passages in which the figures of Dinah and Jephthah's daughter lament their different fates, they are felt to lack any verisimilitude to an actual female voice.[47] In a similar manner, the anonymous prologue also indicates an attitude that an old but pious monk cannot effectively voice a mother's grief over the suffering and death of her son.[48]

'Et iterum audivi vocem de caelo'

The anonymous prologue to the *Planctus* may finally reflect the concept that divine songs are not 'composed' in a modern sense, as exemplified by the persistent Carolingian legend that Gregory the Great dictated chants through the inspiration of the dove of the Holy Spirit, first visualised in the Harker antiphoner (St Gallen, Stiftsbibl., Cod. Sang. 390–391, p. 13, c. 980–1011).[49] Another clear and well-known exemplification of the importance of inspiration is the figure of Hildegard of Bingen in many statements about her revelations and the music associated with them. In the opening of her *Scivias*, Hildegard places the origin of her visions not within herself but from heaven: 'Et dixi et scripsi haec non secundum adinventionem cordis mei aut ullius hominis, sed ut ea in caelestibus vidi, audivi et percepi per secreta mysteria Dei. Et iterum audivi vocem de caelo mihi dicentem: "Clama ergo et scribe sic" (And I spoke and wrote these not by the invention of my heart or that of any other person, but as by the secret mysteries of God I heard and received them in the heavenly places. And again I heard a voice from heaven saying to me, 'Cry out therefore, and write thus!').[50] Later, within the thirteenth vision of Book III, she frequently mentions the celestial source of the songs: 'Audivi … in laudibus civium supernorum gaudiorum in via veritatis fortiter perseverantium, ac in querelis revocatorum ad laudes eorundem gaudiorum, et in exhortatione virtutum se exhortantium ad salutem populorum quibus diabolicae insidiae repugnant' (I heard … the praises of the joyous citizens of heaven, steadfastly persevering in the ways of Truth; and laments calling people back to those praises and joys; and the exhortations of the virtues, spurring one another

---

McLaughlin and Wheeler (ed. and trans.) 2009, p. 81). The quotation is the text of the antiphon for the Benedictus at Lauds on Sabbato Sancto.

[47] See Ruys 2014, pp. 72–74, 80–83, and 85–87.

[48] Klinck 2003 is a balanced general examination of this interpretive issue.

[49] There is a short summary of 'The legend of Saint Gregory' in Earp 2011, pp. 337–41. The illumination from the Harker antiphoner has been frequently reprinted and is included in Treitler 1974, p. 339, which also examines the Gregorian legend. On the iconography of the 'Gregorian' scene and a reevaluation of the Gregorian legend, see the chapter by Parkes in this volume.

[50] Text from Führkötter and Carlevaris (eds.) 1978, p. 6, and translation from Hart and Bishop (trans.) 1990, p. 61.

on to secure the salvation of the peoples ensnared by the Devil).[51] In her *Liber vite meritorum*, she describes that the entire collection of songs was received in a vision: 'Et symphoniam harmonie celestium revelationum, ignotamque linguam et litteras cum quibusdam aliis expositionibus, … mihi ad explanandum ostenderat' (And [this true vision] had revealed … to me for explanation the symphonia of the harmony of celestial revelations and the unknown language and letters with certain other expositions).[52] In her *Liber divinorum operum*, Hildegard also noted that her visions were meant to convey divine matters to humanity: 'Vox de celo facta est ad me dicens: O paupercula forma, … hec que interioribus oculis vides, et interioribus auribus anime percipis, stabili scripture ad utilitatem hominum commenda' (A voice from heaven was created, saying to me: 'O poor little form, … commit to the benefit of humanity through the immutability of writing these things which you see with the inner eyes and perceive with the inner ears of the soul').[53]

In one of her letters to Elizabeth of Schönau, Hildegard mirrors Mary's words to the old monk about his inability to express her feelings and emphasises that only a divine spirit can be fully prophetic: 'Quoniam ipsi exsules sunt, coelestia nescientes, sed tantum mystica Dei canentes; sicut tuba, quae solummodo sonos dat, nec operatur; sed in quam alius spirat ut sonum reddat' (Since these [earthen vessels] are exiles, ignorant of divine matters, but only singing the mysteries of God, like a trumpet which only yields but does not cause sounds; yet, when another blows into it, the trumpet would therefore produce a sound).[54] The divine inspiration was evidently significant in the creation of songs and, as showcased by the *Planctus*, ignoring this medieval perspective has affected the need in modern scholarship to identify an author or composer.

There are ways that modern scholarship has misinterpreted medieval statements concerning creative ownership. One applicable example comes from Hildegard's own *Vita*: 'Sed et cantum cum melodia in laudem Dei et sanctorum absque doctrina ullius hominis protuli et cantavi, cum numquam vel neumam vel cantum aliquem didicissem'.[55] In some recent studies, this passage has been translated as follows, with only minor variations, though it implies a meaning very different from Hildegard's own statements quoted above: 'But I also composed, with their melodies, songs which I also sang in the praise of God and of the saints without the teaching of any man, although no one had ever trained me in either musical notation or voice'.[56]

My concern is with the phrase 'But I also composed, with their melodies, songs … ' and specifically with the word 'composed', which was used by Powell, Führkötter and McGrath, and Silvas and frequently quoted with this reading. Dronke's unaltered

51   Text from Führkötter and Carlevaris (eds.) 1978, p. 614, and translation from Hart and Bishop (trans.) 1990, p. 525.

52   Text from Carlevaris (ed.) 1995, p. 8.

53   Text from Derolez and Dronke (eds.) 1996, p. 45.

54   Text from Van Acker (ed.) 1993, p. 457.

55   Klaes (ed.) 1993, p. 24; Theodericus Epternacensis, PL 197. 104A.

56   Powell 2020, p. 38, adapted from Dronke 1984, p. 145. Similar translations are also found in Palmquist and Kulas (eds.), McGrath and Führkötter (trans.) 1995, p. 52; Silvas (trans.) 1999, p. 160.

translation for this phrase was 'But I also brought forth songs with their melody'[57], and the complete sentence might be more literally interpreted as 'But I also revealed and sang a song with a melody in praise of God and the saints without the teaching of any man, although I had never learned either any neume or song'. The key word here is *protuli* (I brought forth), which generally means 'to bring forth, offer, or reveal something that already exists', as in Ezekiel 12:7: 'Feci ergo sicut præceperat mihi Dominus: vasa mea protuli quasi vasa transmigrantis per diem, et vespere perfodi mihi parietem manu: et in caligine egressus sum, in humeris portatus in conspectu eorum' (His bidding was done; while daylight served, I brought my exile's pack out into the open; then, at nightfall, dug wall through and went out on my dark journey, borne on men's shoulders, plain to view).[58] This has a very different meaning than either the modern English verb 'compose' or the Latin *componere*, which implies an action or activity to make something, as in Exodus 37:29: 'Composuit et oleum ad sanctificationis unguentum, et thymiama de aromatibus mundissimis opere pigmentarii' (And he made oil for the hallowing ointment, and incense of pure spices, with all the art of a perfumer). It is this misunderstanding that is found even in recent studies of Hildegard, and to name her a 'composer' would be to dismiss her own statements, her own 'voice'.[59]

Even if Hildegard is a useful point of comparison, the *Planctus ante nescia* raises different issues. In contrast to Hildegard, whose revealed musical repertoire is known mostly from just two manuscript collections, the *Planctus* was, aside from liturgical chant, perhaps one of the most widely disseminated Latin songs from the Middle Ages to the eighteenth century. From the earliest mention of its elegant diction ('quidam satis eleganter dicit') in Letter 6 from Bec, to its use in the Greater Passion Play from the Codex Buranus (Munich, BSB, Clm 4660/4660a, CB 16*), and the contrafacta in Anglo-Norman and Middle English that used its melody, the *Planctus* was admired for its evocative and dramatic power, though its composer was at most only 'someone' (*quidam*). I believe that it was both the quality of this poem and the increasing discovery of more sources that led both to its attribution (on rather flimsy evidence) to Godefroy of Saint Victor by Oudin in the eighteenth century and its frequent appearance in anthologies and scholarly studies throughout the nineteenth and early twentieth centuries. Unfortunately, in an almost medieval respect for *auctoritas*, scholars following Oudin or the *Histoire littéraire de la France* accepted the author identification without question, though with a few minor bumps concerning which 'Godefroy' was really meant. Dronke in 1988 was probably

---

57 Dronke 1984, p. 145.

58 English quotations from Knox (trans.) 1954. This is clear in Hildegard's usage, for example, *Scivias*, Pars Tertia, Visio Prima, lines 83–84: 'da mihi quomodo possim et qualiter debeam proferre diuinum consilium quod in antiquo consilio ordinatum est' (Grant me to make known the divine counsel, which was ordained of old) (text from Führkötter and Carlevaris (eds.) 1978, p. 329; translation from Hart and Bishop (trans.) 1990, p. 309).

59 See, for example, Bain 2021, p. 209: 'Hildegard is a fixture now in music history courses, and with the largest output of chant that can be ascribed to a Western medieval composer – male or female – so she should be'; and Fassler 1998, p. 150: 'No other twelfth-century composer has left such a large corpus of varied and securely attributable compositions as Hildegard of Bingen'.

the first to seriously begin questioning this attribution; but for many, it was easier to just accept what was now repeated in standard reference works, such as the critical edition of the *Carmina burana* or its recent complete English translation.[60]

While the anonymous letter six from Bec is a primary document for both the dating and significance of the *Planctus*, the anonymous prologue to the *Planctus* creates different problems of belief. It is common to consider stories of this type, whether *vitae* of saints or the *vidas* and *razos* of the trobadours, as fiction. However, similar to re-evaluations of the *vidas* and *razos*, the anonymous prologue may have been a creative way to convey a different type of 'truth' to account for the unique literary qualities of the *Planctus* and to enhance its 'voice' for a reader or listener.[61] In some ways similar to Dronke's hesitations, the author of the prologue struggled with the evocative text of the *Planctus* and that it was almost unbelievable that an old monk would have been able to put into these words the emotions that were felt by the Virgin Mary. This is certainly its dramatic significance when sung by Mary in the context of the Greater Passion Play (CB 16*).[62]

Within the historiography of medieval music, there has always been a compulsion to value compositions by a named composer more than those that were anonymous. Consider the weight that has been put on the words of Anonymous IV concerning Leoninus and Perotinus: what significance would writers of music history books have placed on *Viderunt omnes* and *Sederunt principes* if there had been no name attached? Clearly, there has been excessive value placed on a 'name'.[63]

Perhaps, in a post-modern age, rather than a romantic need to establish 'the author' or 'the composer', it might be possible to accept the perspective of the medieval documents that the source of inspiration was more important than the person. For Hildegard, she was the *amanuensis* for her inspiration, the 'vox de celo' (voice from heaven), and this is the 'voice' we should hear in the songs that she brought forth from her visions. In the case of the *Planctus*, who wrote 'this celestial and mellifluous song' (*huius celestis atque melliflui carminis*) was not significant. More important was for anyone who encountered this uniquely profound expression of motherly grief to hear the 'voice' and inspiration of the Blessed Virgin Mary.

---

[60] Schumann and Bischoff (eds.) 1970, pp. 129–34; Traill (ed. and trans.) 2018, vol. 2, p. 729.

[61] Poe 1995; Meneghetti 1984, especially pp. 325–63; Winiarski 2017.

[62] Schumann and Bischoff (eds.) 1970, p. 164; Traill (ed. and trans.) 2018, vol. 2, pp. 564–65; Dronke (ed. and trans.) 1994, pp. 231–33.

[63] See the discussion of this issue in Van der Werf 1992, along with the added commentaries by Edward H. Roesner, Giulio Cattin, Luigi Lera and John Stinson, and Van der Werf's reply (13–25). Busse Berger 2005, pp. 24–25, briefly discusses Friedrich Ludwig's impact on this issue, and this is examined more extensively in Flotzinger 2007, which discusses the 'Mythos *Notre Dame*' on pp. 37–92. On Anonymous IV's attributions, see the chapters by Everist, Zayaruznaya, and Bent in this volume. On the historiographic emphasis on named composers and ascribed works, see the introduction to this volume.

Appendix 1: Sources for *Planctus ante nescia* and Its Contrafacta

Musical Sources for *Planctus ante nescia*

1. Rouen, BM 666, fols. 94v–96v (12th or early 13th c.; Benedictine Abbey of Saint Ouen)
2. Évreux, BM 2, fols. 3v–4v (early 13th c.; Benedictine Abbey of Lyra)
3. Évreux, BM 39, fols. 1v–2r (early 13th c.; Benedictine Abbey of Lyra)
4. Albi, Méd. Amalric 26, fols. 113r–v, 110v (late 12th/early 13th c.; Aquitanian neumes on drypoint lines with clefs) (text and neumes break off in the middle of the piece, then text continues on fol. 110v without neumes)
5. Paris, Bibl. Mazarine 1002, fols. 235r–237r (late 12th/early 13th c.; Abbey of Saint Victor)
6. London, BL, Add. 36881, fols. 25r–27v (early 13th c.)
7. Munich, BSB, Clm 4660/4660a, fol. IVr (early 13th c.; Brixen Cathedral)[64]
8. Paris, BnF, lat. 5268, fols. 117r–119r (14th c.)
9. Munich, BSB, Cgm 716, fol. 150r (only a short excerpt, attached to a Mittel-hoch-Deutsch *Marienklage*; 15th c.; Benedictine Abbey of Tegernsee)

Text Sources for *Planctus ante nescia*

10. Paris, BnF, lat. 2415, fol. 157r (12th c.; Chartreuse de La Verne; added to Haimo's *Commentarium in Apocalypsim*)
11. Turin, Bnu, E.V.20, fol. 1r (partially burned) (used in AH 20, pp. 156–58 as the sole source) (12th (second half)/early 13th c.; Staffarda (Cuneo), Cistercian Abbey of Santa Maria)
12. Graz, Univ. 409, fols. 70v–71r (*c.* 1200; Benedictine Abbey of Saint Lambrecht)
13. Oxford, Bod. Lib., Add. 44, fol. 80v (early 13th c.; possibly Augustinian Abbey of Wigmore)
14. Paris, BnF, lat. 4880, fol. 83v (13th c.; Benedictine Abbey of Fleury, Saint-Benoit-sur-Loire)
15. Cambridge, GCC 408/414, fol. 220v (13th c.; possibly Dominican)
16. Darmstadt, ULB 397, fragment in front cover (13th c.; Schwäbisch Gmünd)
17. Oxford, Bod. Lib., Rawl. C.510, fol. 5r (13th c.; Benedictine Abbey of Bardney)
18. Budapest, OSK, MNy 79, fol. 199r (*olim* Louvain, Bibliothèque de l'Université, G 200, later signatures: A 6 and IV.28) (late 13th c.)
19. Munich, BSB, Clm 14094, fols. 44v–45r (early 14th c.; later from Benedictine Abbey of Saint Emmeram)
20. Prague, Národní knihovna XII D 8a, fols. 148r–149v (early 14th c.; probably Benedictine Abbey of Saint George)

---

[64] Concerning this provenance, see Brewer 2020.

21.   Karlsruhe, BLB, Cod. Aug. perg. 36, fol. 149r (15th c.; Benedictine
      Abbey of Reichenau)
22.   Namur, MA 104, fol. 77r (15th c.; Premonstratensian Abbey of Floreffe)
23.   Paris, BnF, lat. 3639, fol. 185r (15th c.; possibly Reims)
24.   Paris, BnF, lat. 15163, fols. 229v–230v (15th c.; Abbey of Saint Victor)
25.   Rouen, BM 364, fol. 16r (15th c.; Priory of Notre-Dame de Bonne-
      Nouvelle; att. Bernard)

Contrafacta

1.   *Eyns ne soy ke pleynte fu* (Norman French) and *Ar ne kuthe ich sorghe*
      (Middle English): London, MA, COL/CS/01/001/001, 'Liber de
      Antiquis Legibus', fols. 160v–161v (1274 c.)
2.   *Volek sirom thudothlon* (Ómagyar Mária-Siralom (Old-Hungarian
      lament of Mary), late 13th c.): Budapest, OSK, MNy 79, fol. 134v.

Appendix 2: The Anonymous Prologue to the Planctus ante nescia

After Delhaye 1951, pp. 253–55 (from Paris, BnF, lat. 4880, fol. 83v); some editorial
suggestions and changes in punctuation are added.

Fertur virum religiosum et provecte etatis in cenobio a primeva etate honestis-
sime enutritum atque regularis discipline ad prime eruditum, hanc in senectute sua
exercuisse consuetudinem. Pro nimia devotione atque animi puritate qua pius et
venerabilis senex a primis tyronicii sui rudimentis servabat erga beatam genetricem
redemptoris ac salvatoris nostri, ceteris post matutinorum sollempnia ad requiem
corporum festinantibus, ipse, licet non minus fatigatus, tamen ut eius laudibus libe-
rius vacare potuisset, in ecclesia solus remanebat.

Ubi solo Christo teste sanctissimaque matre eius, ut credere fas est, assistente,
devotam mentem pane pascebat lacrimarum. Desiderium gliscens crebris solabatur
gemitibus atque suspiriis, nichilque terrenum cogitans, ad divina[m] inexplicabili
mentis suspirabat ardore. Inter cetera autem que sic menti affecte dulci se inger-
ebant recordatione, illud altius atque suavius radicatum tenebat ruminans atque
explicans, quanto et quam gravi cruciebatur merore beata illa et intemerata virgo,
videns illud mite et almificum corpus de sacrosancta carne sua procreatum in crucis
stipite protensum, sputis illitum, clavis configi, lancea perforari, mortis denique ferre
supplicium. His et huiusmodi Christi famulus, dum inextinguibili flamma pectus
satagitur, accedere subiit animum ut aliquid de re tam stupenda scribendo, multos
ad lacrymarum umbras[65] provocaret, quibus in meditationibus exardescente igne
felici suavitate rigabatur.

Tum illa beata mater et virgo, cultoris sui miserans anxios estus, benignissima
dignatione misericordes oculos in lacrimis rorantes, attolens vultus, tali perhibe-
tur eam[66] compellasse affatu. 'Quid est, inquit, o mi familiarissime, quod meditaris,
frustra niteris explicare verbis quod sola sum experta. Excedit enim omnis hominis

---

[65] Delhaye 1951, p. 254, reads 'ymbres'.
[66] Delhaye 1951, p. 254, reads 'eum'.

effatum quod in illa fructus uteri mei,[67] quem de spiritu sancto concepi, crucifixione sustinui meroris, doloris et anxietudinis. Verumptamen ne tue devotionis instantia apud Christum doleas inane fuisse, ne me precibus tuis non favere reputes, ne cause-ris lacrimarum tuarum sacrificium non acceptasse, adsum votis tuis et quod tuo non potes conatu vel studio, meo munere consequeris. Scribe ergo quid dictavero, non de tuo sensu propalata, sed ex mea experientia universe parte mundo propinanda.' Quare mox gloriosissime domine parens imperio, dum letus exceptoris fungitur offi-cio,[68] huius celestis atque melliflui carminis ditatur eulogia.[69]

Incipit planctus Sancte Marie matris domini super unicum filium suum penden-tem in cruce, quem ipsa dictavit. *Planctus ante nescia* ...

(It is reported that a man, religious and advanced in age, most decently nourished in the monastery from an early age and also exceedingly learned in the discipline of the Rule, exercised this custom in his old age. In his exceeding devotion and purity of spirit, which the pious and venerable old man from the first rudiments of his novitiate observed towards the Blessed Mother of the Redeemer and our Saviour, while hastening the others after the solemnities of Matins to the rest of their bodies, he himself, although no less tired, so that he would have been able to have more free time for his Lauds, nevertheless remained alone in the church.

There, with Christ as sole witness and his most-holy Mother, as it is meet to believe, assisting, he fed a devout mind with the bread of tears. He consoled the passionate desire with frequent groans and sighs, and thinking nothing earthly, he sighed with fervency to the prophetess of the inexplicable mind. Whereupon, among other things which thus infused themselves with affection to a sweet mind with remembrance, ruminating and also explicating, he held that [desire] rooted more highly and agreeably, by how much and how with grave sorrow that blessed and spotless virgin was crucified seeing that tender and glorious body, begotten from her most holy flesh, stretched out with a stave upon the cross, smeared with spit, fixed with nails, pierced with a spear; in short, to bear the punishment of death. These things, and the like, the servant of Christ, while [his] breast is troubled with an inextinguishable flame, took upon himself to approach [his] intellect, so that, by writing something about a matter so amazing, he would arouse many shadows to the tears with which he was watered in [his] meditations, having been ignited with a sweet, happy fire.

Thereupon that blessed Mother and Virgin, pitying the anxious fires of her wor-shipper, bedewing with most gracious condescension [her] merciful eyes in tears, lifting up [his] face, with such [tears] it was bestowed, having compelled her to speak. 'What is it', she says, 'O my most intimate friend, that you are pondering? In vain do you endeavour to explain with words that which I alone had experienced. For it exceeds the utterance of every man, because in those [things] concerning the fruit of my womb, whom I conceived of the Holy Spirit, I endured a crucifixion of

---

[67] Delhaye 1951, p. 354, reads 'uterinei'.

[68] Delhaye 1951, p. 254 reads 'offitio'.

[69] Delhaye 1951, p. 254 reads 'eulogio'.

grief, of suffering and anxiety. Nevertheless, lest you would grieve vainly of your devotion to have been in that instance in the presence of Christ, nor account me not to favour your prayers, nor should you cause the sacrifice of your tears to not be received, I am mindful to your vows and because you are not able by your effort or study, you will obtain my reward. Write, therefore, that which I shall dictate, not made manifest from your perceptions, but, from my experience, the universal part must be set before the world'. Wherefore, afterwards, obeying the most-glorious Lady's command, while the joy of the amanuensis is performing the office, he is endowed with the gift of this celestial and mellifluous song.

Here begins the lament of the holy Mary, the mother of the Lord, concerning her only son, hanging on the cross, which she herself dictated. *Planctus ante nescia, …*)

3

Petrus de Cruce, Philippe de Vitry, Notational Epochs, and the Spans of Human Lives

> The true length of a person's life, whatever the *Dictionary of National Biography* may say, is always a matter of dispute. For it is a difficult business – this time-keeping; nothing more quickly disorders it than contact with any of the arts.
>
> —Virginia Woolf, *Orlando*

How long do you flourish? This question sometimes pops into my head when I see 'fl.' – the ubiquitous abbreviation for 'floruit' – appended to the name of a composer and combined with a very narrow date range. Within late-medieval musicology, the paradigmatic example is probably Petrus de Cruce. According to the authors of his most recent *Grove* biography, Petrus 'fl[oruit] c. 1290'.[1] There is something almost tragic, or maybe tragicomic, about flourishing – but only c. 1290.

Of course, this is just a shorthand, and its meaning is clear enough: it indicates that we are missing information. The years around 1290 could be the high point of a five-year career, a thirty-year career, or a fifty-year career. Or they could be the high point of nothing; they could instead be reflective of a specific but random pocket of documentation that survived the vagaries of transmission. They could even be the wrong dates: 'c. 1290' might be contested.

The present essay is not an attempt to solve the mystery of Petrus's dates of birth or death. Nor do I wish to fight straw men – I presume that nobody actually thinks Petrus was active only c. 1290; common sense dictates that he must have had a history before and after this. Indeed, a review of the available evidence provides plenty of documentation to support a longer span of activity and influence for Petrus. Given this, I wish to suggest that historiographic forces, even more so than scant documentation, have served to compress Petrus's lifetime and his sphere of influence. Specifically, I argue that notions about the transitional nature of Petrus's notational usage have contributed to a narrative in which his periods of influence and activity were compact. To do this, I align Petrus's case with that of Philippe de Vitry (1291–1361). Vitry would seem to be a bad comparand, given his demonstrably long life. Yet existing scholarship has favoured an account according to which Vitry's

---

[1] Sanders rev. Lefferts 2001.

most important innovations and compositions all stem from a short time early in his career. A fresh look at the datings of Vitry's motets suggests that this was probably not the case, that he in fact composed throughout his long career, and that his earliest compositions were conceived in *Ars vetus* notation.

Ultimately, the forces historiographically constraining the active years of Vitry and of Petrus turn out to be related, both traceable partly to early datings of Jacobus's *Speculum musicae* and rooted in an understanding of a notational and compositional *Ars nova* that rendered Petrus obsolete so that Vitry could flourish – if only for a decade or two. Just as a revised chronology of Vitry's works in turn offers new perspectives on *Ars nova*, thinking about Petrus de Cruce as someone who was active and relevant for a span of time longer than 'c. 1290' casts his notational processes in a different light. Rather than looking like a transitional blip on the radar or a notational 'dead end', Petrus's system is revealed to be largely continuous with the *Ars vetus* described in the treatises of the 1320s and 1330s.[2]

Petrus de Cruce before and after c. 1290

The scant information we have about Petrus de Cruce is pulled from a range of archival and music-theoretical sources.[3] Most influential in terms of his chronology have been some comments made by the theorist Jacobus.[4] In the seventeenth chapter of the famously polemical Book VII of *Speculum musicae* (hereafter SMVII), Jacobus attributed two motets to Petrus in the course of a discussion of the notational habits of the latter's generation (Jacobus calls them *antiqui*).[5] Whereas the system codified by Franco of Cologne c. 1280 divided the breve into two unequal semibreves or three equal ones, Petrus is singled out for occasionally squeezing four, five, six, and even seven semibreves into a breve. To illustrate this notational usage, Jacobus included passages from three motets of which the first two are clearly marked as the work of Petrus. In one, a work whose triplum he says begins 'S'amours ewist point de', Jacobus asserts that Petrus sometimes wrote four semibreves for the span of a breve. He provides two representative passages from the upper voice of this motet. In the other, whose triplum begins 'Aucun ont trouvé', Petrus is said to have used not only four but on occasion five, six, and seven semibreves. Four excerpts of the triplum are given.[6]

---

2   For the most recent articulation of 'the idea that the techniques and style associated with Petrus ... flourished for a relatively brief period', see Bradley 2022a, p. 49 n. 15 and p. 121.

3   See the documentation brought together in Bent 2015a, pp. 32–33, which is more comprehensive than that in Sanders rev. Lefferts 2001.

4   This theorist has traditionally been referred to as 'Jacques de Liege'; on the complicated issues of his origins, see Desmond 2000; Bent 2015a, pp. 45–67, 81–108, 139–56; Wegman 2016.

5   The relevant passage of the *Speculum musicae* is quoted in Bent's chapter in the current volume.

6   Bragard (ed.) 1955–73, vol. 7, pp. 36–38; Wegman (trans.) 2017, pp. 31–32. On the authorship of the third motet cited in this passage, see n. 57 below.

Both of these motets survive, known to modern scholars as *S'Amour eüst/Au renouveler/Ecce* and *Aucun ont trouvé/Lonc tans/Annun[tiantes]*. Together, they open the seventh fascicle of Montpellier, BIU, H 196, the so-called Montpellier Codex, hereafter Mo.[7] This fascicle is usually situated in the 1290s based on paleographical, codicological, and art-historical grounds, although it has also been dated earlier.[8] The pride of place accorded to these two motets in fascicle 7 suggests that their composer, whether he was known to the compilers or not (and presumably he was) was already in high esteem by this point.[9]

Evidence of Petrus's continued relevance is easy to find. Motets attributed to him in recent literature are copied not only in fascicle 7 of Mo but also in the later fascicle 8.[10] This part of the manuscript has been dated to the 1310s or even the 1320s, and it contains works that David Maw associates with a later stage in the evolution of Petrus's style. Accordingly, Maw suggests that Petrus continued to compose beyond the 1290s.[11] *Aucun ont trouvé* and *S'amour eüst* are also copied into Turin, BR, varia 42 (hereafter Tu), a manuscript dated on art-historical grounds between the mid-1320s and the mid-1330s, though it is possibly somewhat earlier.[12] Theorists also continued to discuss Petrus's system and especially the exemplary *Aucun ont trouvé*: it is, for instance, quoted and attributed to Petrus by Robertus de Handlo in his *Regule* of 1326 and also by Johannes Hanboys, perhaps around 1370.[13]

---

[7]   The motets appear as nos. 236 (fols. 270r–73r) and 237 (fols. 273r–75r). On these two motets, see the chapters by Bent and Bradley, the latter for an in-depth analysis of *Aucun ont trouvé*.

[8]   See Bradley and Desmond (eds.) 2018, pp. 1, 5. Note that Mary Wolinski argued for an earlier dating, suggesting that fascicles 1–7 were all envisioned as a unit and 'painted perhaps as early as between the late 1260s and the 1280s'; see Wolinski 1992, p. 282.

[9]   Maw 2018, p. 181 notes that given the preponderance of unica, 'it seems likely that someone close to Petrus de Cruce and his circle assembled this collection' and that several Petronian motets close fascicle 7, excepting a supplement added later.

[10]   This corpus is identified on stylistic grounds based primarily on the use of more than three semibreves in the span of a breve, and although undoubtedly some of the motets associated currently with Petrus were indeed his work, it is worth viewing each attribution critically. For an insightful discussion of the various criteria used to attribute motets to Petrus and the problems they entail, see Bradley 2022a, pp. 77–80, 86–88. She concludes that 'any attempt to pin down Petrus's rhythmic techniques and/or style in order to identify a discrete and definitive body of his compositions is arguably as impossible as it is unproductive' (p. 87). See also the chapter by Bradley for a reflection on Petronian rhythmic style and conceptual aesthetic.

[11]   Maw 2018, pp. 161–63. The author characterises the difference between the style of the motets in fascicle 7 and that of the ones in fascicle 8 as that between 'a phase of discovery' and 'a phase of mastery' (p. 180). On the dating of the eighth fascicle of Mo, see the essays collected in Bradley and Desmond (eds.) 2018, especially Stones 2018, Baltzer 2018, and Curran 2018.

[12]   *Aucun ont trouvé* is on fols. 14r–15v, and *S'amour eüst* is on fols. 24v–27r (original foliation). On the dating of Tu, see Everist 2007, pp. 370–71 n. 18.

[13]   Lefferts (ed. and trans.) 1991, pp. 30–34 on the date of Hanboys, pp. 106–7 for Handlo's citation, and pp. 260–61 for Hanboys's citation. On two further citations, see Bent 2015a, pp. 27–32.

Archival records show that Petrus was paid in 1298 for the composition of a rhymed office for Saint Louis and that he was resident in the palace of the bishop of Amiens in 1301–2.[14] It is also on record that Petrus left a book of polyphony to Amiens Cathedral (a book that, like the first and last fascicles of Mo, began with *Deus in adjutorium*), and this bequest is recorded in a 1347 inventory.[15] This is the first surviving inventory of the Amiens cathedral treasury, and therefore its date does not imply that Petrus died so late. But still, 1347 is the only firm *terminus ante quem* for Petrus's death.

We do not know how long Petrus lived, and since we do not know, it might seem safest to assume that he did not live very long. After all, there is a sense that our medieval forebears had relatively short lives. But although this may be true on average, research into medieval lifespans suggests that there is more to the story. Shulamith Shahar has argued persuasively that the oft-cited notion that medieval people were considered old after the age of forty is a myth, noting that medieval legislative texts often define the onset of old age as sixty to seventy.[16] We know that Vitry died at seventy, and we think that Guillaume de Machaut lived into his late seventies. What if Petrus did too? Even if we never know whether he did or not, I contend that it is a productive question to ask because the potentially awkward spans of human lives can productively reveal historiographic fault lines.

What, then, keeps us from imagining Petrus as a composer who was active in the 1290s, 1300s, 1310s, even possibly the 1320s? The answer turns out to be a function of the interaction between archival and music-theoretical evidence and is centred on the dating of the final book of Jacobus's *Speculum musicae*. Although Ernest Sanders and Peter Lefferts allow for the possibility that Petrus was still alive in the 1320s, they note that, if so, 'he was no longer at the cutting edge of innovation then because Robert Handlo and Jacobus of Liège placed him among their older figures as opposed to the "moderni"'.[17] Indeed, Jacobus explicitly states that Petrus is dead, describing him and Franco together as 'teachers who were so distinguished in their times, and whose memory is deserving of blessing' (*doctores qui temporibus suis fuerunt ita valentes et quorum memoria benedictionem habeat*).[18]

The dating of the final book of the *Speculum musicae*, in turn, is a quagmire: dates as early as 1323 and as late as c. 1350 have been suggested for its completion. As I have

---

14 See Bent 2015a, pp. 32–33, and also the chapter by Bent in this volume.

15 Garnier 1850, p. 265: 'Item [librum] alium organicum. qui fuit magistri Petri de cruce' (another book of organum, which belonged to master Petrus de Cruce). In the 1419 inventory, this book is described in more detail as a 'liber organicus notatus qui vocatur magistri Petri de Cruce. post kalendarium incipit in prima linea littere primi folii. Deus in adjutorium' (a notated book of organum which is called [the book] of master Petrus de Cruce. After the calendar it begins with the words 'Deus in adjutorium' on the first line of the first folio) (Garnier 1850, p. 307).

16 Among other things, it appears that we may be confusing average and modal life expectancy. Medieval people who survived childhood often lived longer than we might think; see Shahar 1993. On the perceptions of 'old age' in the Middle Ages, see also the chapter by Brewer in this volume.

17 Sanders rev. Lefferts 2001.

18 Bragard (ed.) 1955–73, vol. 7, p. 54; Wegman (trans.) 2017, p. 45.

shown in a recent article, the earlier datings for SMVII were based on a misattribution of Jacobus's treatise to Jehan des Murs (Johannes de Muris) and a presumed, now discredited, link with the papal decretal *Docta sanctorum*.[19] Margaret Bent still locates the treatise's completion in the later 1320s (and her candidate for its authorship, Jacobus de Ispania, died in 1332), while Karen Desmond has made an argument for dating it to the 1330s or later.[20] I have suggested dates in the 1340s or as late as c. 1350 for the latest passages in SMVII based on the late notational features witnessed in Jacobus's text (features that include semiminims, dragmas, and half-void notes), and the general similarity between the comparison of *antiqui* and *moderni* between his treatise and the 1351 *Quatuor principalia* by John of Tewkesbury.[21] This does not mean that all of SMVII was written in the 1340s – Jacobus tells us that he revised parts of the treatise.[22] But until we can discern what parts were subject to revision and when, the date of completion is the only reliable *terminus ante quem* for the notational developments mentioned by Jacobus.

The date at which we assume Jacobus to be writing has an obvious impact on our construal of Petrus's biography since, again, a Petrus 'whose memory is deserving of blessing' is highly unlikely to have been alive at the time that at least that particular passage was penned. Hence Bent, who places the completion of *Speculum musicae* in the mid-1320s, reasons that Petrus died 'well before the 1320s' since Jacobus refers to him in the past tense and as being 'of blessed memory'.[23] Obviously, the later a date one subscribes to for Jacobus's Book VII, the later this terminus moves.[24]

---

[19] For a review of the various dates assigned to *Speculum musicae*, Book VII, see Zayaruznaya 2020, pp. 99–106.

[20] Bent 2015a, pp. 53–57; Desmond 2018a, p. 7. In a review critical of Desmond's book, Bent claims to 'have addressed the challenges to existing chronologies posed by [mine and Desmond's] close scrutiny of difficult texts' and to 'offer a first attempt at the fresh evaluation they invite' (Bent 2022a, p. 752). I cannot agree that this review addresses any of the challenges to existing chronologies posed by either my work or Desmond's, nor that Bent offers a 'fresh evaluation'; rather, she restates the reasoning behind the historiographic status quo and tends to misrepresent Desmond's work. For further details, see Desmond 2023.

[21] Aluas 1996. John and Jacobus make the same distinctions between Franconian usage and the ways of the *moderni*: both mistrust arbitrary notation and show respect for figures approved by the ancients, both make disparaging mention of the sub-minim values of semiminim and dragma, and both complain that the *moderni* agree about the notation of the minim but disagree on other points. The attitudes of the writers towards the *moderni* differ insofar as Jacobus sides with the older usage, but I suggest that they seem to be describing approximately the same moment in the development of mensural notation. See Zayaruznaya 2020, pp. 137–38.

[22] See Zayaruznaya 2020, pp. 106, 136.

[23] Bent 2015a, p. 34.

[24] Other passages in the treatise have been read as suggesting that Jacobus knew Petrus personally, and it has been conjectured that this acquaintance took place specifically in Paris in the 1290s, when Jacobus is presumed to have been a student there. Even though this is possible, there is not much evidence for it; see Zayaruznaya 2020, p. 122 n. 87.

In this regard, it is worth noting that Robertus de Handlo, writing in 1326, seems chronologically closer to Petrus than does Jacobus. Handlo situates Petrus between Franco and the *moderni*, rather than grouping him with Franco as Jacobus would do:

> The preceding rule of Franco ... obtains when the value of the brevis does not run beyond the proportion of three semibreves.... . It is, nevertheless, safer and more suitable in motets and in other songs where there are three semibreves [per breve] for a punctus to be added between two and two or between three and three or between two and three or between three and two, as Petrus de Cruce uses it. Singers nowadays do the same.[25]

By 1326, Petrus de Cruce is not a *modernus*, nor would we expect him to be one: the *moderni* of the mid-1320s were beginning to explore a new notational system that would be codified as *Ars nova*. But we may note that Handlo uses the present-tense *ponit* in his description of Petrus as a notator. Although it would be rash to read too much into this, it does not exclude his still being alive in 1326.[26]

Why, then, does the archival record dry up after 1301–2? This too turns out to be at least partially contingent on prior notions of when Petrus was active. For example, it has been conjectured that Petrus might be identified with a 'dominus Petrus de Croy' who was archdeacon of Ponthieu, the northern half of the diocese of Amiens, and who died before October 1336.[27] Bent dismissed this candidate as being 'too late if we are to take literally Jacobus's statement that those he praises are dead'.[28] But again, this is only a problem if Jacobus is indeed writing well before 1336. There may be other reasons to exercise caution in conflating these two persons, but their identity should not be ruled out a priori on chronological grounds.[29] If we imagine a

---

25. 'Regula Franconis precedens ... locum habet quando valor brevis non currit nisi ad proportionem trium semibrevium.... . Securius tamen et verius in motetis et in aliis cantibus ubi semibreves sunt, addatur punctus inter duas et duas, vel inter tres et tres, vel inter duas et tres, vel inter tres et duas, ut ponit Petrus de Cruce. Hoc idemque faciunt moderni cantores' (Lefferts (ed. and trans.) 1991, pp. 100–103; translation modified).

26. Guy of Saint Denis also mentions 'magistrum Petrum de Cruce, qui fuit optimus cantor et Ambianensis ecclesie consuetudinem specialiter observavit' (master Petrus de Cruce, who was the best cantor and particularly observed the custom of the church of Amiens) (Klundert (ed.) 1998, vol. 2, p. 133), but Guy is himself someone who 'flourished', and his dates are partially dependent on those for Petrus; Huglo 2001 gives '*fl* late 13th century and early 14th'. It is worth mentioning that this use of the past tense does not necessarily indicate that Petrus was dead by the time that Guy was writing; compare with the past tense used by the compiler of *Quatuor principalia* in 1351, a decade before Vitry's death; see n. 39 below.

27. See Johnson 1991, vol. 2, pp. 487–88.

28. Bent 2015a, p. 34.

29. Although Johnson (1991, vol. 2, p. 488) warns about onomastic ambiguity relating to the 'de Cruce' and 'de Croy', cautioning that they may in fact be distinct families and that 'any connection between these two individuals remains tentative', he also provides much information that would support Petrus de Cruce and Dominus Petrus de Croy being the same person, including an example in which 'de Cruce' is clearly a Latinisation of 'de Croy' (vol. 2, pp. 485–87).

Jacobus writing this passage in the mid- to late 1340s, his statement could indeed be taken literally and pertain to a Petrus de Croy (d. 1336).

In sum, Petrus's motets (at least ones we can identify as his on the basis of theoretical citations, attributions, and notational usage) were copied into manuscripts between the 1290s and the 1320s–30s; he is listed as an *antiquus* but not necessarily a dead one in 1326; and he is traceable in the archival record at least until the early 1300s, though possibly later depending on our preconceptions about when he lived. Petrus was certainly dead by 1347 and likely by the 1330s.

Philippe de Vitry before and after c. 1980

Philippe de Vitry was not someone who 'flourished' – not in that sense. We know that he was born on October 31, 1291 and that he died on June 9, 1361. But there has been a fair amount of scholarly disagreement about when, within this long life, Vitry was active as a composer.

In contrast with Machaut (c. 1300–77), whose ever-larger complete works manuscripts attest to consecutive layers of compositional output, our main sources for the music attributed to Vitry are either just a bit too early to be informative or frustratingly late.[30] The interpolated *Roman de Fauvel* (Paris, BnF, fr. 146), probably compiled c. 1317–18, sits at the very beginning of Vitry's period of activity – indeed, before his earliest documented appearance.[31] On the other end is the surviving index of the (mostly lost) Paris, BnF, n.a.f. 23190, the first layer of which is dated 1376.[32] Perhaps only slightly later is Ivrea, Bibl. cap. 115, whose copying Karl Kügle has placed in the 1380s or 1390s, though he characterises the majority of its repertory as 'frozen in 1359'.[33] These collections provide rich pictures of the musical landscape while Vitry was in his twenties and in the decades after his death, but they tell us nothing about

---

[30] A handful of Vitry's motets are attributed to him based on the internal evidence of their texts in which the author names himself; several more are attributed by theorists; a third group is attributable based on textual and musical similarities with the first two groups. Whereas citation in the putative '*Ars nova*' treatise once served as evidence of Vitry's authorship (based on the assumption that Vitry cited mostly or exclusively his own works in 'his' treatise), the usefulness of this attributive strategy has been called into question; see Bent rev. Wathey 2001. For detailed information on the attribution of individual motets, see the second appendix to Zayaruznaya forthcoming.

[31] This date of compilation is derived from the close ties between both the interpolated *Roman de Fauvel* and the chronicles in Paris, BnF, fr. 146, which centre on the events of 1314–16 but take into account the coronation of Philip V in January 1317; see Roesner et al. (eds.) 1990. Bent 1998b, p. 48, reminds us that *Fauvel* could be later in the reign of Philip V and might potentially have been finished as late as 1322, though she does not argue for this dating. No events later than those of 1317 are reflected in the manuscript.

[32] See Bent 1990.

[33] Kügle 1997, p. 76. The surviving sources that probably stem from the middle third of the century are too small or too fragmentary to permit much to be said with certainty about their dates or provenance. Kügle 2008 has dated the rotulus Brussels, KBR 19606, which also includes works attributed to Vitry, to the spring of 1335. Although I find this dating plausible, it depends on the identification of a dragon in a decorated initial which is too rubbed for the argument to be considered watertight.

how his work accrued during his lifetime. Thus, the source situation is as supportive of the possibility that Vitry wrote the bulk of his output by age twenty-seven as it is of his having waited until his cushy bishopric in Meaux in 1351 to really dig in. Only *Petre/Lugentium*, which a fourteenth-century hand conveniently identifies as having been written around Christmas in the first year of the reign of Pope Clement VI (thus December 1342 or January 1343) is demonstrably late.

Foundational scholarship on Vitry by Leo Schrade (1956) and Sanders (1975) distributed his works across about three decades, making a distinction between motets included in *Fauvel* and therefore extant by c. 1317, another group not in *Fauvel* but cited in a putative *Ars nova* treatise and therefore in circulation by the 1320s, and a later group likely to be from the 1330s based on their texts and some of their musical features. Vitry thus was thought by these scholars to have had a compositional career spanning from c. 1315 to the early 1340s.[34]

Beginning in the 1980s, however, a new chronology of Vitry's works emerged, put forward by Daniel Leech-Wilkinson first in 1983, then fleshed out in 1995, and followed by Kügle in 1997.[35] The former grounded his chronology in stylistic and notational comparison between several motets whose texts he felt suggested early dates and others in the repertory. Linking *Flos/Celsa* with the 1317 canonisation of its dedicatee, Saint Louis of Toulouse, and placing the fragmentary [...]/*Per grama* in 1316 in the first year of the papacy of John XXII, Leech-Wilkinson suggested that all of Vitry's real innovations were in place before the 1320s. Along similar lines, Kügle identified a decade – or even less – as the span of time in which Vitry wrote some of his most influential works. Based on a combination of textual and stylistic analysis, he assigned a large group of motets to the period c. 1315–20, 'possibly extending to c. 1325'.[36] The idea that most of Vitry's compositional activity occurred between 1315 and 1320 helps cement his role as a young innovator – a view of him already proposed by Sanders and Schrade. Because other fourteenth-century motets (e.g., those of Machaut) are demonstrably later, Kügle accorded much of Vitry's output the status of 'model' motets that were influential on later works.[37]

---

34 Schrade 1956; Sanders 1975.

35 Leech-Wilkinson 1982–83; Leech-Wilkinson 1995; Kügle 1997. Also pertinent here is Ferreira 2008, which includes an appendix addressing issues of dating (28–36). As Ferreira explains (13), this chapter was written in the late 1980s and not significantly revised for publication, which makes it hard to take account of in historiographic terms. Ferreira's datings mostly fall within the narrow window proposed by Leech-Wilkinson and Kügle, though he gives a wider range of c. 1320–35 for *O canenda/Rex* and *Impudenter/Virtutibus*. See also Bent 1998a, which accepts the possibility of later dates for *Flos/Celsa* and [...]/ *Per grama*, giving a range of 1320s to mid-1330s and cautioning against dating motets by their texts without regard for their music.

36 Kügle 1997, p. 118. These datings apply to 'with the exception of *Petre/Lugentium* ... all motets discussed so far' as of p. 118 – that is, the *Fauvel* motets, *Colla/Bona*, *Tuba/ In arboris*, *Douce/Garison*, *O canenda/Rex*, *In virtute/Decens*, *Impudenter/Virtutibus*, and *Vos quid/Gratissima*.

37 See Kügle 1997, p. 138, Table 3.3: 'Some Related Motets of the Ars Nova and Ars Subtilior (arranged in approximate chronological order; models in bold print)'. Motets bolded and placed before c. 1320 include *Tribum/Quoniam*, *Firmissime/Adesto*, *In virtute/Decens*,

But if most of Vitry's compositions were done by c. 1325, what was he up to, musically speaking, during the second half of his seventy-year life? Leech-Wilkinson's suggestion is that during those later decades, Vitry was not compositionally active. *Petre/Lugentium* aside, he was busy doing other things. In this account, Vitry's status as musical innovator is bolstered by the earliness of his output, while biographical details explain the apparent lack of late works. For me, this passage from 'The Emergence of Ars Nova' perfectly encapsulates the precarious and complicated ties between chronology, authorship, and vocational 'identity':

> After the *Fauvel* motets no work associated with Vitry carries a date other than *Flos/Celsa* in 1317 and *Petre/Lugentium* in 1342, and there is no reason other than musicological tidy-mindedness to spread the other pieces out over the intervening years. Indeed, their stylistic similarity, and their marked dissimilarity from *Petre/Lugentium*, suggests exactly the opposite – that they are all quite early. Only if we think of Vitry as primarily a musician – which he surely was not – do we need to assume that he composed at all between his youth and that exceptional late work.[38]

Thus, Leech-Wilkinson explains what might be perceived as a gap in Vitry's composerly activities by recourse to the anachronism of our modern notions about his career and identity. Significantly, the chronology of Vitry's works across his lifespan is directly related here to how we should 'think of him'. If we accept a narrow window of activity, Vitry in fact ends up being someone who 'flourished' in the encyclopaedic sense – a florescence mostly relegated to the years between 1315 and 1325.

A closer look at Vitry's legacy and his output does not support this compressed chronology. To begin with, it might be noted that most of the praise Vitry garnered was from late in his life. In 1350, Petrarch addressed a letter 'to Philippe de Vitry, illustrious musician', and in 1351 the author-compiler of the treatise *Quatuor principalia* called him 'the flower of the whole musical world'.[39] On the other hand, mensural notation treatises dated 1326 (by Robertus de Handlo) and 1336 (by Petrus dictus Palma ociosa) do not mention him.[40] Whatever else he was (and he held many administrative positions over his long life), Vitry's interlocutors clearly thought of him as a musician later in his life.

Moreover, closer attention to both the music and the text of the motets attributed to Vitry suggests that they are not all early. Whatever is in *Fauvel* must date before

---

Flos/Celsa, Vos quid/Gratissima, Tuba/In arboris, Douce/Garison, O canenda/Rex, Impudenter/Virtutibus, and *Almifonis/Rosa*.

[38] Leech-Wilkinson 1995, p. 315.

[39] 'Philippo de Vitriaco clarissimo musico' (Petrarch, *Rerum familiarum* IX, no. 13, γ version, in Laurens (ed.) et al. (trans.) 2003, p. 454); 'minima autem … a Philippo de Vitriaco qui fuit flos tocius mundi musicorum approbata et usitata' (Aluas 1996, p. 382) (for another quotation pertaining to Philippe in the *Quatuor principalia*, see Bent's chapter in this volume).

[40] To be fair, the first of these is a better data point than the second since Robertus names other theorists and composers, whereas Petrus does not. See Petrus dictus Palma ociosa, *Compendium de discantu mensurabili* in Wolf 1914.

c. 1317, but the motets surviving only in later sources are, for a host of reasons, likely to be later. In the case of [...]/*Per grama*, I think it likely that the motet's dedicatee had been misidentified. Previous scholarship had considered him to be John XXII – pope from 1316 to 1344 – and had placed the motet specifically at the beginning of his reign. I argue that the acrostic 'PETRUS' in the motetus points instead to the elevation of Pierre Roger, either to a bishopric or to the papacy as Clement VI, suggesting dates between 1328 and 1342.[41] For *Flos/Celsa*, a motet in praise of Louis of Toulouse, I believe that a too-specific and indeed unlikely occasion had been selected as the motet's origin: Leech-Wilkinson and Kügle placed it between April and August 1317 by linking it to the canonisation of Louis of Toulouse, but there is no reason to associate this motet with that particular event, as Louis was venerated on a number of occasions.[42] *O Philippe/O bone dux* was written in honour of two patrons whom Vitry served in the 1340s.[43] And a close reading of the texts of *Phi millies/O creator* suggests that it was probably composed between the Battle of Poitiers on 19 September 1356 and the Saturn-Mars conjunction of 8 June 1357, and possibly later still.[44] The evidence for Vitry as a composer active mostly in his youth simply does not hold up.

A number of other motets that survive only in sources much later than *Fauvel* were nonetheless placed early because they are cited in the putative *Ars nova* treatise. While this treatise carried a date of c. 1320–25, any motets cited in it had to predate this *terminus ante quem*. But it has been more than twenty years since Desmond described Ulrich Michels's datings of Vitry's *Ars nova* treatise in relation to the works of Jehan des Murs and to the *Speculum* as a 'house of cards'.[45] Absent this link with des Murs's output, the dating of the putative *Ars vetus et nova* treatise is regulated by the dating of the *Speculum musicae* of Jacobus – a treatise that, as we have seen, also sets the date of death for Petrus de Cruce. Jacobus makes clear in SMVII that the *Ars nova* is fully accepted by his contemporaries and that he acts as a lone, aged, and nostalgic champion for an *Ars antiqua*. As noted above, Desmond and I have both suggested later dates of completion for *Speculum musicae*, placing it in the 1330s or later (Desmond) and perhaps as late as c. 1350 (my latest guess).

---

[41] Vitry's *O canenda/Rex* also uses the name of its dedicatee as a motetus acrostic (on this, see the chapter by Bent in this volume). I lay out this line of argumentation in Zayaruznaya forthcoming, chap. 2 ('Crumbling Chronologies'). See also Bent's chapter (n. 80) on the acrostic 'PETRUS' in [...]/*Per grama*.

[42] Leech-Wilkinson 1995, p. 309; Kügle 1997, p. 83.

[43] Kügle identifies this correctly as 'a motet devoted to king Philip VI of France and his son John, duke of Normandy' (Kügle 1997, p. 50) and suggests that it was 'written in connection with John's investiture as duke in late summer, 1333' but with the possibility of its being as late as 1350 (pp. 84, 88). However, he does not link the motet to Vitry; this attribution is tentatively proposed in Leech-Wilkinson 1982–83, p. 9 n. 15, and the work is listed as 'attributed on stylistic evidence" in Bent rev. Wathey 2001.

[44] See Zayaruznaya 2018, pp. 383–84.

[45] The previously established dating of the *Ars nova* texts in relation to Jacobus is laid out in Michels (ed.) 1970, pp. 50–55; see the summary and criticism of this scheme in Desmond 2020, p. 35 n. 64.

Of course, even if we accept that Jacobus is writing at mid-century, that does not mean that the *Ars nova* treatises were written any later. But Desmond's recent work strongly suggests that this was indeed the case. In her 2018 monograph, she proposes a thoroughgoing revision of *Ars nova* and its chronology, especially as it pertains to the works of Jehan des Murs and the Vitriacan *Ars nova* witnesses. Whereas Michels had placed a number of important treatises between 1320 and 1324 (a move necessitated by his early date for SMVII), Desmond's revised timeline is more expansive, distributing the same treatises between 1319 and the 1330s.[46]

With the *Ars vetus et nova* thus potentially representing a later *terminus ante quem* than we had previously believed, the motets it cites that do not survive in *Fauvel* and that use notational features not present in the *Fauvel* motets, like semibreve rests and minim rests, potentially move later as well. The result of all this is that Vitry's compositional activity no longer appears mostly confined to five or ten years, and *Petre/Lugentium* does not look like an outlier anymore. Instead, it becomes plausible that Vitry wrote motets throughout his life.

Petrus's *Ars* and Vitry's *Ars vetus*

According to received chronologies, there was no Vitry before *Ars nova* and also no *Ars nova* before Vitry. As Schrade put it, 'Philippe's activity as a composer can scarcely have had any particular scope before he introduced the novelties [of *Ars nova*]; it is more likely that from the first his work presented a "New Art"'.[47] This idea resulted in the classification of the latest motets in the *Roman de Fauvel* as employing an 'early' *Ars nova* notation – one that does not yet use minims with up-stems and that resolves its semibreves into a set of default patterns.[48] Doing so preserves a rift between Petrus's *Ars vetus* (or 'late-Franconian' or 'transitional' usage[49]) and Vitry's *Ars nova*.

Here, too, recent findings tell a different story. Desmond's reclassification of the (phantom) *Ars nova* treatise as a (lost) *Ars vetus et nova* meshes well with Sarah Fuller's earlier conjecture that the treatise served as a practical guide for singers that were being asked to sing music in both systems.[50] The surviving witnesses to the lost treatise clearly lay out which usage pertains to the older notational system and which to the new, where these differ; and the survival of a number of *Fauvel* motets in later sources confirms that some motets were subject to notational updating in line with the instructions given in the treatises. There is also clear evidence that a number of

---

[46] Desmond 2018a, pp. 27–34, 99–101.

[47] Schrade 1956, p. 344.

[48] For example, see Christopher Page's assertion that the *Fauvel* song *Ay, amours, tant me dure* was 'probably to be read in the newest fashion of the New Art with unsigned semibreves resolved [into patterns]' in Page 1998, p. 356.

[49] Bent 2015a, p. 42, offers both of these terms as alternatives preferable to 'Petronian'.

[50] Fuller 1985, p. 49.

motets now surviving only in *Ars nova* notation were once written without minim stems, in a system that the treatises in question would classify as *Ars vetus*.[51]

The simple fact of the matter is that there is a theoretical system outlined in medieval treatises that accurately describes Petrus de Cruce's notational usage – and that is the *Ars vetus* system as described in texts associated with Vitry. For example, the so-called CSIII Anonymous IV, a treatise found uniquely in Paris, BnF, lat. 15128, mid- to late fourteenth century) explains that the *Ars vetus* uses dots between groups of semibreves, whereas the *Ars nova* does not.[52] These dots seem to have been a Petronian innovation and, in Mo, are found only in the last two fascicles.[53] Indeed, the treatise's example of the *Ars vetus* is comparable to Petrus's notation. Compare Examples 3.1 and 3.2 below: the first comes from CSIII Anonymous IV, where it illustrates the use of dots in the *Ars vetus*; the second is excerpted from the triplum of *S'amour eüst*, attributed by Jacobus to Petrus. (In Example 3.2, the text has been omitted to facilitate comparison with Example 3.1; none of the notated examples in *Ars vetus et nova* treatise witnesses include text.) Soon after this, the Vitriacan text goes on to give instructions for resolving groups of undifferentiated semibreves ranging from two to up to nine, written within a breve of perfect tempus.[54]

Why should we not identify this *Ars vetus* with the *ars* of Petrus? The objection that Petrus only used as many as seven semibreves in a breve whereas the *Ars vetus* goes up to nine does not sustain scrutiny. After all, very few motets written in, say, imperfect tempus, major prolation, ever articulate all six minims within a single breve.[55] And the Barcelona treatise (BAC Cat. 23–4, mid-fourteenth century) actually modifies its quotation from *Aucun ont trouvé* to go up to nine.[56] This suggests that the use of seven semibreves in a breve and the use of eight or nine are clearly continuous and part of the same system – a point underlined also by Jacobus who, depending on how we translate, tells us either that Petrus de Cruce occasionally went up to nine semibreves himself or that another one of the *antiqui* did so.[57]

---

51 Desmond 2018b, pp. 406–7.

52 Reaney (ed.) 1982, p. 38: 'In nova arte non ponuntur aliqua puncta inter semibreves nisi causa alterationis. In vetere autem arte omnes semibreves que ponuntur inter duas quadratas, vel inter punctum et quadratam, vel inter duo puncta, ponuntur pro uno tempore' (in the new *ars* the dot is not placed between semibreves except for the reason of alteration [i.e., perfection]. But in the old *ars* all semibreves written between two square [notes], or between a dot and a square, or between two dots, are written in the span of a breve).

53 This *punctus divisionis* replaces the Franconian *divisio modi*; see editorial discussion in Lefferts (ed. and trans.) 1991, pp. 14–15.

54 Lefferts (ed. and trans.) 1991, p. 39.

55 Or another analogue: Vitry never seems to have written a motet with minor prolation – that does not mean he was not writing within the *Ars nova* system.

56 On this modified citation, see Catalunya 2018, pp. 420–22.

57 Directly after citing two motets and attributing them unambiguously to Petrus, Jacobus gives several excerpts from a third work, now lost, in whose triplum eight and even nine semibreves are sometimes written within a breve span. Depending on how we translate the 'Unus autem alius' that begins the passage, this citation can be read as an attribution to Petrus as well. Wegman (trans.) 2017, p. 32 renders it 'but another [time] he notated',

Example 3.1. Example of *Ars vetus* notation from the *Compendium musicae mensurabilis tam veteris quam novae artis* (CSIII Anonymous IV) (Paris, BnF, lat. 15128, fol. 130r).

Example 3.2. Petrus de Cruce, *S'Amour/Au renouveler*, triplum, breves 5–17 (excluding text) (Mo, fol. 270r).

Another possible objection to the identification of Vitry's *Ars vetus* with the *ars* of Petrus – namely, that Petronian semibreves divided breves into equal parts – is also unconvincing. Petronian motets have been transcribed for decades with tuplets (e.g., dividing a breve into five equal parts) or with an indication that they should be delivered freely, in a *parlando* manner.[58] But as Bent has recently argued, this is a misconception based on Willi Apel's misreading of a passage in Jacobus.[59] In fact, only groups of three (and nine) semibreves divided perfect breves into equal parts – other groupings resulted in patterns of longer and shorter notes.

What were these patterns? For groups of two semibreves, we know that short-long was the norm since this is what Franco records. For larger groups, there is no theoretical evidence contemporary with Mo, fascicle 7. And yet we do have such theoretical indication in the *Ars vetus et nova* – a treatise that is possibly only slightly later than fascicle 8. I do not imply that the *Ars vetus* patterns described in Vitriacan

---

while Bent 2015a, p. 32 understands this passage as referring to a work 'by another composer ('unus alius')'. Bragard (ed.) 1955–73, vol. 7, p. 38: 'Unus autem alius pro perfecto tempore non modo quinque semibreves, sex et septem posuit, sed etiam octo et quandoque novem, ut patet in triplo qui sic incipit: Mout ont chanté d'amours, et cetera' (Another person [or: Another time he] notated for perfect tempus not only five, six, and seven semibreves, but even eight and occasionally nine, as in the triplum that starts: 'Mout ont chanté d'amours, etc'.) (Wegman (trans.) 2017, p. 32, modified). Regardless of how we translate, this passage attests to a continuity between the practice of Petrus and a notational usage in which there are up to nine semibreves in a perfect tempus.

[58] Apel 1942, pp. 322–24; Sanders rev. Lefferts 2001 suggest that the performance of Petronian semibreve groups 'was necessarily too rapid for each semibreve to be measured precisely'. Editions of Petrus's music almost ubiquitously advocate for this interpretation by writing tuplets over groups of four or more semibreves; for a recent example, see Maw 2018.

[59] Bent 2015a, pp. 39–43. See also the Barcelona treatise, which unambiguously states that 'when four, five, six or more [semibreves are placed in one tempus], they are unequal to each other'; Catalunya 2018, p. 436 n. 20.

treatises are a definitive key for unearthing Petrus's rhythms. They probably serve to formalise and ossify a practice that was perhaps initially quite flexible. But once we admit of the continuity between Petrus's usage and Vitry's *Ars vetus*, we can read the instructions provided by the latter as a guide – if not exactly to the patterns intended by Petrus, then at least to the ways in which Petronian semibreves were being resolved when Vitry was coming of age in the first decade of the fourteenth century. At the very least, it would be safe to assume that the users of the latest sources of Petrus's motets could indeed have been guided by a set of defaults similar to those preserved for the *Ars vetus* in Vitriacan *Ars vetus et nova* writings. I would contend that editing Petrus's motets using Vitry's instructions would get us closer to the original sound of Petrus's surfaces than any existing editions have yet done.

Conversely, looking at Vitry as initially a Petronian notator can have great explanatory power, especially over his earlier output. For instance, the motet *Douce/ Garison*, which might originally have been written with undifferentiated semibreves, fills its perfect-tempus breves with between two and seven graphemes (a mix of semibreves and minims in its late unique copy in *Ars nova* notation), and disposes these in ways that overwhelmingly correspond to the *Ars vetus* default rhythms described in CSIII Anonymous IV.[60] It has never been suggested that Vitry might have used Petronian notation – recall Schrade's claim that Vitry's earliest works were already a New Art. But innovation must be relative to something, and Vitry can only have come of age in a notational idiom that is preserved in sources like Tu and the later fascicles of Mo. Petrus's usage epitomised Vitry's *Ars vetus*. From this perspective, the Vitriacan *Ars vetus* system, or at least its perfect-tempus portion, *is* Petronian notation, and the default rhythms Vitry prescribes for undifferentiated semibreves in perfect tempus are likely to be continuous with Petronian practice.

Lives in the History of Notation, Notation in the Histories of Lives

Both Petrus de Cruce and Philippe de Vitry have functioned within our histories of music notation as metonyms for a particular style or system: Vitry is the figurehead of an *Ars nova*, while Petrus is associated with a system that bears his name when we call it 'Petronian'. The idea that each 'represents' a new stage in the history of notation fits into a broader model in which a succession of French composers and theorists – Leoninus, Perotinus, Franco of Cologne, Petrus de Cruce, Philippe de Vitry, Guillaume de Machaut – stand in for distinct stages of notational 'development'.[61]

This move of affiliating particular periods of musical notation or musical style with specific historical persons is neither an uncommon nor an exclusively modern one; we may recall, for example, the way that the more famous Anonymous IV talks of notational rules in use 'from the time of Perotinus Magnus, and in his own time'

---

[60] For this analysis, see Zayaruznaya forthcoming, chap. 4 ('Becoming New').

[61] While Machaut's notational practice is mostly confined to the system of *Ars nova* notation, he is generally seen as looking toward the *Ars subtilior* with his so-called notational licences and with the complexity of a work like *Ma fin est mon commencement*.

(*A tempore et in suo tempore Perotini Magni*).[62] But just because this kind of association is not anachronistic does not mean that it is always clarifying. By mapping technological regimes onto the lives and careers of individuals, we mix two different kinds of periodisation scheme – one technological, the other personal.

These, in fact, operate on their own scales and according to different logics. The dissemination of a new notational technology and its acceptance by a group of people such that it partially or fully supplants an older technology depends on the nature of the innovation itself, on a complicated network of innovators and early adopters, and on the availability of channels of communication between adopters and would-be adopters; it is further modulated by the interests of authorities and organisations.[63] The dates of birth and death of composers, on the other hand, are essentially random. And to those of us writing history, their very randomness makes them potentially instructive when the chronologies in our textbooks turn out to be in tension with personal periodisation schemes that arise from being born at some specific time, from being still alive at some other time, from having lived through something, and then from no longer living through. A life like Vitry's, which spanned seventy years, is at once too long and too short to be comfortably slotted into our histories, and the discomfort is productive.

Consider, then, these two ways of representing what we know about Petrus and his lifespan:

Petrus de Cruce (fl. 1290)
Petrus de Cruce (c. 1270–before 1347)

The first way feels simpler, the second, messier. The first way allows Petrus to remain transitional; the second raises questions about what came before and what came after the experimental motets from the seventh and eighth fascicles of Mo and Tu. The second way, in suggesting that Petrus might have lived on into *Ars nova* times – by no means proving that he did but just raising the question – might point more strongly to the continuities between Petrus's practice and the one that the *Ars vetus et nova* treatises designate as *Ars vetus*.

I contend that Philippe de Vitry and Petrus de Cruce have been subject to related but inverse historiographic processes. In Vitry's case, the documented life is almost too long if we believe that *Ars nova* is a sudden and decisive explosion effected by a young and pioneering Vitry; by offering a biographical explanation according to which Vitry was most active as a composer in the beginning of his life, Leech-Wilkinson's and Kügle's datings render Vitry's influence most concentrated within a short span of time.[64] In Petrus's case, where so little is known about biography, ideas about the transience of the notational system with which he is associated have had the effect of shrinking the composer's life, or at least his influence, to an evanescent moment of flourishing.

---

[62] Reckow (ed.) 1967, vol. 1, p. 46. On the historical and historiographic tendency to affiliate styles or repertories with individuals, see Parkes's reflections in chapter 1, and also the introduction to this volume.

[63] Rogers 1962.

[64] See n. 35 above.

The received chronologies according to which Petrus 'flourished c. 1290' and Vitry did most of his important work in c. 1315–25 depict these composers' realms of activity as wholly distinct. In so doing, they have also tended to depict the notational systems used by each as successive and distinct, both conceptually and in practice. How differently might we treat a topic framed as 'notational systems used by Petrus de Cruce (fl. 1290) and Philippe de Vitry (fl. 1320)' as opposed to 'notational systems used by Petrus de Cruce (c. 1270–before 1347) and Philippe de Vitry (1291–1361)'? The former comparison favours accounts of short, influential but unrelated bursts of innovation; the second offers opportunities to see continuities. Thus, how we understand a composer's output to fall within his life ends up having an impact on how we construct the chronologies of the technological regimes that we associate with that output.

If confronting a revised chronology of Vitry's works partly means re-assessing his relationship with the *Ars nova*, a similar thing should be true of Petrus and the *Ars vetus*. By representing Petrus's sphere of activity as centred c. 1290, we wedge him into a transitional time span between Franco and what have generally been considered to be the earliest glimmers of *Ars nova* in *Fauvel*. One of the historiographic forces compressing Petrus's life might be the idea that he must represent a state between *artes* – that he is 'post-Franconian' but also 'pre-Vitriacan'; he is 'transitional' rather than a terminus in his own right. In thinking of Petrus as active c. 1290, bracketed between two *artes* but not really participating in either one, we might end up occluding the continuities that connect him to both – continuities that point to a much more gradual shift between the two *artes*.

PART II

ASCRIPTIONS, ATTRIBUTIONS, SIGNATURES

4

Composing in the Late Middle Ages: Paradoxes in Anonymity and Attributions

Margaret Bent

Given the value attached to authority from classical antiquity right through the Middle Ages, it is hard to account for the general level of anonymity in polyphonic musical transmission before c. 1400. Why are names rarely or never attached to compositions in the musical sources? Why is it that, suddenly, soon after 1400, composer ascriptions start to appear in polyphonic manuscripts in England, Italy, and France? And why did this change internationally around 1400? Some contemporaries knew who had composed some of the pieces that look so obstinately anonymous in the sources: music theorists, other writers, and later compilers of anthologies, notably the retrospective Italian manuscripts of the early fifteenth century. How did they know? It is not comfortable to assume that those pieces were transmitted on a separate track that has left no trace. There is almost no evidence of intermediary sources with ascriptions that could have been used in preparation of the fair-copy manuscripts. This is true not only for the Italian manuscripts but also for older pieces in the English Old Hall manuscript (London, BL, Add. 57950, hereafter Old Hall), with a number of ascribed pieces whose earlier English concordances are entirely anonymous. This chapter will draw attention to puzzles of this kind and to fluid boundaries between a range of terms that may conceal composers, especially by calling them singers.

Terminology for Musicians and for Composing

Before the fifteenth century, composers were only rarely distinguished from singers, notators, and musicians in general. In the laudatory but often imprecise terminology of a related group of fourteenth-century musician motets, of which more below (see p. 89), members of whole groups (a *collegium musicorum*) are described as *musici*, which seems to be a collective term for theorists, composers, singers, and instrumentalists, sometimes distinguished as such but without discrimination between different manifestations of musicianship. The texts of those motets sometimes present theory as being fulfilled in composition and performance, seeming to reverse the Boethian definition of a true musician as a theorist who cultivates a rational speculative discipline rather than a practitioner, a composer, or singer, a view also embraced in the Guidonian adage *Musicorum et cantorum magna est dis-*

tantia. But as Guido of Arezzo's words are cited and extended in the *Quatuor princi-palia* of 1351, composers are included as '*musici*' and contrasted with those who sing without understanding, a shift in status compatible with the motet texts that honour composers and knowledgeable singers as '*musici*' alongside theorists.[1]

Rob C. Wegman's excellent study of the professionalisation of 'the composer' in the late fifteenth century, and associated terminology, is richly documented from archival sources as well as from the perspective of Johannes Tinctoris and other writings of the later fifteenth century. He traces the transition from craftsman-like 'making' (*facere*), to 'composition', with the loftier creative connotations and implicit status acquired by the word at that later date.[2] But the verb *componere* was widely used in the preceding centuries for musical and literary works and treatises, without those later, grander connotations; and medieval words for 'making' do not seem to have the connotations of mere craftsmanship implied by contrasting it with composition. Leonel Power's early fifteenth-century vernacular treatise 'upon the gamme' was addressed to 'hem that wil be syngers, or makers, or techers'.[3] If any-thing, 'making' implied no less creativity than 'composing'.

Throughout the late Middle Ages, 'composing' was a general word that included 'putting together' the constituents of composite intervals and indeed the making or putting together of counterpoint and compositions. It is common in colophons to treatises, and in reference to authors who have written or compiled treatises, sometimes used synonymously with 'compiling' (*compilare*).[4] It is used as a verb for 'those who compose music' (*qui componunt musicam*)[5] and by the few theorists who assign specific polyphonic pieces to named composers with the verb *composuit*. Anonymous IV writes, 'Viderunt et Sederunt quae composuit Perotinus Magnus' (*Viderunt* and *Sederunt* which Perotinus Magnus composed);[6] elsewhere the verb is *fecit* (made). Jacobus in his *Speculum musicae* writes, 'Nam ille valens cantor, Petrus de Cruce, qui tot pulchros et bonos cantus composuit mensurabiles' (for that excel-lent singer, Petrus de Cruce, who composed so many beautiful and good meas-urable songs), and he goes on to attribute two famous motets to Petrus: *S'Amour*

---

[1]   *Quatuor principalia* I.9: 'Musicorum et cantorum magna est distancia. / Isti dicunt illi sciunt qui componunt musicam. / Nam qui canit quod non sapit diffinitur bestia' (There is a great difference between musicians and singers. They say: those who know how, compose music. For someone who sings what he does not understand is defined as a beast) (Aluas 1996, pp. 209–10). The definition of a true musician derives from Boethius (Friedlein (ed.) 1867, pp. 223–25) and the separation from singers from Guido of Arezzo (Smits van Waesberghe and Vetter (eds.) 1985, p. 95).

[2]   Wegman 1996; Bradley 2022a, p. 56 reflects on the significance of the verbs *trouver* and *faire* in motets by Petrus de Cruce and Adam de la Halle. For 'making/composing/ finding' words in songs, see also Mason 2021. For surveys of the terminology related to composition in this volume, see also the chapters by Bradley, Everist, Desmond, Dolce, and Parkes, and the introduction.

[3]   In London, BL, Lansdowne 763. See Meech 1935.

[4]   For late-fifteenth-century instances of *compilare* applied to the copying of polyphonic music, see Wathey 1988, no. 104.

[5]   See n. 1.

[6]   Reckow (ed.) 1967, vol. 1, p. 82.

eüst/Au renouveler/Ecce and *Aucun ont trouvé/Lonc tans/Annun[tiantes]*.[7] John of Tewkesbury attributes two named motets to Philippe de Vitry (*Cum statua/Hugo* and *Vos quid/Gratissima*: here, the verb is *edidit* [published]), and he further states, 'ut patet in pluribus motetis quos composuit praedictus Philippus, flos quidem musicorum' (as seen in several motets which the aforesaid Philippe composed, indeed the flower of musicians).[8] Prosdocimus de Beldemandis writes, 'Guilielmus de Mascandio quem nominat auctor in littera, fuit in arte musicali magister singularis, in qua arte multa composuit' (Guillaume de Machaut was a unique master in the art of music, in which art he composed many things).[9] Less common before the later fifteenth century is the noun *compositor*, but it was used, for example, in the *Quatuor principalia* to describe Guido's construction of the gamut and monochord, and by Jacobus to describe a composer of discants – that is, a polyphonic composer.[10]

Boundaries between singing and invention were fluid. The training in counterpoint and mensural notation that was required to sing polyphony was the same as the prerequisite for composition. Of those described as singers, many more than we know of must also have been composers, and some compositional ability would often have been taken for granted, given the common training. 'Cantus' is strongly aligned with composition as well as with singing, in poems, treatises, and lists in the texts of motets. A *liber cantus*, *liber de cantu*, or one containing *cantus figuratus*, *figurativus*, or *fractus* is a common way of referring to a book of written polyphonic compositions, made things, *res facta*.[11] The *Libellus cantus mensurabilis* attributed to Johannes de Muris, indeed, calls Guillaume de Machaut a *cantor* in the context of describing his presumably written notational practices.[12]

Words for singing, saying, and inventing were often interchangeable: in the *Aeneid*, Virgil 'sings of arms and the man' (*Arma virumque cano*). In this case, we assume that it means primarily invention (composition), probably some kind of declamation and, less likely, musical singing as we would understand it. The verb *dicere* sometimes unmistakably means 'to sing'. The rubric for the music of one of the complementary underpinnings (*pedes*) of the late thirteenth-century canon *Sumer is icumen in* reads, 'hoc dicit alius pausans in medio' (the other one 'says' this, pausing

---

[7] Bragard (ed.) 1955–73, vol. 7, p. 36.

[8] *Quatuor principalia* IV, I.31, I.32. *Cum statua* is also internally signed. For the attribution of the treatise to Tewkesbury and for the texts and translations (here slightly adapted), see Aluas 1996, pp. 5–29. For another quotation pertaining to Philippe in the *Quatuor principalia*, see the chapter by Zayaruznaya in this volume.

[9] Gallo (ed.) 1966, pp. 83–84. 'Mascandio' was presumably at some stage a misreading of 'Mascaudio'.

[10] Bragard (ed.) 1955–73, vol. 7, p. 5: 'ut est peritus et discretus discantator vel discantuum compositor' (that discanter or composer of discants is expert and judicious). *Quatuor principalia* II.3 and III.4: 'Guido monachus, qui compositor erat gammatis' (Guido the monk, who was the composer of the gamut).

[11] Bent 2014.

[12] Meyer (ed. and trans.) 2000, p. 202: 'Et nota, quod quidam cantores, puta Gulielmus de Mascandio, et nonnulli alii, imperficiunt brevem perfectam minoris prolationis ab una sola minima' (and note that certain singers, for example Guillaume de Machaut, and some others, imperfect the perfect breve in minor prolation by a single minim).

in the middle). In Guillaume Du Fay's early fifteenth-century motet *Inclita stella maris*, a second contratenor part is labelled 'concordans cum omnibus, non potest cantari nisi pueri dicant fugam' (it concords with all the parts, and cannot be sung unless the boys 'say', or utter, the canon).[13]

Composer Ascriptions in Polyphonic Manuscripts before 1400

With certain exceptions, ascriptions to composers in polyphonic manuscripts are vanishingly rare before c. 1400. Poet-composers of monophonic song, named troubadours and trouvères, form a different category; some (not all) of their manuscripts were provided with names of composers long before polyphonic music was similarly ascribed, perhaps because those genres were prized for their poetry and their poets, a category of creator well established by the twelfth and especially the thirteenth century when those repertories began to be formed.[14] The assembled collections of the works of Adam de la Halle and Jehan de l'Escurel include some polyphony, but both left more monophony.[15] L'Escurel's works are ascribed only in the partly classified table of contents of the interpolated *Roman de Fauvel*, Paris, BnF, fr. 146. All the contents of Montpellier, BIU, H 196 (hereafter Mo) are unascribed, but it contains motets by Adam de la Halle which are ascribed in Paris, BnF, fr. 25566, and fascicle 7 of Mo opens with the two aforementioned motets by Petrus de Cruce which are attributed only in theoretical sources.[16]

Machaut is of course a unique case; most manuscripts prepared under his supervision celebrate his authorship.[17] But despite the musicologist's view of him as primarily a polyphonic composer, monophonic songs form a significant proportion of his musical output, and he was then to many a poet first and foremost, consistent with his much larger poetic output, and is so recognised in the triplum text of *Apollinis eclipsatur/ Zodiacum signis*, the first in the aforementioned group of musician motets.[18] Although

---

13   On the interchangeability of saying and singing, see also Marchi 2019, pp. 9–10; Abramov-van Rijk 2009, p. 223 n. 119, reports that the excellent performance of the castrato in the 1607 performance of Monteverdi's *Orfeo* was described with the verb *dire*. A vernacular example in a Montpellier motet is given by Clark 2007.

14   For a discussion of the trouvères as composers of music and text, see the chapter by Dolce in this volume.

15   The ascribed monophonic songs of troubadours and trouvères culminated in the polyphonic rondeaux (as well as motets) of Adam de la Halle, whose works are collected under his name in Paris, BnF, fr. 25566. For an important revaluation of Adam, see Bradley 2022a.

16   On the juxtaposition of these two composers and an analysis of the second Mo 7 motet attributed to Petrus, see the chapter by Bradley in this volume. See also the chapter by Zayaruznaya on the two motets by Petrus.

17   Earp 2021 points out that Machaut's first manuscript (Paris, BnF, fr. 1586) does not identify him, perhaps because he enjoyed steady employment by nobility, but that in his next project, the *Jugement dou roy de Navarre*, he names himself prominently, perhaps because then seeking employment.

18   See now Bent 2023, chap. 16. This interrelated group of at least five fourteenth-century musician motets (see chaps. 15–21) will figure prominently in what follows.

listed there among musicians, Machaut is characterised as one who 'rejoices in poetry' (*gaudet poetria*). Eustache Deschamps described both Machaut and Vitry primarily as poets ('Vitry, Machault de haulte emprise / Poetes que musique ot chier'),[19] and an anonymous author of the *Règles de seconde rhétorique* famously praises them both, Vitry with specific musical terms (that 'he invented the manner of motets, ballades, lais and simple rondeaux, and in music invented the four prolations, red notes, and the novelty of proportions'); Machaut is praised less precisely.[20] Petrarch hailed Vitry as 'a unique French poet' (*poeta nunc unicus Galliarum*) as well as a *musicus*.[21] Gerves du Bus and Chaillou de Pesstain are named as authors of verbal texts within the interpolated *Fauvel* (Paris, BnF, fr. 146, fol. 23v), but its musical composers are not named. Authorship of poetry thus seems to have been privileged over that of music. The extent to which 'poetry' includes music is open, as is the question how far 'singing' includes or implies creation or composition. Poetry, accessible to a wider readership than the specialised notation of music, often had a longer shelf life; the more advanced the musical style, the more quickly it went out of fashion.

Adam's works may have been gathered posthumously, but the exceptional self-promotion that underlay Machaut's complete-works manuscripts was very much in his lifetime. The collected works of Adam in Paris, BnF, fr. 25566 open with an author portrait placed within an initial, and Machaut is variously depicted in the manuscripts of his works, most notably in the famous miniatures at the beginning of Paris, BnF, fr. 1584. Philip the Chancellor was known primarily as a poet, his texts collected in many manuscripts, but London, BL, Egerton 274, dated 1260s, is his only author corpus with musical notation, headed with a rubric declaring his authorship. The contents are all Latin conductus and mostly monophony but also include polyphony.[22] Apart from these, there are no other surviving authorially defined or complete-works polyphonic collections, even small ones, until the retrospective Italian trecento anthologies of the early fifteenth century, grouped by composers, most famously in the Squarcialupi codex (Florence, BML, Mediceo Palatino 87, hereafter Squarcialupi).

Attributions from Treatises, Indexes, Literary, and Archival Sources

The Evidence of Treatises

So how are we able to assign composer names to any music before they appear regularly in manuscripts? The exceptional cases of Philip the Chancellor, Adam de la Halle, Jehan de l'Escurel, and Guillaume de Machaut apart, the few attributions for earlier polyphonic compositions derive almost entirely from treatises and other

---

[19] Queux de Saint-Hilaire and Raynaud (eds.) 1878–1903, vol. 8, p. 178.

[20] Langlois (ed.) 1902, p. 12.

[21] For this and Petrarch's other references to Vitry, see Mann 1987.

[22] Payne (ed.) 2011, pp. xii–xv on attributions to Philip and on 'the role of Perotinus'. See also Rillon-Marne 2012, pp. 229–63.

external writings, and from occasional cases of internal signatures or authorial acrostics. The treatise attributions are to almost the only other composers whose names we can attach to compositions. In the late thirteenth century, Anonymous IV's very specific account of the contributions of Leoninus and Perotinus to the Notre Dame repertory has underpinned accepted historiography; but he also lists a dozen other musicians, singers, and notators or theorists, of whom, apart from Franco of Cologne, we know little and hear less.[23] Robertus de Handlo in 1326 cites a number of notational innovators, presumably composers, otherwise unknown.[24] Some of Vitry's texts are separately preserved and attributed in German humanist poetry manuscripts, thus confirming his authorship of the relevant motets, presumably for both text and music.[25] In turn, other pieces have been attributed by modern scholars to those composers on grounds of stylistic affinity or textual clues, sometimes in conjunction with manuscript groupings. At a later date, the early fifteenth-century treatise in Vercelli, Bibl. Agnesiana 11, definitively attributes to Antonio Zacara da Teramo the ballata *Deduto sey* previously treated as a doubtful work by Johannes Ciconia.[26]

Music examples in treatises, often in late manuscripts, sometimes seem to be transmitted via other theorists, not always referring back to a musical source, and in some cases with clear evidence, from errors or misreporting, that the theorist did not know the musical work firsthand. The successive corruptions in the theoretical transmission of the triplum incipit of Petrus de Cruce's motet *Aucun ont trouvé* are a prime instance of this.[27]

In some cases, it has been assumed that pieces mentioned in a treatise are by the author of that treatise. Those cited in the Vitriacan *Ars nova* treatises, contemporaneously with the innovations that they exemplify, are generally reckoned more likely to be by Vitry. On the other hand, most of the broad range of motet titles cited by Franco or in Franconian digests are generally thought not to be by him. But such inferences are open in both cases to the possibility of later additions and revisions to treatises, where the body of theory was fluid and has proved hard to define. Some manuscript transmissions of the examples in Franco's treatise are very unstable: Christian Leitmeir shows how scribes may arbitrarily invent the music and text of examples to fill space.[28]

The authorial situation for the treatises themselves is very different from that for musical compositions. Many treatises remain anonymous, but some do name authors, often in colophons, as is common in treatises generally. The author of the *Speculum musicae* names himself as Jacobus in a unique authorial acrostic formed of the first letters of each of its seven books, signalled in the proemium. There are even

---

[23] Page 1989, p. 153 lists all of these names in a chronological diagram.

[24] Lefferts (ed. and trans.) 1991.

[25] Wathey 1993b, 1994. For a discussion of the attributions for Vitry's motets, see the chapter by Zayaruznaya in this volume.

[26] Caraci Vela 1997; Bent and Hallmark (eds.) 1984–85, no. 42.

[27] Bent 2015a, chap. 2.

[28] Leitmeir 2005.

occasional examples of what Alastair Minnis called 'the tendency to accept improbable attributions of currently popular works to older and respected writers'.[29] That the author of the treatise of Lambertus was known as pseudo-Aristotle (*cuiusdam Aristoteles*) is a rare instance in music.[30]

The Evidence of Lists and Indexes

Unlike some composer-classified trouvère manuscripts and their tables of contents, entries in indexes in late-medieval polyphonic manuscripts are never classified by composer. Despite composer groupings in some sources, they are more often listed by genre or alphabetically. But indexes do occasionally give composer names, almost exclusively as one of several means to distinguish different settings of the same text. Criteria such as composer, mensuration, and number of voices may differentiate between like-texted Mass movements, and only in such cases, as in the indexes to Bologna, Q.15, Oxford, Bod. Lib., Canon. Misc. 213, Trent, Cast. Buonconsiglio 1379 [92] (aka Trent 92), and Aosta, Sem. mag. 15 (hereafter Aosta).[31] Index attributions usually confirm a manuscript ascription if present but sometimes conflict. They are often the only authority for authorship where no ascription is present in the body of a manuscript.

The only surviving bifolio of Paris, BnF, n.a.f. 23190 (Trémoïlle), contains an index (or rather, a partly classified table of contents) on its first recto. Very few mass movements are included, but two Credos are distinguished from each other by annotating their composers' names. One is by Sortes, presumably referring to the widely circulated Credo ascribed to him elsewhere, the other, previously misread as 'decus', is to 'Denis', presumably Denis le Grant, but in the absence of its music cannot be identified with any extant composition.[32]

Two other listings with named composers are considered to record the contents of lost books of polyphony.[33] One of these is a group of lists in the late-thirteenth-century manuscript London, BL, Harley 978, fols. 160v–161r, headed 'Ordo **** W. de Wint[onia]'.[34] On fol. 160v, *Spiritus et alme*, presumably the Gloria trope,

---

[29] Minnis 1988, p. 11.

[30] Meyer (ed.) and Desmond (trans.) 2015.

[31] For the distinction between indexes and tables of contents, see Bent (ed.) 2008, vol. 1, pp. 89–95 and Bent 2013.

[32] Besseler 1927, p. 241 thought the two words, both misread, might be trope texts. This Credo cannot be identified, but a chace in Ivrea, Bibl. cap. 115 has been convincingly attributed to Denis (see below p. 85). See also Stoessel 2012, and for the Trémoïlle index in general, Bent 2023, chap. 31.

[33] Besançon, BM, I, 716 contains a list of fifty-seven motetus incipits without composer attributions. This list was presumably a table of contents for a late-thirteenth-century collection of three-voice motets now lost. See Bradley 2022a, pp. 82 and 100 n. 13. Only five of the Besançon motets are unica, and most of the motets listed in this table of contents are apparently otherwise extant, principally in Mo and Bamberg, Staatsbibl., Lit. 115.

[34] Discussed and transcribed in Lefferts 1986, pp. 161–65. The second word has been read as *libri*, but this is uncertain. Sean Curran pointed out in conversation that the word might

is followed by the name R. de Burg[ate], and *Postea Ř* by that of W. de Wic[umbe] in the middle of a series of liturgically ordered alleluias. Unsurprisingly, none of these items is specified as polyphonic. A cautious interpretation might not extend authorship to more than the two individual items. Following the alleluias in a second column is a list of 'Cund[uctus]', whose status as monophonic or polyphonic is likewise unknown. On fol. 161r, the ensuing lists of motets have no personal names attached but that they are polyphonic is made explicit by their categorisation according to number of texts and voices. Headings differentiate a group of motets in two parts with one text ('Motetti cum una littera et duplici nota') from those with two texts ('Motetti cum duplici littera').[35] Although London, BL, Harley 978 is thought to report the contents of a lost musical collection (not necessarily all polyphonic), no piece or folio numbers are attached; they might perhaps be present if this were a post facto rather than a prescriptive listing. The plot thickens with an inscription at the end of Oxford, Bod. Lib., Bodl. 125, fols. 98v–99r, following a list of works copied by W. de Wicumbe, a monk of Reading, while seconded to the dependent priory of Leominster in 1245–49. Some of the entries are musical; besides liturgical books and a theory treatise, Wicumbe copied two rolls, one containing three-part, the other two-part compositions (*cantus*) of which he may also be the composer. Fragments from both rolls have been identified (the 'Rawlinson' fragments), including polyphonic alleluias, whose titles, however, have only a small overlap with the Harley listing. This complex situation and the relationship between the two manuscripts is now expertly investigated in an important study by Karen Desmond.[36] The attribution to Wicumbe for the compositions he copied is oblique but highly plausible.

Composers and composition titles otherwise unknown are listed in a second informative testimony, probably of the 1360s, reported by Michael Scott Cuthbert in 2017 and subsequently published by Francesco Zimei.[37] It is a list of some thirty-five titles in the composite manuscript Seville, Bibl. Col. 5-2-25, fol. 23v, which appears to record the prospective contents of a lost book of polyphony, interspersed with a few items that may be treatises. Nearly all the listed titles are Latin, liturgical items including three Sanctus settings, or what may be independently texted motets, none identifiable with known compositions, thus hinting at a significant but largely lost body of Latin-texted trecento works excluded from the later anthologies. Seville,

---

perhaps be *magistri* and also noted other doubtful or erroneous readings.

35 A heading following pieces listed under 'Motetti cum duplici littera' distinguishes a pair of motets that are simply labelled as in two parts ('Item moteti cum duplici nota') but presumably with just one text. That these two motets of the initial type (with two voices and one text) represented a brief interruption or insertion within the larger group of motets with two texts is suggested by the restatement and resumption of the categorisation 'Item cum duplici littera' that immediately follows the pair of 'duplici nota' pieces.

36 Desmond 2020. See also Desmond's chapter in this volume for a discussion of the Rawlinson Fragments and an analysis of the polyphonic alleluias in relation to W. de Wicumbe's authorhip.

37 Cuthbert 2017; Zimei 2018. On the structure of the manuscript, see Cuthbert 2009a.

Bibl. Col. 5-2-25 is exceptional in the fact that at this early date, almost all the titles are ascribed to composers, known and unknown. They include four works by Marchetto, twelve unknown mostly Latin works by 'Magister Ja' or 'Ja[...]bus' and one by a 'Magister Petrus', though Cuthbert is cautious about identifying these with the obvious candidates, Jacopo da Bologna and Magister Piero. Other hitherto unknown composer names, some of which were added later, include frater Terencinus de Verona He[remitarum], [frater] Michael de Pad[ua]. Just three of the Italian texts are known, two of which (a madrigal and a caccia) can be matched to extant compositions.[38] Thus, only a couple of the Italian works that form the bulk or the entirety of the later collected-works manuscripts are represented in the Seville list. This and other evidence, from literary references and fragmentary musical discoveries, hint at the limitations of the retrospective anthologies on which we are so largely dependent for trecento repertory. Those manuscripts almost entirely excluded sacred music and motets, and it is clear that they also excluded composers and works even in the genres that they hitherto appeared to cover so comprehensively.

The Evidence of Archives

Although names of instrumentalists and singers can be harvested from payment records and wills, payments for composition are almost non-existent until the late fifteenth century. One notable exception is the payment in 1298 to Petrus de Cruce for a new office, composed together with others, for the newly canonised Louis IX.[39] This must have been chant. Only the payment, and not any musical sources, allows us to attach a name to this office.[40]

A payment to Francesco Landini in 1379 by the composer Andreas de Florentia, organist at SS Annunziata, 'pro quinque motectis', was tantalising to an earlier generation of scholars when Italians were not thought to have cultivated motets.[41] The five motets have not survived, or at least cannot be identified among extant fragments. Also archivally documented is that Du Fay, at the wish in 1457 of a dying friend and Cambrai canon, Michael de Beringhen, composed plainchant for a new feast recalling six feasts of the Virgin Mary, the *Recollectio Festorum Beatae Marie Virginis*, to words by his colleague Gilles Carlier. There are many sources for this office, which was long in use, but again, the musical sources carry no ascription, and their authorship is known

---

[38] The caccia *In forma quasi* is here attributed to an unknown Frater Enselmus, in Squarcialupi to Vicenzo da Rimini and anonymous in London, BL, Add. 29987.

[39] Bent 2015a, pp. 32–33, reporting Harbinson (ed.) 1976, and Johnson 1991, chap. 6. This gives an excellent account of what can be known about Petrus de Cruce and his role in the Saint Louis office. For another reflection on this payment and an in-depth discussion of Petrus de Cruce's career, see the chapter by Zayaruznaya in this volume. On the Louis IX liturgies and the difficulties in apportioning authorship, see Gaposchkin 2008.

[40] Catherine A. Bradley has drawn my attention to a surprisingly overlooked case, a catalogue compiled in the 1270s by the monk Henry of Brussels, naming a 'Petrus musicae' of Cambrai who made neumas for an office for Saint Elizabeth of Hungary and 'condictus' (potentially polyphonic). See also Haggh (ed.) 1995.

[41] Taucci 1934–35, p. 102.

only from archival records, an account and two charters.[42] Polyphonic works by Du Fay are also archivally recorded, with his name attached, but those payments are not for his compositions but to the Cambrai cathedral copyist Simon Mellet.

Andrew Wathey reports rich pickings from lost books archivally recorded in England, including a payment at Worcester in 1464/65 to Edmundo Syngar for composing a new two-voice mass ('causa compositionis nove misse ad ij vices' [sic]) and from Henry VII to the known composer William Newark in 1493 'for makyng of a song'.[43] These are however from the later fifteenth century when payments for composition become generally more numerous.[44]

There must be many more references to composers and their compositions awaiting discovery in archival documents. A payment may be indirect – namely, in support of the performance of a service that happens to name a composer and work. Anne Walters Robertson has discovered one such: that Johannes Gallioctus from the kingdom of Cyprus was the composer of a 'new mass' performed on Sunday, 8 April 1453, in association with the momentous acquisition of the Holy Shroud by Duke Louis of Savoy and Anne (of Cyprus).[45] 'Galliot', with no first name, is documented among the chaplains and singers at the court of Savoy in the 1440s and could have come there as early as 1434 along with the musicians Anne brought from Cyprus to Chambéry.[46] Might Galiot even have gone to Cyprus from France with Queen Charlotte de Bourbon in 1411? The new reference from 1453 adds his candidacy to those of Jean Hanelle and Gilet Velut as a possible composer of the Cyprus repertory in Turin, Bnu, J.II.9.[47] He would have had to be quite old in 1453 to be a candidate for identification with the composer Galiot of two songs in Chantilly, Bibl. Château 564 (hereafter Chantilly). Since Chantilly is dated after 1400, this is not impossible, but it seems likelier that two men are involved, possibly related.

[42] Haggh 1990, pp. 559–71.

[43] Wathey 1988, nos. 143, 159.

[44] For example, those reported at SS Annunziata in Zanovello 2014 and previous work by Valente Gori and Darwin Smith cited in this chapter, and in Wegman 1996 to Heinrich Isaac, Jacob Obrecht, Clemens non Papa specified as composers.

[45] 'Item magis die octava Aprilis anni presentis pro oblationibus factis per quos supra in missa nova domini Johannis Galliocti de regie chippri ... in ecclesia ... predicti fratrum minorum Rippe ... celebrata' (And again, for the oblations made on the eighth day of April in this year [1453] by [the Duke and Duchess of Savoy] in the new mass of Dominus Johannes Gallioctus from the kingdom of Cyprus ... that was celebrated ... in the church ... of the aforementioned Franciscans of Rive); drawn from a document found in the *Registres du Conseil de Genève* (Archivio di Stato di Torino, Sezioni Riunite, inv. 16, Reg. 102, fols. 351v–352r). This is reported in Robertson 2024, at pp. 180–85. I am grateful to her for sharing her findings in advance of publication.

[46] Bradley (Robert) 1992, pp. 125, 145, 467 and passim, 516.

[47] Velut's presence in Cyprus was known to earlier scholarship, documented together with the newly identified Hanelle by Kügle 2012.

Literary Evidence

It is not only music theorists who name composers. Literary naming could constitute a valuable study in itself; the following are just a few mostly well-known instances. Gace de la Buigne, in his *Roman des Deduis* (written between 1359 and 1377), cites a 'chace des faucons' composed by a musician 'de grant pris', the bishop of Senlis, Denis le Grant. Karl Kügle makes an excellent case to identify this with the only surviving chace, which describes a hunt with falcons, *Se ie chant*.[48] This is an indirect attribution, as the title is not cited.

As well as instrumentalists, Martin le Franc in the *Champion des dames* (c. 1440) names as singers those we know as composers but without naming or attributing specific pieces. Earlier in the century, Johannes Tapissier, Johannes Carmen, and Johannes Cesaris 'sang so well' (*sy bien chanterent*), but they never 'discanted' (*deschanterent*) with such choice melody as Du Fay and Gilles Binchois, who 'followed Dunstaple'.[49] Martin compares a pair of blind rebec players favourably to Du Fay and Binchois (stanza 2037), Du Fay vexed and scowling because he has no melody so beautiful ('Et Du Fay despité et frangne / Qu'il n'a melodie sy belle'). Was it their invention or their execution, or both inseparably, that invited the comparison?

Of the musicians named in Italian poetry, how many might be called composers?[50] Dante in *Purgatorio* meets his friend Casella (d. 1299) who 'sings' Dante's canzone *Amore che ne la mente* and very possibly composed what he sang. The dividing line between composer and performer is not clear; again, singing may sometimes be synonymous with creating. Boccaccio's fictive named performers in the *Decameron* are not identified as composers, but as instrumental accompanists to monophonic *ballate*, they must have had musical training and inventive ability. *Oseletto salvazo* was twice set by Jacopo da Bologna, as a madrigal and as a canonic madrigal. The third terzina names Fioràn, Filippottus, and Marchettus as composers (or makers: *fare, fanno* are the verbs) of *ballate*, madrigals, and motets, with whom modern imitators are unfavourably compared. These are assumed to be Floriano da Rimini, Philippe de Vitry, and Marchetto da Padova. Two of Petrarch's *Epistolae metricae* are addressed to Floriano da Rimini, who is compared favourably to Orpheus. Floriano is thus a third musician immortalised with a nickname by Petrarch and with the most overtly musical (and only mythical) of his classical sobriquets.[51] No surviving

---

[48] See Kügle 1997, pp. 159–60. A lost Credo by Denis is documented above: see n. 32.

[49] In the much-discussed stanzas 2033–34 of Martin le Franc's *Champion des dames*. On their interpretation, see Bent 2004 and Wegman 2003. A famous author portrait of Du Fay and Binchois is in Paris, BnF, fr. 12476. Two poems by Jean Molinet (*Oroison a nostre dame* and *Debat du vieil gendarme et du viel amoureux*, dated by Fallows c. 1470) cite sixty-two chanson titles but without ascriptions (see Fallows 1998).

[50] Many strands that could not be taken fully into account here are pursued in two excellent studies: Abramov-van Rijk 2009 and Jennings 2014.

[51] The others are 'Socrates', the music theorist Ludovicus Sanctus de Beeringhen (= Ludwig van Kempen, 1304–61), chaplain and cantor to Cardinal Giovanni Colonna, and Philippe de Vitry, his 'Gallus', both of whose deaths are commemorated on the flyleaf of Petrarch's Milan *Virgil*, with its famous frontispiece by Simone Martini. See Billanovich 1996, chap. 18, and now, Abramov-van Rijk 2015.

compositions are ascribed to Floriano, though this Petrarchan Orpheus is cited in company with two known composers.[52]

Niccolò de Rossi's sonnet *Io vidi ombre e vivi al paragone*, probably of the 1330s, names twenty musicians, including some long dead (Casella), some of similar date (Marchetto), and some who outlived Rossi (Confortino). Of the others, we have some slight independent testimony only to Floriano and Checolino and perhaps to Magister Piero (if 'Petro mastro' is the composer).[53] In a sonnet by Francesco di Vannozzo (before 1390), *Poi ch'a l'ardita penna*, addressed to Petrarch, 'Confortino', already named in the Rossi sonnet, is not clearly identified but appears to be able to perform and to 'dress' Vannozzo's 'naked' poetry with music to make it more worthy of being sung to Petrarch; this may suggest Confortino was a composer as well as a performer.

Some of the ballatas and madrigals in the *Libro delle Rime* of Franco Sacchetti are headed in later editions as having been set by named composers, including himself (often 'intonata' and/or 'sonum dedit'), so this confirms, unsurprisingly, that some of the works we know in later manuscripts were in named circulation before Sacchetti's death c. 1400. Some of the settings survive, some do not; many of the composers are known but some (including Ottolino da Brescia) are not.

The sonnets in Simone Prodenzani's *Il Saporetto* (c. 1415) give copious musical and performative information[54] and include nearly ninety named pieces, many of which we know from ascriptions in early fifteenth-century sources to be by trecento composers (including Jacopo da Bologna, Bartolino da Padova, and Giovanni da Cascia) but also titles that cannot be identified. But the point for present purposes is that although Prodenzani names composers, known and unknown, to us, they are not directly attached to the titles of pieces cited.[55]

---

[52] Some of this material is also reported in Bent 2015b.

[53] The sonnet names 'Casella, el Guerço e Quintinello, / Mino, Lippo, Segna lor compagnone, / el buon Scochetto, Çovanni e Nerrone, / Parlantino, Bertuci e Çecarello, / Marchetto e Confortino, Agnol cum ello, / Blasio, Floran, Petro mastro, Garçone / Sopra costoro venne Checolino'. Elena Abramov-van Rijk informs me (email, 18 August 2022) of another sonnet by Niccolò de Rossi, *Nella città di senno di Bologna*, entirely dedicated to Checolino and his beautiful singing, and also of a sonnet by Niccolò Quirini (early fourteenth century) containing the words 'O mastro Petro de canto e de nota'. Does this mean singing and notated composition?

[54] See Nádas 1998.

[55] Prodenzani and Sacchetti were case studies in Cuthbert 2009b, a statistically based study of lost repertories and the incidence of concordances, which concluded that 'scholars now need have little worry that they are viewing only a small, possibly unrepresentative sliver of the original written repertory'. He estimates that 75% of Prodenzani's titles are at least provisionally identified (41–42). Cuthbert confines his study to the age of Schism (the two decades either side of 1400) and to works similar to those that survive and thus were likely to have been collected in similar manuscripts. He explicitly excludes Latin-texted motets and sacred music probably originating outside Italy, the earlier period of the Rossi codex (Vatican, BAV, Rossi 215) and Marchetto, older works such as those in the Seville list (Seville, Bibl. Col. 5-2-25), and composers not represented in the retrospective anthologies and from whom no works survive, conceding 'a larger lost repertory of music from mid-century and earlier' (55).

Italian literary naming of composers from whom little or nothing survives, and many unknown text incipits are all the more striking when set beside the large collections of trecento music mostly datable to the early fifteenth century. As noted above, these no longer appear quite as comprehensive as they once seemed, the more evidence comes to light of what was excluded from them.

Musicians Named within Texts of Compositions

Musicians are named in texts of motets and songs from the thirteenth to the sixteenth centuries.[56] The triplum voices of four late thirteenth-century French-texted motets recorded in fascicles 7 and 8 of Mo open by listing the names of musical companions. The triplum texts of *Entre Adam et Hanikel/Chief bien seans/Aptatur* and *Entre Jehan et Philippet/Nus hom/Chose Tassin* are closely related, describing the drunken musical activities of four young friends.[57] The upper voice of *Entre Copin et Bourgeois/Je me cuidoie/Bele Ysabelos* identifies five student companions in Paris, and at least two of these characters reappear in the triplum text of *A maistre Jehan Lardier/Pour la plus jolie/Alleluya*,[58] which addresses eleven individuals by name in addition to other 'bons compaignons' within a Parisian community, possibly a confraternity.[59] The tradition is interconnected and cross-referential, apparently stemming from one widely disseminated piece (*Entre Adam et Hanikel*).

Deus compaignouns de Cleremunde, datable around 1400, is an incomplete anonymous triplum with macaronic text in Anglo-Norman and Latin, in English script.[60] Two musical companions from Clermont, Gwillelmus Malcharte and his brother Alebram, are named and praised as singers and for their personal qualities, suggesting some analogies with *Furnos reliquisti/Equum est*,[61] a piece laden with musical terminology, addressed to the singers' absent singing companion Buclare ('companion' is a recurrent word for a fellow singer). The cantus is in canon; cantus and tenor have different texts, all rhyming in -*are*. At least one can be presumed to be in the voice of the poet-composer, Egardus, named in the text. All of these are 'singers', but as we have seen, that does not preclude authorship.

Some names may hide behind fanciful latinisations (many in the musician motet *Sub Arturo/Fons* were brilliantly decoded by Brian Trowell, such as Nicholaus de

---

[56] There is some overlap in this and following paragraphs with the contents of Bent 2023, chap. 15 (pp. 283–84) and the following chapters.

[57] On the relationship between these texts and the possible importance of Adam de la Halle in instigating an 'Entre' motet tradition, see Bradley 2022a, chap. 3. I am grateful to Catherine A. Bradley for access to her work before publication and for a discussion of these texts. Most of the 'followers', as with the fourteenth-century musician motets, are unica.

[58] On the identification of these names, see Ludwig (1910) 1978, vol. 1/2, p. 599.

[59] See Everist 2018c, pp. 24–28. Also commented by Gómez 1985, pp. 13–15, treating the Mo motets as antecedents for the fourteenth-century group.

[60] Washington, LoC, M2.1 C6 1400 Case, fol. 2r. See Bent 2022b and 2023, p. 397.

[61] Modena, Bibl. Est., α. M.5.24, fols. 35v–36r (Apel with Rosenberg (eds.) 1970–72, vol. 3, no. 295).

vado famelico, 'of Hungerford').[62] Names may be disguised, as the retrograding of Rodericus as 'S Uciredor' in Chantilly and the anagram Borlet yielding Trebol (probably Trebor, in turn the retrograde of Robert) in the same source. The names we have may be nicknames or sobriquets which will not match archival references to an official name. Tapissier's real name was Jean de Noyers; but we lack similar identifications for other names that might also be sobriquets. Such ways of naming may be impediments to identifying composers with documented individuals. Composers may be credited informally or affectionately in music manuscripts that would be seen by fellow performers, reflecting a range of status or authority of ascriptions. First names may be easily recognisable if unusual: exceptionally, we find Leonel or Leonel Power but never just Power. Rebuses, with a note substituting as a solmisation syllable in the name, are quite common, notably for Lantins ('la') and Du Fay ('fa'). 'Prepositus Brixiensis' is unique in being named by his office, not his personal name, which we now know.[63] The Old Hall motet *Are post libamina/Nunc surgunt* is ascribed to Mayshuet. Within the text, he is not named but appears to describe himself as an active distinguished Frenchman, both composer and contrafactor of the motet from French into Latin, to accord with English taste.[64]

In the fifteenth century, Du Fay's rondeau *Hé, compaignons* celebrates his musical colleagues not as singers or composers but simply as 'companions' (including the known composers Hugo and Arnold de Lantins).[65] He greets them informally by their familiar names and drinks to 'Huchon, Ernoul, Humblot, Henry, Jean, François, Hugues, Thierry et Godefrin', in a register similar to those of the thirteenth-century motets. At a more solemn level, Binchois's motet *Nove cantum melodie* enjoins seventeen named colleagues 'favoured by the Muses' to celebrate the baptism in 1431 of Philippe le Bon's son Antoine, count of Charolais; apart from Binchois himself, they are mostly obscure. *Romanorum Rex*, a motet by Johannes de Sarto, lists 'singers' (including himself and Johannes Brassart, known composers) who are to mourn the death of King Albrecht II in 1439. In the second section of Loyset Compere's late fifteenth-century celebratory motet *Omnium bonorum plena*, probably of the 1470s, nearly all the fifteen named musicians are known composers, although they are described there as singers. Josquin Des Prez's *Nymphes des bois* addresses as singers 'Chantres experts de toutes nations', though all are known as composers, solemnly enjoined to mourn the death of Johannes Ockeghem. All four of these works follow the pattern of listing colleagues in the second half of the motet, and in all those cases, those listed are known or assumed to be living at the time. None of these pieces attaches the names of those they cite to a specific composition.

---

[62] Trowell 1957.

[63] Bent 2016.

[64] He cannot be Matheus de Sancto Johanne, as widely stated, but may possibly be the Mucherey who was a singer in John of Gaunt's chapel; see Bent 2023, p. 468.

[65] Besseler (ed.) rev. Fallows 1995, no. 49.

The Fourteenth-Century Musician Motets

These five motets, ranging in date from c. 1330 to c. 1400, have been identified as a related group but have hitherto lacked a detailed study.[66] They differ in register from thirteenth-century predecessors and from Du Fay's rondeau. The intellectual tone is more elevated, the texts are in Latin, the naming more formal, and drink is absent. The motets are ostentatiously, self-consciously clever constructions of text and music, usually anchored in cosmic or biblical reference, with citation and allusion between them, and many shared generic features. Given the resolute anonymity of fourteenth-century musical transmission (apart from Machaut), the most striking of these features is the naming in the triplum parts of a total of about sixty-five musicians, many of whom we have never heard of or who lack any other attestation of musical activity. It is reassuring that a few of those known to us as important for musical practice and theory are prominent, including Johannes de Muris, Philippe de Vitry, and Guillaume de Machaut, all named in *Apollinis eclipsatur* and *Musicalis/Sciencie*.

But what of the others? Of the twelve musicians named in *Apollinis eclipsatur*, none is specified as a composer. Some are explicitly singers, some apparently theorists. Besides Muris, Vitry, and Machaut, Denis le Grant is known as a composer, Henricus Helene as a theorist.[67] Few of the others in *Apollinis eclipsatur*, or in their partial overlap with the twenty named in *Musicalis*, are known or securely identifiable. The seven musicians of *Musicorum collegio/In templo* and the twenty Augustinians of *Alma polis/Axe poli* have also resisted definitive musical identifications. Whether the named musicians were singers, instrumentalists, theorists, or composers is not usually stated except to some extent in *Sub Arturo*, where five of the fourteen are specified as composers. The words used are *res* and *creavit*: they are 'creators' of *res*, or *resfacta* (made things).[68] Apart from the known theorist Johannes Hauboys (doubtless wrongly modernised as Hanboys since the eighteenth century), most of the others are characterised as singers which, as suggested above and as made explicit in Jacobus's description (above) of Petrus de Cruce as 'valens cantor' in the same sentence as the verb *componere*, does not preclude them from being composers. Some of the fourteen musicians in *Sub Arturo* can be identified with varying degrees of confidence. The date has been debated, and I have recently situated it closer to c. 1400 than earlier datings, in line with its musical style and with the latest datable musicians named.[69] It does indeed seem to be retrospective over several generations. What is surprising is that it exceeds the living memory span of about forty years, when singers would have died and their physical voices faded from memory. Does this reflect reputational or institutional memory, or was a 'singer' immortalised in enduring written compositions? As we saw, Rossi's sonnet lists musicians both dead and still living.

---

[66] Reproduced from Harrison (ed.) 1968 and 1980, with an introduction, in Harrison (ed.) 1986. See Bent 2023, chaps. 15–21 for a full study of these motets, their texts, new editions, and what can be inferred about the identity of the musicians named.

[67] See Bent 2023, chaps. 16 and 17, and above, nn. 32 and 48 for Denis.

[68] These five musicians are John of Corby, Thomas Marcon, Richard Blithe, John of Exeter, and William Oxwick.

[69] See Bent 2023, chap. 20 for a full review with bibliography. On the list of musicians in *Sub Arturo*, see also the chapter by Parkes in this volume.

Self-Naming within the Text of a Composition

Did composers also write their own texts? Tight connections between music and poetry, and self-namings in the first person sometimes make it almost inevitable that the same person was responsible for both text and music.[70] Internal namings occasionally break the fourteenth-century silence.

At least three of the fourteenth-century musician motets (*Apollinis eclipsatur, Alma polis, Sub Arturo*) carry composer signatures, usually in the motetus text, self-promotions with similar formulations, some with mock modesty. In *Apollinis eclipsatur*, the author B. de Cluny names himself at the beginning of the second half of the motetus: 'B. de Cluni nitens energia / artis practice cum theoria / recommendans se subdit omnibus' (shining with practical and theoretical art he commends himself to all).[71] He is not otherwise known as a composer. Nor probably is the J. Alanus of *Sub Arturo* despite the claim that he was someone with this very common name who died in 1373. He commends himself as the last and least ('J. Alanus minimus sese recommendat') on his list of 'greats' at the end of a potted history of music theory in the motetus. The anonymous author of *Musicorum collegio* subjects himself to the service of all but this time in the triplum. In the incomplete motet *Arta/Musicus*, which may belong to this group, the mysterious 'Leouns' at the end of the motetus may also be its composer. The shared diction in such formulations is obvious, and more extensive than these samples.

Another authorial signing by an unknown composer within a text is the solmisation piece *Fa fa mi fa* in Karlsruhe, BLB, Cod. Licht. 82, flyleaf, which ends with the composer's signed greeting: John, singer of Liège ('cantore Leodiensi'), requests that he be prayed for, along with the place where he composed the song, Rocamadour ('Rupes Amatoris').[72] Internal signatures by better-known composers include 'Franciscus', if he is indeed 'Landini', assumed to be the author of a single motet voice *Principum nobilissime*: the text includes the words 'me franciscum'. As this is in praise of Andrea Contarini (Venetian doge 1367–82), it is unlikely to be one of the unnamed Florentine motets mentioned above (n. 41). Zacara's *Sumite Karissimi* ends with the (Latin) words 'Zacharias salutes' and in the course of the obscure text encrypts the syllables of the word *recommendatione*. We assume that Machaut wrote his own texts, as for the characteristic vituperative bile of Vitry, both known as poets. As noted above (n. 25), for Vitry there are also text attributions in later humanist manuscripts where his motet texts were evidently valued. Vitry signs himself with 'hec concino Philippus publice' in the motet *Cum statua*, possibly also as *Phi millies/O creator* in the triplum of that motet, and perhaps as (Petrarch's) *Gallus* in *Garrit Gallus/In nova fert* and *Tribum/Quoniam*, where the *Gallus* sings ('concinat') the words of Ovid ('Nasonis dicta'). Authorship of text and music can

---

70 For reflections on the authorship of texts of musical composition, see Everist's and Plumley's chapters in this volume.

71 He is referred to in modern studies as Bernard, but although his twelfth-century namesake makes that a likely choice for a man from Cluny, there is no confirmation that he was Bernard rather than, say, Bertrand or Bartolomeus.

72 See Catalunya 2017, pp. 105, 122.

be assumed in signed texts by Ciconia and at least some by Du Fay.[73] Ciconia names himself in the texts of five of his motets.[74] In Du Fay's motet *Salve flos tuscae*, the last line of the motetus is 'Guillermus cecini natus et ipse Fay', and he famously inserted personal tropes ('Miserere tui labentis Du Fay' and 'Miserere supplicanti Du Fay') in his grand motet *Ave regina celorum*, which his will prescribed for his deathbed, an unprecedented personal statement alongside his funerary monument, prepared before his death, which is now in the Lille museum.

In a few cases, a double attribution apparently separates the authors of text and music.[75] At the midpoint of the motetus text of *Alma polis/Axe poli*, the composer is identified as 'Egidius de Aurolia' (Giles of Orléans, though 'Aurelia' is the usual Latin form), the poet as 'J. de Porta'.[76] In *Argi vices Poliphemus/Tum Philemon* (Aosta, fols. 4v–7r) for Pope John XXII, poet and composer are named, respectively, as Guilhermus and Nicolaus.[77] In one of its sources, the motetus of *Portio nature/Ida capillorum* was headed 'Magister Heinricus' (also mentioned in the text, apparently as poet and composer) but also gives the name 'Egidius de Pusiex', possibly the poet.[78]

Acrostics for Dedicatees and Authors

Most acrostics in texts of compositions are for dedicatees. Jacopo da Bologna's complete and ascribed motet *Lux purpurata/Diligite justitiam* bears in its cantus I the acrostic LUCHINUS, followed by VICECOMES, the Visconti dedicatee.[79] The single cantus I voice *Laudibus dignis merito* is probably also by Jacopo; lines 1–11 of its sixteen lines make the acrostic LUCHINUS DUX. The eight-line motetus of Vitry's motet *O canenda/Rex* has the acrostic ROBERTVS, for the dedicatee Robert d'Anjou, who ruled Naples from 1309 to 1343. The motetus of the fragmentary motet [...]/*Per grama*

---

73 See Holford-Strevens 1997 and 2015.

74 ' ... dignare me Ciconiam' (in *O felix templum*); 'quem Johannes Ciconia canore fido resonat' (in *O Padua sidus preclarum*, thus as a 'singer'); 'El conservet et Maria Johannes Ciconia' (in *Venecie/Michael*, cantus I); 'celum edis hymnis pange eum tuo Ciconia' (in *Albane misse/Albane doctor*, cantus II); 'adesto tuo Ciconia' (in *Petrum Marcello/O Petre*, cantus II). Neither of his two motets for Zabarella is signed.

75 Gardner 2015 cites instances from the thirteenth-century chronicle of Salimbene de Adam, which documents settings by friars of words by others, notably Salimbene's teacher the Pisan Fra Enrico who composed rhythmicised music as well as chant and set to music verses by Philip the Chancellor.

76 Marchi 2019 suggests that some of the secondary names in the double attributions of songs in Chantilly may signal a performer or re-arranger rather than a poet. For a discussion of double ascriptions in Chantilly, see the chapter by Plumley in this volume. Polytextual motets such as *Alma polis* and *Argi vices* are a different case, as the double names are integral to the text and appear to be explicit in distinguishing composer and poet. For *Alma polis*, see Bent 2023, chap. 19, and for *Argi vices*, see p. 627 and chap. 19 n.1.

77 Fischer and Gallo (eds.) 1987, no. 49.

78 Strasbourg, BM 222 C.22, originally fols. 74v–75r. See Zazulia 2018. For possible identities of Henricus, see Bent 2023, p. 338.

79 Elena Abramov-van Rijk informed me (email, 8 April 2021) that Zoltán Rihmer reads the tenth line not as 'verus amator efficax' but 'iuris amator efficax', which restores the word 'vicecomes' in the acrostic, making much more sense than the hitherto accepted 'vucecomes'.

has the acrostic PETRUS.[80] A number of compositions in Chantilly are dedicated to patrons and embody their mottos. In addition, a ballade ascribed there to Cunelier (Jean le Cavelier), *Se Galaas*, presents the name of GASTON (Fébus, third count of Foix) in an acrostic formed, not from the first letters of lines but from proper names: 'Se **G**alaas et le puissant **A**rtus / **S**amson le fort, **T**ristain, **O**gier **N**'Amon'.

Going to a later period, the combined upper parts of Du Fay's motet *Rite maiorem/Artibus* give the acrostic: ROBERTUS AUCLOU CURATUS SANCTI JACOBI. Leofranc Holford-Strevens treats this acrostic not as a dedicatee but as authorial by the poet, commending himself (Robertus) to Saint James's protection in the last line of the poem. The motetus of Du Fay's motet *Fulgens iubar/Purpuera* names Pierre du Castel (alias Pierre de Béthune) in an acrostic as PETRUS DE CASTELLO CANTA; however, he was not the composer.

Most song acrostics are names of women who are, or are assumed to be, dedicatees in songs mostly by known male composers. In at least three songs by Busnois, the name of Jacqueline de Hacqueville is concealed in acrostics or cryptograms.[81] Du Fay's song *Craindre vous vueil* in Oxford, Bod. Lib., Canon. Misc. 213 has the acrostic CATELINE DUFAY, apparently linking the composer's name with that of an unknown woman. All of those are uncontrovertibly by known composers. But very few fifteenth-century songs have acrostics that could be considered authorial. An exception is the acrostic LE GRANT GUILLAUME in *La doulce flour*, discovered by David Fallows. It is assumed to be authorial because Guillaume le Grant is a known composer.[82] Fallows also pointed out to me the MARGUERITE acrostic in the anonymous two-voice rondeau *Mon vray desir* in Bologna, Q.15 (no. 32, R31v–32r, A33v–34r). She is assumed to be a dedicatee – probably correctly – but would that be the assumption if it were not a woman's name?

Authorial acrostics are well known in poems and literary texts, and in music theory (as mentioned) JACOBUS famously explained that he revealed his name through the initials of the seven books of the *Speculum musicae*. In the rare cases when acrostics in musical compositions are authorial, they can constitute exceptions to anonymous transmission. An early instance is in Marchetto's only known surviving composition, *Ave regina/Mater innocencie*, of uncertain date. Marchetto was certainly a composer; the motetus acrostic MARCUM PADUANUM dovetails with 'me' in the last line 'me solvat a peccatis', requesting absolution for himself, confirming that the acrostic here is authorial. That integration also explains why the acrostic is in the accusative: 'me Marcum Paduanum'. As noted above, more of his compositions, non-extant, are listed in Seville, Bibl. Col. 5-2-25. The acrostic 'Rudolfus' embedded in a troped Benedicamus in Munich, BSB, Clm 14274 (Saint Emmeram codex) fols. 47v–48r is hence thought to indicate authorship by Rudolf Volkhardt.

---

[80] Anna Zayaruznaya suggests in this volume (see chapter 3) that this refers not to John XXII but to Pierre Roger (Clement VI), which would make Philippe de Vitry's authorship even more likely. But see Bent 2023, pp. 608–14, where reservations are expressed about this interpretation and alternatives proposed.

[81] See Higgins 1991.

[82] Fallows 1999, p. 231.

Manon Louviot has documented the astonishing case of Frater Johannes Vavassoris, whose highly originally structured motet *Ferre solet/Ana theos de gracia* in Douai, Bibl. Desbordes-Valmore 1105/3 fragment 74.4/1 is signed with an acrostic in the triplum (FRATER JOHANNES VAVASSORIS) and internally dated 1373.[83] He is otherwise known only as a papal scriptor and member of the *familia* of Cardinal Philippe d'Alençon.[84] Another authorial case is the Polish composer Petrus Wilhelmi, whose works are notable for their self-reference; all begin with *P* and are signed with authorial acrostics.[85~]

Grouping by Composer

Italian composer groupings are notable in the San Lorenzo palimpsest (Florence, Arch. di San Lorenzo 2211) and especially in Squarcialupi; there are less consistent or smaller composer groupings in other Italian manuscripts: Lucca, Arch. di Stato 184 and Perugia, Bibl. com. Aug. 3065 (Lucca-Mancini codex), Florence, Bnc, Panciatichiano 26, London, BL, Add. 29987, and Paris, BnF, it. 568.

The two four-voice works ('quadrupla') that Anonymous IV ascribes to Perotinus (*Viderunt omnes* and *Sederunt principes*) open Florence, BML, Plut. 29.1, though this position could also be due to that manuscript's liturgical organisation and prioritisation of four-voice compositions. These and any other possible but unidentifiable composer groupings in the earlier Notre Dame manuscripts are unascribed. Exceptions apart, authorship seems not to have been a primary criterion for ascription, organisation, or classification for the compilers of polyphonic manuscripts, although here for Perotinus and in Mo fascicle 7 for Petrus de Cruce, their compositions are placed – albeit anonymously – at the head of a manuscript or section. In the fifteenth century, the placing of compositions by, for example, Du Fay or John Dunstaple at the head of a section seems likewise to indicate the composers' status. Of interest is the possible grouping of motets by Vitry in the two non-adjacent leaves of Aachen, Stadtbibl., Beis E14. Three of the four motets are by him, excellently studied and interpreted by Anna Zayaruznaya. The fourth motet is *Post missarum/Post misse*, which has no obvious claim on Vitry's authorship; this mandates caution about making attributions on the basis of manuscript groupings.[86]

In the early fifteenth century, we can point to possible Zacara groupings in the Siena fragments, Siena, Arch. di Stato, Framm. Mus. busta n. 1, ins. n. 11, and for Ciconia in the Lucca-Mancini codex (see n. 88 below), where an ascription at the head of the first composition on a page is often taken to apply also to the unascribed piece below it, with or without justification. Some composer groupings may have come about because the pieces arrived together, as perhaps with the clusters

---

[83] Louviot 2021; on this motet as well as for a survey of authorial acrostics (including the example of Marchetto) in late-medieval literature and music, see the chapter by Louviot in this volume.

[84] As noticed by Johanna Thöne, email correspondence, 13 July 2021. For a biographical summary, see Di Bacco and Nádas 1994, p. 56.

[85] Gancarczyk 2006; see also the chapter by Louviot in the present volume.

[86] Zayaruznaya 2018; Bent 2023, pp. 448–52.

of Binchois works in Aosta or English works in Trent codices and Aosta. I have reconstructed a fragmentary English royal choirbook of the 1420s, whose individual isolated leaves show some composer adjacence (of works by Damett, Dunstaple, and Mayshuet), which may indicate planned composer groupings, though there is too little basis on which to take that further.[87] But without other confirmation, to attribute pieces to a composer on grounds of manuscript adjacence is hazardous, especially when dealing with single leaves that couple just two pieces as adjacent. The policy of a manuscript with respect to composer groupings needs to be divined before drawing conclusions: was it a manuscript planned in advance with most of the repertory to hand, or was it a growing anthology, added to as material became available? It is usually possible, at least by the fifteenth century, to distinguish between, on the one hand, the planned assembly of a composer section and, on the other hand, where copying is in order of receipt and therefore more haphazard.

Composer Ascription after 1400

The period around 1400 seems to be a watershed. Manuscripts from the first two decades of the fifteenth century are among the first substantial sources to name contemporary composers. These include the Chantilly, Old Hall, Modena, Bibl. Est., α.M.5.24 and Apt, Trésor 16bis manuscripts, and the Lucca-Mancini and Padua fragments.[88] By the 1420s and 1430s, we have an abundance of ascriptions, as in Bologna, Q.15 and Oxford, Bod. Lib., Canon. Misc. 213. In the latter, several ascriptions to Arnold de Lantins, Antonius de Civitate, and Du Fay carry the word *composuit* or *composita* and even a date. This is not to say that ascription becomes or remains the norm in all genres. Even after 1400, or 1500, when composer names have become more common, many manuscripts remain entirely or largely anonymous. This includes the entire early fifteenth-century English carol repertory.[89] It also applies to song manuscripts. Of the six Loire Valley chansonniers of the 1460s and 1470s, the recently discovered Leuven chansonnier (Leuven, Alamire Foundation 1), along with Copenhagen, DKB 291, 8° and Wolfenbüttel, HAB, Cod. Guelf. 287 Extrav., totally lacks any attributions. In the Nivelle chansonnier (Paris, BnF, mus. Rés. Vmc 57), about half the songs in the main layer carry ascriptions, in Dijon, BM 517, about a quarter of the contents are ascribed, and ascriptions were only added to the first layer of the Laborde chansonnier (Washington, LoC, M2.1 L25 Case) by later scribes. Other song books of similar date with no ascriptions include the chansonniers Cordiforme (Paris, BnF, Rothschild 2973) and Paris, Bnf, fr. 1597, and the manuscript Bologna, Q.16; many others from

---

[87] Commentary and facsimiles in Bent and Wathey (eds.) 2022. The royal choirbook is referred to as 'RC'.

[88] Lucca, Arch. di Stato 184 and Perugia, Bibl. com. Aug. 3065 are together known as the Lucca-Mancini codex. Apt, Trésor 16bis names a dozen or so composers of older repertory, mostly otherwise unknown; the composers of many works left anonymous there (including two motets now attributed to Vitry) are inferred or known from elsewhere. For the Padua fragments, see Cuthbert 2006.

[89] On which see now Fallows 2018. The lone ascription of a carol text as 'quod JD' could refer to anyone but has been tentatively linked to Dunstaple.

the last decades of the fifteenth century and the early sixteenth have very few. Of the later fifteenth-century chansonniers, only Nivelle, Mellon (New Haven, Beinecke 91), Rome, Bibl. Casanatense 2856, and Pixérécourt (Paris, BnF, fr. 15123) are rich in ascriptions, some of them unreliable.[90]

Conflicting attributions are hardly surprising, given how often they may have been transmitted from anonymous copies. Indeed, it is surprising that there are not more. Almost as soon as we have any ascriptions, we get corrected ascriptions, as for example in Paris, BnF, it. 568 and Oxford, Bod. Lib, Canon. Misc. 213. The erased composer ascriptions in the former are judged to have been correct.[91] Of the erased and replaced ascriptions in the latter, some seem to be correctly corrected, others not.

The retrospective Italian manuscripts of trecento repertory date from after 1400, compiled in the 1410s and 1420s with music dating back sixty or seventy years. To varying degrees, they devote sections to individual composers, with ascriptions and, in the case of the Squarcialupi codex, composer portraits. Less self-contained or less comprehensive than Squarcialupi and the palimpsest Florence, Arch. di San Lorenzo 2211 are the composer sections of the Lucca-Mancini codex, Paris, BnF, it. 568, and London, BL, Add. 29987. No collections of Italian polyphony by a single composer, let alone by several, have survived from before 1400; pre-1400 sources, the Rossi-Ostiglia codex (Vatican, BAV, Rossi 215 and Ostiglia, Bibl. mus. Greggiati, s.s.) and smaller fragments are all anonymous, as are all Italian motet fragments before Ciconia except the few mentioned above with internal signatures or acrostics by Marchetto, Jacopo, and Francesco (Landini).

I return to the initial question: in the near-total absence of ascribed compositions in Italian trecento fragmentary sources dating from before about 1380, how did these theorists, authors, indexers, and later composer-ordered anthologisers know who had composed those pieces if they were not ascribed in the musical sources available to them (and later, to us)? How could the apparently comprehensive composer groupings of the large retrospective anthologies, especially Squarcialupi and Florence, Arch. di San Lorenzo 2211, have been assembled and attributed? And on what authority did the Squarcialupi artist make his outstanding composer portraits? Apart from Landini's recognisably similar tomb monument in San Lorenzo, one wonders how, in the 1420s, anyone knew what the older composers looked like. They are shown at the heads of their sections in Squarcialupi at a variety of ages, some with their appropriate liturgical dress, which may be all the artist had to go on; and in the cases of Landini and Zacara, their attested disabilities are faithfully shown. Author portraits within an initial in non-musical manuscripts had long been quite common; the richly illustrated early fourteenth-century Manesse codex of Minnesang poetry has no musical notation but 137 author portraits.[92] Apart from Machaut, the Squarcialupi portraits are apparently the first in manuscripts with music notation since the author/composer portraits in troubadour and trouvère manuscripts.

[90] Anonymity in songs is addressed by Fallows 2018, p. 88 and Alden 2010, pp. 105–6, 155. The issue is addressed by Higgins 1999, pp. 14–15 and Perkins 1999.

[91] Günther 1966.

[92] Heidelberg, Univ., Germ. 848.

The lack of interest in ascribing musical authorship to polyphony in music manuscripts of the thirteenth and fourteenth centuries sits uncomfortably beside a
general respect for authority but applies also to other creative endeavours, though
verbal works, poetry, and visual arts fare somewhat better for authorial naming.

Besides the attributions of non-surviving works to composers noted above, many
composers of the early fifteenth century are known for only one or two works. It
is not credible that they did not write more; this is some measure of what is lost.
Since the same training in active counterpoint was needed for singers and readers of the notation as for composition, it is almost certain that singers could and
often did compose. Marchetto in the early fourteenth century is known for a single
motet, but the Seville list (Seville, Bibl. Col. 5-2-25, fol. 23v) gives more titles by him
that are not extant, and we have names of composers for whom no pieces survive,
though titles are sometimes given. Many named musicians have been passed over in
modern scholarship because they are not explicitly called composers. On the other
hand, there are several composers for whom we depend mainly on the fragile testimony of one manuscript; many others must be lost along with their sources. This
applies not only to (almost) 'one-piece' composers but to (almost) 'one-source'
composers (Ockeghem and Johannes Regis in the Chigi codex (Vatican, BAV,
Chigi C.VIII.234), Johannes de Lymburgia in Bologna, Q.15, Hermann Edlerawer
in Munich, BSB, Clm 14274, Nicholas of Radom in the related sources Warsaw, Bibl.
Narodowa, Lat. F. I. 378 and Warsaw, Bibl. Narodowa III. 8054). Some but not all
of these are local figures whose music had little circulation outside their own region.
But what would we know of Ockeghem and Regis without the Chigi codex?

I have raised a number of paradoxes about anonymity in this brief survey without being able to offer answers. The fluid dividing line in fourteenth-century texts
between singers, composers, and other musical skills that we have come to cate-
gorise and evaluate differently, with different vocabulary, may be more of a barrier
(albeit permeable) to us than it was to them. Its consequence is that music history
has paid more attention to those we assume or know to have been composers than
to those named more generally as musicians or as singers or instrumentalists. The
careers of the likes of Jean and Mathieu Hanelle and presbiter Orpheus de Padua
in the fifteenth century have been overlooked because no compositions ascribed to
them happen to survive.[93] Orpheus would surely have commanded more attention
if we had even one extant composition ascribed to him.

We should probably be more ready to embrace a broader, authorial understanding of what 'singing' and 'voice' might encompass. Although at some level it
remained true that 'musicorum et cantorum magna est distancia', it is clear that
many of those praised in the musician motets were considered to be *musici* whose
compositions were both unlocked by and founded on theory. A surprisingly large
number of composers known to us are cited only as singers. If many of those otherwise unknown 'singers' were indeed composers, we have a large number of names of
potential composers but are left with the frustration of being unable to attach them
to anonymously transmitted compositions.

---

[93] See Planchart 2018 on the Hanelle brothers, pp. 737–38 (Jean), and 16–17, 58–59
(Mathieu); and Bent 2015b.

5

Questions of Signatures and Authorship: Some Elusive Scribes and Artists in Late Thirteenth- and Early Fourteenth-Century France

Alison Stones

Many late medieval manuscripts are signed with the names of people involved in some way in their production, whether they be patrons, commissioners, owners, or makers: scribes, notators, decorators, illuminators, binders.[1] However, such signatures are frequently ambiguous. What do signatures mean, and does their meaning change over time and place? Do they become more or less frequent across time? In this chapter, I examine some cases in the period 1280–1350 in order to demonstrate what degree of certainty or uncertainty surrounds what the signatories actually did. In particular, a critical question concerns the possibility of collaborative work, its nature and extent, especially in cases where only a single name is recorded, whereas variations in the work itself, be it script, decoration, or illumination, suggest the participation of more craftspersons in the making of the book. Can one go so far as to classify such variants as the activities of workshops?[2] The three case studies examined in detail in this chapter will show that the situations vary considerably from case to case, making any generalisation difficult, and that caution is needed when interpreting what is said in relation to what can be seen.

Philippe de Troyes (fl. 1286–90)

The first case study relates to the work of a craftsman who signed his name in several books. Naming himself 'Philippus de civitate Trecensi presbiter' (Philippe de Troyes, priest), he signed the fragmentary notated missel Paris, Bibl. Sainte-

---

[1] For the period 1260–1320, see the lists of illuminators and decorators (pp. 91–95) and of scribes, notators, binders, parchmenters, dealers, and *libraires* (pp. 133–53) in Stones 2013–14, part I, vol. 1.

[2] Whereas religious confraternities were in existence by the late thirteenth century (such as the Confraternity of the Assumption in Rabastens, founded in 1286, whose illustrated charter is partially preserved in Périgueux, MAAP, B. 1721), professional guilds had yet to be formalised. On this, see Cassagnes-Brouquet 2014; Barral i Altet (ed.) 1986–90; Alexander 1992; and the introduction to Stones 2013–14, part I, vol. 1, pp. 17–50.

Geneviève 98 in 1286.[3] The mention of Troyes implies that he was based elsewhere at the time of writing. And what is particularly distinctive about this manuscript is not so much the script and music notation (square notation on a four-line staff ruled in red), both claimed by Philippe in his colophon, but the very beautiful and elaborate pen-flourished decoration, the responsibility for which is not claimed by Philippe in his note (Figure 5.1).

Philippe signed two other manuscripts: an Office for the feast of Saint William of Bourges, inserted into Troyes, MGT 1148, fols. 282r–290r, in which a similar colophon appears: 'Philippus scripsit et cantum notavit' (Philippe wrote and notated the music) (fol. 289r).[4] Here, too, what is distinctive is the pen work. In the four-volume Bible, Oxford, New College 3–6, which he wrote in 1290, the pen work ranges from decoration of text letters (Figure 5.2, New College 3, fol. 8v) to elaborate flourishing used for major initials (Figure 5.3, New College 3, fol. 13r, Genesis). The elaborate colophon of the fourth volume may be consulted in Appendix 1. Again, he makes no mention of the pen decoration in these volumes, suggesting that for him, the writing and noting of sacred texts and music were more important activities than decorating. The Sainte-Geneviève Missal, the Office of William of Bourges and the New College Bible all show Philippe's distinctive writing, full of humorous motifs drawn in ink as part of the ascenders and descenders of the letters. The missal and the Bible both contain the same distinctive large and small pen-flourished initials, leading one to wonder whether Philippe might not have executed them as well. The decoration of his lettering certainly shows him to have been a very competent draughtsman. However, as he does not claim to have done the pen-flourished decoration, nothing can be proven. A further manuscript by the same decorator – perhaps Philippe himself? – has recently come to light: Brussels, KBR 4, a late thirteenth-century copy of the *Grandes chroniques de France*, the first part of which ends with the death of Philippe Auguste in 1223.[5] Whether Philippe de Troyes was also one of the scribes is an open question, as this time, the script is much smaller in scale than in the liturgical books and lacks their decorated ascenders and descenders. At all events, Philippe's work and that of his decorator (if not Philippe himself) are of the very highest quality, putting him/them at the centre of debate about pen decoration, its makers, and its relation to script on the one hand and illumination on the other hand.[6] Was Philippe operating only in Champagne or also in Paris? A reflection of his initials is

---

3   This wording occurs twice: at the beginning at fol. 1v as shown in Figure 5.1 ('Incipit liber iste quem Philippus de civitate Trecensi presbiter beneficatus in ecclesia Trecensi scripsit et cantum notavit anno Domini millesimo ducentesimo octogesimo sexto orate pro eo Artificem commendat opus non propria lingua. Non redimit victum cumulata scientia morum') and again at the explicit (fol. 145v). See Stones 2013–14, Cat. III-83, with previous literature.

4   See the folio at https://initiale.irht.cnrs.fr/en/decor/57726https://bvmm.irht.cnrs.fr/iiif/7000/canvas/canvas-1244133/view.

5   Kindly drawn to my attention by François Avril and Marguerite Debae (personal communications). The manuscript is online at https://uurl.kbr.be/1905894.

6   See Stones 2020.

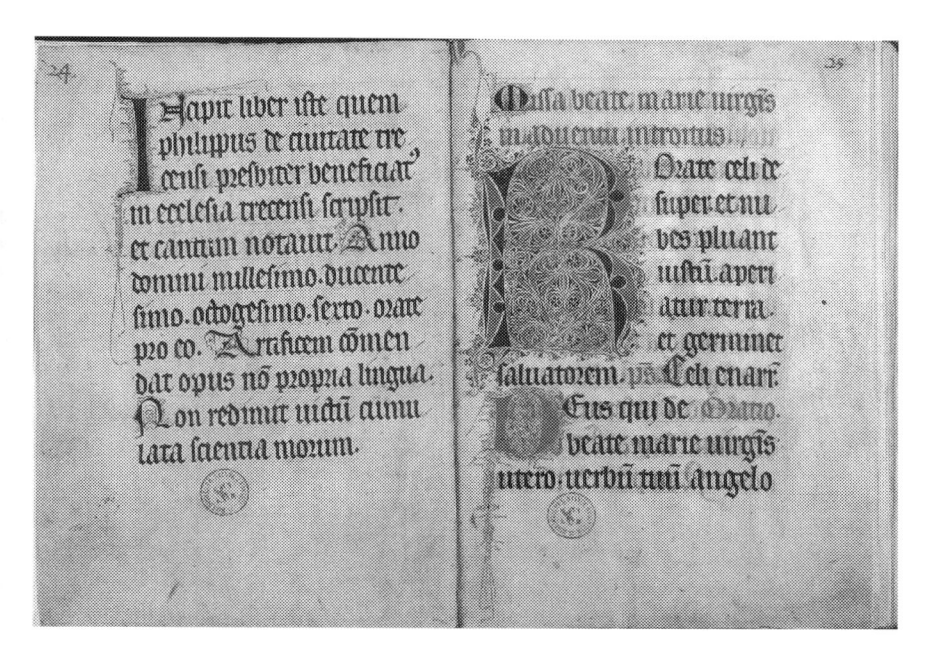

Figure 5.1. Paris, Bibl. Sainte-Geneviève 98, fols. 1v–2r: colophon written by Philippe de Troyes and opening of the Mass of the Virgin for Advent (photo: IRHT). By permission of the Bibliothèque Sainte-Geneviève, Paris.

Figure 5.2. Oxford, New College 3, Bible, fol. 8v: hooded male bust figure holding book (photo: author). New College Library, Oxford, MS 3, f. 8v © Courtesy of the Warden and Scholars of New College, Oxford.

Figure 5.3. Oxford, New College 3, Bible, fol. 13r: I initial for Genesis (photo: author). New College Library, Oxford, MS 3, f. 3r © Courtesy of the Warden and Scholars of New College, Oxford.

also to be found in the *Bible historiale*, Paris, BnF, fr. 160,[7] whose major illustration is by the artist known as the 'Papeleu Master', a principal participant in the *Bible historiale*, Paris, Arsenal 5059, written by Jean Papeleu in 1317, most likely in Paris.[8] The possible involvement of Philippe's decorator in this book also suggests that perhaps the same flourisher began his career by working in a minor capacity on some books made for the Dominicans and for other patrons in Paris in the 1260s and 1270s, graduating from executing a pen-flourished initial on a single page to being responsible for all the flourishing in at least two manuscripts, with some collaborative contributions in between.[9] But unless more evidence comes to light, we shall never know if all this work was done by Philippe de Troyes or someone else whose style was closely related, or even whether any of the decoration was executed by Philippe in addition to script and music notation.

The fact that Philippe claims responsibility for both the writing and notating of three works, together with the possibility that he could also be the author of the decoration, calls for comparison with the evidence available elsewhere in the same period.[10] In some cases, the task of writing and that of notating were clearly divided between different individuals: thus, Baudewins, in Flanders (Ghent ?), wrote a troper while Pierot le noteur provided the notation;[11] likewise, Prevost le noteur was paid in 1278–79 for notating the summer part of a breviary and a troper written by Baudouins li cliers.[12] Nevertheless, as witnessed in other cases, Philippe was not alone with the ability to perform both tasks: in 1341–42, Maistre Jehan was paid from the accounts of Sainte Waudru in Mons for writing and notating; Jehan de Naste (the same person?) was paid in the same year for exactly the same work;[13] and in 1347–48, Nicolon le Lateur was paid for writing and notating a new antiphonary, while the illumination was done by B. de Souchies.[14] Finally, we have evidence that one individual could also perform the decoration: Matheus, monk of Saint-Jean-d'Aulps, not only wrote and notated but also illuminated an antiphonary in 1319.[15]

---

7   Online at https://gallica.bnf.fr/ark:/12148/btv1b10538908q/f11.item.

8   Stones 2013–14, Cat. I-62 with previous literature. The manuscript it online at https://gallica.bnf.fr/ark:/12148/btv1b550095679.

9   For more on this flourisher, see Stones forthcoming.

10   For these and other references, see particularly Dehaisnes 1886; Rouse and Rouse 2000; Busby 2002; Stones 2013–14, part I, vol. 1, pp. 81–132.

11   Stones 2013–14, part I, vol. 1, p. 134. See also the chapters by Plumley, Everist, Doudet, and Bent in this volume on the issue of collaborative composition as regards music and dramatic works.

12   Stones 2013–14, part I, vol. 1, p. 149.

13   Dehaisnes 1886, vol. 1, p. 340: 'Compte de l'église Sainte-Waudru de Mons, rendu par Jean de Lens, de saint Rémi 1341 à saint Rémi 1342'.

14   Dehaisnes 1886, vol. 1, p. 361: 'Compte de la fabrique de la collégiale Saint-Amé de Douai, du 24 juin 1347 au 23 juin 1348, par N. Du Quesnoy, chanoine'.

15   Dehaisnes 1886, vol. 2, p. 559.

Master Honoré (fl. 1289–1312)

Master Honoré is documented from 6 February 1289 to January 1312 and was dead by June 1313.[16] The *Decretum Gratiani*, Tours, BM 558 (Figures 5.4 and 5.5), was purchased from him in Paris on 6 February 1289 and so annotated by its owner: 'Anno domini M CC LXXX octavo, emi presens Decretum ab Honorato illuminatore morante Parisius in vico Herenenboc de Bria, precio quadraginta librarum parisiensium' (In the Year of Our Lord 1288 I purchased the present Decretum from Honoré the Illuminator living in Paris in Herenenboc de Brie street, for the price of forty Parisian pounds). Further annotations in the manuscript identify the purchaser as 'Guillelmus': his name is now illegible on fol. 350v in the note he wrote in 1290 on receiving his licence to teach canon law, but on fol. 350r, although his surname is no longer legible, it can be read in an ex libris written in the top margin: 'Iste liber est michi Guillelmo' (This book is mine, William).[17]

The Paris tax rolls from 1292 to 1300 record the taxes paid by 'Honoré l'enlumineur' (Honoré the illuminator) the sum of x sols in 1292; by 'Mestre Honoré, enlumineeur' (Master Honoré, illuminator), the sum of xii sols in 1296; by 'Mestre honoré d'amiens' (Master Honoré of Amiens), the sum of viii sols in 1297; by 'Honoré d'amiens, enlumineeur' (Honoré of Amiens, illuminator), ix sols in 1299; and by 'Mestre Honoré enlumineeur' (Master Honoré, illuminator), ix sols in 1300.[18] Property transactions indicate that he was still alive in 1312 and tell much about his holdings, wealth, and family, notably his son-in-law Richard de Verdun, also an illuminator; as Honoré is not recorded in the 1313 tax roll, he was presumably dead by then.[19] He was paid xx livres parisis in 1296 for the king's illuminated books, as indicated by the mention 'Honorato illuminatore pro libris regis illuminatis' (to Honoré the Illuminator for illuminating books for the king).[20] An earlier payment in the same record refers to the very large sum of cvii livres and x sols paid to an unspecified person, for a breviary intended for the king – the manuscript referred to in this payment is undoubtedly Paris, BnF, lat. 1023, and the king was Philippe IV le Bel. But these records, as Rudolf Blum pointed out,[21] are separated by other records and need not be connected at all. Similarly, the purchase of the Gratian *Decretum* now in Tours from the illuminator Honoré does not say that the manuscript was actually illuminated by him, merely that it was purchased from him; and indeed, its style is not recognisable in the breviary (compare Figures 5.6 and 5.7 to Figures 5.4 and 5.5).

Blum was writing in 1948, at a time when Anglo-French scholarship was not prepared to pay undue attention to opinions in German. In another decade, the artist

---

16 Section adapted from Stones 2009 and the entries in Stones 2013–14, Cat. I–43 (Paris, BnF, lat. 1023, breviary) and Cat. I-45 (London, BL, Add. 54180, Cambridge, Fitzwilliam 192 and Fitzwilliam 368, which together form a copy of the *Somme le roi* by Frère Laurent d'Orléans).

17 Rouse and Rouse 2000, vol. 2, p. 164.

18 Baron 1968, pp. 43, 50.

19 Rouse and Rouse 2000, vol. 1, pp. 26–36.

20 Fawtier (ed.) 1930, p. 21, no. 407.

21 Blum 1948.

Figure 5.4. Tours, BM 558, Gratian's *Decretum*, fol. 1r: emperor ordering scribe to write, in the presence of a lawyer, a soldier, a friar, and other people (photo: IRHT). © Bibliothèque municipale de Tours.

Figure 5.5. Tours, BM 558, Gratian's *Decretum*, fol. 143r: 'Causa quatuor' on whether an excommunicate may accuse an ecclesiastic; bishop accused (photo: IRHT). © Bibliothèque municipale de Tours.

and the books were inextricably linked by Eric G. Millar in his 1959 volume and by Carl Nordenfalk in his famous article of 1964, which brushed aside any question about what exactly the documents said.[22] Most recently, Richard Rouse and Mary Rouse have traced Honoré through a wide range of documents and built up a clear picture of his holdings, wealth, and family.[23] But attributions to his hand all remain speculative, however convenient a catch-all his name may still be.

The illumination of the breviary Paris, BnF, lat. 1023 is the work of several artists. The frontispiece painter (fol. 7v), the best of them, who may well be Honoré in person, is the artist also responsible for the London and Cambridge copy of the *Somme le roi*[24] and one of the most consummate painters of his time. He was also responsible for the psalter component of the breviary which is exceptional for the subtlety of its iconography and for the sophistication of its style, close to the artistic level of the frontispiece (compare Figure 5.6 (frontispiece) with Figure 5.7 (psalter section)). The frontispiece is on much thicker parchment than the extremely thin vellum used in the rest of the book, but that need not mean it was not an intrinsic part. Indeed, it epitomises the emphasis on the kingship of David that is strongly brought out in the psalm illustrations as a whole and references as well the status

[22] Millar 1959; Nordenfalk 1964.

[23] Rouse and Rouse 2000, especially vol. 1, pp. 126–36.

[24] Stones 2013–14, Cat. I-45, listed in n. 16 above.

Figure 5.6. Paris, BnF, lat. 1023, Breviary of Philippe le Bel, fol. 7v: anointing of David; David killing Goliath. Bibliothèque nationale de France.

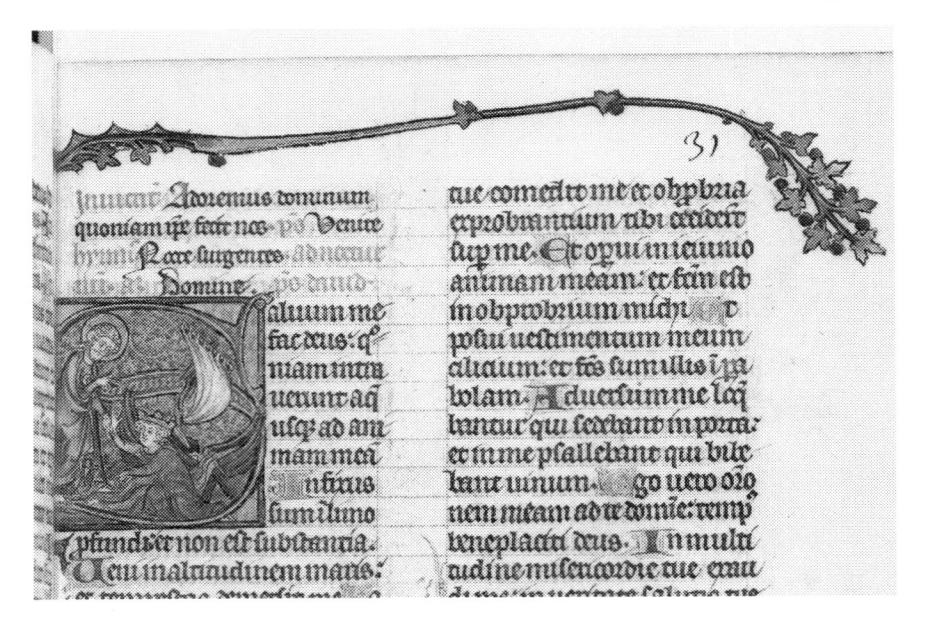

Figure 5.7. Paris, BnF, lat. 1023, Psalm 68, fol. 31r: King David in waters, his ship capsized, rescued by the Lord. Bibliothèque nationale de France.

of the book's royal patron. In the top register, the youthful David, identified by an inscribed plaque placed beneath him, is anointed by Samuel (wearing a pointed hat with cusped upturned brim), who holds him by the hair and raises his arm to pour oil on the kneeling youth who faces forwards holding his crook under his arm, his hands in prayer. God in a cloud, top left, blesses; Isaiah, veiled, looking at the anointing but turning away, heads a crowd of men emerging from the gates of Bethlehem on the right. Below, King Saul stands forward as a knight (shield *or a dragon sable*) on the frame, another knight behind him at the foot of a hill with trees, watching David sling at Goliath (shield *gules a carbuncle or*), feet on the frame and facing the viewer, feeling with his right hand the stone at his head. On the right, David is depicted in profile, raising his sword to decapitate the bare-headed dead Goliath. Marginal inscriptions, similar to those used in the *Somme le roi*, identify Samuel, Isaiah, Bethlehem, Saul, David, Goliath, and David.

Technically, the page is a masterpiece of subtle colours very finely modelled and complemented by a sophisticated play of liquid gold (the surcoat of Saul in the lower register), burnished gold with black linear designs (the corner motifs and Saul's shield), gold with delicate scrollwork (in the upper background) and a gold and blue with fleur de lis lozenge pattern (in the lower background). Glair seems to have been used on some of the draperies to give it shine, especially around the black shading on David and Isaiah, and on greys and pinks of the figures on either side. The hair of Samuel is modelled in blue and dark maroon, almost brown, and his robe is flecked or stippled in black, while David's tunic in the lower register is a grey-blue tending towards mauve without quite becoming mauve; there is a lighter blue perhaps painted on white and also modelling on the oil-horn, where dark green has been painted on black – otherwise, greens are paler. Dark colours are contrasted with pink and orange.[25] Sewing holes in the top margin indicate that this precious page was once protected with silk. The psalter initials are remarkable for their portrayal of David as privileged king, highly appropriate in a royal commission, and the psalm initials can also be attributed to the painter of the frontispiece (fol. 31r, Figure 5.7).

At the Temporal occurs a change in colour scheme, with the introduction of a dark mauve tone first used on the cloak of Isaiah (fol. 70v), and a lozenge background motif.[26] These changes may be due to the participation of another artist, and they are also found in the Christmas initial (fol. 86v), followed by a change to a lighter palette again for Easter (fol. 165v), Ascension (fol. 187v), and Pentecost (fol. 193v), where the figure style is similar to that of the psalter. At the Sixth Sunday (fol. 212r), another change is introduced, with the use of extremely small initials, much less polished, together with figures in a distinctly cruder style. Hereon, it would appear that the work is no longer by the artist of the great frontispiece and the psalter. Yet another hand participated for the illustration of Saint George (fol. 319v) – attributable to a painter known as the Méliacin Master – and this initial with its knight in armour is closest, in that artist's work, to the *Roman de Jules César* in Rouen, BM 1050.[27] The Méliacin Master also painted the martyrdom of Saint Peter Martyr (fol. 321v) but not Saint Mark on fol. 320r. There may be another change of hand at fol. 351v, and at fol. 389v a much less competent draughtsman takes over, although even in this section the frontispiece artist makes an occasional appearance, as in the lovely head terminal on fol. 402v, noted by Ellen J. Beer in 1959.[28] The distribution of initials in a smaller format appears to be haphazard except in the month of June in the Sanctoral where there is a cluster in this format, perhaps reflecting the participation of a particular (lesser) artist. We know from the tax rolls mentioned above that Richard de Verdun, Honoré's son-in-law, in 1319 along with Johannes de la Mare illuminated three new antiphonaries for the Sainte-Chapelle. They were notated by Guillelmus and bound by Nicolaus; a fourth volume was notated by Pierre, but none is extant.[29] Whether these individuals were involved in Paris, BnF, lat. 1023 or not, the essential point, however, and one that has not been adequately stressed in previous literature, is that this great book was a collaborative effort.

A second work by the frontispiece painter has survived in London, BL, Add. 54180 (Figure 5.8) and Cambridge, Fitzwilliam 192 and Fitzwilliam 368, as noted above.[30] It

---

[25] So far as I know, this page has not been subject to technical analysis, a practice coming to the fore in recent years; see, for instance, Panayotova (ed.) 2016; Panayotova and Ricciardi (eds.) 2017–18.

[26] The manuscript is online at https://gallica.bnf.fr/ark:/12148/btv1b90665543.

[27] Stones 2013–14, Cat. I-36.

[28] Beer 1959, p. 23 nn. 31, 32, and plate 62 (fol. 402v).

[29] Maillard (ed.) 1961, vol. 2, no. 13187; Vidier 1901, p. 339; Rouse and Rouse 2000, vol. 2, p. 77.

[30] Stones 2013–14, Cat. I-45a–b and n. 16 above.

Figure 5.8. London, BL, Add. 54180, *La Somme le roi*, fol. 136v: Misericord and Avarice above Abraham receiving two angel pilgrims and the good woman measuring oil. © British Library Board, Additional MS 54180, fol. 136v.

is a copy of the *Somme le roi* made for King Philippe IV le Bel between 1285 and 1305 (probably c. 1290–95). The *Somme le roi* is a treatise on Virtues and Vices composed by Frère Laurent d'Orléans, confessor to King Philippe III le Hardi, for the edification of the royal children. Illustrations were an intrinsic part of the educational programme, making the moralistic text more readily comprehensible.[31] Thirteen miniatures survive from this copy, two of them separated and now part of the Cambridge manuscript. The volume in the British Library contains the arms of King Philippe IV le Bel on fol. 97v and those of his wife, Jeanne de Navarre, on fol. 14v.[32] The presence of this heraldry allowed François Avril to identify this book as the 'good copy' itemised in Blanche de Navarre's will of 18 March 1396: 'Nostre bon livre de la Somme le roy, qui fu au roy Phelippe le Bel, et est bien enluminé' (Our good copy of the *Somme le roi* which belonged to King Philippe le Bel and is nicely illuminated).[33]

The beautiful scrollwork in gold on gold, lavishly used in the backgrounds, the elegant figures with fine modelling on the drapery, the astute placing of architectural and foliage elements, and the bright palette, together with a similar use of identifying inscriptions, set this manuscript firmly alongside the magnificent frontispiece of the Breviary of Philippe le Bel in Paris, BnF, lat. 1023, for which a payment in 1296 has long been associated with the name of Master Honoré as noted above. But as with the Breviary of Philippe le Bel, attribution to the hand of Master Honoré himself still remains speculative. The case of Honoré is but one of many examples where documents mention individuals by name, but matching those names to surviving manuscripts and illustrative programmes remains hypothetical in the absence of signatures on the actual manuscripts.[34]

The case of Jean Pucelle, named along with Anciau de Cens and Jaquet Maci, in the Billyng Bible, Paris, BnF, lat. 11935, is more explicit than the references to Honoré in the sources mentioned above: on fol. 642r, between the lines of the explicit 'Robertus de Billyng me fecit. Amen' (Robert de Billyying made me. Amen), annotations were added in red: 'Jehan Pucelle, Anciau de Cens, Jaquet Maci, il hont enluminé ce livre ci. Ceste lingne de vermeillon que vous vees fu escrite en l'an de grace mcccxxvii en un jeudi darrenier jour d'avril veille de mai' (Jean Pucelle, Anciau de Cens, Jaquet Maci, these are the names of the people who illuminated this present book. The line in red that you can see was written in the year of Our Lord 1327 on a Thursday, the last day of April, the vigil of May 1). But even in these manuscripts, separating out what was due to each individual named is no easy task.

---

[31] For the manuscript tradition and a survey of the illustrations, see Brayer and Leurquin-Labie (eds.) 2008.

[32] The manuscript is online at https://www.bl.uk/manuscripts/Viewer.aspx?ref=add_ms_54180.

[33] Delisle (ed.) 1885b, p. 30, no. 202; Avril 1998, pp. 276–77.

[34] A notable case of such wishful thinking is that of Richard and Jeanne de Montbaston, for whom a huge oeuvre has been recreated with not a shred of specific evidence; there is not a single extant manuscript that contains a signature in either name. See Rouse and Rouse 2000, vol. 2, p. 203, Appendix 9A. On the difficulty of linking documented names to musical works copied in the sources, see the chapter by Bent in this volume.

Pierart dou Thielt (fl. 1349–53)

We are on firmer ground with the one signed and dated work by Pierart dou Thielt. The colophon to the *Queste del saint Graal*, Paris, Arsenal 5218, fol. 91v, claims that he wrote, illuminated, and bound the volume in 1351:[35] 'Chius livres fu par escrips le nuit nostre dame en mi aoust la mil trois cens et li. Si l'escripst Pierars dou Tielt, et enlumina et loia' (The writing of this book was finished on the evening of the feast of the Assumption in mid-August [15 August] in the year one thousand three hundred and fifty-one. And Pierars dou Thielt wrote it, illuminated it, and bound it). Below, in darker ink, at a larger scale, are the words 'Explicit li queste del saint Graal', introduced by a highly competent pen-flourished initial *E* (Figure 5.9) to which I return below.

The illustration is sparse: an opening miniature relating to the events at the beginning of the story, leading up to the knighting of Galahad, son of Lancelot, who will be the Grail winner (Figure 5.10). On fol. 10r, Galahad rides up to a White Abbey with a shield *argent* (white) *a cross gules* on the altar; on fol. 88r is the much-reproduced image of the Grail procession.[36] The rest of the decoration of Paris, Arsenal 5218 consists of painted champie initials in gold and colours, and of the occasional marginal figures and animals drawn in pen.

The Arsenal *Queste del saint Graal* is Pierart's only signed manuscript. But we know that he occupied the post of keeper of manuscripts at the Benedictine Abbey of Saint Martin of Tournai, from 1349 to 1352 or 1353 during the abbacy of Gilles li Muisis.[37] Where else can his work be found? First in books made for Gilles, which are closely related stylistically to Pierart's signed work in Paris, Arsenal 5218. The works of Gilles, primarily chronicles of his abbacy, are contained in four manuscripts: Kortrijk, Stadsbibl., Goethals-Vercruysse 135, *Tres tractatus* with six miniatures; Brussels, KBR IV 119, a miscellany with twenty-four miniatures; Brussels, KBR 13076–77, *Tractatus quartus* with six miniatures but severely retouched, including at fol. 50v of KBR 13076, the famous miniature depicting the cataract surgery performed on Gilles by the surgeon John of Mainz; and Paris, BnF, n.a.f. 1789, *Liber compilatus*, unillustrated.[38] The miniatures in these manuscripts are all similar to the work of Pierart dou Thielt and are most likely by him.[39]

The Epistle and Gospel books in Brussels, KBR 456–57 raise different questions. Also owned by Gilles li Muisis, they are sparsely illustrated with pen drawing that at first sight bear no relation to the work of Pierart, which consists of figured miniatures and historiated initials (Figure 5.11).[40] But in Pierart's *Queste* manuscript,

---

[35] See particularly Avril 1981, p. 348, no. 301; Walters 1996; Delcourt (ed.) 2009, p. 194, no. 86, with previous literature.

[36] Online at https://gallica.bnf.fr/ark:/12148/btv1b7100017d/f179.item.

[37] D'Haenens 1959a, p. 259.

[38] *Tractatus primus*, edited in De Smet (ed.) 1841, pp. 115–30; *Tractatus secondus* (*De consuetudinibus*), edited in D'Haenens (ed.) 1959b; *Tractatus tertius* and *Tractatus quartus*, edited in Lemaître (ed.) 1906.

[39] See Caullet 1907–8; Martin 1909; D'Haenens 1959a; Stones 1998, pp. 564–65.

[40] Stones 1998, Figures 23, 27, 28, 29.

Figure 5.9. Paris, Arsenal 5218, *Queste del saint Graal*, fol. 91v: colophon and explicit. Bibliothèque nationale de France.

Paris, Arsenal 5218, there is also an important pen-flourished initial found at the *E* of the explicit (Figure 5.9). It is a beautifully drawn pen-flourished initial in black and brown ink. Was it also the work of Pierart and could it be related to the pen-flourishing in the Epistle and Gospel books? One could argue that the Arsenal initial is his work because he says on the line above that he wrote, illustrated, and bound the book. But the counter-argument is that the ink is different, the lettering larger in scale, and the initial is of a type that is found nowhere else in the manuscript. And it is not particularly close in drawing style to the pen work in the Epistle and Gospel books. As a consequence, whoever else might have executed this initial and those in the Epistle and Gospel books is doomed to remain anonymous.

A second avenue to explore is the famous Bodley *Roman d'Alexandre* in verse (Oxford, Bod. Lib., Bodl. 264), one of the most distinguished books of the fourteenth century.[41] Its first colophon on fol. 208r says that the writing of the manuscript was completed on 18 December 1338, and a second colophon on the same page claims that the illumination was completed by Jehan de Grise in 1344. This manuscript was written and illustrated in Flanders, possibly at Bruges, or more likely at Tournai, and it has been conjectured that it may have been made for King David II of Scotland because the major protagonist, Alexander the Great, is frequently depicted bearing the arms *or*

---

[41] Here, I resume what is said in Pérez-Simon and Stones (eds.) 2019, pp. 68–104. The manuscript was fully reproduced (in black and white) in James (ed.) 1933. The manuscript is available at https://digital.bodleian.ox.ac.uk/ objects/60834383-7146-41ab-bfe1-48ee97bc04be/.

Figure 5.10. Paris, Arsenal 5218, *Queste del saint Graal*, fol. 1r. Miniature: the damsel arrives at Arthur's court in search of Lancelot; Lancelot, a squire, and the damsel ride to the nunnery where Galahad has been brought up; he puts on his armour. *A* initial: the hermit and Lancelot before courtiers at table. Border: apes trapping birds with net and cord. Bibliothèque nationale de France.

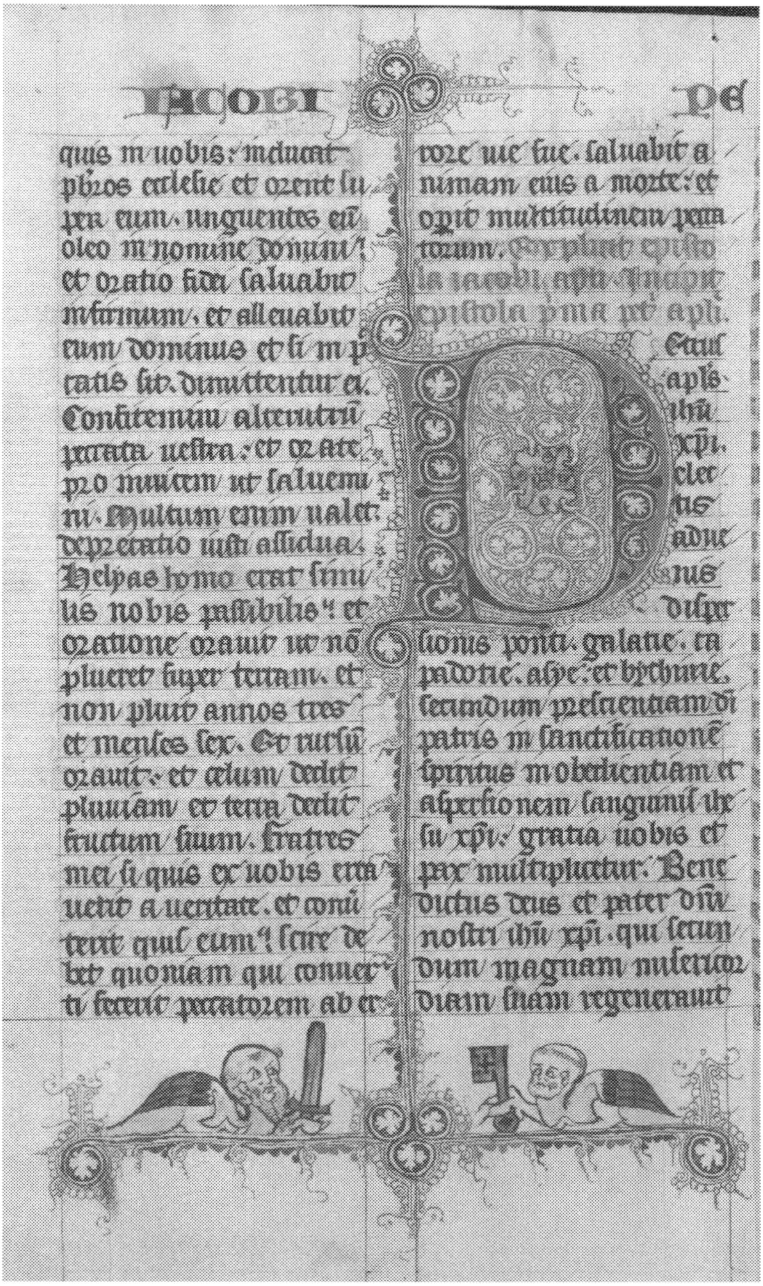

Figure 5.11. Brussels, KBR 456, fol. 125v: evangeliary, 'First Epistle of Peter'. *P*, pen-flourished initial and border; on bottom border two tonsured hybrids holding sword and key. By permission of the KBR – Ms. 456–57.

Figure 5.12. Oxford, Bod. Lib., Bodl. 264, *Le Roman d'Alexandre*, fol. 50r: Alexander's voyage to the bottom of the sea in a glass barrel. Border: birds, hare, bagpiper, two youths riding pony and hound, two groups of youths watching a cockfight. A four-line foliate initial *T*. Three two-line initials with female faces. Image: Bodleian Libraries, University of Oxford. Creative Commons licence CC-BY-NC 4.0.

a lion gules, similar to the arms of Scotland but lacking a bordure.[42] Several artists took part, and it is far from clear what part Jehan de Grise played in the enterprise. Avril recognised one participant as Pierart dou Thielt, although he did not specify exactly which illustrations he thought were made by him.[43] Domenic Leo has attempted a division of hands, but we do not entirely agree. Stylistic attribution can be a subjective affair.[44]

In my view, some of the most notable miniatures in this manuscript can be attributed to Pierart: Alexander's submarine adventure (fol. 50r, Figure 5.12) and Alexander's flight (fol. 80r), and perhaps also Alexander at the deathbed of Darius (fol. 49r). The section from fols. 54v to 57r would also appear to be Pierart's work, and he seems to have been an occasional contributor thereafter, painting a figure here and there (fols. 66r, 67v, 72v), the faces in some minor initials, and probably many of the border scenes. His work is notable for his faces outlined in brown ink with short curly hair and considerable modelling. Avril attributed several further manuscripts to Pierart: part of the *Roman de la rose* in Tournai, Bibl. ville 101, written in 1330;[45] part of the Breviary of Maubeuge, Cambrai, Le Labo 133 (with the Master of the Ghent Ceremonial of 1322, Gent, Univ. 233);[46] the addition to the Evangeliary of Saint Martin of Tournai in Washington, LoC, De Ricci 127;[47] a *Pamphile et Galathée*, Brussels, KBR 4783, and a Book of Hours, Brussels, KBR IV 453.[48] To this list I have added two volumes of Vincent of Beauvais's *Speculum historiale* with foliate initials, Brussels, KBR 79 and KBR 118, and the *Somme le roi* of 1358 in Lille, MM 366.[49] *Le Roman de Lancelot du Lac, La Queste del saint Graal*, and *La Mort Artu*, Paris, BnF, fr. 122, written in 1345, is also part of this general stylistic current if not directly due to Pierart,[50] and *Les Vœux du paon* and *Le Restor du paon* in New York, Morgan, G.24 is also close to Pierart's style, as noted by Avril,[51] while the full-page miniatures in the *Roman d'Yvain ou le chevalier au lion* of Chrétien de Troyes and the *Atre perilleux* (Paris, BnF, fr. 1433) might be seen as anticipating elements of Pierart's style.[52]

Defining the oeuvre of Pierart dou Thielt is a complex affair. First, we have his signed work, a touchstone against which to measure non-signed works. Much of the reconstruction proposed above is based on stylistic analysis and is subject to the uncertainty that is intrinsic to the method. But in the absence of signatures and specific

---

[42] The heraldry is similar to, but not the same as, that of David II of Scotland. See E. W. B. Nicholson's General Description and History of the Manuscript printed by M. R. James as an introduction to his own text expressing a note of caution (James (ed.) 1933, Introduction).

[43] Avril 1981, pp. 348–49.

[44] Leo 2013, pp. 263–71.

[45] Avril 1981, p. 303 no. 250, and pp. 301–2 no. 249, respectively.

[46] Avril 1981, pp. 300–301 no. 248.

[47] Avril 1981, p. 348.

[48] Avril 1981, p. 348.

[49] Stones 1990, p. 302 n. 3.

[50] See Delcourt (ed.) 2009, pp. 163–65 no. 66 by Alison Stones.

[51] Avril 1981, p. 349 no. 302; Leo 2013 passim. The manuscript is online at https://www.themorgan.org/manuscript/76974.

[52] Stones 1998, p. 564 n. 104; Stones 1993, p. 259 n. 127.

claims to authorship, stylistic analysis is still the best and most reliable tool for the art historian. As the late distinguished scholar Robert Suckale has put it, 'it is however not possible to completely reject stylistic analysis. It cannot be excluded from the practice of the art historian'.[53]

The multi-tasking activities that Pierart claims for himself were not unique, as we saw with Philippe de Troyes. There are many other cases, both earlier and later. For instance, Willelmus, monk of Andres (OSB, diocese of Thérouanne), says a century earlier, 'I wrote, illuminated, bound, and corrected the present book' (*presentem librum scripsi, illuminavi, ligavi, ligatumque et emendatum*).[54] Nicolas le Breton, working in Paris in 1316 was paid for 'illuminating, notating and completing' (*illuminatus, notatus, et completes*) a new gradual for the count of Savoie, plus an additional sum for rebinding the exemplar.[55] In 1338, Stephanus Gissardus was paid in Cambrai for 'binding, illuminating and repairing several books' (*pluribus libris ligandis illuminandis et reparandis*).[56] Most specific is the payment to Maistre Robert, illuminator of Valenciennes, in 1343–44, where distinctions are made between the sizes and scales of illuminated letters and whether they are historiated or not:

> For 1168 small letters received on Saint Martin's day (11th November), @ 11 *compengnons* per 100. Item, 145 letters size I, @ 1 *compengnon* per letter; item, for 4 letters size II @ 2 *compengnons* per letter; item, for 4 historiated initial letters @ 10 *compengnons* per letter, adding up to 2 sols 6 deniers, totalling 39 livres 15 sols. Item, to the same, on the Friday after Christmas Day, 1300 and a half and a quarter of small letters, according to the above price; item 121 letters @ size I, item 12 letters @ size II, item 14 historiated initials, adding up to 39 livres 15 sols.[57]

The examples selected here represent something of the variety and complexity of the process of attribution. The definition of artistic personalities is full of pitfalls for

---

53 'Auf Stilkritik gänzlich zu verzichten ist jedoch nicht möglich. Sie ist aus der Praxis des Kunsthistoriker nicht weg zu denken', cited from Robert Suckale 2006, p. 275 by Stones 2013–14, part I, vol. 1, p. 18. For a reflection on stylistic analysis as a tool for attributing works when it comes to music, see the chapter by Everist and the introduction to the volume. See also Desmond's, Bradley's, and Brewer's chapters for other examples of practical application of stylistic analysis in relation to authorship of particular works.

54 Saint-Omer, BA 112, Martyrology, fol. 27r, cited by Dehaisnes 1886, vol. 1, p. 66.

55 Edmunds 1990, nos. 6–7; Rouse and Rouse 2000, vol. 2, p. 99.

56 Dehaisnes 1886, vol. 1, p. 330: 'Compte de la fabrique de la cathédrale de Cambrai, du 24 [juin 1338] au 23 juin [1339], par Guillaume De Montcornut, chanoine'.

57 ' ... pour XIc et LXVIII petites lettres, rechiutes le jour Saint Martin, parmi XI compengnons le cent. Item, C et XLV lettres d'un point, parmi I compengnon de le lettre; item pour IIII lettres de II poins, parmi II compengnons le lettre; item, pour IIII lettres ymagenées pour ystores, parmi X compengnons le lettre, montent, compengnon pour ii s. vi d. (total) xxxi l.xv s. Item, a lui, le venredi après le jour dou Noel, XIIIc et demi et I quart de petites lettres, par le fuer devant dit; item, VIxx et une lettre d'un point; item, XII lettres de II poins; item, XII lettres ymagenées pour istores montent xxxix l. xv s' (Dehaisnes 1886, vol. 1, p. 346 ('Compte de l'église Sainte-Waudru de Mons, rendu par Jean De Leuse')). The term *compengnon* is identified as 'monnaie' (unspecified coinage) by Dehaisnes. The overall meaning of the passage is not entirely clear.

the unwary. Today, art historians are less concerned to establish certainty than in previous generations and are more prepared to acknowledge the limits of what can be known from what survives. The key is to distinguish what is certain from what is speculative and to take due account of both. Another question raised by the three cases examined here is whether it can be said that notions about artistic authorship underwent decisive change between the late thirteenth and the mid-fourteenth centuries, the period represented in this chapter. To a certain extent, the answer is yes, as in the latest example by Pierart dou Thielt, supplying us with the decisive signature, complete with explanation of what exactly he did. He nonetheless signed only a single manuscript, whereas his style can be detected in other books that lack his signature, and even in the signed Arsenal manuscript there is room for questioning, in relation to the explicit initial on the one hand and in relation to the broader context and definition of Pierart's unsigned work on the other hand. One could even go so far as to claim that the uncertainty surrounding the artistic personalities of the decorator of the works written and noted by Philippe de Troyes, and of Master Honoré, the latter known primarily from documents and not from actual manuscripts, still persists into the mid-fourteenth century – and well into the Renaissance.

Appendix 1: Philippe de Troyes's Colophon in the Third Volume (fol. 435v) of the Bible Oxford, New College 3–6

Edition after Coxe 1852, vol. 1, p. 2.

In calce, 'Volumen istud tertium scripsit Philippus presbiter / Natus urbe Trecensium existens naturaliter / Sed in hoc beneficium sortitus spiritaliter / Hinc cum Maria Filium Ihesum laudemus partier.

Anno Dei millesimo Qui summus regit omnia / Simul et ducentesimo ex quo venit in propria / Octogesimo decimo finita est pars tertia / Biblie benignissimo dante Cui sit gloria / Amen.

Artificem commendat opus non propria lingua. Non redimit victum cumulata sciencia morum. Sapientia sine eloquentia est quasi cytharam habens in sinu clauso. Ave Maria.

(At the end. This third volume was written by Philip, priest, born a native in the city of Troyes, but in the present benefice obtaining spiritual favour. Let us from thence offer similar praise to Mary's son Jesus.

In the year one thousand of Our Lord, who reigns over all things, two hundred more from He who came to his own, in eighty and ten the third part was finished. The most blessed bible was given to the one to whom glory be. Amen.

Skill commends the work not its own tongue. The sum of scientific knowledge does not redeem the victor. Knowledge without eloquence is like a silent cithara. Hail Mary.)

PART III

MEDIEVAL CONSTRUCTIONS OF AUTHORITY AND OF THE AUTHORIAL PERSONA

6

Encoded Signatures: Devotion and Artistic Self-Presentation in the Motet *Ferre solet* (1373)[1]

Manon Louviot

Douai, Bibl. Desbordes-Valmore, 1105/3 fragment 74.4/1 (hereafter the Douai fragment) is a music fragment composed of two parchment bifolios.[2] It contains two complete motets, one three-voice Gloria, and two voice-parts most likely from two different motets. The music for all of these is written in black (and, in one motet, red) mensural notation, perhaps by a single hand, and all the texts are in Latin. The exact provenance of the fragment is unknown, but circumstantial evidence situates it in northern France or Flanders.[3] The *terminus post quem* of the fragment is 1373, as is evident from one of the complete motets, *Ferre solet/Ana theos de gracia*, which is the focus of this chapter.

Ferre solet is a four-voice *unicum* copied on fols. 3v–4r.[4] Its Marian topic is conveyed through the melody of the tenor, which quotes an *Ave Maria* antiphon for the Annunciation (CAO 1539),[5] and through the newly created poem of the triplum, which

1   This chapter is available under the Open Access licence CC–BY–NC–ND. I dedicate this chapter to the memory of Daniel Saulnier, who supported my first steps in this work with his characteristic kindness, confidence, and wise insight. The production of this chapter received support from a European Research Council (ERC) Consolidator Grant under the European Union Horizon 2020 research and innovation program (Grant number 864174), in the context of the project 'BENEDICAMUS: Musical and Poetic Creativity for a Unique Moment in the Western Christian Liturgy c. 1000–1500', led by Catherine A. Bradley. Thank you to Catherine A. Bradley and Johanna-Pauline Thöne for their comments on earlier drafts. I am especially grateful to Anne-Zoé Rillon-Marne and Gaël Saint-Cricq for their insight and thoughtful editorial leadership. My deepest gratitude goes to Nicholas David Yardley Ball, for his critical engagement and his careful language proofreading. Unless otherwise mentioned, all translations are mine.

2   Images are available on DIAMM, thanks to the kind permission of the library: https://www.diamm.ac.uk/sources/3939/#/. For a detailed description of the fragment with musical transcription, see Louviot 2021.

3   See Louviot 2021, pp. 128–29.

4   The Douai fragment also transmits a *solus tenor*, whose function in *Ferre solet* is discussed in Louviot 2021, pp. 114–16.

5   See Cantus Index at http://cantusindex.org/id/001539. The full prayer reads, 'Ave Maria gracia plena Dominus tecum benedicta tu in mulieribus et benedictus fructus ventris tui'.

praises the redemptive powers of the Virgin Mary in a sophisticated Latin register. The meaning of the motetus's poem, while clearly devotional in character, is hard to understand. The music features a fair amount of sophistication on the rhythmic, melodic, and structural levels, with syncopated lower voices governed by changes of proportions and mensurations as indicated by two canons copied on fol. 4r.[6]

The poems set by the triplum and the motetus have a similar structure, as shown in Appendix 1: they are composed of octosyllables, grouped in eight (triplum) and five (motetus) sestains with an *aabaab*, *bbcbbc*, and so forth rhyme scheme. Each poem encodes a certain amount of text, two by means of acrostics and one by means of a telestich. A clerical status and a name are ciphered in a fragmented letter acrostic in the triplum: FRATER is a continuous acrostic, formed by the first letter of each of the first six poetic lines (see bold capitalised letters in Appendix 1), then JOHANNES is encoded through the first letter of each first and third, fourth and sixth poetic line (so each first and third poetic line of each triplet); finally, VAVASSORIS uses the first letter of every third poetic line. The first syllable of each poetic line of the motetus encodes a date of composition as well as a claim of authorship (see bold capitalised letters): ANNO DOMINI MILLESIMO TRECENTESIMO SEPTUAGESIMO TERCIO FECIT ISTUM MOTETUM (he made this motet in the year of our Lord thirteen seventy-three). Finally, the last syllable of each line of the motetus forms the opening words of the Marian prayer used in the tenor voice (see bold letters).

The scribe was obviously skilled in this kind of copying. The five pieces of the Douai fragment are copied with care and precision, in particular in the alignment of text and music.[7] Moreover, the copyist took care to visualise the acrostics in their use of capital letters. This is especially visible in the triplum in which only some of the initial letters are part of the acrostic.[8] Such careful work certainly suggests a scribe well aware of the acrostics, perhaps even an authorial copy.

While the motet uniquely contains a self-identification, a date of composition, a claim of authorship, and a prayer to the Virgin Mary, only circumstantial information is known about the identified maker, Frater Johannes Vavassoris. He was active around 1373, and his name suggests Norman origin;[9] he was part of the regular clergy (as indicated by the title 'frater'), and, to judge by his mastery of Latin, he had a university background.[10] Ongoing archival research has not yet yielded a precise identification, on account of the difficulty in matching the author of *Ferre solet* with

---

[6]   See the musical analysis in Louviot 2021, pp. 112–14, 121–23. A discussion of the canons is found at 116–21.

[7]   On the efforts spent on the alignment of text and music, see Louviot 2021, pp. 96–97, 112.

[8]   The same copying strategy is, for that matter, used in the motet voice copied on the following verso (fol. 4v), which also includes a fragmented letter acrostic (SANCTUS LAMBERTUS).

[9]   Yver 1990.

[10]   Louviot 2021, pp. 128–29.

homonyms documented either in the university records[11] or in the papal archives.[12] Nevertheless, *Ferre solet* allows us to explore the performance of identity, even when we do not know who exactly is behind this name.

This chapter questions what the self-identification of Frater Johannes Vavassoris in a Marian motet tells us about the perceptions of his work and of his creative and spiritual individuality. First, I explore similarly hidden names in fourteenth-century poetry to highlight the functions of authorial encodings and better understand the self-presentation of Vavassoris, seemingly unique in late-medieval music. Then, to set the intellectual context for Vavassoris's encoded signature, I analyse how encoding names in literary productions interact with their target audience. Finally, I compare *Ferre solet* and its copy in the Douai fragment with self-representations in medieval sacred art and uncover the multi-layered relationship between the maker Johannes Vavassoris, his devotion to Mary, and the audience of his motet. By setting the uniqueness of the information ciphered in the motet against contemporary artistic and intellectual contexts, this chapter offers new understandings on the self-presentation of the composer in the fourteenth century.

Encoded Signatures as Authorial Affirmation

To date, the only comparable example to *Ferre solet* is Marchetto da Padova's motet *Ave regina/Mater innocencie*.[13] Probably composed early in the fourteenth century – that is, almost seventy years before *Ferre solet* – Marchetto's *Ave regina* contains two acrostics: the first word of each distich in the triplum forms the same Marian prayer as in *Ferre solet* in full, while the first letter of each verse of the motetus poem forms MARCUM PADUANUM, presumably the name of the composer.[14]

---

[11]   Indeed, several people sharing this name are documented as students of northern French colleges and universities in the 1370s, but there is either no connection to a regular status (leaving the identification at best hazardous), or the homonyms are described as part of the secular clergy and therefore cannot identify themselves as 'frater(s)'. See, among others, Courtenay and Goddard (eds.) 2013; Denifle and Chatelain (eds.) 1894, p. 461; Durand 1910, p. 586; and Gorochov 1997, p. 708.

[12]   The various 'Johannes Vavassoris' active in the late fourteenth century and mentioned in papal documents from both Rome and Avignon are never associated with musical activity. Although this does not preclude that some of them may have had musical training and given that 'Johannes' was a very common name and 'Vavassoris' a very common surname, any more precise claim of identification would be premature. See the mentions, for instance, in Di Bacco and Nádas 1994, pp. 51 and 56; and Hayez and Hayez (eds.) 1979, p. 55. Many thanks to Giuliano Di Bacco, David Fiala, and Fañch Thoraval for the stimulating discussions about the identification of 'Frater Johannes Vavassoris' during MedRen 2015 in Brussels and during the year 2019 (personal email communications). In that regard, my position is more cautious than that adopted by Margaret Bent and Johanna Thöne (as is clear in Bent's chapter in the current volume).

[13]   The motet is transmitted in Oxford, Bod. Lib., Canon. Class. Lat. 112, fols. 61v–62v and has been edited in Fischer and Gallo (eds.) 1976, no. 37. The motet is discussed in more details in Robertson 1995, especially pp. 300–304.

[14]   The motet is assumed to have been composed in 1305, probably for the consecration of the Scrovegni Chapel: see Gallo 1974. See also Robertson 2012. Other motets encoding

However, the use of authorial acrostics was very common in medieval poetry throughout Europe. Below, I discuss a few examples that have similarities to the literary encoding mechanisms of *Ferre solet*. By focussing on the ways and the reasons why the acrostics were formed and sometimes signalled, and ultimately on their functions, I illustrate and illuminate contemporary authorial strategies in other art forms, shedding further light on the literary signature found in Vavassoris's motet.

Geographically close to the presumed origin of Johannes Vavassoris is the poet Jean de Le Mote (fl. 1330–50), who was praised alongside Guillaume de Machaut and Philippe de Vitry as one of the best *faiseurs* (makers) of his day.[15] He wrote *Le Parfait du paon*, a continuation in 3,921 verses of two previous poems on the legend of Alexander the Great (*Vœux du paon* by Jacques de Longuyon and *Restor du paon* by Jean le Court dit Brisebarre).[16] At the end of his poem, Jean de Le Mote inserts his name (JEHAN DE LE MOTE) in an acrostic composed of the first letters of lines 3906–18 and signalled at lines 3905–6: 'Mon non couvertement vœl en ces viers atraire. / Je conmenche mon non, Diex me gart de contraire!' (I want to draw discreetly [attention] to my name in these verses. / I start my name, may God prevent me from contradicting [myself]!).[17] Line 3905 claims discretion ('couvertement'), and the acrostic is indeed a hidden device, pointing at a posture of humble authorship. Of course, this comes in contrast to the unambiguous signal of the authorial encoding right in the next verse ('Je conmenche mon non'), and with the playful acknowledgement of contradicting himself. This acrostic certainly functions as an

---

a Marian prayer through acrostics can be found, for instance, in Turin, Bnu, J.II.9: *Assumpta gemma/Gratulandum* (fols. 60v–61r) and *Aurora vultu/Ave virginum* (fols. 61v–62r). These motets do not contain any authorial identifications. To my knowledge, *Ave regina* is the only other fourteenth-century motet containing an authorial acrostic. Fourteenth-century motets are rarely ascribed, even by other means than acrostics. For a brief (though incomplete, as Marchetto's motet is not mentioned) overview, see Boogaart 2018, pp. 159–60. Authorial acrostics in Latin motets are more common in the fifteenth century. Such an example is Petrus Wilhelmi in the motet *Pneuma/Veni/Dator/Paraclito*: in the quadruplum, the first letters of the first six words cipher the name PETRUS; in the triplum, the first letters of the first eight words cipher the name WILHELMI, and the first letters of the first ten words of the motetus cipher the city DE GRUDENCZ. For a discussion and bibliographic references on Petrus Wilhelmi, see Gancarczyk 2006. See the chapter by Bent in the current volume on Marchetto's acrostic and for a survey of acrostics and other authorial self-naming devices in late-medieval polyphonic compositions.

[15] Jean de Le Mote is described as such next to Machaut, Vitry, as well as Colart Haubiert (whose output is unknown today) in a poem written in 1350 by Gilles li Muisis, an abbot and poet from Tournai (on Gilles, see also the chapter by Stones in this volume). Jean de Le Mote was affiliated to various bourgeois, princely, and royal courts, including the comital house of Hainaut, and the patronage of Philippa, wife of King Edward III of England. On Jean de Le Mote, see Plumley 2013, especially chaps. 6 and 7, and Menegaldo 2015.

[16] *Le Parfait du paon* (and another poem, the *Voie d'enfer et de paradis*) were commissioned by Simon de Lille, the royal goldsmith to King Philippe VI of France. A modern edition is available in Carey (ed.) 1972. See also Rouse and Rouse 1997, and Plumley 2013, pp. 201–12.

[17] Carey (ed.) 1972, p. 168.

authorial affirmation, perhaps to prove to his commissioner, Simon de Lille, that he was indeed the rightful author. In addition, verse 3919 dates the poem of the year 1340 (though not in an acrostic): 'l'an mil .iij. .C. .xl. volt ceste branche faire' (in the year 1340 I want to do this branch), clearly defining his poem as a ramification ('branche') of the previous versions of the legend of Alexander the Great. Inscribing his name as an acrostic therefore also ensured that he would become, and remain, part of this literary continuation.

A more complex acrostic can be found in the 1343 *Pharsale* by Niccolò da Verona, a highly literate Italian poet who was active in the fourteenth century.[18] Written in Franco-Italian, the epic poem retells the story of the battle of Pharsalus (during which Caesar defeated Pompey) and is based on the early thirteenth-century chronicle of Caesar, the *Faits des Romains*. *Pharsale* is composed of 3,166 alexandrines divided into 117 laisses (a type of stanza of varying length, treating a single theme or idea). Towards the end, Niccolò da Verona signed, dated, and acknowledged his patron at lines 1934–37: 'Nicolais le rima do pais Veronois / Por amor suen segnor de Ferare marcois / E cil fu Nicholais, la flor des Estenois, / Corant mil e troi cent ans e qarante trois' (Niccolò rhymed it, he of the Veronese lands / Out of love for his lord, the Marquis of Ferrara / And this man [also] was Niccolò, the flower of the Este / In the year one thousand three hundred years and forty-three).[19]

In addition, the first letter of laisses 3–96 (ninety-four letters in total) recomposes three of these signature verses (lines 1934–35 and 1937). The laisses are of varying and unpredictable lengths, and therefore, the acrostic is spread out irregularly, making it very difficult to notice. Moreover, there is no indication in the text that the three signature verses are also encrypted as an acrostic. John F. Levy hypothesises that the acrostic functions like a 'hidden copyright mark' which 'would still be retrievable' even if Niccolò's signature verses, located visibly at the end, are removed.[20]

Niccolò da Verona was not the first poet to cipher an entire poem as an acrostic in another work. He may have drawn this idea from Giovanni Boccaccio (1313–75). Sometime between 1342 and the beginning of 1343, the Florentine poet wrote the *Amorosa visione*, a narrative allegorical poem of fifty *canti* organised in *terza rima* (three-line stanzas with a fixed three-line rhyme scheme). Taken together, the initial letters of all the *terza rima* throughout the fifty *canti* (1,503 letters in total) form three sonnets, which led this acrostic to be described by modern scholarship as the longest in Western literature.[21] The final line of the first sonnet thus created provides the name of the author: GIOVANNI E DI BOCCACCIO DA CERTALDO. This first sonnet is dedicated to Boccaccio's presumed lover, Maria d'Aquino, whose first name is also ciphered through an additional acrostic composed of the initial letter of the first, third, fifth, seventh, and ninth lines, therefore creating an acrostic within

[18] On Niccolò da Verona and his works, see Lelong 2011.

[19] Levy 2013, pp. 206–11 for a discussion of the function of the acrostic and p. 206 for the translation.

[20] Levy 2013, pp. 209–10, 216.

[21] See, among others, Wilkins 1951, p. 101; Kirkham 2001, p. 123. For the dating of the poem, see Branca (ed.) 1974, p. 6.

an acrostic.[22] In most surviving manuscripts, the three sonnets hidden as an acrostic in *Amorosa visione* are spelled out before the main text. They are themselves prefaced by an explanation of their interaction with the poem and their author. It is not known, however, if such special prefatory emphasis originated with Boccaccio: 'tre infrascripti sonetti si contengono per ordine tutte le lectere principali de rittimy della infrascricta amorosa visione e pero che in quelli il nome dell autore si contiene altramenti non sicura di porlo: sonetti sono questy' ([In] the three sonnets written below are found in the order all the first letters of each *terza rima* [tercets] of this poem written below, *Amorosa visione*. And because in those [three sonnets] is contained the author's name, no effort has been made to name him elsewhere. The sonnets are as follows).[23]

Therefore, as Levy has observed, the function of a self-identifying acrostic is not limited to that of a signature. Such an acrostic can also, or indeed primarily, serve as 'a virtuoso performance intended to call attention to itself and what it asserts about its author', a function evidently at the core of the sophisticated acrostics of the motet *Ferre solet*.[24]

Encoded Signatures as Interaction between Author and Audience

Playing with encoded signatures is characteristic of the fourteenth century, and these authorial acrostics are only one of the many 'forms of oblique "naming by not naming"'.[25] Other literary means were explored by poets, of which the most well-known examples are probably the anagrammic signatures of Guillaume de Machaut (c. 1300–1377). The instructions that reveal them can be easy and straightforward, like at the beginning of *Confort d'ami*, a narrative poem of 4,004 lines, dated from 1357, at lines 35–40: 'Si osteras premierement / Une sillabe entièrement / Au commencier dou ver onsieme / Et une lettre dou disieme / Pres de la fin; la les saras / Quant .i. petit y museras' (So first eliminate / One whole syllable / From the beginning of the eleventh verse / And then cut out a letter from the tenth / Near the poem's end; you'll recognize them / After just a little thought).

But the instructions can also be much more intricate, like at the end of another narrative poem, *Le Jugement dou roy de Behaigne* (2,079 lines, *terminus ante quem* 1342), at lines 2055–63: 'Mais en la fin de ce livret feray / Que qui savoir / Vorra mon nom et mon seurnom de voir / Il le porra clerement percevoir / En darrein ver dou livret et veoir, / Mais qu'il dessamble / Les premières .vij. sillabes d'ensamble / Et les lettres d'autre guise rassamble, / Si que nulle n'en oublie ne emble' (But at the end of this book, I will see to it / That anyone / Eager to learn my name and surname / Will be able to recognize them clearly / In the book's last verse, see them there. /

---

[22] The acrostic of MARIA has been noticed by scholars very early on. See, for instance, Booth 1909, p. 81.

[23] Huot 1985, p. 110. The text reproduced here is drawn from the manuscript Wellesley, WCSC, P858, fol. 1r (https://repository.wellesley.edu/object/wellesley16255). See also Levy 2013, pp. 208–9.

[24] Levy 2013, p. 209.

[25] De Looze 1991, p. 164.

Let him simply remove / The first seven syllables from the whole / And reassemble them in another fashion, / Neglecting or omitting none).[26] The last verse of the book is, 'A gentil mal cuide humble secours'. Unscrambling the first seven syllables ('A gentil mal cuide hum'), one can read 'Guillemin de Machaut'.[27] Interestingly, this signature also has an explicit authorial function, as is evident in lines 2055–59.

Laurence de Looze identifies further functions of this signature: that of a 'ludic evocation of earlier anonymity' as well as a 'witty fiction that depends on the complicity of writer and reader'.[28] Indeed, as is quite clear from the more complex anagrammic example of the *Jugement*, even if the reader is invited to discover or recreate the author's name, they can only do so if they already know the solution and, therefore, in which order exactly to 'reassemble [the letters] in another fashion'.[29] This perspective on literary creation in which the reader is actively involved in recreating the author's name from the anagrammic passage is, according to De Looze, 'emblematic in fourteenth-century French letters'.[30]

This recreational act was emulated in other countries too. An interesting comparison for *Ferre solet*, because it is also in Latin, is the *Vox clamantis* by the English poet John Gower (c. 1330–1408). The allegorical poem deals with the peasant uprising of 1381, focussing in particular on the sufferings and corruption of the Church and of England.[31] Towards the end of the prologue of the first book, at lines 21–24, the reader finds instructions on how to compose the poet's name, a device, it has been suggested, he learned through the works of Machaut:[32] 'Primos sume pedes Godefridi desque Iohanni / Principiumque sui Wallia iungat eis / Ter caput amittens det cetera membra, que tali / Carmine compositi nominis ordo patet' (Take Godfrey's first letters and bequeath them to John / Let Wales conjoin to them its beginning / Beheaded, let 'ter' grant the remaining letters / Showing, when combined, the name's arrangement).[33]

---

[26] Text and translation adapted from Palmer (ed. and trans.), with Smilansky (ed.) and Leo (comp.) 2019: http://d.lib.rochester.edu/camelot/text/palmer-machaut-the%20debate%20series-judgment-of-the-king-of-bohemia.

[27] See Hœpffner 1906, p. 405. On anagrams in the Middle Ages and the Renaissance, see Higgins 1991.

[28] De Looze 1991, p. 169.

[29] De Looze 1991, pp. 162–78 discusses further the shifts of strategies of (non-)naming throughout the Middle Ages. More examples from Guillaume de Machaut, his contemporary Jean Froissart, and a later comparand Christine de Pizan, can be found at pp. 171–76.

[30] De Looze 1991, p. 176.

[31] Minnis 1988, pp. 170–71; Kirkham 2001, p. 124.

[32] Sáez-Hidalgo, Gastle, and Yeager (eds.) 2017, in particular chap. 23 by Peter Nicholson (Nicholson 2017), and chap. 26 by Robert J. Meindl (Meindl 2017).

[33] Text and translation from The Gower Project Translation, last edited by Robert J. Meindl on 9 November 2022: http://gowertranslation.pbworks.com/w/page/149185233/Vox%20Clamantis%20Book%20I. This signature is often mentioned as an acrostic, but this is clearly an anagrammic signature.

The desire for solid attributions that are engraved within the work itself – rather than changeable paratextual ascriptions that can vary across the copies of a work – and for interactions with the reader goes far beyond poetry. It was particularly favoured in preaching sermons and in thematic sermons – that is, those based on and developing a single theme from Scripture.[34] For instance, and for now remaining in England, a certain Robert of Basevorn wrote the *Forma praedicandi* c. 1322. One of the most well-known *artes praedicandi*, the *Forma* discusses the composition of the modern form of sermons, in particular distinguishing between an 'English' and a 'French' method.[35] In the introductory section, Robert announces an acrostic composed of 'the capital letters' providing the name of the dedicatee, his own name, and his status. The initial letters of the fifty chapters indeed spell out DOMINO WILLELMO ABBATI DE BASINGWERK ROBERTUS DE BASEVORN (To Lord William, Abbot of Basingwerk, Robert of Basevorn).[36] Robert of Basevorn wrote this text in response to sermons preached by impostors who were not recognised by the Church and did not have the legitimacy to write such texts. Thus, the acrostic here functions not so much as a ludic interaction with the reader than as an assertion of his authority and of his legitimacy as a writer of sermons.

The thematic sermons were very widespread in academic centres like Oxford or Paris and were also used as an opportunity to play with an author's name. At French universities, for example, the candidate for the title of doctor opened his defence with a public debate on a theme chosen from Scripture, the same process as the thematic sermon. In the fourteenth century, the chosen theme could contain an onomastic allusion to the candidate's own name. For instance, Dionysius de Montina (licensed in theology at Paris between Christmas 1374 and 2 February 1375) drew his topic from Acts 17:34: 'in quibus et Dionysius Areopagita' (among them was Dionysius the Areopagite). The chosen topic quotes his first name (Dionysius) verbatim, while 'Areopagita' refers to the 'hill of Ares' in which the Greek 'pagus' designates a rocky hill, therefore echoing the 'montina' (mountain) of Dionysius's family name.[37] Obviously, this 'made the selection of the theme very difficult', but it was a means to 'show the rhetorical capacities of the new Latinist'.[38] Playful, intellectual games around authors' names therefore also served to demonstrate one's academic skills.

Thus, although unusual in fourteenth-century motets, hidden authorial signatures were very common in other literary forms. The examples considered above demonstrate different and possibly overlapping functions of authorial acrostics and anagrams, including authorial affirmation, hidden copyright, artistic or rhetorical

---

[34] On the *Artes praedicandi*, see Briscoe and Jaye 1992 and Wenzel 2015.

[35] The text has been edited in Charland 1936 at pp. 231–323. See also Akae 2008.

[36] Text and translation from Baltzell Kopp 1971, p. 111. Note that the acrostic does not explicitly reveal the status of Robert as the author.

[37] Trapp 1956, p. 270. More examples of 'heraldic mystifications' (a term coined by Trapp) have been gathered by Ueli Zahnd at https://puns.zahnd.be/index.php. On Dionysius de Montina, see Sullivan 2004, p. 260.

[38] Trapp 1956, pp. 270–72. See the summary of university trajectories in the decades around 1400 in Courtenay 2011.

performance, interaction with the reader, assertion of legitimacy, or literary affiliation. Additional information, like dedicatee or date, can strengthen or clarify these functions. This points at interactions in the development of authorial consciousness and at a shared use of well-known literary devices like acrostics and anagrams to explore the possibilities granted by hidden authorial signatures.

In northern France and in England, the phenomenon was in all likelihood particularly lively not only in artistic forms but also within rhetorical contexts (theology, preaching, universities), which might reinforce the hypothesized Norman origin and university background for Johannes Vavassoris.[39] In any case, it seems very likely that Vavassoris was aware of such literary devices and conferred a multi-layered function on the ones he deployed in *Ferre solet*. In this motet, the acrostics were intended for authorial affirmation, artistic performance, and as I will show in the following section, devotional expression.

Encoded Signatures as Devotional Expression

The motetus of *Ferre solet* contains a telestich: the last syllables of each poetic line, grouped in threes, form the opening words of the Marian prayer: AVE MARIA GRACIA PLENA. Four other motets cipher the Marian prayer, though always as an acrostic. In addition to the early fourteenth-century motet *Ave regina* by Marchetto da Padova mentioned above, later examples include two Marian motets in the manuscript Turin, Bnu, J.II.9. This book was copied in the first half of the fifteenth century, perhaps in northern Italy, and possibly following a commission by King Janus of Cyprus (r. 1398–1432).[40] In the motet *Aurora vultu/Ave virginum* (fols. 61v–62r), the words AVE MARIA GRATIA PLENAE are ciphered using the first letter (triplum) or the first word (motetus) of each poetic line. In *Assumpta gemma/ Gratulandum* (fols. 60v–61r), the first syllables of each quatrain form the words AVE MARIA, and the prayer is continued similarly in the motetus (GRATIA PLENAE).[41] Finally, the motet *Benedicta/Ave mater*, ascribed to Gilet Velut in a manuscript of fifteenth-century polyphony (Oxford, Bod. Lib, Canon. Misc. 213, fols. 102v–103r), similarly encodes the prayer over the two voices, starting here in the motetus: the first words of each sestain produce AVE MARIA GRATIA PLANA DOMINUS TECUM, and the first word, or group of words, of each sestain in the triplum continue BENEDICTA TU IN MULIERIBUS BENEDICTUS FRUCTUS VENTRIS TUI (note that the first word of the last sestain is not 'Iesus', as in the original prayer, but 'expiatis', as if to keep the focus on Mary).[42] These four motets are all quite far

---

[39] Hanly 1997.

[40] The dating and provenance of the manuscript are most recently discussed in Kügle 2012. The manuscript and its cultural context are analysed in Clément et al. (eds.) 2021.

[41] In both texts, there is a repetition of one letter in the middle of the acrostics (therefore rendering, in the triplum A VE E MA RI A, and in the motetus GRA TI A P PLE NAE). See Hoppin 1957, p. 99. On the devotional expression in these two motets, and in Turin, Bnu, J.II.9, see Thoraval 2021, pp. 157–64.

[42] Hoppin 1957, p. 99. The manuscript is available online at https://digital.bodleian.ox.ac. uk/objects/a4120d22-b62f-4b57-861d-43c839c790a0/.

away chronologically from 1373, the date encoded in *Ferre solet*, but by encrypting the same words from the same prayer, they underline that composing acrostic on the Marian prayer was a relatively widespread practice in motet compositions.[43]

However, *Ferre solet* is significantly different from these four motets. It is the only motet that combines the ciphered text with the use of the prayer (words and melody) in another voice, namely the tenor. Moreover, only *Ferre solet* combines an acrostic and a telestich in the same voice, the use of a telestich itself being seemingly a quite unusual practice. More subtly, the intended topic of *Ferre solet*, while broadly laudatory, is blurred by its complex Latin register, its unusual cultural references, and the recourse to numerous metaphors, which contrasts with the evident Marian praises found in the other four motets. There is once more a fundamental difference between *Ferre solet* and its closest comparand, Marchetto da Padova's *Ave regina*, which combines the acrostics of the prayer and a name (while the other three motets are anonymous or are ascribed through an addition at the top of the page): the unique presence of a clear claim of authorship ('fecit istum motetum') and also of a date (1373).

Additionally, *Ferre solet* as transmitted in the Douai fragment is unique in its highlighting of the encoded acrostics. As mentioned above, the letters composing the acrostics are capitalised. Moreover, the telestich is highlighted by means of a brief explanatory rubric copied on fol. 4r, in a leftover space after the motetus and before the contratenor and *solus tenor*. The rubric reads, 'lege finalez sillabas huius dicta[minis] / Ave maria gracia plena legi in illis T[enoribus]' (Read the last syllables of this poem / *Ave maria gracia plena* to be read in these tenors). The rubric is particularly interesting because it not only draws attention to a feature of the poem that could not otherwise be highlighted visually but also makes explicit the connection between the telestich and the tenor, which uses the Marian prayer.

While this is the only known copy of fourteenth-century music that draws attention to its own ingenuity and at the same time claims ownership of it, this attitude is very common in medieval art.[44] An illuminating comparison to the literary self-representation of Vavassoris is the scribal self-portraits added to skilfully decorated books. For instance, the scribe of an eleventh-century manuscript of Saint Jerome's *Commentary on Isaiah* drew himself at the end of the book with the accompanying mention of his name, Hugo, and the description 'imago pictoris et illuminatoris huius operis' (image [or reflection] of the painter and illuminator of this work).[45] The claim of craftmanship can be strengthened by a self-representation of the scribe

---

43 This Marian prayer was not the only liturgical text to be used in acrostics. For instance, the closing versicle 'Benedicamus Domino' is ciphered twice in the upper voices of the four-voice motet *Belial vocatur/Belial vocatur/Belial vocatur/Tenura* (transmitted in Burgos, Las Huelgas, s/n (c. 1320–30), at fols. 82r–83r): a first time through the first syllables of each word and a second time through the first letters of each word. The final verse of the text quotes the closing versicle in full. See Saint-Cricq 2010, vol. 1, pp. 109–10.

44 See Kessler 2019. See the chapter by Stones in this volume on authorial colophons as regards the copying and decoration of gothic manuscripts.

45 Oxford, Bod. Lib., Bodl. 717, fol. 287v: https://digital.bodleian.ox.ac.uk/objects/99379ed1-a0c0-4a5d-b31a-eb9a9ed30f40/surfaces/fca2ae02-799a-4b0a-800a-e4bb60ceeode/. For a discussion of this manuscript and Hugo Pictor, see Gameson 2001.

at work on the very manuscript, as is the case of Frater Ruffilus or Rainaldus and Oliverus in another source, who depicted themselves within beautifully illuminated initials.[46] The devotional dimension of self-portraits by scribes is sometimes made explicit: for instance, Engilbertus represents himself in a twelfth-century homiliary literally praying to Christ within his work, his prostrated body forms the tail of the letter Q of 'quod'. The claim for the copy of the manuscript is made clear through the caption 'pictor et scriptor' (painter and scribe).[47] In spite of the chronological distance, these illuminations and *Ferre solet* share at least two common features: the self-representation within their own sacred work and the ostentatious refinement of the work over which responsibility is being claimed. The intertwining of the quality of a sacred work and the power of the devotion is typical of medieval sacred art, and the literary inscription of Vavassoris's signature and claim of authorship over the motet can be understood through this perspective. Vavassoris represents himself in a sacred motet and claims the authorship of the skilfully composed piece, perhaps hoping that his artistry will be an acceptable gift to the Virgin Mary. From this perspective, the intricacy of the motet and its visual highlighting can be understood as a way to enhance the efficacy of the Marian prayer.[48]

In contrast to these illuminations, however, the authorial signature of Vavassoris is hidden, in particular when the motet *Ferre solet* is performed aurally. What happens to the devotional self-representation when the motet is performed? How can we reconcile the affirmation of authority over artistic ingenuity and devotional expression when the signature is hidden to the auditory perception?

Comparisons of the inscriptions in *Ferre solet* and inscriptions on church bells may provide further insight into these questions. Medieval inscriptions of all kinds (liturgical, authorial) on these liturgical objects were very common in the Middle Ages, and like motets, bells could be both silent and sonorous objects. But just like acrostics and telestichs in a motet, inscriptions on church bells are hidden to human perception, even when the object itself is sonorous. Analysing church bells, Vincent Debiais has shown that 'it is the bell itself, which, by ringing, disseminates the message of the inscription and sings the praise to Christ' (c'est la cloche qui, en sonnant, propage le message de l'inscription et chante la louange au Christ).[49] The poetic

---

[46] Frater Ruffilus depicts himself at work on the initial *R* with his tools standing next to him, in the Passionary of Weissenau (Cologny, Bodmer 127, fol. 244r, twelfth century; https://www.e-codices.unifr.ch/en/list/one/fmb/cb-0127. On Ruffilus, see Berschin 2010 and Michon 1987. 'Rainaldus scriptor' and 'Oliverus pictor' depict themselves writing and painting the initial *O* in *De laudibus sanctae Crucis*, preserved in Douai, BM 340, fol. 9r (second half of the twelfth century; <http://initiale.irht.cnrs.fr/codex/8349). See Gameson 2005.

[47] Trier, Stadtbibl. 261-1140 2°, fol. 153v. An excerpt of the folio featuring the self-representation of Engilbertus is digitised at https://www.trierer-buecher.de/restaurierungen/homiliar-des-paulus-diaconus/. On Engilbertus, see Mariaux 2015, p. 407.

[48] The combination of artistry and prayer in motets becomes more widespread in the fifteenth century, as had been demonstrated in Blackburn 1997. For further details on painting and praying, see Palazzo 2016.

[49] Debiais 2009, p. 208. See also Ingrand-Varenne, Pallotini, and Raaijmakers (eds.) 2023, which was published after the writing of the present chapter.

devices of *Ferre solet* also are not perceptible when listening to the polytextual motet, but when singers perform it, they disseminate the message of the inscription – that is, Vavassoris's Marian prayer – regardless of whether the inscription is perceived by human ears or not.

Ferre solet and its written state in the Douai fragment highlight a complex phenomenon that combines both artistic self-staging and the function of the motet as a formalised expression of prayer. The comparands given in this chapter reveal that specifically in *Ferre solet*, some kind of balance is negotiated between these two functions, which may differ from earlier and contemporary examples.

Indeed, studying Marchetto's *Ave regina*, Alberto Gallo and Anne Walters Robertson have argued that the acrostic naming of Marchetto da Padova (assuming it is indeed an authorial acrostic) is not so much a confirmation of the personality of the musician or of the fact of his composition, as it is an act of prayer, a personal participation of the musician in the religious meaning of his work.[50] This explains why the name is in the accusative ('marcum paduanum'), positing Marchetto as the recipient of the beneficial effects of the prayer.[51] By contrast, in *Ferre solet*, Frater Johannes Vavassoris names himself in the nominative, as the subject of the verb *fecit*.[52] This grammatical difference combined with an active verb perhaps makes it a staging that is more focused on the fact of his authorship than that of Marchetto da Padova.

Vavassoris's position is given visual prominence too, since his motet such as it appears in the Douai fragment is the only example that features visual highlighting and an explanatory rubric of the encoding mechanisms. In this sense, the signature in *Ferre solet* can be understood better in comparison with literary works, like those of Jean de Le Mote or Robert of Basevorn. On the one hand, Vavassoris draws the devotional function of the motet into a confirmation of his artistic self-presentation. On the other hand, the visual clues in the Douai fragment interact with the readers, supplying them with the tools necessary to recognise the sophisticated poetic and musical devices by which this self-presentation is integrated within the rest of his composition.

Appendix 1: Texts and Translation of the Motet *Ferre solet*

The texts are reproduced from Louviot 2021, pp. 162–64, with a translation by Leofranc Holford-Strevens. Words that resist translation are rendered as ??? and the lone illegible word as ***.

---

[50] Gallo 1974 and Robertson 2012.

[51] Gallo 1974, p. 304.

[52] See Bourgain 2001, pp. 361–74, especially p. 362; Kessler 2019, especially pp. 61–62.

Triplum

[**F**]erre solet cor Gaudium		The heart is wont to rejoice
Recipiens presidium		in receiving protection
A sumpto vitis (colore) liquore		from having taken the juice of the vine.
Totum vulgus concivium		The entire mass of fellow citizens
Exultat cum convivium	5	exults when it fills
[**Rep**]let suum hoc humore		its banquet with this liquid.
Jesus nostri pro amore		Jesus for love of us
botrus insolito more		was the grape bunch in unusual manner
Oppressus est torculari		crushed in the wine press.
Heu nostro pro vigore	10	Alas, for our vitality
[dur]o perpessus dolore		having suffered with hard pain,
Adhuc vinum se vult dari		he still wishes himself to be given as wine.
Nostra fides debet fari		Our faith ought to proclaim
quod pro nostro salutari		that for our salvation
Natus fuit de [virgi]ne	15	he was born of the Virgin,
Eos que est sine pari		the dawn that is without peer
celo lucens terre mari		shining for heaven, earth, and sea
Siderum ab origine.		from the origin of the stars.
Vitis vera [y]magine		The vine by a true image
fertur terna propagine	20	is borne by a threefold shoot
[quam] pincerna pharaonis		that Pharaoh's cup bearer
Agnovit sumpno germine		recognised in his sleep by its growth.
sic crevit quod examine		It has so grown that on testing
pree[st] gemmis uva bonis		the grape excels with good buds.
Vere [Virgo] dei donis	25	Truly [the Virgin] by God's gifts
tulit unam de personis		bore one of the Persons,
que est deus ac deitas		who is God and Godhead,
Abbas non divisionis		the father not of division
immo summe unionis		but of supreme union,
in [trini]tate unitas	30	unity in trinity.
Satis videtur veritas		It seems sufficiently the truth
quod aucta celi civitas		that the citizenry of heaven
in hujus assumptione		has been increased in her Assumption.
Sursum clamet humilitas		Let humility cry upwards,
tua [nam]que castitas	35	for your chastity
digna est electione		is worthy of being chosen,

Omni exaltatione
atque dominatione
super omnia sidera
Rose flores non tam bone   40
sunt [sub] vitis ditione
veni et nobis impera

Iure tua sunt supera
cito nobis da federa
mater misericordia   45
Sic quod vana hec [o]pera
transeundo per prospera
gustemus vinum glorie

of every exaltation
and domination
over all the stars.
The flowers of the rose are not as goodly
under the command of the vine;
come and rule us.

The things above are rightly yours;
swiftly give us covenant,
mother of mercy,
so that, passing by these vain works
through things propitious,
we may taste the wine of glory.

Motetus

Ana theos de gracia.
Noys ac providencia.
Domini almum procul ave
Mite ac[c]epit u***ya
Nitens deica usya   5
Milethum cui fertur ave.

Leoni nam gentem huma
Si non valet plus quam spuma
Monet que te maculari
Trenara sunt ad infima   10
Censura fera[tu]r yma
Te[gens] mergens in mari

Sileant cum prudencia
Momenti in presencia
Septim inunda sic hos flagr[a] 15
Tu quod cum pertinacia
Animati superbia
Gemant omnes et nos fragra

Sinu tuo ut sagaci
Mo[re] sacra nos pingaci   20
Tergas tua mundicia
Cipressus rore vinaci.
Odor sapor de te nasci.
Fere possu[nt] qui omnia

God of grace,
mind, and intelligence
received the Lord's life-giving *Ave*
mildly from afar
Gleaming with the divine essence
to whom the *Ave* is borne [to Miletus].

For bury the people to the lion
if it is not worth more than foam
that warns you are being stained
they are at the depths of Taenarum.
Let the censure be borne to the bottom,
hiding, plunging in the sea.

Let them be silent with prudence
in the presence of the movement
seven whips flood these thus
Thou, because with pertinacity
animated by pride
all may groan and

that in your wise bosom
???
Cleanse with your cleanliness
cypress with winous dew
Smell and taste to be born of thee
which can do pretty well everything

Citra deum innant im**ple**.	25	This side of God they float, fill
Istringos nos et adim**ple**.		us ??? and fulfil
Tumulum cordis pincer**na**		the tomb of the heart O cup bearer
Morum corda nostra re**ple**.		fill our hearts with sound morals
Te si gracie ut sup**ple**		thee if of grace as fill
Tum rimantur sempiter**na**	30	then they search for things eternal;

Tenor

Ave maria gracia plena dominus tecum benedicta tu in mulieribus Alleluya

(Hail Mary, full of grace, the Lord is with you; blessed are you among women. Alleluia.)

7

The (Critical) Reception of Adam de la Halle's Motets by Petrus de Cruce and His Circle

Catherine A. Bradley

Adam de la Halle is one of the best-known thirteenth-century composers. He was not only a creator of monophonic songs of various kinds as well as of lyric and poetic texts and dramatic *jeux* but also of polyphonic rondeaux and motets. Despite Adam's fame and the survival of a complete works compilation of his wide-ranging oeuvre in Paris, BnF, fr. 25566 (hereafter Ha, dated to the early 1290s), concrete biographical details remain elusive. Adam undoubtedly came from Arras, and it is generally supposed that he was born in the mid-1240s. He may have studied in Paris, and scholars – notably Carol Symes – have suggested that he died abroad, in Sicily, before 1290.[1] The *opera omnia* collection of Adam's works in Ha is unusual in its thirteenth-century context. Although groupings of songs by a single author are typical of trouvère chansonniers, the section of Ha devoted to Adam is remarkable in its scale and scope as well as in its internal organisation by genre.[2] The inclusion of polyphony by Adam is, moreover, wholly exceptional: Ha is the only extant trouvère author collection to contain groups of polyphonic works, and thus Adam is 'the only thirteenth-century trouvère to whom polyphony is explicitly attributed in a music manuscript'.[3] It is, therefore, entirely thanks to Ha that we know Adam

---

[1] For a recent view of Adam's dates, see Symes 2019, pp. 28–32. See also Bradley 2022a, pp. 49–56. For a recent summary of the rich non-musicological literature on Adam's biography, see Ibos-Augé 2018a, pp. 230–33. This chapter builds on material previously published in Bradley 2019 and Bradley 2022a.

[2] On authorial song collections, and in relation to Adam's *opera omnia*, see Haines 2019, especially pp. 112–20.

[3] Saltzstein 2019 (ed.), introduction, p. 4. As Saltzstein notes (n. 16), several monophonic songs ascribed to Gautier de Coinci have polyphonic concordances, but it seems unlikely that Gautier was the composer of these song melodies, still less of their polyphonic settings. The authorship of polyphonic settings remains an open question in the case of Guillaume d'Amiens: two monophonic rondeaux ascribed to him in Vatican, BAV, Reg. lat. 1490 (hereafter Vat) appear, without ascription, in a three-voice polyphonic context in Paris, BnF, fr. 12786 (hereafter PaB). On this, see Everist 2019, p. 333. See also Saint-Cricq 2019 on the presence monophonic songs ascribed to Robert de Reims within polyphonic motets, and – more broadly – on the phenomenon of song attribution and quotation in relation to motets.

to be the composer of five vernacular motets.[4] Three of these five compositions are preserved also within thirteenth-century motet collections – notably, Montpellier, BIU, H 196 (hereafter Mo) – but none of them is ascribed to Adam, since such books never record composer attributions.

As a composer of songs, Adam seems to have been especially esteemed – apparently posthumously – in the 1290s and early 1300s. Perhaps this was thanks to his skill as a 'self-promoting songwriter' in the fashioning of his own legacy,[5] or it may have been because an early death attracted attention and increased his reputation.[6] Adam's rondeaux and rondeau refrains were frequently quoted in the layer of the thirteenth-century motet repertoire preserved in the seventh fascicle of Mo (copied c. 1290).[7] His refrains are similarly prominent as interpolations in the romance *Renart le Nouvel* (dated in the early 1290s).[8] And his *grands chants* were cited within the late thirteenth- or early fourteenth-century *Dit de la panthère*, with the status of authoritative texts on love.[9] Indeed, Adam's thirty-six *grands chants* were very widely transmitted, with not a single unicum surviving among them.[10] And a group of them was retrospectively appended – probably in the early fourteenth century – to the chansonnier de Noailles (Paris, BnF, fr. 12615), to follow the songs of other Artesian greats.[11]

This chapter argues that Adam's motets were, in contrast to his songs, rather less revered by a younger generation of motet composers active in the 1290s and early 1300s, including Petrus de Cruce.[12] Petrus's motet *Aucun ont trouvé/Lonc tans/Annun[tiantes]* was repeatedly cited by medieval theorists, from whom alone its attribution to Petrus is known.[13] I demonstrate that Petrus's famous triplum opens

---

[4]   On Ha and on the complex reception and status of Adam de la Halle as a creator of dramatic works, see the chapter by Doudet in this volume. For further reflections on Adam, see also the introduction and chapters by Everist and Bent.

[5]   Haines 2019, p. 119.

[6]   See Bradley 2022a, pp. 55–56.

[7]   On Adam's presence in Mo 7, see Bradley 2022a, pp. 7–40. Polyphonic rondeaux do not appear to have had an established written transmission in the thirteenth century. Only three (late) thirteenth-century rondeaux collections survive, and it is possible that the notation of two of them may have been motivated by a desire specifically to preserve works by Adam: the group of sixteen rondeaux ascribed to Adam in Ha and the fragmentary leaf Cambrai, Le Labo, B 1328 (hereafter CaB). CaB seems to come from an author corpus for Adam, since it records a *jeu-parti* by Adam and the same first four of his polyphonic rondeaux in the same order as collected in Ha. There is also an unnotated and unattributed collection of thirty-four polyphonic rondeau in PaB, which includes four works elsewhere ascribed to Adam. On polyphonic rondeaux and their sources, see Everist 1996.

[8]   On probable quotations of Adam in *Renart le Nouvel*, see Saltzstein 2019, pp. 354–55. On a date of post 1291 for *Renart le Nouvel*, see Haines 2010b, pp. 25–34.

[9]   On quotations of Adam in the *Dit de la panthère* – dated between 1290 and 1328 – see Huot 1987, pp. 193–94, 201–2.

[10] See Ragnard 2019, pp. 189–92.

[11] Saint-Cricq with Doss-Quinby and Rosenberg (eds.) 2017, pp. xvii–xviii.

[12] On the relative chronology of Adam and Petrus, see Bradley 2022a, pp. 48–50.

[13] On theoretical citations of *Aucun ont trouvé* and their attributions, see Bent 2015, pp. 27–32; Catalunya 2018, pp. 420–22. There is an additional unattributed citation of this

with a previously unnoticed quotation of the triplum of Adam's motet *Aucun se sont loé/A Dieu commant/Super te*. Petrus's quotation of Adam seems here to set up a direct comparison between the two composers, and one in which the music and text of Adam's triplum are unflatteringly positioned as representative of an outdated and less expressive mode of composition.

This interpretation is corroborated by the circumstances in which another of Adam's motet incipits – the motetus opening of his *Entre Adam et Hanikel/Chief bien seans/Aptatur* – is quoted: as the triplum explicit of an anonymous and unique motet in Mo fascicle 8, *Se je sui/Jolietement/Omnes*. The appearance of Adam's incipit in *Se je sui/Jolietement/Omnes* has long been noted but without scrutiny of the broader musical and textual context in which the quotation is framed.[14] I argue that the triplum of *Se je sui* sets up its closing quotation of 'Chief bien seans' in such a way as to cast Adam's motetus as musically old-fashioned and poetically hackneyed. Moreover, I propose that the choice in *Se je sui/Jolietement/Omnes* of a particular version and arrangement of the 'omnes' tenor, and in combination with a female-voiced motetus text, may constitute an additional and as-yet-unsuspected allusion to another of Adam's motets, *De ma dame/Dieus comment porroie/Omnes*. As in Petrus's *Aucun ont trouvé*, the evocation of Adam's motets by the unknown composer of *Se je sui/Jolietement/Omnes* seems to be competitive and unfavourable. That this negative attitude to Adam is shared with a work known to be by Petrus invites a reconsideration of the status of *Se je sui/Jolietement/Omnes* as a composition either also by Petrus himself or someone in his circle.

Adam and Petrus are, to date, the only late thirteenth-century composers with securely attributed motets. It is not only satisfying and intriguing to be able to posit a direct quotational link between them, but it also indicates that composer's identities had a significance within cultures of motet creation that is belied by the entirely anonymous appearance of extant polyphonic motet collections. By uncovering and interrogating unsuspected traces of compositional personalities and interactions within late thirteenth-century motets, this chapter seeks to underline and to understand the significance of such authorial traces for a reception of composers and their creations in the Middle Ages.

Quoting Adam's *Aucun se sont loé* in Petrus's *Aucun ont trouvé*

Adam de la Halle's motet *Aucun se sont loé/A Dieu commant/Super te* (preserved in Ha and in the seventh fascicle of Mo) opens with a polyphonic self-quotation (see Example 7.1).[15] Adam's motetus begins by quoting the refrain text and

---

triplum incipit in the recently discovered treatise in Philadelphia, FLP, Lewis E 39, fol. 1r–v (on fol. 1r). The attribution of *Aucun ont trouvé* to Petrus by Jacobus, in *Speculum musicae*, is discussed in Bent's chapter in this volume. On attributions and references to Petrus, and for a discussion of his life and career, see also the chapter by Zayaruznaya.

[14] See, for example, Falck 2001; Ibos-Augé 2018b, p. 211.

[15] I transcribe the medieval perfect long as a dotted minim in duration. In the interpretation of semibreves, I follow the ternary division of the breve espoused by Franco, rendering pairs of semibreves as unequal and consistently interpreting the first as the shorter or

Example 7.1. Opening of Adam de la Halle's motet *Aucun se sont loé/A Dieu commant/ Super te* (Mo 7, no. 263, fol. 288r–v).

melody of his three-voice rondeau *A Dieu commant*, while the motet's surrounding triplum and tenor voices recreate the harmonic context of the original rondeau.[16] Notwithstanding accommodations to the new generic context of the motet (a plainchant tenor quotation and an independently texted and fast-moving triplum), *Aucun se sont loé/A Dieu commant/Super te* gives a strong aural impression of Adam's rondeau source. The motet's polyphonic self-quotation – replicating musically the three voices of Adam's polyphonic rondeau at its outset, quoting and recasting the rondeau's refrain text to frame a new motetus voice that explicitly describes and names Adam's hometown of Arras – serves to place Adam's identity, and his status as the creator of *Aucun se sont loé/A Dieu commant/Super te*, centre stage.

The very beginning of Adam's motet triplum is itself replicated at the outset of the triplum of Petrus de Cruce's *Aucun ont trouvé/Lonc tans/Annun[tiantes]*, recorded in Mo 7 and in Turin, BR, varia 42 (hereafter Tu; see Example 7.2, which reproduces the clarificatory dots or strokes of division that mark breve units in the original nota-tion). Fascicle 7 of Mo opens with a pair of motets that are attributed to Petrus in theoretical treatises, where they exemplify the rhythmic innovation with which he is credited: the division of a perfect breve into more than the maximum number of three component semibreves previously permitted in Franco of Cologne's *Ars cantus mensurabilis*.[17] The first motet in Mo 7, *S'Amour eüst/Au renouveler/Ecce* (no. 253, extant also in Tu), is attributed to Petrus only by the fourteenth-century theorist

<hr />

'recta' semibreve of the pair (in parallel with Franco's practice for breves). Lacking any clear medieval theoretical prescription, I maintain the overall triple conception of the breve for groups of four or more semibreves, applying the fast-notes-first principle established for *conjuncturae*. Ligatures are shown by square brackets and *conjuncturae* by dashed slurs. Plicae are indicated by a dash through the stem and editorial insertions are given in square brackets. Accidentals and dots of division are reproduced as in the manuscript source. Original text spellings are retained in transcriptions of a particular manuscript source, but capitalisation and line numbers are editorial. Refrain texts are italicised. Motet titles follow the standardised version established in Gennrich 1957.

16   For a comparison of Adam's polyphonic rondeau and motet, and for evidence of the direction of quotation, see Bradley 2019, pp. 466–75. See the complete edition of Adam's rondeaux in Wilkins (ed.) 1967.

17   On theoretical discussions of Petrus's motets and his relationship to Franco, see Bent 2015, pp. 21–27. See also Zayaruznaya's chapter in this volume.

Example 7.2. Opening of Petrus de Cruce's motet *Aucun ont trouvé/Lonc tans/ Annun[tiantes]* (Mo 7, no. 254, fol. 273r–v).

known as Jacobus, and its triplum does not exceed groups of four semibreves within the perfect breve unit. Its neighbouring composition in Mo 7, *Aucun ont trouvé/ Lonc tans/Annun[tiantes]*, by contrast, does not feature any four-semibreve groups but instead goes further in fitting as many as five, six, and seven individually texted semibreves within the space of a perfect breve.

The first five notes of Petrus's rhythmically radical *Aucun ont trouvé* triplum are an exact musical match for the opening of Adam's *Aucun se sont loé* (marked by boxes in Examples 7.1 and 7.2). The two tripla are rhythmically and melodically identical and at the same pitch level (beginning on *f*). Shared poetic elements are shown in bold in Examples 7.1 and 7.2: the opening word 'Aucun', the shared '-é' past participle ending ('loé'/'trouvé'), and the initial conjunction 'but' ('mais'/'més'). Though brief, the correspondence of both music and text in Adam's and Petrus's incipits is strikingly exact, and it is underlined by the identical harmonic outline of bar 1 of both motets (with the same opening *F/c/f* sonority that progresses to *a/e*). Although the melodic profile of this triplum opening is not especially distinctive in the wider context of Mo 7 and 8, only these two motets have it in common. Textually, the opening word 'Aucun' is found in two further late thirteenth-century motets: *Aucuns vont souvent/Amor, qui cor vulnerat/Kyrie eleison* (no. 264, which directly follows Adam's *Aucun se sont loé* in Mo 7 and is also preserved in Tu) and *Aucun, qui ne sevent servir Amour/Iure tuis/[Virgo] Maria* (a unicum in Mo 8, no. 317).[18] Neither of these two 'Aucun' motets has any direct musical or further poetic connections with Adam's and Petrus's incipit, but significantly both tripla are among the small number of motets in Mo that may be described as Petronian, since they follow Petrus in their division of the perfect breve beyond Franconian limits, here into as many as six

---

[18]   See the comparison of 'Aucun' motet incipits in Bradley 2022a, pp. 44–45.

syllabic semibreves.[19] This suggests that the 'Aucun' text opening became somehow linked with Petrus's multi-semibreve style, a convention that could, in turn, have encompassed the awareness that Petrus himself inherited the incipit from Adam.

Petrus's *Aucun ont trouvé* triplum seems to be a direct musical and textual response to Adam's *Aucun se sont loé*, and the principal divergence between these two 'Aucun' incipits is telling is this regard. Where Adam's three-semibreve group is melismatic (carrying the single syllable 'se'), Petrus's is syllabic (setting the three syllables 'ont trouvé'). This encapsulates precisely the difference between their musical styles. Syllabic semibreves are the hallmark of Petrus's known motets, but two of Adam's five motets do not feature individually texted semibreves at all, and the remaining three rarely reach, let alone exceed, Franco's three-semibreve limit.[20] Petrus's addition of individual syllables to Adam's formerly melismatic semibreves appears pointed in the context of his triplum text, which begins as follows: 'Some [*Aucun*] have composed [*trouvé*] their songs from habit / but I have been given occasion / by Love, who re-emboldens my desire / so that I have to make [*faire*] a song' (see lines 1–4 in Example 7.2).[21] Petrus therefore explicitly sets his own process of composition in opposition to 'Some' who remain unnamed, but the very word 'Aucun', together with its accompanying musical material, identifies Adam. Adam's motet incipit stands in *Aucun ont trouvé* as an evocation of an older manner of song-making that is explicitly contrasted with – and here actually updated in – a newer syllabic semibreve style.

Petrus's portrayal of Love in *Aucun ont trouvé* is profoundly positive: it is Love that moves him to sing and inspires his song, which serves in turn as a means of communicating his respect, both for his beautiful lady and for Love itself.[22] The two additional Petronian tripla *Aucuns vont souvent* and *Aucun, qui ne sevent servir Amour* take a similar position.[23] Both defend Love against 'Some', who speak ill of Love only because they do not fully understand it and do not love loyally or deeply. Like *Aucun ont trouvé*, *Aucun, qui ne sevent servir Amour* explicitly links Love and song, declaring at its conclusion that song is itself the testimony to the power of true love. All of these multi-semibreve tripla stand in sharp contrast to Adam's *Aucun se sont loé*, which is a diatribe against Love. Although 'Some have praised Love', Adam blames it for pain and ultimately advises against loving loyally, since it leads inevitably to disappointment. The three Petronian tripla, then, exploit the opening triplum word 'Aucun' to the same rhetorical end as Adam: the attitude to Love of 'Some' who remain abstract is briefly characterised at the outset, as a basis to launch an extended, contrasting, and personal reflection. But the Petronian tripla go on to turn the message of Adam's motet on its head, taking the here equally well-worn but notably opposite position of praising rather than denouncing Love, and moreover

---

[19] For full details of the total of nine such motets in Mo, see Bradley 2022a, p. 78.

[20] See details of Adam's use of syllabic semibreves in Bradley 2022a, p. 9.

[21] This translation is adapted from Maw 2018, p. 181.

[22] On this, see also Maw 2018, pp. 181–83.

[23] See the respective editions and translations of these motet texts in Tischler (ed.) 1978–85, vol. 4, p. 86, nos. 263 and 264; and pp. 108–9, no. 317.

aligning a true understanding of Love with the inspiration, intensity, and implied superiority of their song making.

By texting the semibreves of Adam's 'Aucun' incipit and contradicting Adam's position on love, Petrus's *Aucun ont trouvé* opens with what seems like a manifesto for his style and philosophy of song vis-à-vis Adam's. In this context, it is tempting to propose that Petrus's choice of the initial verb 'trouver' – literally 'to find', but here meaning 'to compose' (employed in the same sense as in the noun trouvère) – could have carried an additional significance.[24] Even within the repertoire of vernacular songs, which often reflect on the act of their own creation, the usual verb to describe the act of composition is 'faire' (to make), while 'trouver' is employed only rarely.[25] As in songs, motets in Mo overwhelmingly prefer the phrase 'faire un chant' or 'chanson', occasionally specifically referring to the 'making' of a 'quadruble' or 'treble' or 'motet'.[26] In conjunction with a quotation of Adam's 'Aucun' incipit – itself more common as the first word of a song than of a motet – the selection of the particular verb 'trouver' in the first line of *Aucun ont trouvé* is therefore noteworthy.[27] Not only does it enable a shared '-é' past participle ending with *Aucun se sont loé* and create a lexical variety that additionally heightens the sense of contrast between Adam's and Petrus's modes of composition, but it might also invoke Adam's principal identity as a trouvère songwriter. Petrus, in his motet, seems therefore to embrace the inspiration of Love to 'make' polyphony in a new way, one that responds to and departs from that of a trouvère like Adam, whose own rejection of Love is invoked here as an old-fashioned style in which songs were 'found', out of habit.

---

[24] I have found only three additional instances in Mo where 'trouver' is used in the sense of 'to compose'. Two are in a construction where it is explained that Love 'me fait cest chant trouver' (i.e., Love 'makes me compose this song', in the triplum of Mo 5, no. 115 and motetus of Mo 7, no. 256). The third is in the motetus of Mo 7, no. 292, where again Love is the motivation 'de chanchon trouver', and 'trouver' falls at the end of a line, rhyming with other '-er' endings.

[25] Mason 2021, p. 240, identifies 122 songs that use the verb 'faire', while only twenty-six employ 'trouver', and the expression 'commencier' (to commence) a song is more typical, used in thirty-three songs. 'Commencier chanson' is very uncommon in motets, but it is used by Petrus in the motetus of Mo 7, no. 253.

[26] The use of the verb 'faire' in conjunction with 'chant' or 'chanson' is found, for instance, in the tripla of Mo fascicle 3, no. 42; fascicle 5, nos. 95, 116, and 128; fascicle 7, no. 293; and fascicle 8, nos. 316 and 324. Mo 3, no. 50 has 'ai fet un novel deschant', while Mo 2, no. 30 uses 'faire' to refer to a 'quadruble'; Mo 5, no. 82 states that it 'would like to make a little motetus/motet' (*voil faire un motet petit*); and Mo 5, no. 116 (as well as 'fere chançon') refers specifically to making a 'treble'. Mo 5, no. 131 states that 'cest treble fis acorder a deus chans' (this triplum has been made to accord with two voices), an expression shared with Mo 5, no. 114, which explains that 'Amours … me fet ce treble acorder' (Love … makes me accord this triplum). See the discussion of several of these Mo motets that reflect on their own processes of composition in Rose-Steel 2011, pp. 50–57. On medieval terminology for composition and composers, see the introduction to the current volume and chapters by Bent, Desmond, Everist, Parkes, and (for the composition of dramatic works) Doudet. See also Dolce's discussion of the terms 'tro(u)ver' and 'trouvère'.

[27] On 'Aucun' as a song incipit, see Bradley 2022a, pp. 46–47.

Quoting Adam's 'Chief bien seans' in the Anonymous Motet *Se je sui/Jolietement/Omnes*

Entre Adam et Hanikel/Chief bien seans/Aptatur was Adam de la Halle's most widely transmitted motet. Although none other of Adam's motets is preserved in more than three independent music manuscripts, this composition survives in six.[28] Its motetus incipit was also cited, although incorrectly in connection with a different melody, in the treatise *De arte discantandi* by the theorist known as Anonymous V.[29] *Entre Adam et Hanikel/Chief bien seans/Aptatur* does not contain any apparent self-quotations, but Adam exceptionally refers to himself by name in the third person at both the outset and conclusion of the motet.[30] The triplum opens by naming four friends, of whom Adam is the first, depicting jollity, music making, and dancing among them. The motetus is an extended description of the physical beauty of a lady, moving downwards from her 'shapely head' (*chief bien seans*), to her 'rounded stomach' (*boutine soulevant*) and 'all the rest' (*et plus li remanans*), to close with the declaration that 'Adam is taken' (*que pris est Adans*).

It is unsurprising, then, that a reference to Adam made by the unknown composer of the unique Mo fascicle 8 motet *Se je sui/Jolietement/Omnes* should involve a quotation from *Entre Adam et Hanikel/Chief bien seans/Aptatur*, as Adam's most widely transmitted and directly self-referential motet. *Se je sui/Jolietement/Omnes* presents, at the close of its triplum, the text and music (transposed up a fifth) of the incipit 'Chief bien seans' of Adam's motetus. Example 7.3 gives the opening of *Entre Adam et Hanikel/Chief bien seans/Aptatur*, for comparison with the last bar of the triplum of *Se je sui/Jolietement/Omnes* in Example 7.4. The 'Chief bien seans' incipit is unstable across transmissions of Adam's motet, both in the orthography of its text and, notably, in the details of its melody (all extant versions of the motetus incipit are given in Example 7.3).[31] The quotation of the incipit at the end of *Se je sui* offers another orthographic variant, with the spelling 'cief'. Musically, the version of the incipit in the Mo 8 motet quotation seems best to match the fragmentary and incomplete copy of *Entre Adam et Hanikel/Chief bien seans/Aptatur* in Vorau, BAC 23 (Frag. 118D), the opening of whose motetus is itself closely related to the version preserved in Mo 7 and Ha. The final plica in the Mo 7 and Ha version (marked by a dashed box in Example 7.3 and also present in Tu) is understandably omitted in the context of the Mo 8 quotation, since the 'Chief bien seans' phrase functions here as an ending rather than a beginning.

Musical and textual quotations are central to the compositional ethos of motets throughout the thirteenth century. However, such quotations are usually of refrains

---

[28] For details of the transmission of Adam's motets, see Bradley 2022a, p. 9.

[29] The treatise survives only in the margins of Paris, BnF, lat. 15139 (hereafter StV), with the citation of Adam's motetus incipit on fol. 275r.

[30] See the complete texts and translations in Tischler (ed.) 1978–85, vol. 4, pp. 83–84, no. 258.

[31] Example 7.3 includes the version of the motetus incipit text in StV, in the margin of fol. 275r, where it is cited with an incorrect melody in the context of the treatise ascribed to Anonymous V, *De arte discantandi*.

Example 7.3. Opening of Adam de la Halle's motet *Entre Adam et Hanikel/Chief bien seans/Aptatur* (Mo 7, no. 258, fol. 280v, with variant versions of motetus).

or songs rather than snippets of other motets.[32] As Anne Ibos-Augé has observed, the practice of quoting motets in motets is a rare and apparently late thirteenth-century phenomenon.[33] Moreover, the particular voice part in which quoted motet material (usually an incipit) appears is normally respected in its quotation: most often it is tripla that quote triplum incipits (as also in *Aucun ont trouvé*).[34] The quotation of Adam's 'Chief bien seans' at the close of *Se je sui* is an exception to this trend, and as such the motetus incipit's appearance in its new triplum context is notable. On musical grounds, the decision to place this quotation in the triplum voice also appears significant: Adam's 'Chief bien seans' phrase could feasibly have sounded at pitch over the final *G–F* progression of the 'omnes' tenor, presented in the same range as the end of the *Jolietement* motetus and without the need for transposition up a fifth.[35] Indeed, Adam's 'Chief bien seans' incipit would have been much more in

32 Ibos-Augé 2019, p. 265 emphasises that 'Chief bien seans' is not a refrain but rather a 'fragment' quoted in homage to Adam.

33 Ibos-Augé 2018b identifies five examples of motets that quote motets (including *Se je sui/ Jolietement/Omnes* but not *Aucun ont trouvé/Lonc tans/Annun[tiantes]*).

34 Ibos-Augé 2018b shows that the triplum of *Par une matinee/O clemencie/D'un joli dart* (Mo 8, no. 309) is a patchwork of four triplum incipit quotations, while the motetus of *Au tens nouvel/Chele m'a tollu/J'ai fait tout nouveletement* (Mo 8, no. 312) is comprised of three different motetus incipits and two triplum incipits.

35 The presentation of 'Chief bien seans' at pitch in the motetus at bar 18 would produce an unsupported *G–c* fourth at the start of this bar; however, bar 17 also opens with the interval of an eleventh between tenor and motetus (i.e., an octave and a fourth between the outer voices). Although the final *G–F* cadence of the 'Chief bien seans' would sound in unison with the tenor, the upper voices elsewhere shadow the tenor at the octave fairly frequently (e.g., the triplum at the cadence in bars 8–9).

keeping with the slower-moving and melismatic profile of the motetus in *Se je sui/ Jolietement/Omnes.*

In the context of the triplum, Adam's motetus incipit has the textual and musical effect of appearing in quotation marks. Poetically, the first-person text *Se je sui* opens, very similarly to *Aucun ont trouvé*, with the poet's declaration that he is moved to sing by the true love of a beautiful and worthy lady: 'If I am happy and singing / it is with reason / because the beautiful, good, and knowing [lady] / gives me occasion' (see lines 1–4 in Example 7.4).[36] *Se je sui* then goes on to reflect on the beauty and virtues of the lady before closing with a return to the theme of song making, stating that 'I must indeed be serviceable / and make a song / because [her] beauty is a hundred times more / than is expressed by "a shapely head"' (lines 28–31). The poet, therefore, unequivocally compares his song specifically to Adam's *Chief bien seans*, asserting the superiority of his own expression. *Chief bien seans* offered a straightforward and detached, third-person description of a beautiful lady, with the emphasis strongly on her physical characteristics throughout, and perhaps a closing insinuation that Adam's desire for her was consummated. *Se je sui*, on the other hand, is personal and self-reflective, taking a loftier tone as regards love and the lady's good character, and making it plain that the lady, as yet, only promises – in her eyes or her regard – the noble reward and delight of true love that the poet desires, and which inspires his song. That *Se je sui* ends by openly quoting and disparaging *Chief bien seans* invites these two complete texts to be read against each other and underlines the marked differences between them.

Adam's quoted motetus also stands out musically in the context of the *Se je sui* triplum. There is a striking contrast between the densely presented text of this triplum – which is entirely syllabic and proceeds exclusively in semibreves and breves – and the noticeably slower-moving profile of the triplum's final quotation from Adam. The rhythmic values of this closing quotation shift, for the first time in *Se je sui*, to breves and longs.[37] Moreover, while the triplum *Se je sui* is freely declaimed, Adam's motetus incipit outlines the typical pattern of the third rhythmic mode. The quotation's single semibreve group is distinguished in *Se je sui* by the fact that it is purely decorative rather than syllabic, representing the first and only melisma of the entire triplum. Musically, therefore, *Se je sui* is distinctly more modern – with its non-modal, more rapid, and relentlessly syllabic text declamation – than Adam's modal and melismatic *Chief bien seans* motetus. By the triplum text's self-declared estimation, this newer syllabic style enables and represents a more expressive form of song than Adam's.

---

[36]   *Se je sui* shares the expression 'm'en done ochoison' with *Aucun ont trouvé*. In the latter triplum, it is also Love that 'gives occasion' to the poet to sing ('més a moi en doune ochoison'). The identical and possibly Picard orthography of 'ochoison' in both of the tripla as copied in Mo is also notable.

[37]   This invites comparison with the quotation in Machaut's ballade no. 12, *Pour ce que tous*, of the Denis le Grant refrain *Se je chant* (also the opening text of the motetus of Mo 7, no. 277), on which see Kügle 1997, pp. 158–62. In Machaut's ballade, the *Se je chant* quotation is similarly set apart by its longer note values.

Example 7.4. The anonymous motet *Se je sui/Jolietement/Omnes*
(Mo 8, no. 316, fols. 364v–365v).

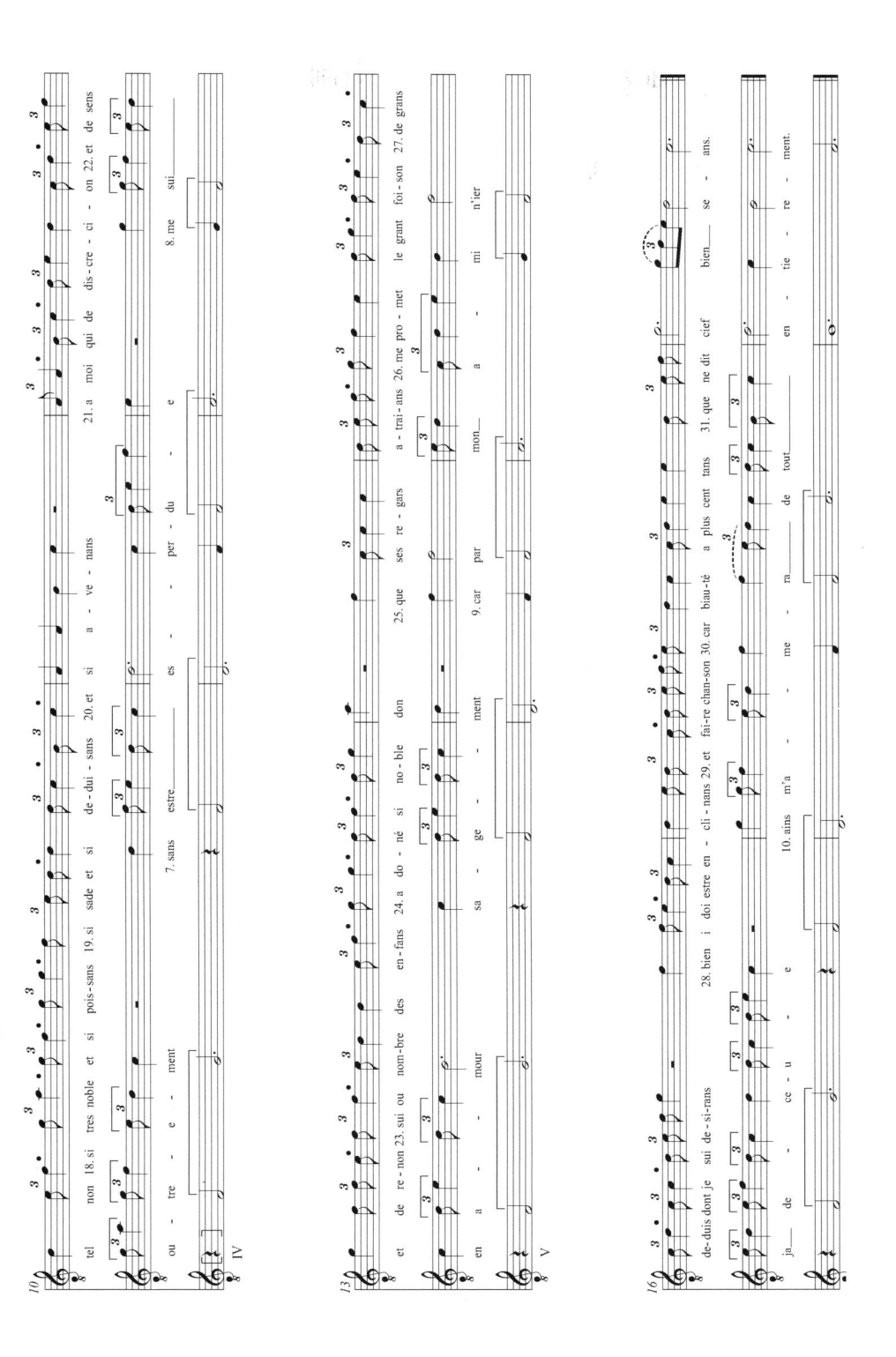

Adam's *De ma dame/Dieus comment porroie/Omnes* and the Motetus and Tenor of *Se je sui/Jolietement/Omnes*

The triplum of *Se je sui/Jolietement/Omnes* may not be the only voice in this motet to refer to and assert its superiority in relation to Adam. Demonstrably atypical features of both the *Jolietement* motetus and the 'omnes' tenor in this Mo 8 unicum may also constitute rather more oblique evocations of Adam and, specifically, another of his motets, *De ma dame/Dieus comment porroie/Omnes* (extant in Mo 7, no. 279 and Ha and included in the table of contents to the now-lost motet book Besançon, BM, I, 716).[38] The motetus of *Se je sui/Jolietement/Omnes* is one of a very small number of thirteenth-century motet texts in a female voice: its first-person text speaks (in line 9) of a male sweetheart ('mon ami'). A total of only twenty texts among the 325 motets of Mo are in a voice that is unambiguously female, although such texts are most prevalent in Mo 8, with six examples in this final fascicle (including *Se je sui/Jolietement/Omnes*), three of which appear side by side.[39] There are just three female-voiced motet texts in fascicle 7, and in all three cases the use of the female voice is inspired by the quotation of a rondeau by Adam: the motetus of *Mout me fu grief/Robin m'aime/Portare* (Mo 7, no. 265) quotes in its entirety the *Robin m'aime* rondeau sung by Marion in Adam's *Jeu de Robin et Marion*; the motetus of *Dame bele et avenant/Fi, mari, de vostre amour/Nus n'iert ja jolis* (no. 271) quotes from Adam's female-voiced *malmariée* polyphonic rondeau *Fi, mari*; and the motetus of Adam's own motet *De ma dame/Dieus comment porroie/Omnes* contains a self-quotation of another of his female-voiced polyphonic rondeaux, *Dieus comment porroie*. The use of the female voice in motets was not only often inspired by this mode of enunciation within rondeaux, but within the context of Mo fascicle 7, it seems to have been strongly and indeed exclusively linked to Adam.[40] Thus, in *Se je sui/Jolietement/Omnes* – whose triplum ends with a direct quotation of a motet by Adam – the presence of a female-voiced motetus text may also have recalled Adam's frequent use of this narrative voice, not only in his rondeaux but also in the motet *De ma dame/Dieus comment porroie/Omnes*. Adam's *Dieus comment porroie* motetus is voiced by a woman who sings principally of her physical desire for her lover, addressing her 'little belt' (*ceinturele*).[41] The motetus's female protagonist in *Se je sui/Jolietement/Omnes*, by contrast, describes the loyalty of her lover (line 5 in Example 7.4), closing by emphasising that he will never deceive her and loves her entirely (lines 9–10). These female-voiced motetus texts continue the trend in which Adam's motets

[38] On Besançon, BM, I, 716, see also Bent's chapter in this volume.

[39] See the list in Grau 2010, p. 184. I add to Grau's corpus Mo 8, no. 323, whose tenor 'non veul mari' is in the female voice. Mo 8, nos. 323–25 therefore constitute the run of three motets containing female voices.

[40] Two further motets in Mo seem to have inherited their use of the female voice from rondeau quotations, though with no link to Adam: the motetus and triplum voices of *Li jalous/Tuit cil/Veritatem* (Mo 5, no. 169) and *S'on me regarde/Prennes i garde/He, mi enfant* (Mo 8, no. 325). See the discussion of the rondeau quotations in these motets in Bradley 2022b, pp. 415–25, 430–36.

[41] See the complete text and translation in Tischler (ed.) 1978–85, vol. 4, pp. 92–93, no. 279.

espouse a view of love that emerges as comparatively worldly or base, in sharp contrast to the relative idealism of Petrus's *Aucun ont trouvé/Lonc tans/Annun[tiantes]* and of *Se je sui/Jolietement/Omnes*.

The possibility of a connection between *Se je sui/Jolietement/Omnes* and Adam's *De ma dame/Dieus comment porroie/Omnes* is heightened by the fact that these motets share the same tenor melody. 'Omnes', the only tenor used twice among the five motets ascribed to Adam, is employed to striking and exceptional effect in his *De ma dame/Dieus comment porroie/Omnes*. This motet is multi-sectional and unique in the thirteenth-century repertoire because it features two different established melodic versions of the 'omnes' plainchant melisma.[42] Adam creates an unusually intricate large-scale structure by treating his 'omnes' tenor(s) to a total of three different rhythmic arrangements, each repeated four times, and with refrain quotations appearing at structural junctures (the end or beginning of a new pattern).[43]

The choice of the 'omnes' tenor in *Se je sui/Jolietement/Omnes* is old fashioned by the standards of Mo 8, whose motets tend to favour vernacular song tenors or to inaugurate new chant tenors without an established history of polyphonic treatment in earlier organa and clausulae, or indeed earlier motets. The anonymous creator of *Se je sui/Jolietement/Omnes* employed, moreover, a nine-note version of the plainchant melisma (with two internal iterations of the home or final pitch, *F*, as in Example 7.4, bar 2, for instance) exploited by Adam in four tenor cursus of his *De ma dame/Dieus comment porroie/Omnes* but much less common than the ten-note version (with three internal iterations of the *F* final), also used by Adam in eight other cursus of this same composition and in most other late thirteenth-century motets.[44] Just as in Adam's *De ma dame/Dieus comment porroie/Omnes*, the Mo 8 motet *Se je sui/Jolietement/Omnes* presents the 'omnes' melisma in three different rhythmicisations (that of the opening cursus in Example 7.4; the pattern shared by cursus II, IV, and V; and the arrangement in cursus III and VI). However, in the Mo 8 motet, all of the tenor statements save the initial one open with an unexpected and rhythmically disorientating breve rest at the start of each tenor cursus.[45] In the context of the closing 'Chief bien seans' quotation in the *Se je sui* triplum – as well as the use of the female voice in the *Jolietement* motetus – the choice, melodic version, and rhythmic arrangement of the underlying 'omnes' tenor might all have been understood to constitute a further reference to Adam's motets. Once again, the invocation of Adam was an unfavourable comparison: it served further to underline the novelty

---

[42] On different versions of the 'omnes' tenor, see Bradley 2019, pp. 452–55.

[43] On the structure of this motet vis-à-vis its refrain quotations, see Ibos-Augé 2019, pp. 268–71. See also Bradley 2022a, pp. 19–20 and the edition of this motet in Tischler (ed.) 1978–85, vol. 3, pp. 112–15.

[44] Just six out of twenty-three 'omnes' motets use the nine-note, two-*F* version of the chant, while fifteen use the ten-note, three-*F* form. In late thirteenth- or early fourteenth-century sources, only three motets use the two-*F* version: *Dieus ou porrai/Ce sont/Omnes* (in Mo 7, Bamberg, Staatsbibl., Lit. 115 – hereafter Ba –, Vat, and Tu); *Je ne chant pas par renvoiserie/Talens/Aptatur/Omnes* (in Ba); and *Apello cesarem/Omnes* (in Oxford, New College 362).

[45] See the discussion of this tenor rhythmicisation as unusual in Wolinski 2018, p. 193.

of *Se je sui/Jolietement/Omnes*, drawing attention to its daring tenor rhythmicisation as more modern than in Adam's *De ma dame/Dieus comment porroie/Omnes*.

Se je sui/Jolietement/Omnes: A 'Petronian' Motet?

Whatever the degree to Adam was invoked in *Se je sui/Jolietement/Omnes*, whether explicitly only in the triplum or implicitly in all three voices, the unknown composer of this Mo 8 motet took a very similar attitude to Adam's motets as Petrus did in *Aucun ont trouvé*. The triplum *Se je sui* certainly shares its textual topos and declamatory style with the two known works by Petrus,[46] and this Mo 8 unicum was suggested by Richard Crocker, on purely stylistic grounds, as one of Petrus's possible compositions.[47] However, *Se je sui/Jolietement/Omnes* has typically been excluded from any 'Petronian' corpus because of the fact that it does not appear to divide its perfect breves into more than three semibreves but rather respects Franco's limit, making use of only pairs and trios of syllabic semibreves. As copied in Mo 8, the only surviving manuscript source, the triplum breve units that are clearly demarcated throughout by dots of division invariably contain either two or three semibreves. Yet there are two triplum phrases that, as recorded in Mo 8, must be erroneous. If the breve units indicated by dots in the manuscript are respected, the triplum phrases in bars 1–2 and 5–6 are too long for the amount of musical time that they can occupy vis-à-vis the lower voices.

In his edition of *Se je sui/Jolietement/Omnes*, Hans Tischler corrected both of these triplum phrases in different ways, and his readings are provided above the stave in Example 7.4 (which retains his duple division of the breve for semibreve pairs).[48] At the end of bar 1, Tischler converted a group of two semibreves within the time of a breve to a group of three (marked by a box in Example 7.4), with the consequence that the groupings of semibreves in the following three breves were reconstrued, contradicting the further three dots of division marked in the manuscript. In bar 5, Tischler's solution required two adjustments to the triplum as copied in Mo 8 (marked by boxes): the first was a change of pitch (from *b* to *a*) and the second the conversion of a breve-length *c* – copied in the manuscript as a square rather than a diamond-shaped note – into a semibreve, to form part of a three-semibreve unit.

---

[46] *Se je sui/Jolietement/Omnes* (Mo 8, no. 316) also immediately precedes in Mo the Petronian motet *Aucun, qui ne sevent servir Amour/Iure tuis/[Virgo] Maria* (Mo 8, no. 317), discussed above.

[47] Crocker 1990, p. 670. Maw 2018, p. 162 n. 5 doubts Crocker's ascription of this motet to Petrus on the grounds of its 'faster tenor rhythm and closer rhythmic mesh of motetus and triplum' in relation to other motets in the more established 'Petronian' corpus. On Petrus's stylistic traits, see also Zayaruznaya's chapter in this volume.

[48] Tischler (ed.) 1978–85, vol. 3, pp. 182–85. Tischler's solution is very close to that previously offered by Rokseth 1936, pp. 214–16. At the start of the problematic passage in bars 1–2, where there are two groups of semibreve pairs in the manuscript, Tischler accommodates an 'extra' semibreve by re-grouping the initial semibreves as a trio followed by a pair, whereas Yvonne Rokseth opted for a pair followed by a trio. In bar 5, Rokseth's rhythmic solution was the same as Tischler's, but unlike Tischler she tolerated a dissonant *F/c/b* sonority and did not change the triplum pitch *b* to *a*.

Both of Tischler's resolutions of these corrupt triplum passages – especially that in bar 5 – required multiple adjustments to the notation in Mo 8: several of the breve units marked by dots and their internal semibreve grouping are adjusted, a pitch is altered, and a breve is exchanged for a semibreve. The transcription of the triplum in Example 7.4 proffers alternative solutions for these passages in both of which only a single dot of division – the aspect of the notation that seems most susceptible to error or confusion – is disregarded in each instance, compressing two of the demarcated breve units into the space of a single breve. In bar 2, this results in a four-semibreve group at the end of the phrase, while in bar 5 it produces a five-semibreve group at the beginning of the phrase (both marked by boxes in Example 7.4).[49]

The solutions in Example 7.4 are more economical than Tischler's, requiring fewer adjustments within the phrases as a whole and without having to override pitches or rhythmic identities. However, they involve the introduction of 'Petronian' groups within a triplum that is otherwise 'Franconian'. Tischler was squeamish about groups of more than three syllabic semibreves within the time of a breve, actively eliminating in his edition of a motet in Mo's 'old corpus' (*Par une matinee/Mellis stilla/Domino*, fascicle 3, no. 40) two four-semibreve groups clearly indicated in the Mo triplum, and in its concordance in Paris, BnF, n.a.f. 13521 (hereafter Cl).[50] I have previously sought to undermine a strict distinction between 'Franconian' and 'Petronian' practices, demonstrating that melismatic four-semibreve groups were – and especially outside Mo – relatively common decorative features of late thirteenth-century motets and rondeaux.[51] I have also emphasised the fact that tripla that do not reach Franco's maximum limit for the breve – with exclusively pairs of texted semibreves – are the norm in Mo and other late thirteenth-century sources, while those that mix different kinds of texted semibreve groups – pairs, trios, and beyond – are in a relative minority.[52] Given that *Se je sui* is in this latter category and is one of the most syllabically dense tripla in the entire thirteenth-century motet repertoire, the introduction of a four- and a five-syllable group in order to resolve the problem of two corrupt phrases seems worth entertaining. Potentially, the scribe of this motet in Mo 8 was copying from a version of the piece in which dots of division were fairly sparing, as is the house style in the main body of Mo fascicle 7. Here, semibreve pairs are adopted as the implicit default unit and chains of semibreves are clarified only when it is necessary to distinguish pairs from other semibreve groupings (of three or more). If the Mo 8 scribe of *Se je sui* were adding dots to a less proscriptively notated

---

49   After the initial semibreve pair in bar 5, the dot of division in the Mo 8 triplum (fol. 365r, first system of left-hand column) is also extremely faint in appearance, apparently in a lighter or different ink than the dots immediately following.

50   Tischler (ed.) 1978–85, vol. 2, pp. 13–15. The analysis of *Par une matinee* in Cl in Curran 2013, pp. 81–84 respects the original notation and takes seriously the need to accommodate these two four-semibreve groups within the breve unit. See also pp. 209–10 for a comparison of the Mo and Cl tripla.

51   See Bradley 2022a, pp. 79–80, 84–88. See also Bradley 2023, pp. 20–26.

52   See Bradley 2022a, pp. 80–81. See also Desmond 2018c, pp. 141, 149–50. Desmond's categorisation of fascicle 8 motets according to texture and rhythmic characteristics distinguishes as a group those motets with three or more texted semibreves.

triplum (of the kind found in Mo 7), he could have failed to identify or understand the triplum's lone four- and five-semibreve group in bars 2 and 5, mistakenly introducing clarificatory dots within these larger groups. This would be in keeping with the fact that the scribe was elsewhere overzealous and somewhat inconsistent with dots in *Se je sui*, on three occasions inserting an unnecessary and uncharacteristic dot of division before a breve.[53]

Hypothetically, then, *Se je sui/Jolietement/Omnes* could be a Petronian motet in the strictest sense, with a syllabic triplum that divides its breves into more than three semibreves. Yet, even if the solution for the triplum with Petronian semibreves is rejected, this motet still shares the stylistic and conceptual aesthetic of Petrus's *Aucun ont trouvé*. Both tripla feature striking syllabic declamation at the semibreve level as well as self-reflective texts about song making and comparative invocations of Adam de la Halle's motets, opposing syllabic and melismatic modes of text setting. The relatively unusual use of varied tenor rhythmicisations found in *Se je sui/ Jolietement/Omnes* is also a feature of Petrus's two known motets (although both of these pieces use just two different tenor patterns rather than three).[54] *Se je sui/ Jolietement/Omnes*, then, shows awareness of, and seems actively to participate in, the same kind of Petronian musical, poetic, and indeed quotational practices exemplified in works that can – on the basis of external theoretical evidence – be securely attributed to Petrus. If *Se je sui/Jolietement/Omnes* was not actually by Petrus himself, it was clearly a composition by someone who knew and admired Petrus's motets.

This chapter has scrutinised attitudes to Adam's motets as revealed in the motets of his close but probably later contemporaries. As emphasised at the outset, the rather negative light in which quotations from Adam's motets are cast contrasts with a more straightforwardly positive broader reception of his songs, refrains, and polyphonic rondeaux. Why did a slightly younger generation of Petronian motetists take a different and explicitly combative attitude towards Adam's motets in particular? The five anonymous motets in Mo fascicle 7 that quote rondeaux and refrains by Adam do not do so in an obviously disparaging or comparative context. Rather, they seem to follow in the footsteps of Adam's own practices of (polyphonic) self-quotation and to pay homage to Adam.[55] Stylistically, however, these five Mo 7 motets are broadly comparable also with Adam's own motets in the same fascicle. None could be deemed Petronian in any sense, and only one of them features occasional syllabic semibreve trios, unlike the tripla *Aucun ont trouvé* and *Se je sui*.[56] Along with a shift in attitude towards Adam, these two Petronian tripla are

---

53   Throughout, and correctly, dots of division are not usually placed before breves in the triplum, but they are exceptionally provided before breves on three occasions (as reproduced in Example 7.4): at the start of bar 4, after the first semibreve trio, after the semibreve trio in the middle of bar 10, and after the final semibreve pair at the end of bar 10.

54   On this technique in the context of Mo 7, see Bradley 2022a, p. 118.

55   For a list of these motets and details of their quotations, see Bradley 2022a, pp. 12–13.

56   There are three syllabic three-semibreve groups in the triplum of Mo 7, no. 269, that quotes Adam's *Hé resveille toi* refrain in its tenor.

also set apart from other motets that quote Adam, not only stylistically but also by the genre from which they quote: motet incipits rather than rondeaux or refrains. Perhaps Petrus and participants in the Petronian style resented Adam's widespread fame and success because of what they considered to be his lack of skill specifically as composer of motets. Equally, Adam may have been quoted in densely syllabic tripla principally as representative of a particular mode of motet creation, as the embodiment of an older and now outdated musical and poetic idiom against which Petronian tripla defined themselves as new and superior. Even if derogatory, the invocation of Adam in this context is proof of a complex reception for his works and status. Adam remained a compositional figure with whose lineage the creators of Petronian tripla wished openly to associate themselves and against whom they felt the need to measure and prove themselves. These hints of a competitive and critical attitude to Adam's motets – expressed through quotation – ultimately confirm, rather than deny, his influence and legacy.

PART IV

THE COMPOSING WORKSHOP

8

In the Writing Workshop: Composing for the Stage in French during the Long Fifteenth Century

Estelle Doudet

The author is dead: a pilgrim, protagonist of the play *Le Jeu du pèlerin*, declares he has seen the tomb of Adam de la Halle in Italy. His claim sparks a discussion with two other characters about the 'clerc net et soutieu' (the elegant and subtle scholar)[1] whose talents were appreciated even by the princes. Is it true that Adam, a poet, a musician, and a playwright who 'savoit dis et chans controuver' (who knew how to invent speeches and songs),[2] is deceased? Which of his works will be remembered? How can we be sure that the 'canchons, / partures et motés entés' (songs, jeux-partis, and motets *entés*)[3] attributed to him are really his own? During the comic *Jeu*, Adam's authorial status seems to oscillate between truth and fiction, while the memory of his works appears both extensive and fragile among those who remember them.

Le Jeu du pèlerin is an anonymous interlude dating from the end of the thirteenth century. It was interpolated in *Le Jeu de Robin et Marion* in Paris, BnF, fr. 25566, the main collection of Adam de la Halle's works.[4] As an early example of a play-with-in-the-play, the brief *Jeu* anticipates the implicit and, in part contradictory, trends in the long-standing historiographic narrative about the pre-modern performing arts. On the one hand, it indicates that the aura of the 'great author', alongside the discussions on attribution, were phenomena already evident in French-speaking

---

[1]   Langlois (ed.) (1924) 1958, p. 70, lines 23, 37.

[2]   Langlois (ed.) (1924) 1958, p. 70, line 37.

[3]   Langlois (ed.) (1924) 1958, p. 73, lines 90–91.

[4]   The sole extant version of *Le Jeu du pèlerin* is contained within this manuscript: the initial scene of 133 lines serves as a prologue to Adam's *Robin et Marion* (fols. 37v–39r); a subsequent addition of seventy lines is interposed between Robin's lines 698 and 699 (fol. 47r–v); a final addition of eighteen lines is inserted between Robin's lines 723 and 724 (fol. 48r). The original text of *Robin et Marion* is curated in Badel (ed.) 1995, pp. 206–85 (with an English translation in Axton and Steven (comp. and trans.) 1971). For the supposition that *Le Jeu du pèlerin* might have been authored by Adam himself, refer to Brusegan 2004. Regarding Paris, BnF, fr. 25566 and the intricate reception and stature of Adam de la Halle as a progenitor of musical compositions, see the chapter by Bradley in the present volume. For additional insights into Adam, consider the introduction and chapters by Everist and Bent.

territories during the thirteenth century. On the other hand, it reinforces the notion that between the mid-twelfth and mid-sixteenth centuries, being an author was precarious. Only a select few writers, such as Adam de la Halle and Jean Bodel in the thirteenth century, could be seen as examples of dramatic composers. Similarly, only a handful of performers, like the renowned actors Pierre Gringore and Jean de Pontalais in the early sixteenth century, could be seen as forerunners to Molière. In this regard, dramatic compositions written and enacted in Old French (twelfth and thirteenth centuries), followed by Middle French (fourteenth to early sixteenth century), would ostensibly predate the emergence of the playwright and the professional actor, both of whom are held to emerge, even originate, in the seventeenth century, according to this established narrative. How might we then understand the paradox of a history of theatre built around the 'great playwrights' subsequent to the Middle Ages, which would be, at the same time, a history that excises the 'great playwrights' from the Middle Ages?

The author is dead, Roland Barthes said provocatively in 1968.[5] His statement was intended to serve as a catalyst for re-evaluating the concept of authorship (*auctorialité* in French). Within this framework, it becomes imperative to regard as authors not solely the solitary geniuses who conceived singular works but also those who embraced a more collaborative creative approach, whether manifested over time through cultural legacy or enacted within communal networks of creation and distribution. This enables us to reassess the historical dynamics of theatrical authorship, by which I mean herein the unique methodologies and self-crafting practices employed by playwrights and the broader concept of theatrical *auctorialité*, a term encompassing cultural impact, social standing, and legal obligations accorded to an author. These ways of working are known to us today from dramatic works, archival documents (financial accounts, political and judicial decisions) and narratives (chronicles, fictions). However, such documentation is sparse for the twelfth and thirteenth centuries and for part of the fourteenth. By contrast, both plays and archives are numerous and well-preserved in French-speaking regions for the long fifteenth century (1380–1530). It is therefore this period, also called Middle French, that will be my focus.[6]

---

[5]   Barthes (1968) 1984 (English translation in Barthes 1977).

[6]   In this chapter, I have opted to minimize the use of the terms 'medieval' and 'Renaissance' for two main reasons. Firstly, these concepts are steeped in a value system forged by nineteenth-century theatrical historiography: medieval theatre was often perceived as primitive, while Renaissance and classical theatre were seen as more refined. However, such a value system is now outdated. Secondly, the surviving sources present limitations (with fewer than ten plays and limited archives, primarily from the city of Arras before 1300, compared to over five hundred plays and thousands of documents preserved in all French-speaking regions after 1400). These limitations hinder our ability to demonstrate a direct continuity in theatrical writing, staging, and production between the periods around 1200 and 1400, although such continuity is likely. Conversely, recent research indicates that despite shifts in dramatic aesthetics, the techniques of theatrical composition explored in this chapter remained consistent in France until the 1630s. On these epistemological issues, see Bouhaïk-Gironès and Doudet 2024.

The Middle French period is particularly interesting because it was a time for lexical revolution in the field of authorship. During that period, a new term, *composer*, surfaced to denote two distinct forms of expertise: an artistic skill allowing composers to arrange and organise textual and/or audio-visual elements, and a social proficiency involving navigating circumstances and meeting collective expectations. If the author refers etymologically to the authority (*auctoritas*), being a composer implies a certain mastery of the art of building relationships (*com-ponere*), both between the different components of a text and between the persons who work together to put on a show. In this sense, surveying those who composed for the stage in the Middle French period means investigating the functioning of a writing workshop.[7]

The notion of a 'writing workshop' was proposed in 1989 by Bernard Cerquiglini. He defined it in terms that have remained famous among medievalists: 'This continual rewriting of a work that belonged to whoever prepared it and gave it form once again. This constant and multifaceted activity turned medieval literature into a writing workshop. Meaning was to be found everywhere, and its origin was nowhere'.[8] The writing workshop invites us to renounce the ideas of origin and genealogy in favour of the vision of 'constant and multifaceted activity' undertaken by the makers of medieval texts. From Cerquiglini's perspective, however, the writing workshop was a metaphor, which aimed to draw attention to the collective dimension of medieval *auctorialité*. As far as music and theatre are concerned, the writing workshop is not a mere image. It concretely describes complex collaborative creative processes, whose sociological, economic, and legal aspects must be closely examined.[9]

I will begin by examining the emergence of the verb *composer* and the noun *compositeur* in French, which came to designate those who wrote for the stage, and by exploring the rhetorical practices these terms may have denoted. Once this semantic framework is established, I will lay out various modalities of theatrical composition in Middle French language, including reuse, seriality, and montage, which contributed to the adaptability of the theatrical text. Collaborations among artists also entailed concrete forms of social interactions and economic negotiations, at times fruitful, at times challenging, among those involved in composing dramatic performances. Ultimately, while the concept of the writing workshop indeed debunks the notion of the solitary genius, it does not undermine the author function (*fonction auteur*), as defined by Michel Foucault as a tool for social legitimization and legal control.[10] In fact, I will demonstrate that this dimension was significant for fifteenth-century French-speaking theatre, as individuals who served as public speakers, regardless of their roles as theatre makers, were already held accountable for the ideological and emotional impact of performances on audiences.

---

[7] For an examination of this concept and that of *faire oeuvre* in French, see Bouhaïk-Gironès and Doudet 2014, §3–4.

[8] Cerquiglini 1999, p. 33 (French version in Cerquiglini 1989, p. 57).

[9] For a thorough examination of these aspects in fifteenth- to eighteenth-century French theatre, refer to Chaouche et al. 2017. For a similar approach applied to other medieval corpora in Latin and other languages, see Coste 2021.

[10] Foucault 1977 (French version in Foucault (1969) 2001).

What Composing Means

In Paris, BnF, fr. 25566, the lyrical and dramatic works that Adam de la Halle 'fist' [wrote] conclude precisely where the singular known version of *Le Jeu de saint Nicolas*, 'que Jehan Bodel fist' [crafted by Jehan Bodel], begins (fol. 83r).[11] An identical verb, *faire*, characterizes the authorship of the two most renowned playwrights of the thirteenth century.[12]

From the end of the thirteenth century, the lexicon of literary endeavour underwent two distinct transformations.[13] On the one hand, the existing action verbs were complemented by new nouns: from *faire* (to make) were derived the *faiseur*, the *facteur*, and in a specifically theatrical sense, the *fatiste*, the one who wrote a play by reusing textual materials. 'Selon ce qu'il plaist au faiseur' (according to the maker's taste) is a common phrase in Eustache Deschamps's *L'Art de dictier*, the first work of poetry dedicated, in 1392, to artificial music and to 'the other music called natural' – that is, to versification in French.[14] On the other hand, between 1300 and 1500, the lexicon used to describe authors underwent significant diversification; *auctor, actor, escripvain, poete, rhetoricien, orateur, composeur*, and *compositeur* emerged. Written around 1460 and printed in 1500, *L'Instructif de seconde rhétorique*, the initial French rhetorical treatise to reference dramatic writing, frequently employs the verb *composer*.[15] Fifty years later, the performer and playwright Pierre Gringore presented himself to Queen Mary of England, whose royal entry into Paris he orchestrated in 1514, as a follower of the 'orateurs, facteurs et compositeurs modernes en françoys' (orators, makers, and modern composers in French).[16]

If the surviving documents are to be believed, *composer* and *compositeur* were therefore common terms for theatre artists as early as the fifteenth century, while they seem to have become commonplace for musicians a century later. These words are indeed found in all kinds of documents commenting on theatrical practices. They fall from Philippe de Vigneulles's pen as the Metz chronicler described his fellow citizen Charles Cauvellet, 'qui estoit homme fort ingenieulx, compousoit bien et juoit farces et moralités' (who was a witty man, who composed well, and played farces and morality plays) but who was condemned for his involvement in

---

[11]   Bodel's original play is in Henry (ed.) 1981 (English translation in Axton and Stevens (comp. and trans.) 1971).

[12]   For comprehensive examinations of medieval terminology concerning composition and composers as applied to music, see the introduction of this volume as well as specific chapters therein by Bent, Bradley, Desmond, Dolce, Everist, and Parkes.

[13]   Doudet 2008.

[14]   Deschamps defines 'artificial music' as a 'science that enables, with the assistance of the aforementioned hexachord, the production of diverse correct notes from steel, iron, wood, and metals.' (Dauphant (ed. and trans.) 2014, pp. 582–635, cit. artificial music p. 588, cit. 'faiseurs', pp. 590, 602, and passim). On Deschamps's notion, see also the chapter by Plumley in this volume.

[15]   Buron et al. (eds.) 2015, p. 109, lines 1183–84.

[16]   Brown (ed.) 2005, p. 127.

a conspiracy in 1491.[17] In town accounts they frequently surface, whether in French or regional languages, to designate the artists who received payment; it was the case in Avignon, where nine ecus were paid to 'al mestre qui a composset une farce ho la moralytat a 5 personnagez' (to the master who composed a farce, along with the morality play with five characters) for a show performed at the city hall in 1519.[18] Finally and obviously, the playwrights called themselves *composeurs* or *compositeurs*, sometimes with insistence. The young Orléans lawyer Jacques Milet, who wrote the monumental *Histoire de la destruction de Troie la grant* in 1450, reiterated this term in the concluding epistle of his play ('Moy dessus nommé compositeur et translateur de l'istoire precedent' [I, the composer and translator of the aforementioned history above]) as well as in his prologue:

Then I commenced contemplating
the authoring of the history of Troy
and embarked on composing it
striving to do so to the best of my capability... .
I attest that I have spared no effort
in composing with precision,
and I humbly entreat that the *Histoire* I have compiled,
the commencement of which ensues,
be received graciously.[19]

Milet's claim reflects the increasing theorisation of authorship that took place in most literatures in modern European languages during the late Middle Ages. In *De vulgari eloquentia* at the beginning of the fourteenth century, Dante distinguished between poets and inventors (*poeti, inventori*) and verse makers (*rimatori*), a term encompassing writers – potentially poets as well – who handle the technical aspects of writing.[20] In the following decades, this difference went hand to hand with a hierarchy in *auctorialité*, 'poets' having been granted a greater reputation than 'makers'.[21] But Milet's testimony makes it possible to specify this semantic framework in the case of theatre: by rhyming *composee* and *disposee*, the playwright draws attention to the fact that mastering the rhetorical skill of *dispositio* is the *compositeur*'s specific task. The young author did not of course invent the Trojan legend, but he was the first to stage it in French, which required him to reorganise the episodes of the legend, to redraw the characters, and to produce a new versification adapted to theatrical performance. *Dispositio* and *elocutio* appear here as complementary to that of

---

[17] Doudet 2018, p. 555.

[18] Doudet 2018, p. 509.

[19] 'Lors je me prins a pourpenser / De faire l'istoire de Troye / Et a mon povoir composer, / Tout au mieulx que faire porroie... . / Protestant que riens ne desrogue / A chose par droit composee, / En requerant d'umble pensee / Qu'on prengne en bon entendement / L'istoire par moy disposee, / Dont s'ensuit le commencement' (Paris, BnF, fr. 24333, fols. 8r–9v, lines 273–76 and 323–28).

[20] Fenzi with Formisano and Montuori (eds.) 2012.

[21] Armstrong and Kay 2011, p. 11.

inventio, which involves the original conception of the subject, and to that of *actio*, which concerns staging and performance.[22]

The rhetorical significance of the verb *composer* in Middle French is evidenced by various sources. One of the most noteworthy instances to have attracted scholarly interest[23] involves the collaboration between Jean Marchand and Pierre Gringore, who jointly orchestrated the official entries of French kings and queens into Paris for over fifteen years (1500–1517). Marchand was identified as a master carpenter; the records of the royal ceremonies consistently designate him as such. Gringore was both a playwright and an actor; he received payment for his role as a 'compositeur' (composer) in 1501 and 1502, as 'facteur et inventif' (maker and inventor) in 1504, as 'historien et facteur' (historian and maker) in 1514, and as 'compositeur et historien' (composer and historian) in 1517.[24] Although their exact meaning eludes us, these terms denote complementary rhetorical skills, all of which Gringore mastered, yet which several writers could have shared under different circumstances. In any case, the notion that 'composer' may have encompassed both stage writing and adherence to certain theatrical techniques now prompts us to delve into the realm of theatrical composition.

The Means of Composing

Theatrical texts are by nature characterised by their capacity to evolve. From an author's lines to an actor's words and ultimately to a reader's pages, a multitude of opportunities for textual mobility abound. This subject has been extensively explored by historians for the modern period.[25] However, medieval dramatic cultures have received far less scrutiny, despite the fifteenth century being a golden era for the performing arts and the advent of the printing press in Europe. This period is inherently intriguing for investigating how such mobility functioned as well as the writing and editing techniques it entailed. Here, I will demonstrate that the available sources permit us to embrace a genetic approach to pre-modern and early modern creative processes, a methodology that specialists in modern and contemporary theatre have largely neglected and deemed nearly impracticable to follow.[26]

A few years ago, I was fortunate enough to discover, in a late fifteenth-century manuscript (Paris, BnF, n.a.f. 6514), the longest role for an actor currently known in pre-modern European performing arts. This is the role of Homo (the Man), the principal character in the morality play *L'Homme pecheur*; the manuscript was created for its rehearsals. It enables a comparison with the printed editions of this extensive

---

[22] Also, refer to the chapter by Everist in this volume, which explores the language of rhetoric as it pertains to musical composition.

[23] Bouhaïk-Gironès 2012; Doudet and Lu 2020.

[24] Hindley (ed.) 2000, pp. 20–26.

[25] Chartier 2014.

[26] Thomasseau 2010.

penitential morality play, in Paris around 1494–99.[27] The exceptional preservation of two versions of the same work, one designed for the stage and another for the book market, sheds light on the different rhetorical techniques used by those who prepared the scenario and lines for performance and those who prepared the text for reading.[28]

The role reveals a play that is shorter and more concentrated than the printed version, staging about twenty characters; their interactions seem carefully organised by brief stage instructions which as yet remain obscure. The printed volume, on the other hand, presents a play animated by about sixty characters, whose lines are adorned with oratory effects and complex versification. It would be reductive to consider these witnesses merely as the short and long versions of the same play. Rather, an examination of the stage directions reveals two different dynamics of theatrical *composition*: the role was written to guide the actor, to prepare his memory and his body for the performance, much as a musical score might do today; the print was designed to allow buyers to imagine retrospectively a show that most had not seen, by offering them a highly spectacular text in terms of rhyming and stage design.

Such flexibility in writing existed even before the plays were performed and continues to be an essential dimension of a dramatic text from its inception. Among the *composition* modes often used by *fatistes* was the technique known as *faire par personnages*, which was very popular during the fourteenth century. Most of the plays preserved in French from this period are the result of dramatisation, adapting texts for the stage that already existed in a narrative or a lyrical form.[29] *L'Estoire de Griseldis en rimes et par personnages* (1395) is the theatrical adaptation of the famous tale by Petrarch about the patience expected from married women, translated by Philippe de Mézières.[30] Likewise, the forty *Miracles de Notre Dame par personnages*, preserved in Paris, BnF, fr. 819–820, were inspired by the rich European tradition of versified narratives about the Virgin.

The *Miracles*, likely crafted and performed on a yearly basis in Paris from 1339 to 1382, showcases two additional prevalent modes of composition: montage, entailing the incorporation of disparate elements into the dramatic text (in this instance, excerpts from sermons and sung rondels, alongside numerous polyphonic motets and liturgical items); and serial reuse of textual and/or audiovisual components, such as the recurrence of rondels across various plays.[31] Such writing practices imply a cumulative *auctorialité* as the composers follow one another by recycling the same

[27] At least four editions of *L'Homme pécheur* from the 1490s–1510s have been preserved, with Vérard's being the oldest. See USTC 49908, 70307, 70306, 49883. No modern edition.

[28] The role has been edited in Bénichou-Samson 2014; for a more detailed study, see Doudet 2020.

[29] Dramatisation, the adaptation of pre-existing lyric or narrative texts for the stage, is a process exemplified by Adam's *Robin et Marion*, which presents sung pastourelles. However, this particular writing technique should not be conflated with theatricality, defined as the capacity of a text to be performed, a trait that was widespread in the twelfth and thirteenth centuries. Concerning the performative aspect of numerous debates and dialogues likely composed by jugglers in Old French, see Menegaldo 2010.

[30] Roques (ed.) 1957.

[31] Edition of the *Miracles* is in Paris and Robert (eds.) 1876–83. For study on the *rondels*, see Gros 1988; on the musical pieces included in the plays, see Wilkins 1974.

material.[32] They also suggest a collective authorship since the *Miracles* seem to have been written and performed within the Confrérie de Saint-Éloi (the guild of Parisian goldsmiths) although the exact history of their creative process is still unknown.[33]

Sources from the fifteenth century, which are considerably more abundant, afford a clearer view of the operation of the writing workshop, albeit with many details still shrouded in obscurity. The serial reuse of certain scenes is particularly striking in the case of the addresses to the public in the prologues and epilogues of the plays. The inaugural French morality play, *La Moralité du jour saint Antoine*, staged at the Collège de Navarre in Paris in January 1427, commences with four stanzas wherein a 'doctor' directs the audience's focus towards the penitential enactment about to unfold:

> *The Doctor*
> Listen, you who must heed,
> sons of Adam. We believe ourselves so wise
> that we refuse to heed anything
> beyond preserving our old ways of life.[34]

The same verses, this time recited by Christ himself, reappear in the prologue to *Mystère de saint Sébastien*, a play produced in the Lyon region in the last third of the fifteenth century:

> *Christ*
> Listen, if you seek wisdom,
> you proud people. You believe yourselves so wise
> that you refuse to heed anything
> beyond preserving your old ways of life.[35]

Although the precise modes of circulation of these lines across varied contexts remain unclear, they attest to the presence of rewriting networks employing efficient recycling methods. The same seriality, as depicted through the montage technique, can be discerned in the epilogues of plays that culminated with songs. In the Rouen collection, the most important theatrical anthology copied in French during the sixteenth century, many of the seventy-five farces and moral plays end with the

---

[32] For discussions on cumulative authorship and *auctorialité* in music composition, see the introduction of this volume and chapters by Parkes and Everist.

[33] On the production context of the *Miracles*, see Clark 1994; Maddox and Sturm-Maddox (eds.) 2008.

[34] 'Entendez qui devés entendre, / Filz Adam. Nous sommes tant sages / Que ne voulons a riens entendre / Fors maintenir noz vielz usages'. *La Moralité du jour saint Antoine* (edited in Doudet (ed.) 2019, cit. p. 65, lines 1–4) is preserved in a single manuscript (Paris, BnF, fr. 25547, prologue fol. 313r).

[35] 'Entendés si voulés aprandre, / Orgullieulx. Si vous estes sages, / Vous ne voulés en rien entendre / Fors maintenir vous vieulx usages.' *Le Mystère de saint Sébastien* is also known in a single version (Paris, BnF, n.a.f. 1051, prologue fol. 1v) and has been edited in Mills (ed.) 1965, cit. p. 3, lines 49–53).

line 'une chanson pour dire adieu' (a song to say farewell), which announces that the actors will leave the stage to music.[36]

Different constraints can explain why montage, seriality, and reuse techniques were chosen. The first aspect is associated with the expectations of those who commissioned and financed the performance. In this regard, it is unquestionably the mystery plays, the most lavish spectacles of the fourteenth, fifteenth, and sixteenth centuries, typically arranged by the civic and religious authorities of urban centres, that provide us with the most abundant documentary evidence. We know, based on the records of the performance, that the Burgundian city of Seurre asked André de La Vigne to write a new *Mystère de saint Martin* in 1496. La Vigne composed the 11,000 lines of the play in less than five weeks.[37] But purchasing such original creations was costly. Among other things, it meant hiring renowned *orateurs* like La Vigne (who had previously worked for Charles VIII, king of France[38]) and talented *poètes* capable of producing excellent quality work with a high speed of execution. Many organisers of mystery plays thus opted to purchase an existing text and have it reworked by *fatistes*. In 1501, the city of Mons acquired the *Passion* performed in Amiens the previous year. Likewise, in 1510, Châteaudun town councillors acquired a play depicting the life of Christ, which had already been staged in Amboise in 1507. They tasked the *fatiste* Aignen Charuel with expanding and enhancing the text, with the assistance of a team of copyists.[39]

A second form of constraint involves adapting plays to meet new staging demands or criteria. The textual material must then be reorganised according to the principles of *amplificatio* and *abbreviatio* to match the number of actors available to perform them. The Rouen collection encompasses two versions of *La Farce du poulier*, one featuring four roles and the other with six roles. These versions were likely tailored for commercial theatrical troupes, which frequently assembled four to six actors during the long fifteenth century.[40]

Indeed, company directors and actors also took part in the writing workshop. Exceptionally, a few of their workbooks have been preserved in the Middle French period. They underscore the potential impact of a third type of constraint on theatrical writing, a phenomenon Christian Biet termed the *séance* (the session). This

---

36 The Rouen collection (Paris, BnF, fr. 24341) does not include any musical notation; on the serial reuse of this musical announcement, Doudet 2018, pp. 292–93.

37 Duplat (ed.) 1979, p. 118, minutes of the Seurre performance (Paris, BnF, fr. 24332, fol. 260r–v).

38 La Vigne's title in the minutes is 'facteur royal' (Duplat (ed.) 1979, p. 118). He was recruited by the Savoy court immediately after the performance: see Brown (ed.) 1989, pp. 1–13.

39 For the Mons Passion, see Runnalls 2002; Châteaudun *Passion* has been lost, except for a fragment in Paris, BnF, n.a.f. 1445. However, the financial records of the performance have been preserved (see Couturier and Runnalls (eds.) 1991).

40 Paris, BnF, fr. 24341, fols. 132v–144v; the play with six characters has been edited in Tissier (ed.) 1997, pp. 183–234. The adaptation of the number of characters to the available actors for performance likely persisted as a theatrical technique, although well-preserved documentary evidence for earlier periods, particularly before the fifteenth century, is lacking. For insights into this hypothesis regarding Bodel's *Jeu de saint Nicolas* and other thirteenth-century plays, see Dominguez 2008.

pertains to the interactions between the stage and the audience.[41] The manuscript Florence, BML, Ashburnham 116 was, along with Florence, BML, Ashburnham 115, owned by the artist Jazme Oliou in the 1470s. Oliou inscribed his name multiple times ('Jaquemart bon compagnon' fol. 1r, 'Jacobus Olivi' fols. 3v, 28v) in this two-volume workbook, which comprises a repertoire of six plays, several songs and poems, and even a medical recipe 'ad habendum bonam vocam' (to acquire a good voice). One of the plays, *Le Jeu d'argent*, is transcribed with numerous additional scenes, three prologues, and two epilogues, evidently tailored to suit the diverse audiences Oliou and his troupe anticipated encountering in Avignon. For instance, the concluding address to a 'roiale magesté' (royal majesty), a possible reference to René d'Anjou and his court, was crossed out on folio 28r and substituted with a farewell to 'toute la compaignie' (the entire company).[42]

It is noteworthy that until recent decades, numerous modern editors of medieval theatre have downplayed this unexpected textual fluidity. At times, they have not mentioned the myriad traces left by the writing workshop in the manuscripts, such as the alternative versions inscribed in the margins or the graphical symbols denoting deletions and additions. Occasionally, they have attributed a *lectio textualis* status to these traces, deeming them either commendable or less persuasive based on their interpretation of the *intentio auctoris*, the author's intention.[43] Today, it is imperative to shift our perspective on these pieces of material evidence. What they tangibly reveal to us is not solely textual variation; rather, more surprisingly yet also more intriguingly, they unveil a process of creation.

Composers at Work: The Challenges of Collaboration

In 1468, George Chastelain, the official historian and *orateur* of the Burgundian ducal court, collaborated with the municipalities of Valenciennes and Mons to stage a play dedicated to the memory of Charles le Téméraire's deceased father, titled *La Mort du duc Philippe*. In 1473, Jean Molinet, a poet, and Simon Marmion, a painter, collaborated to produce 'comedies' in Valenciennes celebrating the knights of the Golden Fleece.[44] Guillaume de Gamaches, a schoolmaster in Beauvais, collaborated with the cantors of the cathedral, actors hired by the bishop, and the company of the Momeurs du Mont-Pinard to organise a performance commemorating the peace of Arras in 1483.[45] In the 1480s, Katherine Bourlet, a nun in the convent of Huy (Liège), undertook the task of transcribing and adapting for the stage famous penitential texts from the fourteenth century, such as *Le Pèlerinage de vie humaine*, in collaboration with several anonymous Carmelites.[46]

---

[41] Biet 2009.

[42] Hindley (ed.) 2019, p. 470, line 1515.

[43] The 1929 and 2019 critical editions of *Le Jeu d'argent* epitomises these different approaches, developed in Hindley (ed.) 2019, pp. 312–20.

[44] Doudet 2018, p. 591.

[45] Doudet 2018, pp. 590–91.

[46] Doudet (ed.) 2012, pp. 306–25, 525–650.

A single decade's documentation of the performing arts in a single French-speaking region is sufficient to recognize the vast diversity of social statuses, cultural backgrounds, and economic incentives among those involved in composing theatre during the long fifteenth century. Despite this diversity, all these testimonies share a common thread: the individuals mentioned had to *composer* in the second sense of the word in French, which means to negotiate their roles as authors within collectives. This often resulted in dealing with complex and occasionally tense situations. The challenges raised by the sharing of authorship and, possibly, the contest for *auctorialité* before, during, and after the performances are questions I will try to address by taking two examples of collaborative work: *La Résurrection* performed in Angers in 1456 and *Les Trois Doms* in Romans in 1509.

In late May 1456, prompted by René d'Anjou, a three-day performance was organised, depicting the resurrection of Christ and its implications for humanity. The handwritten manuscript of the play, meticulously crafted in anticipation of the performance, 'does not specify who the author is', as noted by the modern editor.[47] However, the financial records delineate the duties for which the three principal individuals overseeing the performance were compensated. The largest payment was allocated to Jehan du Prier, the most prominent show producer in King René's court.[48] He received no less than one hundred gold ecus to 'convertir és faintes et despense du mistere' (convert this money into manufactured items and costs), for designing the staging, the scenery, the special effects, and financing their production. Pierre de Hurion received ten gold ecus for 'avoir habillé les personnages de la Resurrection' (for having reworked the characters of the play and rewritten their lines from an existing canvas). This task of composition suited Hurion's talents, as he was referred to as a 'habile imitateur' (skilled imitator) in *L'Instructif de seconde rhétorique*.[49] Finally, Jehan Daveluys was paid eight ecus for 'mettre au net le pappier de la Resurrection, et y avoir faict les adicions' (making a clean copy of the manuscript and inserting the additions to it). The example illustrates a well-organized collaborative working process, where various actions related to composition are allocated to distinct tasks and skills.[50] From what we can discern, the *Résurrection* was a success, memorable enough to be utilised thirty years later as a selling point, as I will elaborate below.

As early as the summer of 1508, the city councillors of Romans made the decision to stage a production called *Les Trois Doms* to honor the saint-martyrs Severin, Exupere, and Felicien. The initial task of writing the play was assigned to Grenoble canon Sibout Pra. After a few weeks, the town commissioners in charge of supervising Pra's work declared themselves dissatisfied. They then called on Master Chevalet, the most renowned *fatiste* in the Rhone region at the time, who agreed

---

[47] Servet (ed.) 1993, p. 9. For a new edition and comment of these documents, see Bouhaïk-Gironès 2023, pp. 99–104.

[48] Runnalls 1981.

[49] Buron et al. (eds.) 2015, p. 119, lines 12–13. On Hurion, consult H. Haug 2013.

[50] For insights into collaborative efforts in music, see the chapters by Plumley, Everist, and Bent in this volume; for art history, see Stones's chapter.

to help.[51] However, after Pra and Chevalet spent a few days working together, the latter decided to cease writing in collaboration 'pour ce qu'ilz ne volit pax besognier avesque ledit chanoine Pra' (because he did not want to work with this Canon Pra). While Pra and his clerk continued to work alone until May 1509, Chevalet was again called on at that time to 'radouber' (improve) some episodes, in particular the roles of the executioners for which this *fatiste* was famous. The persistent rivalry between the two authors and the ensuing textual flux are visibly evident in the manuscript copy of the mystery play (Paris, BnF, n.a.f. 1261), which incorporates the alternative lines composed by Chevalet in its margins.[52]

The 1456 performance of the *Résurrection* in Angers and the 1509 production of *Les Trois Doms* in Romans both illustrate some of the situations where the *compositeurs* were led to negotiate the sharing of their authorship, with contrasting results. Whereas the working process in Angers appears to have been efficient, with each collaborator being assigned a distinct form of authorship and thus complementary *auctorialité*, the unsuccessful collaboration in Romans reflects the uncomfortable situation in which the playwrights found themselves. The conflict between Pra and Chevalet should not merely be attributed to a clash of personalities, as a psychological perspective might imply, but can be analysed in sociological terms. They were writers with unequal reputations, whose talents were pitted against each other by those who commissioned their work. However, this example is compelling because it illustrates that collective authorship is a dynamic process in which playwrights are not the sole actors. Indeed, the failure can also be seen as a consequence of ineffective team management by the Romans officials, whose lofty expectations and excessive control exerted pressure on the artists.[53]

The work processes in Angers and Romans shared a common feature, which should not be overlooked. In both instances, the actors responsible for performing the plays intervened in the text they were to recite and adjusted their lines to suit their preferences. The changes 'que aucuns des joueurs d'iceluy mistere y cuiderent adjouster a leurs plaisances' (that some actors had added at their pleasure) have been censured by the reviewers of the *Résurrection* manuscript.[54] On the contrary, the roles that Chevalet rewrote at the request of wealthy Romanais such as Etienne Combez des Coppes were incorporated into the copy of *Les Trois Doms*, indicating the influence that the town's prominent figures exerted over the theatrical endeavour, which they likely regarded themselves as co-authors of.

Indeed, during the fifteenth century, some plays had no other *compositeurs* than the communities that decided to stage them. In December 1496, Chalon-sur-Saône

[51] On Chevalet's theatrical *compositure* and career before and after 1509, see Servet (ed.) 2006, pp. 14–15.

[52] For a comprehensive analysis of the unsuccessful collaboration between Pra and Chevalet, see Bouhaïk-Gironès and Doudet 2014, §7–25.

[53] The commissioners in Romans were also discontented with the painter François Thevenot and proposed that he expedite his work by collaborating with an artist from another town, an offer that he declined (Bouhaïk-Gironès and Doudet 2014, §26; Bouhaïk-Gironès 2023, p. 61).

[54] Servet (ed.) 1993, p. 12.

city council decided to express its gratitude to Saint Sebastian by performing a show dedicated to him a few months later.[55] Twelve members of the council, who were prominent figures in the city, were elected to undertake three missions. Firstly, they were tasked with 'veoir et corriger la ryme' (reading and improving the writing) of an already acquired text, signifying that these officials assumed the role of composers in the rhetorical sense of the term. Secondly, they were responsible for creating 'les chaffaulx, secretz' (the stage and special effects) and ensuring that all the necessary equipment for the performance was manufactured. Last but not least, they were tasked with directing the actors, assigning roles, and overseeing rehearsals in such a way that 'ceulx qu'ils cognoistront non estre souffisans pour jouer le personnaige a eulx baillé, qu'ilz pourront changer et bailler aultres personnaiges' (if they find out that some actors are not talented enough to play their characters, they could give them other roles).[56] What makes this example unique is that the writing, scenography, and staging of the mystery play were undertaken by the city council itself. In contrast, on other, more common occasions, the composition process relied on the collaboration of various actors within the cities. This collaborative approach is exemplified by the Lille procession, one of the most renowned performative events in French from that era.[57]

Hall of Fame, Walk of Shame: Standing and Accountability

In the 1490s, the printer Antoine Vérard published the *Mystère de la Résurrection* as a text allegedly from 1456 and 'composé par maistre Jehan Michel et joué à Angiers triumphamment devant le roy de Cecile' (composed by Master Jehan Michel and performed triumphantly in Angers before the king of Sicily). Michel had indeed composed a renowned adaptation of Arnoul Gréban's *Passion*, a reworking that was staged in Angers in 1486. However, he was not involved in any capacity with the team commissioned by René d'Anjou thirty years prior. As Vérard was known for his unscrupulous publishing strategies, we can presume that his erroneous attribution was intentional. Theatre is a commercial art, and theatrical authorship carries economic implications: fame translates into financial gain.

It can also entail complications. Since theatre is a public art, the creators of a production bear responsibility for its impact on the public sphere. This investigation will therefore conclude with the following question: how did the justice system of the long fifteenth century address the criminal liability of playwrights, considering the intricate dynamics of the creative process that I have just delineated? A few trials involving fifteenth-century French-speaking composers and actors have been

---

[55] The play has not been preserved, unlike that of the Lyon region on the same subject, mentioned above. But Chalon's municipal registers make it possible to reconstruct its creation process.

[56] Chalon-sur-Saône city archives, cited in Bouhaïk-Gironès and Doudet 2014, §28.

[57] Attested from 1270 and continuing until the middle of the eighteenth century, the Lille procession was overseen by the city council. However, in this instance, the shows were organized by entertainment experts, including leaders of joyful urban societies, and the plays were likely written by local clerks and/or performers. Seventy-two plays have been preserved in a single manuscript dating from the end of the fifteenth century (Wolfenbüttel, HAB, Cod. Guelf. 9 Blankenburg) and edited in Knight (ed.) 2001–11.

documented. I will briefly summarize two legal cases where the charge was *lèse-majesté*, an attack on the honour of the crown. Although this was a very serious accusation, both cases concluded significantly with the release of the detainees.

Jehan Savenot and his company were arrested in 1447 for having criticised the military policy of the king of France during a comic farce, part of the *Mystère de saint Éloi* performed in Dijon.[58] They informed the prosecutor that they were not accountable for the lines considered scandalous. They asserted that they had purchased a script from another company, unaware of any wrongdoing, as the play had previously been successful. Above all, Savenot pretended to ignore 'qui a esté le fateur et celui qui a ditte laditte farce' (who has authored and published the said farce). The director likely understood that asserting authorial responsibility and then making it impossible to attribute the play to a specific author was a crucial argument in his defence. This indeed presented a significant challenge for the prosecution, which struggled to identify a culprit. Consequently, the case was dropped.

When Henri Baude was arrested in 1486, along with the four lawyers who performed in his play which attacked the corrupt advisers of King Charles VIII, he did not deny that he was the author. On the contrary, the playwright wrote to his patron Jean II de Bourbon that 'il a fait qu'on a fait / jouer une brievfe moralité' (he arranged for a short morality play to be put on), with emphasis on the action verb *faire*.[59] While claiming its authorship, Baude cunningly shifted his *auctorialité*, or legal liability in this case, onto an institution beyond suspicion. He emphasised that the performance had been duly authorised by the Parisian Parliament and subsequently expressed discontent regarding the criminal procedure initiated against him by the royal court, considering it unjust. Baude, who was himself trained as a lawyer, based his argument on the fact that the prerogatives of the different institutions that were 'gardes et protecteurs' (guardians and protectors) of the public sphere overlapped and conflicted. Furthermore, he questioned who exactly possessed the legal competence to adjudicate composers and performers. Indeed, at that time, individuals who composed for the theatre had a rather fluid social identity and typically belonged to multiple social spheres: to the church as literati, to urban communities as citizens, and sometimes to the courts when engaged as administrative employees or remunerated artists. This intractable issue, coupled with the likely intervention of Baude's patron, ultimately resulted in the release of his group between July and December 1486.

As these two examples illustrate, fifteenth-century justice was evidently ill-equipped to contend with the argumentative strategies employed by show producers, playwrights, and actors, drawing from their multifaceted authorship and intricate *auctorialité*, not to mention their multifarious social status. When facing the risk of a conviction, the artists accused knew how to turn these dimensions into an advantage. But as those who wrote for the stage asserted their status throughout the sixteenth century, legal frameworks for regulating theatrical activities became more consolidated. Around and after 1562, with the onset of the Wars of Religion in French-speaking regions, the control apparatus was strengthened for both theatrical

---

[58] Documents edited and studied in Bouhaïk-Gironès 2003 and Bouhaïk-Gironès 2012.

[59] Baude's correspondence with Jean II de Bourbon and the trial records are edited in Quicherat (ed.) 1856, pp. 113–20. The case is re-examined in Bouhaïk-Gironès 2007, pp. 143–49.

and musical performances. Paradoxically, the gradual replacement in French of the *faiseur de jeux* (theatre makers) by the *poète dramatique* (dramatic poet), which traditional historiography dates from the late sixteenth and early seventeenth century, was contemporaneous with a judicial and social control of hitherto unseen force for the artists. Yet, the working processes specific to the writing workshop that I have tried to describe for the long fifteenth century never ceased to exist.[60]

Since the beginning of the twenty-first century, those who compose for the stage have increasingly been given or have claimed the names of *faiseurs de théâtre*, of *écrivains de plateau* (theatre makers, stage writers), rather than authors or dramatists.[61] Post-modern and post-dramatic approaches have criticized two supposedly typical aspects of the nineteenth- and twentieth-century European theatre: the sacred character of the theatrical text, which would not suffer any change, and the dominant role of the stage director, who would impose his vision on the actors. Instead, a continuous theatrical writing before, during, and after the performance is promoted and an *auctorialité* distributed equally between the theatre makers. It is noteworthy that in contemporary French theatrical culture, this demand for change is expressed in terms identical to those developed during the fourteenth and fifteenth centuries, when the *faiseurs* and *compositeurs* of plays thrived.

However, this recent movement should not be construed as an unconscious return to the Middle Ages. In reality, the writing workshop, along with the issues of cultural legitimisation, economic competition, and legal liability that collaborative authorship and complex *auctorialité* entail, have been constant themes throughout the history of European theatre. This raises the question as to whether the now obsolete text-centrism and the outdated tyrannical figure of the 'great author' are not challenges for theorists and historians rather than hindrances for theatre practitioners.

Undoubtedly, the 'great author' is a fascinating figure that sparks the imagination. Although the thirteenth century has scant surviving documentation of theatrical practices, the most notable manuscripts invited their readers to recall a few celebrated musicians, poets, and playwrights by portraying them as fictional characters. The scribe of Paris, BnF, fr. 1635 chose to present both *La Repentance Rutebeuf* and *La Repentance de Théophile* with identical titles and layouts. In the former, the poet confesses to the Virgin (fols. 2va–3ra), while in the latter, the main character of Rutebeuf's play *Le Miracle de Théophile* performs a similar prayer (fol. 83rb).[62] In Paris, BnF, fr. 25566, the sequence in which Adam de la Halle's works are transcribed – from the poet's youthful devotion to love and music, to the ironic self-reflection portrayed in the theatrical plays and finally to the aging writer's contemplation on death – delineates the idealised life of the devout Christian, while layering subjective experiences to captivate the readers' attention.[63] The mythologising of authors has been, and continues to be, a fundamental technique throughout the history of music, theatre, and literature.[64]

---

[60] Chaouche et al. (2017), pp. 31–37.

[61] Lehmann 2006; Tackels 2015.

[62] Zink (ed. and trans.) 2001, pp. 331–40, 568–74.

[63] Huot 1987, pp. 64–74; Badel (ed.) 1995, p. 10.

[64] I am grateful to Sarah J. Brazil for proofreading this chapter.

9

Facere, Componere, Invenire: Reassembling the Composer in the Long Thirteenth Century

Mark Everist

Composing, living as a composer, and the status of composition in the long thirteenth century are today fundamental objects of inquiry. Yet it appears sometimes impossible to discuss the concepts without falling foul of (post-)Enlightenment models of originality and creativity. The obvious tropes of the great composer are today perhaps subject to some scrutiny, although discourses are still, in the third decade of the twenty-first century, structured around Leoninus, Adam de la Halle, and Philippe de Vitry. Furthermore, the mechanics of composition are hard to separate from such established paradigms of inquiry as compositional process, reworking, and arrangement.[1] Studiously avoiding such terms as 'composition' and 'composer' in contemporary scholarship, however, seems as problematic as using them in unmediated ways more familiar from nineteenth- or twentieth-century musicography. An attractive alternative might be an understanding of the practice – of both *ars* and *techne* – of creating pieces of music derived from a number of sources: (1) what we know about the activities of individual actors (poets, composers, scribes, performers, and others); (2) comprehension of what surviving compositions, their sources, and their interactions reveal; and (3) a grasp of how musicians of all sorts talked and wrote about living as a composer. In short, 'being a composer' – or a 'compositional actor' – and the act of 'composition' are concepts that need recuperation for the Middle Ages in general and the long thirteenth century in particular.[2]

Theorising the Medieval Composer

By the third quarter of the thirteenth century, those who wrote about music were obsessed by innovations in rhythm and were content to talk about counterpoint as if it were essential but straightforward. But such theorists rarely spoke about the act

---

[1] Central to understanding the resonance of the term 'composition', its cognates and near synonyms are Bandur 1996 and the entries 'compositio' and 'compositor' in Bernhard (ed.) 1992–2006.

[2] The 'reassembling' of the medieval composer that the title of this chapter appropriates, and the coinage of the term 'compositional actor', invoke actor network theory of the mid-2000s, and especially Latour 2005, much discussed in studies of music since 1945 but with little penetration of repertories before 1900. See Piekut 2014; Born and Barry 2018.

of composition – or about works as compositions (as opposed to examples of rhythmic, notational, or contrapuntal practice) – and few were interested in music other than how it was at the time of the writing or, more frequently perhaps, how it might be in the future; Anonymous IV is a rare and well-known exception.[3] The language of rhetoric – of *dispositio, progressio, elocutio,* and *pronunciatio* – which was so important in earlier attempts to write about music,[4] yielded in the mid-thirteenth century to terms that seem to promise much for modern exegesis: the three infinitives of this chapter's title, *facere, componere,* and *invenire.*

Tracking these three terms through theoretical writings from Johannes de Garlandia to Johannes de Grocheo, from around 1260 perhaps to c. 1300, is less disappointing than one might expect. There are obvious risks in the close reading of terminological fragments, ripped bleeding from their logical and grammatical contexts, but such close readings simply point to not merely the wide range of terms that seem to describe what a compositional actor did in the Middle Ages but also to the interchangeability of those terms.[5] Whereas Garlandia used both *facere* and *componere* endlessly to talk about assembling ligatures, for example,[6] his immediate successor, Lambertus could say that 'and these [sounds] are investigated by showing their uses and comparisons between each other, and how every melody is *composed* from them' (et de hiis tractat ostendendo utilitates et comparationes eorum inter se, et quomodo ex hiis *componitur* omnis melodia) (emphasis mine).[7]

The author of *Ars cantus mensurabilis,* Franco of Cologne, appears to be clearer when he says that 'whoever wishes to *make* a conductus, first he must *find* the most beautiful melody [*cantus*] as possible' (Quia qui vult *facere* conductum, primam cantum *invenire* debet pulcriorem quam potest],[8] which then serves as its tenor. The use of the term *invenire,* however oblique in this usage, echoes broadly with the range of lexical convention around the terms *trouvère* and *troubadour,*[9] and *facere* has little ambiguity. The senses of 'make' and 'find' are here aligned with some precision. But the Anonymous of Saint Emmeram develops the usage of *invenire* to bring it even closer to such modern uses as 'invention': 'And note that its [discant's] *invention* was a necessity in this art, and this is because without it we were not able in any way to have a perfect knowledge of the concord in disparate melodies' (Et nota, quod eius *inventio* fuit necessitas in hac arte, et hoc est, quia sine ipsa in diversis cantibus

---

3   For Anonymous IV's role as a historian, see the exchanges triggered by Van der Werf 1992 and responses in the same volume by Edward Roesner (13–15); Giulio Cattin and Luigi Lera (15–16); John Stinson (17–21).

4   Sachs 1990. See also the chapter by Doudet in the current volume on the language of rhetoric as applied to drama composition.

5   For other surveys of the medieval terminology related to composition and composers, see the introduction to the current volume and chapters by Bent, Bradley, Dolce, Desmond and Parkes, and Doudet for the composition of dramatic works.

6   Reimer (ed.) 1972, vol. 1, p. 62.

7   Meyer (ed.) and Desmond (trans.) 2015, pp. 12–13.

8   Reaney and Gilles (eds.) 1974, pp. 73–74.

9   For a survey of the medieval occurrences of the term *trouvère,* see Dolce's chapter in this volume.

perfectam).[10] It was left to Grocheo to pick up on Lambertus and to deploy the word *componere* as a term that means something close to what might be understood as 'composition' today when he wrote that 'to *compose* ductia and stantipes is to determine the sound in ductia and stantipes through *puncta* and correct *percussiones*' (*componere* ductiam et stantipedem est sonum per puncta et rectas percussiones in ductia et stantipede determinare][11] and when he praised 'those who by natural industry and practice, have learned such cantus and know how to *compose* it' (aliqui qui ex industria naturali et per usum, talem cantum cognoscunt, et *componere* sciunt).[12] Like the author of *Ars cantus mensurabilis*, Grocheo reserved the use of the term *facere* for the construction of a tenor, alongside the use of *componere* as the term for the composition of a duplum.[13]

The wide etymological and semantic ranges of the terms *componere, facere, invenire*, and a host of others correspond to the equally wide range of competencies that constitute or impinge on the medieval practice of composition. It is self-evidently dangerous to assume that networks of practice remain unchanged from one century to the next. Indeed, it could be argued that the changes in such networks in fact define and delineate chronological segments in the history of medieval music more generally. The inventory of competencies that might be considered elements in a network of compositional practice could include writing poetry, creating monophonic music, creating polyphonic music, writing down music of all sorts, singing, writing down words, writing new words to old music and old words to new music, and assimilating pre-existing music and poetry to new contexts. Any or all of these competencies, in any combination, could make up the artistic persona of the compositional actor.

The technical competencies exhibited by compositional actors also extended to the management of the organisation of such large and celebrated codices, as for example, the Florence manuscript (Florence, BML, Plut. 29.1), the codex St Gallen, Stiftsbibl., Cod. Sang. 339, the Machaut manuscript Machaut Vg, or the Chansonnier Saint-Germain-des-Prés (Paris, BnF, fr. 20050).[14] Such inventories of competencies

---

[10]   Yudkin (ed. and trans.) 1990, p. 274.

[11]   Mews et al. (eds and trans.) 2011, p. 74.

[12]   Mews et al. (eds and trans.) 2011, p. 76.

[13]   'Sic enim unus iacet super alium ad modum tegularum et cooperturae domus et sic continua abscisio fiet. Volens ultimo duplum componere debet minutam abscisionem supra tenorem facere et ei aliquoties consonare' (Thus one part lies upon the other in the manner of tiles and of the roof of a house and thus continuous *abscisio* may be accomplished. He who wishes to compose a duplum to this must make a minute *abscisio* above the tenor and make it somewhat consonant) (Mews et al. (eds and trans.) 2011, p. 57).

[14]   These manuscripts were celebrated for different reasons in early philological and musicological studies. Before the advent of consultation online, the chansonnier Saint-Germain-des-Prés was one of the earliest manuscripts to have been published in facsimile (Meyer and Raynaud (eds.) 1892), while the Florence manuscript has been at the centre of scholarship on the music of the long thirteenth century since its announcement to the musical world in Delisle 1885a. The study of St Gallen, Stiftsbibl., Cod. Sang. 339 was the inaugural volume of the series 'Paléographie Musicale' (Monks of Solesmes (eds.) 1889).

are easy to draw up but much more difficult to theorise. What the Middle Ages hand down in terms of data about compositional actors and the act of composition problematises the nature of the act even more. The surviving composer corpora are instructive: those of Guillaume de Machaut,[15] Hildegard of Bingen,[16] Jehan de l'Escurel,[17] and Adam de la Halle[18] spring immediately to mind. And close behind comes the manuscript organisation of vernacular secular song with its hierarchy of composers. But is the status of each of these composers celebrated in these codices the same? There is much to be said for looking at the Machaut and Adam de la Halle corpora in similar ways – both created poetry, both were involved in the production of romance, both composed monophonic and polyphonic music, but how should the composer collections of Gace Brulé, of the Chatelain de Couci, or especially of Thibaut de Navarre be aligned with this tradition? Here, the presence of multiple melodies for the same lyric suggests that compositional acts involve rather more some sort of collaboration or competition than in the case of Machaut or Adam de la Halle.[19]

Questions of collaboration focus many ideas about *facere, invenire,* and *componere*. Relationships between Philip the Chancellor and Perotinus are instructive, for example, and Anonymous IV's attributions to Perotinus overlap with secure medieval attributions to Philip the Chancellor.[20] The overlaps do not involve the polyphonic conductus or even the motet but in a single – but rightly famous – monophonic conductus *Beata viscera*, four monophonic prosulae based on single voice parts from Perotinus's organa quadrupla, again attributed to him by Anonymous IV, and the recent discovery that Perotinus's *Alleluya V Posui adiutorium* quotes words and music from Philip's *Veritas equitas*.[21] Presumably Perotinus 'set' Philip the Chancellor's poem, *Beata viscera*, in the same way that Schubert set Goethe or that Berio and Boulez set E. E. Cummings. And it may also be assumed both that

---

Until very recently, Machaut Vg enjoyed almost legendary status because of difficulties of access. This has now been remedied by the publication of Earp, Leo, and Shapreau (eds.) 2014.

[15]   Earp 1989.

[16]   Two surviving manuscripts can claim the status of an author corpus: Wiesbaden, HLB 2, and Dendermonde, SPP, Cod. 9.

[17]   Arlt 1998.

[18]   Paris, BnF, fr. 25566. See Huot 1987, pp. 64–74.

[19]   The idea that the names appended to the works in the surviving chansonniers are those of the aristocratic poets and not necessarily those of the composers underpins the pathbreaking work on the transmission of trouvère song by Hendrik van der Werf in the 1960s and 1970s: Van der Werf 1965, 1972, and Van der Werf (ed.) 1977–79. For a discussion on trouvères as composers of music and/or text, see Bent's and especially Dolce's chapters in this volume.

[20]   For Anonymous IV's approach to questions of attribution in the conductus repertory, see Everist 2017. For Perotinus and Philip the Chancellor, see Payne 198, 1991, vol. 2, pp. 534–54. It should be clear on the basis of the thrust of this chapter that the recent proliferation of attributions to Philip the Chancellor on the basis of stylistic similarity should be treated with suspicion, such as in Traill 2003, 2006a, 2006b.

[21]   Payne 2017.

Philip took Perotinus's melodic lines and texted them and that the latter removed words from the former's conducti and just used their music. But such correspondences raise a number of further questions: Did Perotinus *always* set poetry written by others? Was Philip the Chancellor's poetic ambition restricted by *either* writing words to pre-existing music *or* writing poetry that he expected to be set musically by someone else? The danger of extrapolating more broadly from these slender data is clear: it is perhaps too easy to assume that someone who could deploy measured music and its resultant structures with the virtuosity that Perotinus exhibited was not capable of writing the poetry in those conducti that Anonymous IV ascribes to him. If Perotinus did not write the poetry to such widely known works as *Salvatoris hodie*, *Dum sigillum*, and *Relegentur ab area*, the complexity of those compositions – and their very close relationship between word and note – demands the hypothesis of a sort of collaboration that goes far beyond that found in *Beata viscera* or the prosulae on which Perotinus and Philip the Chancellor are known to have collaborated.[22]

Questions of composition and the activities of composers have focussed to a large degree on the attention paid to named composers and an emphasis on questions of attribution. The former certainly reflects modern concerns with avoiding the re-inscription of nineteenth- and twentieth-century thinking about composition onto the Middle Ages, since in focussing on named medieval composers there is the risk of replicating the nineteenth-century emphasis on canonic composers at the expense of the overlooked *Kleinmeister* or *petits maîtres*, so called. But this is much less an issue – necessarily, because so much is anonymous – in the extensive repertories of the conductus, most of the organum repertory and almost all the motet repertory.

Anonymity is inflected by chronology. Although there is no question that works without ascription are certainly more common before 1300 than after,[23] perhaps a more intriguing question is the degree to which anonymity may have been less complicated in the Middle Ages than in the later history of music and that searches for alternatives to anonymity might obscure other medieval preoccupations and values in music and poetry.[24] There is no shortage of alternatives to the simple binary opposition between ascribed and anonymous works. Terminologies used by art historians attempt to circumvent objections to cut-and-dried attributions. Such locutions as 'follower of a', 'workshop of b', 'pupil of x', 'school of y', or 'attributed to z' are more than familiar. Moreover, to move to the world of the decorated page, such formulations as 'Master of the Berry Apocalypse' or 'Master of the Bedford Hours',

---

22   For reflections and examples of large-scaled and multi-faceted collaborations, see Doudet's chapter for the composition of dramatic works, Stones's for manuscript decoration, and Plumley's for chanson composition.

23   On the inflection of anonymity and manuscript ascriptions by chronology, see the chapter by Bent in this volume.

24   This puts into perspective the sometimes febrile attempts to expand the number of attributed works to already named composers from Perotinus to Petrus de Cruce. In the case of the latter, Hans Tischler ((ed.) 1978–85, vol. 1, pp. xvi–xx) attributes every work in Montpellier, BIU, H 196 that deploys more than three semibreves in the triplum to the composer.

are mainstays of fifteenth-century art history,[25] and the 'Johannes Grusch' atelier is a well-known cornerstone in the same chronology as that of thirteenth-century sources of polyphonic music.[26] Indeed, such formulations have been used for the fourteenth-century motet.[27] These attributional strategies take a single securely attributed work or small group and attempt to anchor unattributed works to it on the basis of style. But an overview of Adam de la Halle's polyphonic music (especially the motets) is instructive in this regard, since at every turn, especially in the motets, if they were not attributed to Adam by a relatively unambiguous rubric 'li motets Adan', anyone would struggle to distinguish any single work from the vast repertory of anonymous motets in the seventh and eighth fascicles of the Montpellier codex (Montpellier, BIU, H 196) and related sources.[28] Adam's motets are so heterogeneous that they would not, were they not securely ascribed, be attributed to the same composer under any circumstances. In short, then, stylistic similarity – which every scholarly generation likes to think it can identify – does not necessarily map onto the identification of a single creative voice. Such art historically derived groupings as 'The Master [*sic*] of the Royal Motets' appear much more problematic when viewed in this light: of some value when identifying stylistic groupings but treacherous in terms of attribution and authorship.[29]

A consequence of these observations is to stress the various contingencies in play as a theory of medieval composition begins to emerge. A plausible place to start might be to interrogate the opposition between polyphony and monophony that is so deeply and – some might say – perniciously embedded in such scholarly tools as RISM used daily, although less inscribed in patterns of thought deployed more recently in work on motet and chanson. But thinking about questions of *componere*, *facere*, and *invenire* permits an effortless leap over this crude opposition: the network of competencies alluded to earlier not only rejects division into monophony and polyphony but allows those competencies to suffuse all types of music; to give very simple examples, contrafactum is no more the exclusive property of the polyphone than centonisation is the monopoly of the monophone.

Theorising the compositional act(or) usefully profits from revisiting another opposition: of simultaneous and successive composition. This is not to advocate a return to the analyses of the 1980s[30] but an attempt to open up a discussion of how a simple network of poet and compositional actor might work – the *Beata viscera* example is instructive – or, and more to the point, what happens when the compositional act involves, for example, both the poetry and music of a polyphonic chanson, a rhymed office, or a monophonic conductus? Does the composer write their own

[25] Meiss 1974, vol. 2, pp. 368–72; Campbell (ed.) 2009.

[26] Branner 1972; Baltzer 1972.

[27] For the 'School of Vitry' and 'Follower of Vitry', see Leech-Wilkinson 1982–83, p. 18.

[28] Everist 2019. For a reflection on stylistic analysis as a tool for attributing works, see the introduction to this volume and the chapter by Stones when it comes to art history.

[29] Leech-Wilkinson 1995, p. 316 and passim.

[30] Examples are legion, but citation of a couple of them are instructive: Obst 1983; Leech-Wilkinson 1984.

poem and then 'set' it as if it had been written by someone else, or do they work in a more cohesive way, moving back and forth between the manipulation of syllables and pitches? Further reflection might invoke questions of chronology, topography, and genre to argue quite reasonably that such answers are contingent on time, place, and musical type. Such theorising is also contingent on textual instability: not the type of paleographical disturbance between one source and the next but the larger types of volatility – that is, the existence of the same song in both three and four voices and of the same chanson with different strophes, the permutations of voice parts in the motet, contrafactum of all sorts and in all genres, and the constant substitution of clausula in the organum repertory. Opinions vary in almost all of these domains: for example, the traditions of thought around the *solus tenor* on the one hand[31] and on the other hand how to interpret the chronologically late mensural readings of the notation of various sorts of vernacular monophony.[32] Medieval texts are inherently unstable, but it is a further step to ask what this means in terms of the competencies of the composer: Does the composer who takes a Parisian two-voice organum and attempts to impart mensural signs to its notation around 1300 necessarily need to have been able to compose such a piece in the first place? Could they even read the original notation of, say, the two-voice *Alleluya V Epulemur in azimis* when they updated it to something approaching the mensural?[33]

And if theorising the composer is rendered complex by invoking textual instabilities, composers, performers, simultaneities, and successivities, the position is varied even further by thinking about notated and unnotated music. So much of what is understood of the work of the compositional actor – compositional processes, techniques, and conventions – is derived from close readings of works, manuscripts, and transmissions – and so, little from external features that the unwritten becomes even more of a challenge as compositional acts are probed and analysed.

Naturas Deus regulis 1: Intertexts

As an indication of how the act of composition might in fact be 'probed and analysed', the constellation of works around the variable-voice conductus *Naturas Deus regulis* may serve as an example. Variable-voice conducti are in two *partes*: the first (usually either the first stanza or the first two stanzas – as in the case of *Naturas Deus regulis* – of three) is set for three voices, and the rest of the work is set for two.[34]

---

[31] Differences of opinion around the *solus tenor* (the appearance of tenor and contratenor as a single voice part in a fourteenth- and fifteenth-century motet) hinge on whether it relates to questions of performance or composition. See Davis 1967; Bent (1981) 2002.

[32] Here, the issue is whether mensurally notated versions from around 1300 inform the rhythm of works from a century earlier that were copies in non-mensural notation, organum duplum and the *musica cum littera* of conductus. See Everist 2023.

[33] *Alleluya V Epulemur in azimis* is one of the works copied in the fragments preserved in Copenhagen, DKB 1810 4⁰ that rewrites the original modal notation using mensural shapes; see Bergsagel 1990.

[34] The sources and structure of the five surviving variable-voice conducti are considered in Everist 2020.

Broadly speaking, versions of the five variable-voice conducti in the manuscript Wolfenbüttel, HAB, Cod. Guelf. 628 Helmst. (hereafter W1) are presented with the three- and two-voice sections in order,[35] whereas in Florence, BML, Plut. 29.1 (hereafter F), they are divided into two, the three-voice sections being copied with the three-voice conducti and the two-voice sections with other two-voice works.[36]

The *Entstehungsgeschichte* of *Naturas Deus regulis* is complicated by the fact that it shares a terminal 'Benedicamus Domino' section with another conductus: the three-voice *Leniter ex merito*.[37] Although this complicates the history of the work's genesis, such melodic correspondences within the conductus repertory and between the conductus and other genres are not unknown. What is even more remarkable in the case of *Naturas Deus regulis* is that large parts of the poetry of its first stanza share images and specific lexical usages with an account of a miracle that purportedly took place during the Danish invasion of Abingdon Abbey in the late ninth century and reported in the later copy (what Hudson calls the B text) of the Abingdon Chronicle in the 1230s.[38]

Any understanding of the network of actors involved in such a work as *Naturas Deus regulis* requires a calibration of surviving and inferred sources against dates. For this repertory, most of the dates are broadly secure and are set forth in Figure 9.1. Considering the sources for the conductus, the earliest surviving witnesses are the two versions in W1 copied in the 1230s in Saint Andrews and the version in F, copied in Paris between 1245 and 1255.[39] The remaining sources ('terminal MSS' in Figure 9.1) either stem directly from the latter or more probably from an intermediary source now lost (b): Madrid, BNE 20486 (hereafter Ma), Wolfenbüttel, HAB, Cod. Guelf. 1099 Helmst. (hereafter W2), and Münster, ULB 382 (the last being one of several fragments from the reconstructed Soest manuscript);[40] in any case, they probably date from after F. It seems as if F and W1 descend independently from a source, now lost and identified as α in Figure 9.1, and that dates from a generation earlier: the 1210s. The only surviving source for this generation of manuscript copying is a collection of conducti (unrelated to the constellation of works around *Naturas Deus regulis*) is Troyes, MGT 1471 for which the poetry but not the stave lines or notation was entered into the manuscript.[41] Whether the exemplar for *Naturas Deus regulis* (α) is its original source or whether the work dates from before the 1210s with an origin in W1 is impossible to say, given the state of the surviving witnesses. None of the five variable-voice conducti betray any evidence of date in their

---

[35] Fols. 98v–101r.

[36] Fols. 211v–214r and 286v–287v. For the manuscript distribution, texts, and translations of the variable-voice conductus, see Everist 2018b.

[37] *Leniter ex merito* is preserved twice in W1, fols. 16r–v and 81v–84v (these two versions will be discussed below) and once in F, fols. 224v–225r, and its text alone in Oxford Bodleian Library, Rawl. C.510. There is also a fragmentary version in Cambridge, Jesus College, QB1.

[38] Hudson (ed. and trans.) 2002–7, vol. 1, pp. 270–71.

[39] For the dating of W1 in the 1230s and its location, see Everist 1990, with additional support from Baltzer 2008. The dating of F in Baltzer 1972 has not been contested.

[40] Maschke 2020.

[41] Bevilacqua 2016.

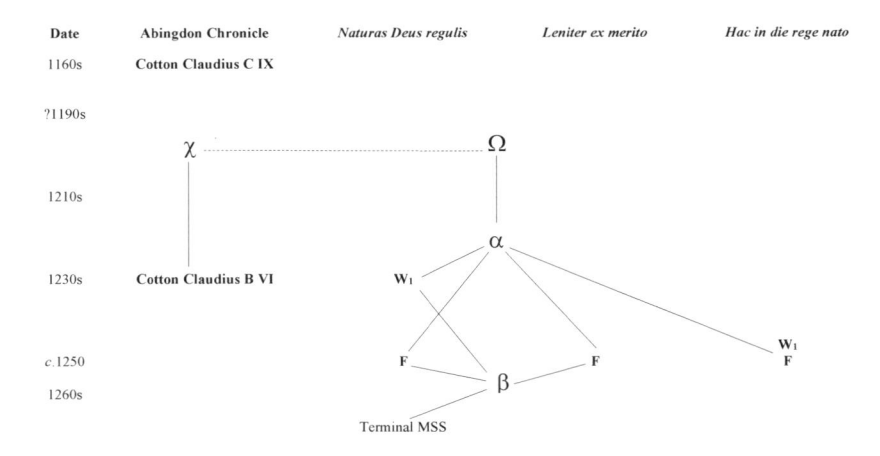

Figure 9.1. *Naturas Deus regulis* and related works: sources and chronology.

poetry. The situation is rendered more complex by the fact that the variable-voice quality of *Naturas Deus regulis* is reflected in different ways in different sources. The three terminal sources for the work – Ma, W2, and Münster, ULB 382[42] – preserve two-voice versions of the first two stanzas, and the latter source transmits a fragmentary two-voice version of the first stanza; none of the three retain anything of the work's variable-voice qualities as copied in W1 and F.

Both sources for the variable-voice version of *Naturas Deus regulis* end with a 'Benedicamus Domino'. In W1, this section ends the two-voice version of the work and is itself set for two voices. In F, however, not only is there a two-voice version of the 'Benedicamus Domino' at the end of the two-voice section of *Naturas Deus regulis*, but there is also a three-voice version at the end of the separate three-voice section of the piece. This three-voice 'Benedicamus Domino' is also found at the end of one of the two versions of *Leniter ex merito* in W1 but is absent from the three-voice setting of the work in F.

The 'Benedicamus Domino' *cauda* employs a plainsong in the tenor. In itself, this is not particularly striking: there are around two dozen conducti that conclude their poetry with the words 'Benedicamus Domino'; some of these seem to have had the text added later, while for others it is an integral and non-separable part of the text. Some works borrow various forms of plainsong for the 'Benedicamus Domino', whereas others ignore the chant tradition.[43] The 'Benedicamus Domino' *cauda* that ends *Naturas Deus regulis* and *Leniter ex merito* derives its tenor from the chant of the gradual *Benedicta et venerabilis* ℣ *Virgo Dei genitrix* (Example 9.1).[44] The

---

[42] Fols. 107r–109v, 96r–99r, and back flyleaf, respectively.

[43] For a discussion and inventory of conducti that make use of the 'Benedicamus Domino', see Everist 2018a, pp. 199–213.

[44] The identification was made in Bukofzer 1953, p. 82. Manfred Bukofzer's subsequent interpretation of the correspondence as the presence of a clausula is unwarranted: see

Example 9.1. Comparison of (a) 'Benedicamus domino' that ends *Naturas Deus regulis* and *Leniter ex merito* (F, fols. 287v and 225r) and (b) gradual *Benedicta et venerabilis V Virgo Dei genitrix* (Monks of Solesmes (ed.) 1961, p. 1265).

conductus tenor borrows the chant from the syllable '-go' of 'virgo' in the verse of the gradual and employs it for the syllable 'Do-' of 'Domino'. There is no textual variance between the tenor in the four presentations of the *cauda*: the versions of *Naturas Deus regulis* and *Leniter ex merito* in W1 and the two- and three-voice presentations embedded in the F version of *Naturas Deus regulis*. There is, however, no other witness to a polyphonic setting of the fragment, but it is possible that a monophonic version of this 'Benedicamus Domino' melody may well have circulated but for which no source survives.

The two-voice conductus *Hac in die rege nato* is also related to the complex of pieces orbiting around *Naturas Deus regulis* (see Figure 9.1). It is a widely celebrated conductus because it cites the incipits (all textual and some musical) of a large number of other conducti.[45] In the middle of his well-known account of the books of polyphony known to him, Anonymous IV mentions only three two-voice conducti by name: *Ave Maria, Pater noster commiserans*, and *Hac in die rege nato* 'in which', he rightly says, 'are contained the names of several conducti and similar things'.[46] The final citation of this piece matches the opening line 'Naturas Deus regulis' and therefore brings the work into the ambit of both *Leniter ex merito* and *Naturas Deus regulis* itself.

Robertson 1988, pp. 50–51.

[45] The work is preserved in just two sources: W1, fols. 174v–176v and F, fols. 332r–333v.

[46] ' ... in quo continentur nomina plurium conductorum, et similia' (Reckow (ed.) 1967, vol. 1, p. 82).

Also given in Figure 9.1 are the sources for the Abingdon Chronicle. All evidence points to the original text having been written sometime in the 1160s with the earliest witness (London, BL, Cotton Claudius C IX, hereafter Cotton Claudius C IX) being copied shortly afterwards. An enlarged copy of the chronicle (London, BL, Cotton Claudius B VI, hereafter Cotton Claudius B VI) was copied in the second quarter of the thirteenth century, at almost the same time as W1. This is important because it is this particular version of the chronicle that preserves the account of the ninth-century miracle that shares text with *Naturas Deus regulis*.[47] The text of the relevant passage of the chronicle – the *explanatio miraculi* – is as follows:

> Hec sunt Christi opera, omni laude digna, cui nichil est difficile. Qui licet **naturas** singulas **certis astringi regulis statuerit**, et sic providerit ut **a prescriptis formulis natura** eodem **nullo possint conatu ultra naturam progredi, vel per se citra regredi**, tamen earum **Auctor** quando vult, et ubi vult, et sicut vult, per quamlibet naturam, tam rationalem quam irrationalem.[48]

The text shared with *Naturas Deus regulis* is set in bold, as it is in the poetry of the conductus itself:

Naturas Deus **regulis**	God **ordained that natures**
Certis astringi statuit.	**Be bound by fixed laws,**
Et **a prescriptis formulis**	And **that he would not by any means be able**
Nullo conatu potuit	**To go beyond Nature**
Ultra naturam progredi	**From the prescribed formulae**
Vel per se citra regredi;	**Or to retreat within them through himself;**
Sed his ligari vinculis	But by these chains the **Author**
Ipsorum **Auctor** noluit,	Of these laws was unwilling to be bound,
Qui retrahit et tribuit	He who in turn takes away and gives
Naturis, quod vult, singulis.	To individual natures what he wills.
Sic ergo nostris seculis	Thus to our age, therefore,
Mortalis nasci voluit.	He wanted to be born mortal,
Quod eternus apparuit.	Because he had been made manifest as eternal.[49]

The lexical correspondences are clear, and – apart from the poem's authorship of the *regulae certae* and some slight changes of tense and mood – the meaning of

---

47 For a discussion of the sources of the Abingdon Chronicle, see Hudson (ed. and trans.) 2002–7, vol. 1, pp. xxii–vi and xxxvii–ix. I am grateful to Professor Hudson and to his colleague Professor Robert Bartlett for an informative exchange on the subject of the sources for the Abingdon Chronicle and of its relationship with *Naturas Deus regulis* (private communications to the author, 12–24 May 2022).

48 'These are the works, worthy of all praise, of Christ, for whom nothing is difficult. Although He has decreed that each **nature be bound by certain rules**, and thus provides that **by such regulations these natures cannot through any effort move beyond their nature or of themselves move back from it**, however their **Author**, when He wishes and where He wishes and as He wishes, may wondrously elucidate His marvels through any nature, both rational and irrational'. (Hudson (ed. and trans.) 2002–7, vol. 1, p. 47).

49 F, fol. 211v (based on Anderson's translation (see n. 53 below) with modifications).

both passages is largely the same. As will become clear, a reason is required for the appearance of the *explanatio miraculi*, and the inferred witness (c) in Figure 9.1 takes account of this. Questions of filial or collateral transmission between the conductus and the chronicle are paramount and are central to the following account of the compositional history of *Naturas Deus regulis*, its related works, and the compositional actors involved in this network of musical and poetic practice.

Naturas Deus regulis 2: Compositional Practice

The levels of intertextual complexity found in *Naturas Deus regulis* are rare in the conductus repertory. Poetic intertexts between conducti and biblical, patristic, or antique sources are common, but references as those in *Naturas Deus regulis* to such near-contemporary texts as the Abingdon Chronicle are significantly rarer.[50] References to text and occasionally the music of the liturgy – in the form here of the citation of the 'Benedicamus Domino' – are not unknown in the repertory. But the convergence of such a number of intertextual trajectories, while they make the identification of 'solutions' to such questions as compositional priority and even agency difficult, provides a valuable environment to interrogate the question of reassembling the composer in the Middle Ages.

Identifying the network of compositional practice in *Naturas Deus regulis* implies building an inventory of the actors involved, analysing the relationship between them, and defining their competencies. Actors, their relationship, and their competencies overlap and inform one another, and to illustrate how this might work, analysis could begin with the least complex: the three terminal transmissions of *Naturas Deus regulis* in two voices in Ma, W2, and Münster, ULB 382. It is too simple to argue that these sources merely constitute terminal readings in a complex source-critical tradition. The act of reducing three-voice polyphony to two-voice works and then copying it in a form (layout, notation, script, and *ordinatio*) not dissimilar to the more extensively preserved sources that are found in other parts of the tradition – conducti for two voices – constitutes its own art. A fundamental question is whether all three of the scribes independently removed the triplum from *Naturas Deus regulis*. Given the relative simplicity of the action, it is not at all impossible, but the inferred witness β in Figure 9.1 permits the suggestion of a lost source from which all three derive; it is not, however, impossible that one of the three could have served as the exemplar for the others. This means, in terms of competencies, that the scribes of Ma, W2, and Münster, ULB 382 could have been just that – scribes and nothing more – and that perhaps one of them, or the scribe of a now-lost source (inferred as β), felt capable of removing the triplum and the 'Benedicamus Domino' from their exemplar.

---

[50] The editions of the texts of the conducti edited in Anderson (ed.) 1979 document a number of biblical, patristic, and classical references. Whether this is Anderson's work alone is unclear. Two of the volumes (1, i and 2, i) cite the assistance of Alan Trelour, then reader in comparative philology at the University of New England, who may also have been responsible for some of the identifications.

With three, or perhaps four, actors and their competencies described, a broader picture of the compositional network of *Naturas Deus regulis* is possible. Figure 9.2 rewrites the data from Figure 9.1 in a way that identifies all the possible actors in the network and the ways in which they might interrelate. Here, *Naturas Deus regulis* again sits in the centre with the Abingdon Chronicle on the left, *Leniter ex merito* and *Hac in die rege nato* on the right; as in Figure 9.1, the diagram attempts to reflect chronology from the 1160s to the 1260s. A key chronological overlap exists between the B scribe of the additions to the Abingdon Chronicle (Cotton Claudius B VI, where the correspondences with *Naturas Deus regulis* are found) who was active in the second quarter of the thirteenth century and the copying of the W1 transmissions of *Naturas Deus regulis* and *Leniter ex merito* in the 1230s. However, although the W1 scribe records the earliest witness to the two conducti, the scribe of Cotton Claudius B VI makes the latest intervention in the text of the Abingdon Chronicle, notwithstanding the fact that the original composition of the chronicle and the two conducti could be coterminous in the 1190s (the likely but not necessarily earliest possible date for the conducti).[51]

The argument for at least two generations of activity between the composition of *Naturas Deus regulis* and *Leniter ex merito*, and their copying in W1, is strong. The chronology, provenance, and textual traditions of W1 and F require the presence of the scribe of an inferred witness (a) who must have been responsible for both conducti, indeed for most of the shared repertory in the two manuscripts; and the scribe of the inferred source a stands at least at one remove from the archetype (W) and its scribe. *Hac in die rege nato* must also have been copied in a source that predates a (since it too is also found both in W1 and F), quite possibly by the scribe of W, since *Hac in die rege nato* cites part of *Naturas Deus regulis*.

The last line of *Hac in die rege nato* quotes not only the first line of *Naturas Deus regulis* but also the pitches of the counterpoint, transposed down a fourth, of the lowest two voices. Since this identification runs counter to every description of the piece from Anonymous IV to Robert Falck's index of the genre from the 1980s, Example 9.2 gives the detail.[52] With such an elaborate and precise citation, *Hac in die rege nato* and *Naturas Deus regulis* could *not* have been composed at the same time and copied into the inferred source a; it is more likely that *Naturas Deus regulis* must have existed before so that *Hac in die rege nato* could have cited it – no later than in the inferred source a. *Hac in die rege nato* provides strong evidence for such a close relationship between poet and musician that they might have been the same person. It further strongly suggests that the individuals responsible for the pitches and rhythm of *Naturas Deus regulis* and *Hac in die rege nato* were *not* the same person since autocitation appears not to be the aesthetic imperative of the latter.

---

[51] The earliest datable conductus is *In Rama sonat gemitus*, which makes reference to the exile of Thomas Beckett, archbishop of Canterbury between 1164 and 1170. See Sanders 1984, pp. 505–30 and Payne 2001. A reading of the technical resources dated by Payne and found in the two conducti suggests a dating in the 1190s for *Naturas Deus regulis* and *Leniter ex merito*.

[52] See Anonymous IV's description above at p. 181 and n. 46; Falck (1981, p. 208) claims that 'only the first reference, to *Hac in die Gedeonis* … , is a musical quote'.

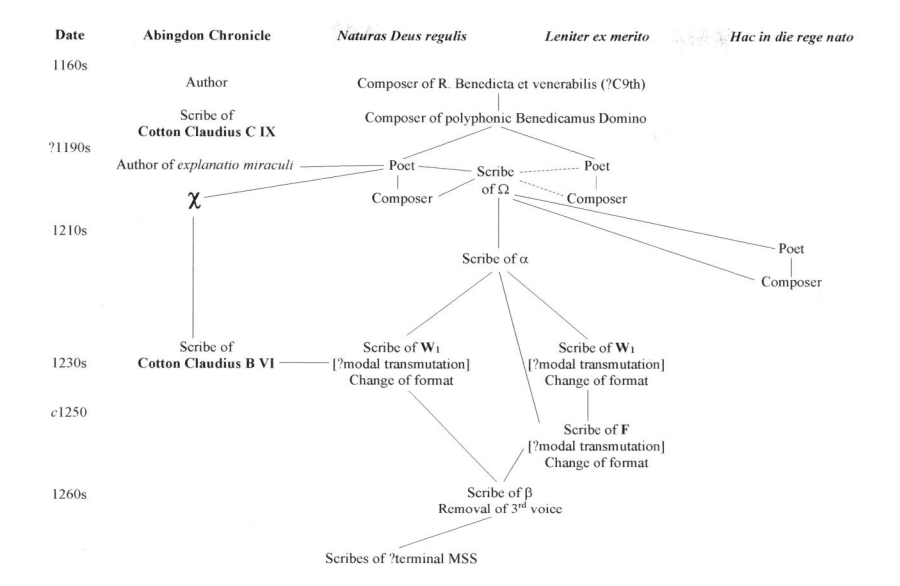

Figure 9.2. *Naturas Deus regulis* and related works: actors in the compositional network.

Example 9.2. Citation of musical incipit of (a) *Naturas Deus regulis* in F, and of (b) *Hac in die rege nato* in F.

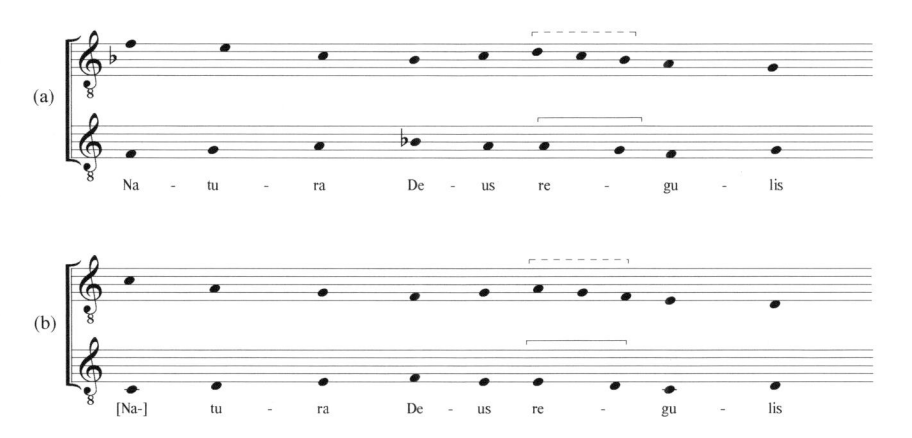

The search for the acts of composition for *Naturas Deus regulis* and *Leniter ex merito* leads to a chronological point at least as early as a generation *before* the copying of the inferred source a that served as the exemplar for W₁ and F. The two conducti are very different: *Naturas Deus regulis* is an ambitious, variable-voice composition, playing off a range of numerical proportions in the durations of its *caudae* across its three through-composed stanzas. By contrast, although *Leniter ex merito* is not as musically simple a work as the syllabic *Fas et nefas ambulant*, which follows it in F, it is a far cry from the complexity of the variable-voice conductus. Syllabic for the most part, *Leniter ex merito* modestly adorns its last four poetic lines and musical phrases with very short *caudae*; the first three of six *longae trium temporum* (hereafter LTT), the last of ten.⁵³ In its elaborate use of *caudae, Hac in die rege nato* is much more akin to *Naturas Deus regulis*, but its poetic and musical priorities obviously lie elsewhere. The poetry of the three works is similarly different. *Leniter ex merito* is a simple three-stanza lyric set strophically, with all three stanzas set to the same music, while *Naturas Deus regulis* consists of three stanzas of which the third is considerably elongated; *Hac in die rege nato* consists of two highly irregular stanzas resulting from its centonate construction.

Two of the three conducti – *Naturas Deus regulis* and *Leniter ex merito* – could have been created either by the same composer or different ones in the generation before being copied by the scribe of the inferred source a. The same competencies are required but simply in different measure. The ability to create two-voice syllabic polyphony is central to *Naturas Deus regulis*, and composing for three voices is also essential for both works. But the control over *discantus* – the technique required to create the measured and untexted *musica sine littera* – is as slender for *Leniter ex merito* as it is prodigious for *Naturas Deus regulis*. *Hac in die rege nato*, although probably dating from a generation after at least *Naturas Deus regulis*, shares many of its characteristics.

Each of the three conducti has a different ambition, however. The compositional actor responsible for *Leniter ex merito* barely exceeds an aspiration to go beyond the simplest syllabic three-voice texture, whereas the individual who assembled *Hac in die rege nato* not only exploits lengthy textual and musical quotations (this is unique in the repertory) but puts these in a frame replete with lengthy *caudae* that creates a numerical structure as complex as any two-voice conductus in the repertory. Whoever was at work in *Naturas Deus regulis* goes even further and exploits the variable-voice texture in an equally complex numeric environment. Whether a single compositional actor was, or could have been, responsible for all three works is unlikely for chronological reasons. However, the view that an individual working over a creative lifetime lasting from c. 1180 to c. 1220 could not have had the musical imagination to create all three works needs to be tempered with the equally valid

---

⁵³ All three works are edited in Anderson (ed.) 1979–, respectively, vol. 1, pp. 69–91; vol. 1, pp. 114–17; vol. 4, pp. 74–80; and in Tischler (ed.) 2005, passim. In both cases, the non-mensural *musica cum littera* is rendered in an erroneous metrical if not modal form, and in many cases the structure of the *musica sine littera* is distorted by the insistence on a 6/8 metre and the consequently irregular length of rests. Both errors are extensively probed and documented and historical reasons given to explain them in Everist 2018a, pp. 91–126.

observation that, even within the range of the three conducti presented here, the extent of musical competencies is relatively narrow, and the work of a single compositional actor cannot be ruled out. To accommodate all three works, however, it would be necessary to hypothesise compositional acts in two periods of activity, perhaps twenty years apart, and also for autocitation.

Poetic actors at work in this complex of conducti are equally varied. The centonisation in the work of the poet of *Hac in die rege nato* is a fundamental additional competency beyond the conventional deployment of end-accent, rhyme, and line length (syllable count) that underpins the composition of *rithmus*. It also argues, for the same reasons as the music, that the compositional and poetic actors at work in *Hac in die rege nato* were *not* the same as those who created the conducti cited there. The poetic impulse in *Leniter ex merito* additionally hinges on the borrowing of a couplet from the fifth of Ovid's *Heroides* (Oenone to Paris), cleverly divided between the first and fourth stanzas of the conductus as follows:

Ovid, *Heroides*, **Letter 5,** lines 7–8	*Leniter ex merito*, **beginning of stanzas 1 and 4**[54]
Leniter ex merito quicquid patiare, **ferendum** est;	(I) **Leniter ex merito / Ferendum** quod patimur; / …
Que venit indigne **pena dolenda** venit.	(IV) **Pena dolenda** venit / **Que venit** immerita. / …
[**Calmly must we bear** whatever suffering is **our desert**;	[**Calmly must we bear** / Whatever suffering is **our desert**; / …
The **penalty that comes** without deserving brings us **sorrow**.]	The **penalty that comes** without deserving / Brings us **sorrow**. / …]

Classical reference in conductus texts is significantly rarer than allusion to biblical or patristic sources but not unknown.[55] Aside from having the knowledge of Ovid's *Heroides*, the poet of *Leniter ex merito* has to be able to divide Ovid's elegiac couplets into two separate utterances and to transform them first into seven-syllable proparoxytones and in the fourth stanza into seven-syllable paroxytones and proparoxytones. The poet also has to modify Ovid's conjugations, moods, and wider lexical choices – 'immerita' for 'indigna', for example – and also to display an aesthetic sense capable of eliding the preoccupations of Ovid's abandoned fountain nymph into a clearly sacred poem that evokes the Garden of Eden at the end of the first stanza as easily as it evokes the Phrygian woods at its beginning.

Unlike the instances of *Hac in die rege nato* and *Leniter ex merito*, it is far from clear how the shared text between *Naturas Deus regulis* and the Abingdon Chronicle, as has already been set forth, came into being: a collateral borrowing from a common source or the chronicle borrowing from the conductus or vice versa. It seems unlikely that the editor or scribe of the version of the Abingdon Chronicle in Cotton Claudius B VI invented the ninth-century miracle and its *explanatio miraculi* which

---

54 F, fols. 224v–225r.

55 This example is identified in Anderson (ed.) 1979–, vol. 1, p. xl. See Showerman (trans.) (1914) 1947, pp. 58–59.

shares its text with *Naturas Deus regulis*. They likely had a source (indicated as г in Figures 9.1 and 9.2) whose substance could well have originated in the ninth century but whose precise text of the *explanatio miraculi* was a relatively recent addition. Indeed, the textual tradition of the revised chronicle text – origins in lost sources from the 1190s and copying in the 1230s – may well have mirrored that of *Naturas Deus regulis* itself.

While the same questions about compositional actors might be asked about poetic ones – does this constellation of conducti stem from one or several compositional voices? – a perhaps more pressing question concerns the overlap between compositional and poetic actors: whether the same individual write both text and music. The most restrictive view would have the music and poetry of *Naturas Deus regulis*, *Leniter ex merito*, and *Hac in die rege nato* created by a single individual; the counter-argument has however already been given: that it is unlikely that either the poetry or music in *Hac in die rege nato* was written by the same person as any of the works (and this includes *Naturas Deus regulis*) that it cites. The most generous view of the question would have separate poetic and compositional actors for each of the three conducti and separate individuals contributing poetry and music. To these six would have to be added scribes and performers, who might also have overlapped with any of the other actors, compositional or poetic.

A final constellation of compositional actors surrounds the construction of the 'Benedicamus Domino' chant and its incorporation into *Leniter ex merito* and *Naturas Deus regulis*. Even if the chant dates from after the late eighth-century core of the gradual repertory, *Benedicta et venerablis. V Virgo Dei genitrix* was still several hundred years old when an individual took part of the chant as the basis for the counterpoint on the words 'Benedicamus Domino' which is shared between the two conducti. But although this individual clearly does not form part of the same network of compositional actors currently under discussion, the person responsible for aligning the gradual fragment with the conductus exhibited some additional musical competencies. They were able to extract the chant fragment so that its syllable '[vir]-go' matched the destination syllable 'Do-[mino]' and to impart a metrical rhythm to serve as the basis of part of the *cauda* in *Leniter ex merito* and *Naturas Deus regulis*. As Example 9.1 has shown, not only is the excision of the chant meticulously executed, but the melodic fragment is then interpolated into a fully metrical context *sine littera*. The absence of any monodic or polyphonic freestanding 'Benedicamus Domino' based on the same chant fragment would at least allow the individual to be (one of) the same compositional actor(s) responsible for the rest of the musical work.

When the putative exemplar, inferred source α, for both W1 and F was copied, perhaps in the 1210s, the poetry and music of all three conducti had already been composed. It seems likely that *Hac in die rege nato*, given that it cites one of the other two works, was a later composition perhaps originating at the time of the copying of α with *Naturas Deus regulis* and *Leniter ex merito* being copied into α from what might be considered the archetype W or other closely related sources. This suggests that the network of compositional and poetic actors spans both the generations of α and W, stretching from the 1190s to the 1210s. Performers as supplementary actors in this network cannot be ignored, but they play a lesser role as compositional actors in conductus *cum caudis* than they do, for example, in two-voice and especially sustained-tone florid organum.

For the conductus, however, it is not quite so clear how a performer might play a role in the network of compositional activity. The levels of contrapuntal complexity in the *cauda* argue against anything other than a literate compositional impulse largely uninformed by performative input (which could include the arts of memory, improvisation, or both). In the same way, either the careful setting of a pre-existing poem or the simultaneous creation of poetry and *musica cum littera* seems to imply a more cerebral than an improvisational inclination on the part of the compositional actor. A possible exception involves the use of the *punctus organi* at cadence points at key structural intervals, where the manuscript variations and the variants within a single transmission betray a wide range of difference, and here, manuscript readings are most likely dictation of varied performances by others, heard and recorded, rather than any form of non-literate compositional act.[56]

If the creative network that ensnares the three conducti under discussion here extends from the copyist of W to that of a, it also needs to extend to the copyist of W1 in the 1230s and of F c. 1250, since the creative acts there go beyond mere copying and involve modal transmutation, questions of *ordinatio*, the transmission of the 'Benedicamus Domino' shared by *Naturas Deus regulis* and *Leniter ex merito*, and the question of the textual material shared with the Abingdon Chronicle. *Naturas Deus regulis* is found in W1 and F in modally different versions. Chronology of sources is no guide to priority in this case, since the original version of the work is first found in W and the modally transmuted version survives in one of the two surviving sources; this is a classic requirement for the possibility of *recentiores non deteriores*: where the more recent source may be as close or closer to the archetype than the older witness.[57] The modal transmutation applies necessarily only to the *caudae* – the *musica sine littera* – but in a such a complex piece as *Naturas Deus regulis*, there are passages that run from as few as five to as many as over seventy LTT. F matches W1 in a fair number of instances – where the modal structure and the resultant durations are the same – but there are also places where *caudae* in a 'short' mode (I or II) in W1 are transmuted into a 'long' mode III, V, or I with sustained *extensio modi* in F. A good example is the very beginning of the two-voice section, which sets the first syllable of the beginning of the third stanza: 'Pauper mundum ingreditur'; here, W1 gives a mode I *cauda* of 18 LTT whereas F transmutes this into a mix of mode V with occasional *fractio modi* (or mode I with sustained *extensio modi*) resulting in a *cauda* of 35 LTT, almost double the length (Example 9.3).[58]

Which constitutes the original and which the transmuted copy matters less in the present context than the question of the competencies of whoever made the changes: whether on the rue Saint-Jacques for F or on the north-eastern coast of

---

[56] For the *punctus organi*, see Everist 2018b, pp. 127–50.

[57] *Recentiores non deteriores* is a key element in classical Lachmannian textual criticism. See Trovato 2014, pp. 125–28.

[58] The modal transmutation seems not to influence or to be influenced by the textual differences between the two manuscripts ('Pauper mundum ingreditur' in W1 and 'Hic per mundum ingreditur' in F), although the two readings (and the fact that the version in F might well have been some sort of palimpsest) certainly complicate interpretation of the passage.

Example 9.3. 'Pauper mundum' cauda from (a) *Naturas Deus regulis* in F, and (b) *Naturas Deus regulis* in W1.

the north-east Atlantic archipelago for W1. Knowledge and deployment of modal rhythm are more important than control over contrapuntal progression as the revising compositional actor carefully rewrites the notation, changing ligatures and inserting additional *tractus* to separate out LTT. The individual displays as much musical acumen as any 'original' composer manipulating effectively the same tools. With the perceived sense of Paris as more a centre for modal polyphony than Saint Andrews, one might argue for the slavish copying from a related exemplar in Scotland and the creative reimagining of the *caudae* in Paris. Given the further modification of the *ordinatio* of the work (splitting the three- and two-voice sections and placing them in the appropriate part of the manuscript), the compiler of F might well have thought that further disciplining the contents of their exemplar might have aligned well with the overall plan of the book.

Compositional action during the copying of W1 and F also affects the question of sharing of the 'Benedicamus Domino' *cauda* between *Naturas Deus regulis* and *Leniter ex merito*. As far as the latter is concerned, the scribe of F simply omits the *cauda*, while in W1, there are two versions: a version with the 'Benedicamus Domino' *cauda* in the second fascicle and one without in the sixth. The subject of generic manipulation, *Leniter ex merito* is treated as a simple three-voice conductus and copied with others in the sixth fascicle of W1, whereas the version with 'Benedicamus Domino' is placed in fascicle 2 alongside organa tripla – including other 'Benedicamus Domino' settings – and other loosely liturgical works in three parts. The compositional actors at work in W1 were not only directing the form of *Leniter ex merito*, but they were also using the conductus to manage the *ordinatio* of the manuscript.

The fate of the 'Benedicamus Domino' *cauda* in the hands of the compositional actors at work on *Naturas Deus regulis* was more complex. In W1, where the variable-voice work is copied from beginning to end without a break, the 'Benedicamus Domino' *cauda* is found at the end of the two-voice section and accordingly set for two voices. The compositional actor in F, on the other hand and perhaps as a consequence, choosing to divide all the variable-voice conducti into three-voice and two-voice sections, presents the 'Benedicamus Domino' *cauda* twice: once for three voices at the end of the three-voice section and once for two voices (the lower two of the three-voice version) at the end of the two-voice section of *Naturas Deus regulis*. The later sources for *Naturas Deus regulis* – Münster, ULB 382, Ma, and W2 – either preserve the first two stanzas only or are fragmentary, and no 'Benedicamus Domino' *cauda* is in evidence. But the compositional actors in W1 and F made a good deal of the 'Benedicamus Domino' *cauda*, using it to define genre or both reducing the number of voices from three to two and changing the structure of the work.

The network of compositional actors that enmesh *Naturas Deus regulis*, *Leniter ex merito*, and *Hac in die rege nato* encompasses the placing together of notes (what later centuries would happily and restrictively call 'composition'), the deployment of syllables, rhyme, and end accent in the creation of poetry, the notation of the resulting design on the membrane page, subtraction of voices, attribution of genre, *ordinatio* of the codex as a whole, the use of modal transmutation, the reuse of plainsong, centonisation, the shadowy echoing of text from a twelfth-century English chronicle, and the not-so-shadowy homage to Ovid. This inventory of competencies embraces a greater or lesser number of individuals whose skills overlap one with another in ways to which the vicissitudes of history no longer provide access. But the network of compositional actors at work in just these three conducti points to the wider range of activity, collaboration and aesthetic responsibility that a broader, more medieval definition of 'composer' allows.

The history of the conductus from its origins to the middle of the thirteenth century helps focus several broader questions about compositional acts and compositional actors in the Middle Ages. It helps move the discussion on from simple statements about the inadequacy of extrapolating principles from post-Enlightenment composition to the Middle Ages and to reimagine the range of competencies that medieval composition might, if not encompass, at least overlap with; it also assists with resolving anxieties about authorship and attribution. To point to 'scribal' activity that overlaps with some sort of creative manipulation of words and/or notes is not to remove the possibility of slavish copying of texts that allows the deployment of classic text-critical methodologies to which most music sources from the long thirteenth century seem so resistant, but it does point both to the multidisciplinary environment in which so much creation in the period took place and the collaborative nature of much of that work.

As the examination of language in theoretical accounts of composition has shown, usages change not so much over the course of centuries but over decades, and nowhere is this clearer in the changes evidenced by different generations of manuscript copying; the ways in which creative networks around the three conducti discussed in this article require analysis according to the changes between the archetype W, the inferred manuscript a, and the earliest layers of surviving copies in W1 and F show clearly how continuity and change demand knowledge of movement from one decade to the next and how they in turn inform understanding of the history of the compositional network.

PART V

COMPOSERS AS COMMUNITIES

10

W. de Wicumbe as a Composer of Alleluya Rondelli[1]

Karen Desmond

W. de Wicumbe was a monastic composer active in mid-thirteenth-century England.[2] According to his own witness, he wrote plainchant and polyphony. In a compilation of his 'labours' (*opera*), Wicumbe reports a list of theological, liturgical, musical, and other items that he 'copied' or 'wrote', 'corrected', and 'excerpted' (*scripsit*, *correxit*, and *excerpsit*), while he was temporarily resident at Leominster Priory, in the west of England, for four years.[3] Wicumbe, who describes himself as a monk of Reading Abbey (Leominster Priory was a dependent cell of Reading), copied this list with a dry pen on a blank opening near the end of a twelfth-century Reading Abbey manuscript, Oxford, Bod. Lib., Bodl. 125 (hereafter Bodl. 125), fols. 98v–99r.[4] On the basis of the individuals from Reading Abbey mentioned by Wicumbe in this list of labours, Richard Sharpe convincingly dated Wicumbe's four years at Leominster to the years 1245–49 (and thus also providing a secure date, in the second half of the 1240s, for the production of the items listed by Wicumbe).[5] Items on the list that pertain to Wicumbe's musical and compositional activities include his copying of a troper and a processional, a Mass for the Virgin Mary, a computus that included a theory treatise on music, a diurnal with calendar, composing music for a history of Saint Margaret (the text was written by a 'Brother Hugo de Wicumbe'), and the production of two rolls (*rotuli*) of polyphony.[6] Wicumbe uses

[1] This chapter is available under the Open Access licence CC–BY–NC–ND. The writing stages of this chapter were funded in part by a major grant from the National Endowment for the Humanities ('Polyphony and Practices of Music Writing in Worcester Cathedral Priory, c. 1150–1350', FEL-281888-22), and by the European Union (ERC, BROKENSONG, 101088317).

[2] On W. de Wicumbe, see most recently Desmond 2020.

[3] The list was first published in Madan 1924. Further studies also published the complete list: Schofield 1948, 84; Sharpe et al. (eds.) 1996, pp. 461–63; Coates 1999, pp. 81–82.

[4] Some scholars expand 'W.' to the most likely 'William': in what follows, however, I simply use his Latin toponym 'Wicumbe'.

[5] Sharpe et al. (eds.) 1996, p. 461.

[6] Bodl. 125, fol. 98v; transcription from Coates 1999, pp. 81–82 (bold emphasis mine): '**scripsit** librum a[d opus] precentoris scilicet troparium et processionale simul… . **Scripsit** eciam librum ad missam de sancta Maria super proprium pergamenum suum. **Scripsit** eciam

the same verb *scribere* (to write) to describe all these activities, with the exception of *componere* (to compose), which he uses to characterise the production of the Saint Margaret *historia* on a text by Hugo de Wicumbe, which he (W. de Wicumbe) set to music (the verb he uses to describe his addition of music notation is *imponere*; see the words in bold in note 6).[7]

Copying and composing music was just one of W. de Wicumbe's monastic activities. He appears at some point to have served in the role of precentor at Reading Abbey. Although the list of labours is written in the third person, the general scholarly consensus is that it was written by Wicumbe, and since Wicumbe consistently refers to himself in the list as 'W.', Coates reasonably proposed that the instances of 'W. precentor' are likely self-references.[8] Knowledge of the central role of the precentor – other terms include cantor and *armarius* – within monastic community life has greatly increased in recent years. Margot Fassler writes that by the twelfth century, the cantor had become 'one of the most important persons in the religious community: he supervised all aspects of music-making, he was in charge of the library and the scriptorium, and he oversaw and directed the celebration of the liturgy'.[9] Other medieval figures linked to the copying and composition of music who occupied the precentor's office include for example Roger de Chabannes (d. 1025), cantor at the Abbey Saint Martial in Limoges, who was the uncle and teacher of the prolific music scribe and composer Adémar de Chabannes (988 or 989–1034), and in England, Symeon of Durham, cantor and historian at Durham Cathedral Priory (c. 1090–1129).[10] Along with leading the musical life of his community, the duties of Reading's precentor would have included the care for and the maintenance of the

---

compotum o[ptimum] cum quodam tractatu de musica... . Item [quendam] librum diurnalem parvum cum Kalendario compendiossime abbreviatum... . Item hys[toriam] beate Margarete [dictamine] fratris Hugonis de Wicumbe **composuit**. Notam [cantus] ipse W. **imposuit**. **Scripsit** [eciam duas rotulas unam continentem] triplices cantus organi numero, aliam [continentem] duplices cantus numero' (he copied a book [for the work] of the precentor, namely a troper and processional... . He also copied a book for the Mass for holy Mary on his own parchment. Also he copied a[n excellent] computus along with a certain treatise on music... . And a [certain] small diurnal book substantially abbreviated, with a Calendar... . Also he composed a history of blessed Margaret [on the text] of Brother Hugo de Wicumbe. The same W. added the [musical] notation. He [also] wrote [two rolls one of which contained] in number three-voice organal settings, the other two-voice settings).

7 For other surveys of the medieval terminology related to composition and composers, see the introduction to the current volume, chapters by Bent, Bradley, Everist, Dolce, and Parkes, and Doudet for the composition of dramatic works.

8 Coates 1999, p. 61. I have proposed that Wicumbe may have held this role in either the 1240s or 1250s between the precentorships of J. of Abingdon and Richard of Sutton (Desmond 2020, pp. 642–43 n. 12).

9 Fassler 1985, p. 29. For a recent collection of essays that focuses on the important role of the cantor in medieval society and with detailed case studies of specific cantors, see Bugyis et al. (eds.) 2017.

10 Grier 1995 and Rozier 2017, respectively.

community's books, which accords with the description of the labours Wicumbe listed in Bodl. 125.[11]

Wicumbe has been linked to specific extant music manuscripts. Given Wicumbe's statement that he 'wrote' (*scripsit*) two rolls of polyphony, Luther Dittmer proposed that Wicumbe was the composer of the music compositions copied in two fragmentary rolls and of those in an incomplete polyphonic *libellus* copied in a hand also found in the two rolls.[12] The fragments are catalogued as Oxford, Bod. Lib., Rawl. C.400* (hereafter Rawl. C.400*), fols. 1–10 and Oxford, Bod. Lib., Lat. liturg. b.19 (hereafter Lat. liturg. b.19), fol. 4 – hereafter the complete set of fragments will be referred to as the Rawlinson Fragments.[13] Christopher Hohler linked the rolls to Reading, and Andrew Wathey confirmed this provenance and dated the copying of the music (at least on the second rotulus) to before December 1256.[14] Finally, Wicumbe has also been proposed as the composer of some or all of the polyphonic compositions listed in a blank opening of another Reading Abbey manuscript, London, BL, Harley 978 (hereafter Harley 978), fols. 160v–161r, given the ascription on fol. 160v of at least some of the compositions listed to a 'W. de Wic.'.[15]

But beyond physical artefacts, some musicologists have attributed the development of a specific formal structure of polyphonic alleluya to Wicumbe and have proposed that a series of alleluyas included in the Worcester Fragments, which have a similar overall form to the twelve Rawlinson alleluyas and some of which are among

---

[11] On the role of cantor in the production and custody of books as documented in Anglo-Norman England, see Webber 2017.

[12] Dittmer 1954. In addition to linking the 'W. de Wicb' of Bodl. 125 to these surviving sources (pp. 35–37), Dittmer provided, for the first time, a reconstruction of the fragments and their contents, including transcriptions of the texts and music (pp. 20–28). For an analysis of the two text and music hands of the Rawlinson Fragments, see Desmond 2020, pp. 657–61.

[13] The Rawlinson Fragments that survive are (1) a 'text booklet' of two contiguous bifolia (Rawl. C.400*, fols. 1–4); (2) the 'first rotulus' that now survives incomplete as four small rectangular fragments of parchment (Rawl. C.400*, fols. 5–8); and (3) the 'second rotulus', now also incomplete and in three fragments, with music copied on one side and various texts in various hands on the reverse (Rawl. C.400*, fols. 9–10 and Lat. liturg. b.19, fol. 4). The top half of the second rotulus, Lat. liturg. b.19, fol. 4, was among a box of liturgical fragments up for auction at Sotheby's and was recognised by Andrew Wathey as the missing part of the second rotulus. See Barker-Benfield 1983, p. 116 and Wathey 1993a, pp. 73–74. Table 10.1 below (p. 202) lists the contents of the fragments. In addition, a motet and polyphonic responsory were copied on the recto of the second rotulus.

[14] The same music and text hand is present across all three sources, and notes regarding purchases of grain at Reading and nearby Wokingham are recorded in a contemporaneous hand on the verso of the second rotulus. See Hohler 1978, p. 19; Wathey 1993a, pp. 73–74.

[15] Given the Reading provenance of both manuscripts, Bertram Schofield made the connection between 'W. de Wicb.' of the Bodl. 125 list and the 'W. de Wic.' of Harley 978: see Schofield 1948. On Harley 978 and its list of polyphonic compositions, see especially Handschin 1949–51; Dittmer 1954, pp. 39–45; Wibberley 1976, pp. 180–81; Lefferts 1986, pp. 161–80; Taylor 2002; Deeming 2015a.

the Harley 978 list of polyphonic compositions, may also be by Wicumbe.[16] These alleluyas, in the Rawlinson and Worcester Fragments, all have a sectional structure where chant-based sections are prefaced with passages of freely composed polyphony, which function as preludes, interludes, and postludes. In addition, a specific compositional technique associated with insular style, rondellus, was used consistently in the freely composed preludes and in some of the interludes of the Rawlinson alleluyas; the preludes of the Worcester alleluyas showcase a related technique, voice exchange, likewise non-chant based.[17] It implies that this particular way of structuring alleluyas, with the insertion of these freely composed sections based on rondellus or voice exchange, could perhaps be a fingerprint of Wicumbe's compositional style. On the other hand, Nicky Losseff cautions that 'unfortunately *nothing* that is extant can unequivocally be ascribed to him [Wicumbe]' (emphasis mine).[18]

In the following, to address this gap in understanding, I present reconstructions of the most distinctive passages of the Rawlinson alleluyas – their rondelli. I analyse the style and structure of these passages, including a previously unrecognised extensive rondellus that serves as an interlude between the respond and verse in one of these settings. Unfortunately, this reconstruction and analysis is complicated by the fragmentary survival of these alleluyas: extensive portions of parchment are lost from the first rotulus, and for the six alleluyas of the text booklet, their scribe copied the texts but never added the staves or the music notation. I conclude with some thoughts on the attributions of these alleluyas to a single individual in light of this musical analysis and the available extra-musical evidence, including palaeographical and codicological evidence presented in a previous study of the fragments.[19] First, however, a brief description of the insular rondellus is necessary.

---

[16] On the structural and stylistic similarities between the alleluyas of the Rawlinson and Worcester Fragments, see Dittmer 1954, pp. 29–35. Ernest Sanders (2001) states that the attribution of the Rawlinson and Worcester alleluyas to Wicumbe 'seems entirely consistent with the available evidence' and that the surviving fragmentary compositions and those not extant but listed in Harley 978 were probably composed by Wicumbe. Dittmer (1954, 36) further suggested that 'W. de Wicb' was connected to Worcester, proposing an identification with a certain William of Winchecombe, prebend of Saint Andrew's Church in Worcester in 1283. Coates (1999, p. 62) proposes, however, that the identification with Winchecombe is inconsistent with the palaeographical evidence. Wicumbe's activity now appears to be earlier than the dates we associate with the Worcester Fragments, which are generally dated to the late thirteenth and early fourteenth centuries. For the historical implications of the dating of Wicumbe's activity to the 1240s, see Desmond 2020, pp. 644–46, 697–701.

[17] Although Sanders does not go as far as to attribute this technique to Wicumbe, he does want to at least locate the earliest examples of it in the west of England, the region where Dittmer and Sanders posit Wicumbe's activity: 'most of the English sources that for the first time transmit rondelli or other pieces with rondellus or *Stimmtausch* features come from localities little more than twenty miles east of Wales, while Odington had lived only fifteen miles from Worcester' (Sanders 1963, p. 84).

[18] Losseff 2004.

[19] Desmond 2020.

Rondellus Technique in Insular Music

Terminological issues arise in any discussion of rondellus. These relate to the difficulty in assigning insular compositions to generic categories.[20] In the case of 'rondellus', the term is used both to refer to an overall genre and a compositional technique.[21] Frank Ll. Harrison used the genre label 'rondellus-conductus' to refer to compositions that are freely composed and lack a cantus firmus but that incorporate some passages of rondellus technique; for pieces such as *Ave miles celestis curie* that are based on a cantus firmus but use voice exchange in the upper voices, he labelled 'rondellus-motets'.[22] Peter Lefferts, in his tabulation of thirteenth-century compositions that use rondellus, distinguishes between three types of composition: (1) conductus that incorporate passages of rondellus (which he terms 'conductus-rondellus'), which were copied either in score or in parts;[23] (2) polyphonic settings of alleluya plainchants that incorporate passages of rondellus; and (3) independent rondelli and 'rondellus-motets' that were copied in parts.[24]

Walter Odington (fl. 1298–1316) gives us the most extensive medieval description of rondellus. At the end of his *Summa de speculatione musicae*, he works through a series of terms relating to polyphonic music, offering definitions, some discussion, and examples of each of these terms in this order: rondellus, conductus, copula, motet, and hocket.[25] Some of these can be understood as genres, some as compositional techniques, some as both. Odington introduces rondellus as a species of discant, thus, as a specific texture or technique of polyphonic writing. Rondellus can be written 'with or without text' (*cum littera vel sine*), and the melody that one voice sings is echoed by all the voices in order. His detailed definition is as follows, and he concludes it with a short music example of a rondellus not extant in any other source, *Ave mater domini*:

> Rondelli must be composed as follows. The most beautiful melody possible should be conceived, and then organised following any of the above-mentioned modes, with or without text. That melody will be performed and joined to other

[20] On the problematic issue of genre in thirteenth-century insular polyphony, see Williamson 2016, especially pp. 154–71 on the rondellus. For a detailed discussion of the term in medieval texts, see Reckow 1972–2006.

[21] The other meaning of 'rondellus', to mean a refrain song, essentially a Latin translation of the French term *rondeau*, will not be considered here, but see Falck on Ludwig's use of the term to describe the monophonic Latin refrain songs in Florence, BML, Plut. 29.1 (hereafter F) (Falck 1972, p. 39).

[22] Frank Ll. Harrison 1959–60. As an introduction to his analysis of fourteenth-century voice exchange techniques, Lefferts gives a useful summary of rondellus and voice exchange in the thirteenth century, highlighting some of these issues of terminology (Lefferts 1986, pp. 28–33). On *Ave miles celestis curie*, including a discussion of its generic classification, see Colton 2017, pp. 28–29.

[23] Lefferts (1986, p. 29) sees the origins of rondellus and voice exchange techniques in the 'constructivist techniques of contrapuntal invention found in conductus *caudae*'.

[24] Table 6 in Lefferts 1986, p. 31.

[25] Hammond (ed.) 1970, pp. 139–46.

melodies in two or three voices, proceeding through consonances, so that when one [melody] ascends the other descends or the third [melody descends], so that they don't descend or ascend at the same time, except perhaps for the sake of greater beauty. And one by one the melodies are declaimed, thus:[26]

Figure 10.1. The *Ave mater domini* rondellus cited in Walter Odington's *Summa de speculatione musicae*. Cambridge, CCC 410, fol. 34v. By permission of The Parker Library, Corpus Christi College, Cambridge.

Odington's example is written out in score. Its rondellus technique is easily visible since the texted portion (the second period of rondellus) is echoed through the voices successively beginning with the lowermost stave. The key feature of rondellus (and the one that distinguishes it from a *rota* or round, like the famous *Sumer is icumen in*) is that all voices begin together: we hear all three melodies that will comprise the rondellus at once. The three separate melodies to be sung by all three voices are then exchanged in order, until all three melodies have been sung in each voice. Thus, while the experience of a performance moving through time is progressively different for each of the three voices, since they each sing three different melodic phrases, the listener hears essentially the same passage of polyphonic music stated three times (allowing for the difference in timbre of each of the three singers, however, which may become especially evident when each voice takes its turn singing the text). The form of Odington's example has two periods of rondellus as follows:

---

[26] 'Rondelli sic sunt componendi. Excogitetur cantus pulchrior qui potest et disponatur secundum aliquem modorum praedictorum cum littera vel sine, et ille cantus a singulis recitetur cui aptentur alii cantus in duplici aut triplici procedendo per consonantias, ut dum unus ascendit alius descendit vel tertius, ita ut non simul descendant vel ascendant nisi forte causa maioris pulchritudinis. Et a singulis singulorum cantus recitentur, sic:' (Hammond (ed.) 1970, p. 141, translation mine).

	sine littera	*cum littera*
Voice 1:	BCA	EFD
Voice 2:	CAB	FDE
Voice 3:	ABC	DEF

Rondellus technique is specifically distinguished from the more general technique of 'voice exchange' (*Stimmtausch*).[27] Many thirteenth- and fourteenth-century insular motets have extensive passages or sections with voice exchange, usually between two upper voices, and supported by one or two lower voices that sing a short melodic and rhythmic ostinato (the *pes*, literally the 'foot'). Voice exchange between two voices is also found in compositions copied in continental manuscripts. Rondellus technique, however, is confined to those textures where melodies are exchanged in order between *all* voices in the texture, most commonly between three voices.[28] Rondellus defined in this way appears to be restricted to thirteenth-century insular compositions, and the technique does not seem to have persisted into the fourteenth century.[29] Nor is rondellus a technique found in compositions copied on the continent.[30]

The Rondelli of the Rawlinson Fragments

The booklet and the first rotulus of the Rawlinson Fragments transmit twelve polyphonic alleluya settings (see Table 10.1). One, a setting of the *Alleluya V Post partum virgo*, has concordances in the Worcester Fragments and the Montpellier Codex (Montpellier, BIU, H 196, hereafter Mo);[31] the remaining eleven are unica. Texts for six alleluyas are copied in the booklet: its two contiguous parchment bifolios have

[27] For an in-depth musico-analytical study of *Stimmtausch* in the insular repertory and its antecedents, see Büttner 1990.

[28] A related type of composition, the *rota*, where the voices enter in turn (i.e., unlike the rondellus, they do not begin together) is uncommon: there are two examples in the thirteenth-century insular repertoire: *Sumer is icumen in* (which also incorporates a *pes* in voice exchange) and *Munda Maria* (WF 21). See Sanders 1963, pp. 85–86.

[29] The abandonment of the technique may be related to the expansion of voice ranges in fourteenth-century polyphony (Lefferts 1986, p. 30).

[30] Losseff 1994, pp. 100–101. Robert Falck (1972) proposed that a series of compositions in F demonstrate voice exchange, and possibly even canonic techniques. However, even though voice exchange may be present, Sanders (1978, p. 173) countered that the rondellus and *rota* are not found in continental sources and must be recognised as 'quintessentially English medieval phenomena'.

[31] The triplum and tenor parts are extant in a fragmentary codex of polyphony copied at Worcester Cathedral (Worcester, CL, Add. 68, frag. xxxviii, fol. 4v), now known as Worcester Reconstruction I. Another version of the work survives in another fragmentary codex from Worcester (Worcester, CL, Add. 68, frag. xxxv, fol. 3v, 1r), now known as Worcester Reconstruction II. This version is transposed (from D to G), and only the triplum and tenor voices for the freely composed introduction are extant. The introduction also survives separately in a continental source: it is copied, with a contrafact Marian text, *Alle psallite cum luya*, in the eighth fascicle of Mo (fols. 392r–393v, no. 338). For an analysis of the introduction to this alleluya and its voice exchange technique, see Büttner 1990, p. 203.

Table 10.1. The contents of the Rawlinson Fragments.

Source	Call number, folio	Text scribe	Music scribe	Music compositions
The 'text booklet'	Rawl. C.400*, fols. 1r–4v	A	–	*All. V Post partum virgo* *All. V Nativitas gloriose* *All. V In conspectu angelorum* *All. V Fit Leo fit Leonardus* *All. V Hic Franciscus* *All. V Fulget dies*
Rotulus 1	Rawl. C.400*, fols. 5r–8v	recto: B verso: A	recto: B verso: A	(recto) *All. V Dies sanctificatus* *All. V Hic est discipulus* *All. V Vidimus stellam* *All. V Adorabo ad templum* (verso) *All. V Assumpta est Maria* *All. V Post partum virgo*
Rotulus 2	Lat. liturg. b.19, fol. 4r–v Rawl. C.400*, fols. 9r–10v	recto: A verso: various (*possibly including B*)	recto: A	(recto) *Mirabilis Deus invisibilis/* *Ave Maria/Ave Maria* *Descendit de celis* (verso) Various texts (see Wathey 1993a), including *History of Saint Margaret*

texts for three voices laid out in separate parts, but neither the stave lines nor the music notation were copied. The two bifolios, along with the fragments of the two rotuli, were recycled to fashion a cover (termed a 'limp cover') for a fourteenth-century bishop's pontifical, made for the bishop of nearby Salisbury.[32] The binder cut the left and right margins from each of these bifolios; thus, on every page, text from either at the beginning or end of each line of the alleluyas is missing. In addition, the binder cut off the top and bottom margins from each bifolio, so one to three staves are missing from each folio. Figure 10.2 shows a reconstruction of one opening from this text booklet (fols. 3v–4r), where I have added the missing staves and labelled the compositions and voice parts copied on this opening.[33]

Another six alleluyas were copied (see Table 10.1), again in separate parts, on one of the two fragmentary rotuli (hereafter the 'first rotulus'): four alleluyas were copied by another scribe on the side of the rotulus catalogued by the Bodleian as its recto, and two more alleluyas were copied on the verso by the same scribe that copied the text booklet (see Figure 10.3 and compare the similarity of the hand with Figure 10.2).

[32] Desmond 2020, pp. 652–56.

[33] Since the two bifolios were arranged within one upside-down relative to the other, more staves are missing from the top of the inner bifolio. My codicological analysis of the Rawlinson text booklet is the subject of a forthcoming article ('W. de Wicumbe's Polyphonic Troper').

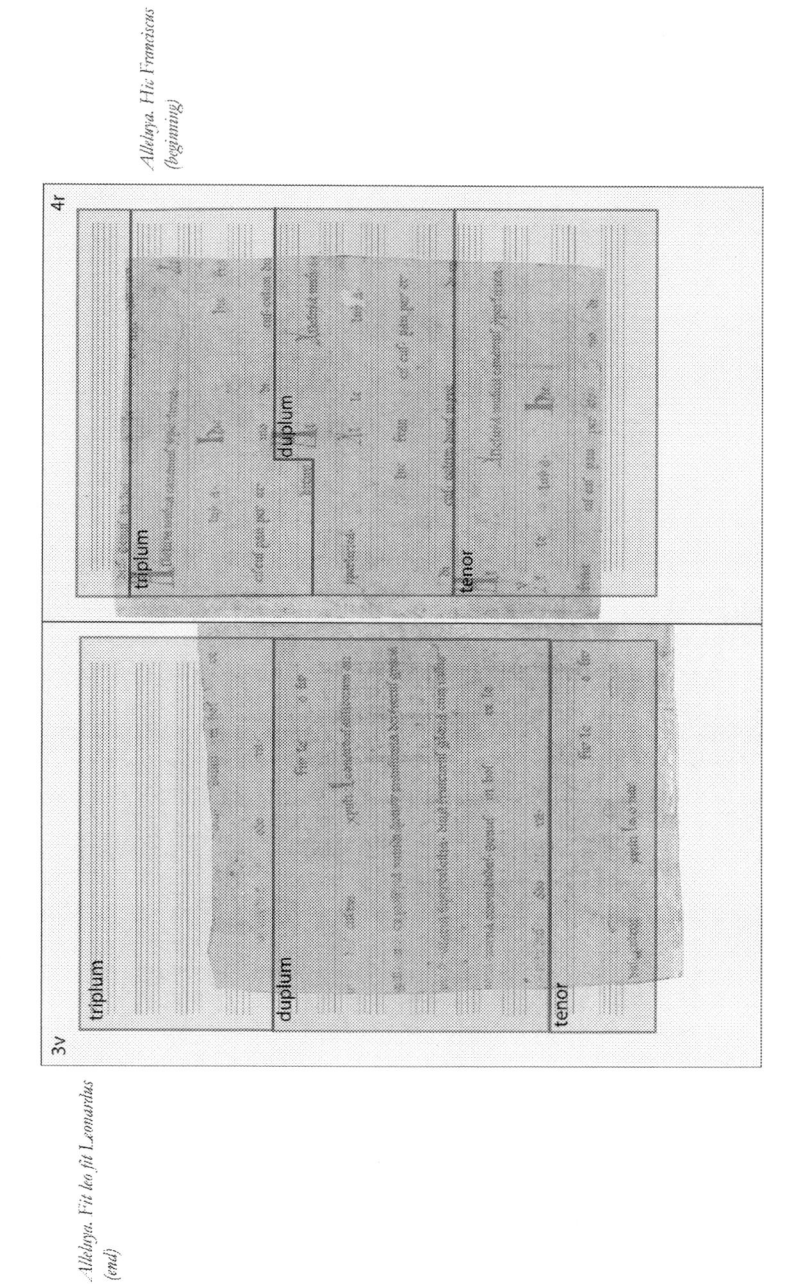

Alleluya. Fit leo fit Leonarius (end)

Alleluya. Hic Franciscus (beginning)

Figure 10.2. A reconstruction of one opening from the Rawlinson text booklet. The missing staves are added. Oxford, Bod. Lib., Rawl. C.400*, fols. 3v–4r. Image: Bodleian Libraries, University of Oxford. Creative Commons licence CC-BY-NC 4.0.

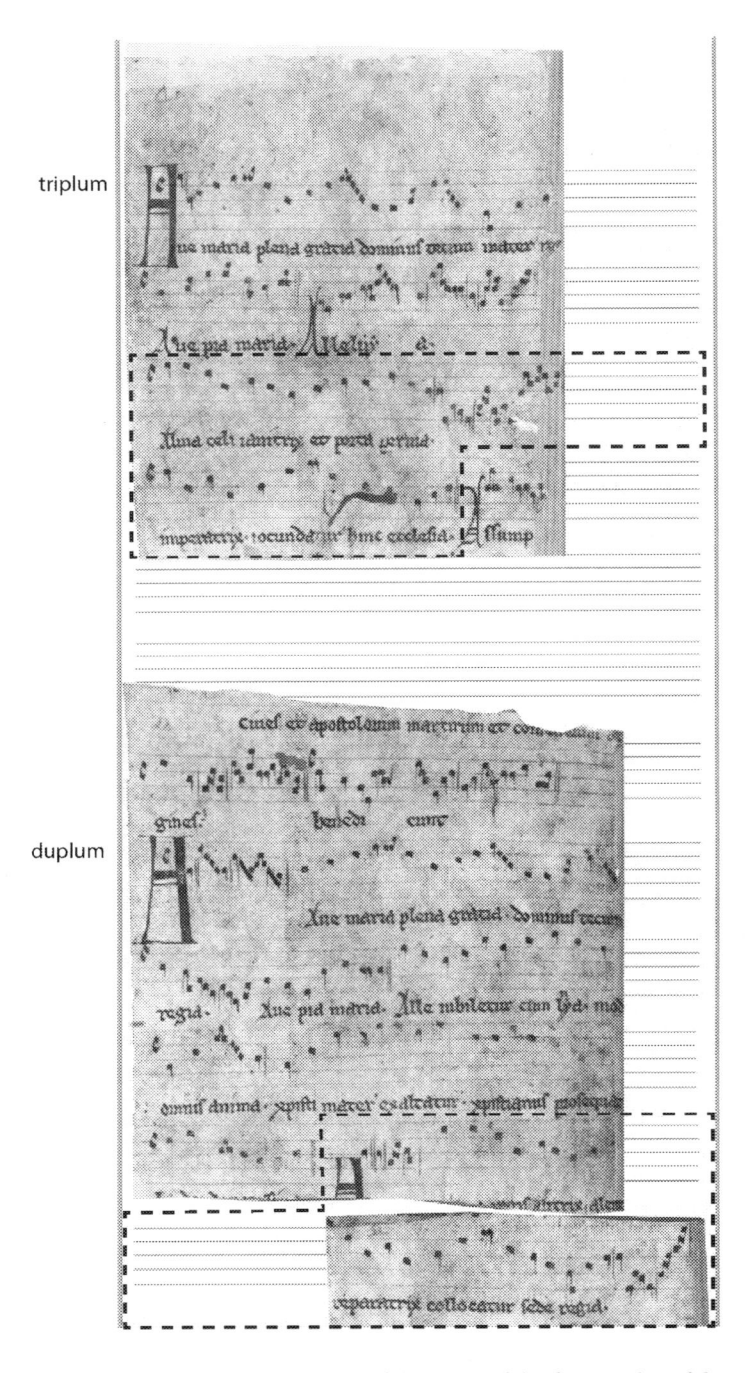

Figure 10.3. Reconstruction of the verso of the first rotulus of the Rawlinson Fragments. Dashed boxes highlight the rondellus interlude. Oxford, Bod. Lib., Rawl. C.400*, fols. 5v–7v. Image: Bodleian Libraries, University of Oxford. Creative Commons licence CC-BY-NC 4.0.

Thus, two main text and music hands are present in Rawlinson Fragments: I have presented elsewhere evidence for the hypothesis that W. de Wicumbe was likely the more accomplished scribe (Scribe A in Table 10.1), who copied the text booklet, and the text and music of the two alleluyas on the verso of the first rotulus, which I propose was copied *before* the side now labelled recto.[34] Scribe A (W. de Wicumbe) also copied a motet and a polyphonic responsory on the recto of the second rotulus. Thus, Scribe A's hand is present on all three sources of the Rawlinson Fragments. Subsequent to Scribe A's copying, a second text and music scribe, Scribe B in Table 10.1, copied the four alleluyas on the now labelled recto of the first rotulus.[35]

In addition to the setting of the plainchant pitches of the 'Alleluya' portion of the respond and the verse to polyphony, each of these twelve alleluyas has freely composed polyphony (non-chant based) that prefaces the settings of both the plain-chant respond and the verse (see Table 10.2).[36] The texts for eleven preludes are extant since only the beginning of the triplum for the final alleluya of the text book-let (*Alleluya V Fulget dies*) is preserved, and although space was left for the prelude text, Scribe A never filled it in. While the interludes of the *Alleluya V Dies sanctifi-catus* (first rotulus, recto) and the *Alleluya V Post partum virgo* (text booklet, and with a concordance in the Worcester Fragments) consist of a single short phrase sung before the setting of the verse, which do not feature either rondellus or voice exchange, one alleluya has a more extensive interlude of 45 L between the respond and the verse (*Alleluya V Assumpta est Maria*, first rotulus, verso) that is a rondellus.[37] The *Alleluya V Dies sanctificatus* (first rotulus, recto) has two written-out postludes, apparently sung before the repeat of the respond: the first is a lengthy postlude of 38 L that features voice exchange, and a second alternate shorter postlude (without voice exchange or rondellus) is also provided. The preludes, interludes, and post-ludes that feature rondellus or voice exchange are listed in Table 10.2.[38]

The resultant quadripartite form of the written-out polyphony for most of these alleluya settings has been described by both Dittmer and Sanders.[39] It consists of (1) a prelude, (2) a respond setting, (3) an interlude, and (4) a verse setting. In liturgical performance, however, the form would also include the repeat of the

---

34 Desmond 2020, p. 460 n. 45.

35 I also hypothesised that the hand that copied some of the texts of the verso of the second rotulus, including the Saint Margaret history, may belong to Scribe B, who I tentatively identified as Hugo de Wicumbe (Desmond 2020, pp. 659–61).

36 In Table 10.2, all the rondelli are preludes except those explicitly marked as interludes or postludes in the 'incipits' column. A dash (–) indicates that not enough content survives to make a determination for the particular cell in question.

37 The interludes of most of the remaining text booklet settings also appear relatively short (two occupy a half stave and one a full stave), although the interlude to the *Alleluya V Fit Leo fit Leonardus* seems relatively lengthy: it is the portion with the text 'Fit Leo fit Leonardus cultor Christi' in Figure 10.2 that occupies just over one and a half staves.

38 The shorter interludes of most of the settings consist of single short phrases that do not use rondellus or voice exchange technique and so are not considered within the scope of this chapter and not included in Table 10.2. For this reason, neither is the alternate postlude of the *Alleluya V Dies sanctificatus* included in Table 10.2.

39 Dittmer 1954, pp. 29–35; Sanders 1965, p. 34.

Table 10.2. Formal and stylistic aspects of the Rawlinson rondellus

Sources	Incipits (triplum, duplum, tenor [base plainchant])	Rondellus	V/E with pes	Order	Poly-textual	Phrase length	Verse syllable counts	First & last sonority	PC first note & final	Length
Text booklet, Rawl. C.400*, fol. 1r–v	Ave magnifica Maria. Ave mirifica Maria. Al [POST PARTUM VIRGO]		✓	tr-du	✓	6 L x2 8 L x2 10 L x2 4 L	9 13 17 5	D, E	C, E	52 L
1v–2r	[Al] Alleluya. Ave Maria mater pia. [Alleluya Ave Maria mater pia] Alleluya Alleluya Ave Maria [mater] pia. [NATIVITAS GLORIOSE]	✓		du-te-tr	–	x3	13 + 7	–	F, G	–
2v–3r	- Al Alleluya per … -omino cum latria [Al] … iam cantatur in ecclesia patria [IN CONSPECTU ANGELORUM]	✓		te-du-tr	✓	x3	–	–	C, E	–
3r–4r	Alleluya dulci cum armonia Al Alleluya dulci cum armonia Al Alleluya dulci cum armonia. [FIT LEO FIT LEONARDUS]	✓		tr-du-te	–	x3	11 + 8 + 8	–	–	–
4r–v	Alleluya musica canamus yperlirica. Al Alleluya musica canamus yperlirica. Al Alleluya musica canamus yperlirica. [HIC FRANCISCUS]	✓		tr-du-te		x3	7 + 8	–	C, D	–
4v	[Al] - - Alleluya. Fulget dies [FULGEBUNT?]	(✓)		–	–	–	–	–	–	–

Rotulus 1, recto, Rawl. C.400*, fols 5r–7r	*[Alleluya] Christo iubilemus.* *[Alleluya Christo iubilemus]* *Al 'pes' Alleluya Christo iu[bilemus] [DIES SANCTIFICATUS]*	✓		tr-du-te	✓	10 L x3 6 L	10 + 6 + 7 5	*D, C*	*C, D*	36 L
5r–7r	*Alleluya Christus nobis datus est* *Alleluya Christus nobis datus est* *Alleluya [DIES SANCTIFICATUS] (POSTLUDE)*		✓	tr-du		6 L x2 9 L x2 8 L	11 7 + 10 6 + 7	*D, C*	*C, D*	38 L
7r	*[A]lleluya clare decet decantare* - *- [HIC EST DISCIPULUS]*	✓	–	tr-du-te	✓	1 L 9 L? x3 2 L?	–	*D, C(?)*	*C, D*	(30 L)
8r	*[Adoremus ergo natum matre]* *[Adoremus ergo natum matre]* *A 'pes' Adoremus ergo natum matre [VIDIMUS STELLAM]*	✓		tr-du-te	✓	6 L x3 2 L?	4 + 4 + 7?	*D, C(?)*	*C, D*	(20 L)
8r	*[A]ve sanctitatis speculum maria.* - *- [ADORABO AD TEMPLUM]*	(✓)		tr-du-te	✓	6 L x3 6 L? x3 3 L?	12 ? ?	*G, G*	*G, G*	(39 L)
Rotulus 1, verso Rawl. C.400*, fols. 5r–7v	*Ave Maria gratia plena* *[A] Ave Maria gratia plena* *- [ASSUMPTA EST MARIA]*	✓		tr-du-te	✓	1 L 12 L x3 8 L	1 10 + 10 7	*D, C*	*C, E*	45 L
	… regis alitrix *Alma celi ianitrix* *- [ASSUMPTA EST MARIA] (INTERLUDE)*	✓		te-du-tr	✓	1 L 6 L x3 10 L x3 2 L	1 7 + 6 ? + 8 + 5	*D, D*	*C, E*	51 L
8v	- - *- [POST PARTUM VIRGO]*	–	–	–	–	–	–	–	*C, E*	–

respond and the passages of the plainchant that were sung monophonically by the choir. A complete performance of one of these polyphonic alleluyas was likely organised as follows:

> *Soloists:* Freely composed polyphonic prelude
> *Soloists:* The word 'Alleluya', set to three-voice polyphony
> *Choir:* Alleluya + jubilus, sung monophonically
> *Soloists:* Freely composed polyphonic interlude
> *Soloists:* The verse, set to three-voice polyphony except for final melisma
> *Choir:* Final verse melisma, sung monophonically
> *Soloists:* Freely composed polyphonic postlude *or* repeat of freely composed polyphonic prelude
> *Soloists:* Repeat of the word 'Alleluya', set to three-voice polyphony
> *Choir:* Alleluya + jubilus, sung monophonically

Like the majority of the surviving insular polyphonic alleluya settings, these Rawlinson alleluyas may be understood as 'prosulated' in that the manner of their textual additions shows an affinity with the composition and performance of the plainchant alleluya prosula.[40] In the plainchant alleluya prosula, newly composed texts were added to the melismatic passages of the base plainchant. These prosulas were generally of two kinds: one was a prosula on the alleluya respond; the other was a prosula on the alleluya verse (hereafter I will term these 'respond prosula' and 'verse prosula'). The verse prosula often incorporated the entire text of the base plainchant verse within the newly composed text. Stylistically, the verse prosula's text was often assonant with the vowel sounds of the base plainchant's melismas. Its function was to elaborate or clarify the often-paratactic base plainchant text. The respond prosula, on the other hand, had an introductory function that served to exhort the choir in their singing of the alleluya's wordless melisma (*jubilus*) that closes the respond. Some of the texts of these respond prosulas echo each of the vowel sounds of 'Alleluya' (A-E-U-A), but frequently their texts are simply assonant with the 'A' vowel and feature musical imagery of resounding heavenly praise.

The freely composed preludes of the polyphonic Rawlinson alleluyas serve exactly this exhortatory function (the complete texts of the text booklet rondelli are given in Table 10.3; the texts of the rondelli on the rotulus are in Appendices 1.1–1.6).[41] Their verse lines

---

[40] Desmond 2020, pp. 661–88. These settings might also be considered to exemplify the practice of troping more generally, since they include newly composed music in the freely composed sections and in the polyphonic voices added to the chant. I have used the term 'polyphonic prosulation' to refer to the technique of adding new words and voices to these plainchant alleluyas (Desmond 2020). With reference to monophonic plainchant and troping practices, Andreas Haug (2018, p. 263) makes a case for using the umbrella term 'tropes' to denote additions of either text or music that do not alter the formal structure of the preexisting chant. For editions of alleluya prosulas (texts only), see Marcusson (ed.) 1976 and Odelman (ed.) 1986, and the studies on them in Marcusson 1979; Steiner 1969; Wilton 1998.

[41] In Example 10.1 and Appendices 1.1–1.6, reconstructed passages are indicated with smaller noteheads and smaller font. In most cases the reconstructions are secure because of the rondellus form: that is, even if only one voice part survives, it can suffice to reconstruct a three-voice rondellus. In some alleluyas, I have provided a few conjectured notes if, for

Table 10.3. Texts of the text booklet rondelli, aligned to show the entry order of the texted voice

Triplum	Duplum	Tenor
Alleluya V Post partum virgo		
Ave magnifica mari- -a. Ave salvifica deigera mari- -a. Ave [gratifica mun]doque salutifera mari- -a. Ave mari- -a.	A- -ve mirifica mari- -a. Ave mundifica puerpera ma[ri- -a.] Ave glorifica luce corusca supera mari- -a Ave maria.	Al-
Alleluya V Nativitas gloriose		
[Al-] Alleluya. Ave maria ave mater pia. Ave [plena gra-]tia.	[Alleluya Ave maria ave mater pia. Ave plena grati- -a.]	Alleluya Alleluya Ave maria [ave mater] pia. Ave plena grati- -a.
Alleluya V In conspectu angelorum		
[...]	Al Alleluya per [...]-omino cum latri- -a	[Al- ...] iam cantatur in ecclesia patri- -a
Alleluya V Fit Leo fit Leonardus		
Alleluya dulci cum armonia resultet in ecclesia pro leonardi gl[ori- -a]	Al Alleluya dulci cum armonia resultet in eccle[sia pro] leonardi glori- -a	Al Alleluya dulci cum armonia resultet in [ecclesia] pro leonardi glori- -a
Alleluya V Hic Franciscus		
Alleluya musica canamus yperliri- -ca.	Al Alleluya musica canamus yperliri- -ca.	Al Alleluya musica canamus yperlirica.

are irregular, although most often featuring odd numbers of syllables due to the ubiquitous trochaic (first-mode) rhythms in the syllabically texted upper voices (see the 'verse
syllable counts' column in Table 10.2).[42] The text content consists of mostly declamatory
exhortations. All of the preludes to the Marian alleluyas echo repetitions of 'A-ve, A-ve,
A-ve' at the beginning of each of their lines of text, hailing the Virgin, and assonant with
the first two syllables 'Al-le' of the word 'Alleluya' (see the respond prosulas of *Alleluya V
Post partum virgo*; *Alleluya V Nativitas gloriose*; *Alleluya V Adorabo ad templum*; *Alleluya
V Assumpta est Maria*). The textual content of the others mostly focuses on the explicit
invocation of music and sweet harmony (e.g., *dulci cum armonia, musica canamus yper-
lirica, terrea celestia resultent dulci cum symphonia* in the *Alleluya V Fit Leo fit Leonardus*).
The primary rhyme sound – the final syllable of each text phrase – is almost invariably
'-a,' assonant with the first and last vowels of 'A̲lleluy a̲', with the exception of the prelude
to the *Alleluya V Dies sanctificatus* (Appendix 1.3), whose texts are constructed around
assonance with all four of the alleluya vowel sounds (A-E-U-A). Beyond their insistent
and repetitive 'a' vowels, the compositional techniques of rondellus and voice exchange
used in these polyphonic preludes, interludes, and postludes evoke a sound world of an
encircling and echoing song of praise.

Of the Rawlinson preludes, one features no rondellus: as shown in Table 10.2,
the prelude to the *Alleluya V Post partum virgo* is structured around three periods
of voice exchange of increasing length in the upper two voices above a *pes* tenor,
concluding with a 4 L coda (see 'phrase length' in Table 10.2). The *Alleluya V Dies
sanctificatus* also features voice exchange, not in its prelude, which is built on rondellus, but in its postlude, which has two periods of voice exchange of increasing length
and concludes with an 8 L coda (see Table 10.2).

The most ambitious of the Rawlinson rondelli is the interlude between the respond
and verse of the *Alleluya V Assumpta est Maria*. Although only a portion of the triplum
and an even shorter portion of the duplum survives (marked with dashed boxes in
Figure 10.3), enough survives to allow for its reconstruction, demonstrating that this
interlude is based on two periods of rondellus and is the longest of all the Rawlinson

---

example, two of the rondellus phrases are known, and there are a few notes missing in
the third, but they can be reasonably reconstructed based on the melodic contour and
the implied harmonies (see, e.g., the first four measures of the D phrase in Appendix
1.2). If a passage genuinely cannot be reconstructed since it is missing from all three
voice parts, I have left those passages blank (as I have done in Appendix 1.4, where the
B phrase is completely missing and only the A and the end of the C phrases survive).
Dittmer (1954, pp. 46–55) previously reconstructed some of these compositions, but
there are significant differences in my reconstructions, including some of the pitch
and text content and interpretations of the rhythmic notation. Dittmer transcribed the
Alleluya V Hic est discipulus and *Alleluya V Adorabo ad templum* in binary metre (these
are his items B and D; he had not identified the base plainchants for these two settings).
On my identifications of these two base plainchants, see below (n. 56). Dittmer did not
reconstruct the *Alleluya V Assumpta est Maria* interlude nor the second period of the
Alleluya V Adorabo ad templum prelude.

[42] In reference to a closely related repertory, Losseff (1994, p. 103) has suggested that
the irregular phrase lengths in the conductus with rondellus serve to create 'drive and
tension' in their overall form. In Losseff's case study, however, the poetic texts are regular
and the musical phrases are irregular.

rondelli with a total length of 51 L (see Appendix 1.2, and the 'phrase length' and 'length' columns of Table 10.2). This *Alleluya V Assumpta est Maria* also has a lengthy prelude of 45 L, with a 12 L rondellus phrase passed between the three voices, and a coda of 8 L (see Appendix 1.1). Although unfortunately not enough of the verse is extant to reconstruct this alleluya completely, it was likely at least as extensive as, if not longer than, *Alleluya V Dies sanctificatus*, which has a total length of 237 L (see Appendix 1.3 for the 36 L rondellus prelude of this work).[43] My reconstruction of the *Alleluya V Adorabo ad templum* demonstrates that it also had two periods of rondellus (Appendix 1.6), but at the other end of the scale, two of the Rawlinson rondellus preludes consist of one short phrase passed between the three voices and a short coda (see Appendices 1.4 and 1.5). Although it is impossible to reconstruct the preludes for which no music survives, on the basis of the surviving text, the rondellus prelude of *Alleluya V Hic Franciscus* looks to have been of the short variety: it includes, like the prelude to the *Alleluya V Vidimus stellam* (Appendix 1.5), a single fifteen-syllable line of verse passed between the three voices (see the image of this rondellus on fol. 4r in Figure 10.2). By contrast, the prelude to the *Alleluya V Fit Leo fit Leonardus*, has a longer text (27 syllables) passed through the three voices. This line of text must have been set either as one long rondellus phrase (like the 12 L phrase found in the prelude to the *Alleluya V Assumpta est Maria*) or with the text split into two periods of rondellus.

If the texted portion of the rondellus is labelled as the A phrase, the most common ordering of voices that sing the A phrase first is triplum-duplum-tenor (see the 'order' column in Table 10.2). For example, the *Alleluya V Assumpta est Maria* rondellus prelude may be represented as follows (with the A phrase that carries the text highlighted in bold font):

Triplum	**A** B C
Duplum	C **A** B
Tenor	B C **A**

There are three exceptions to this ordering of voices. In the *Alleluya V Nativitas gloriose* prelude, the particular spacing of text indicates that the order in which the voices sing the texted phrase is duplum-tenor-triplum. In the *Alleluya V In conspectu angelorum* prelude, as well as in the interlude of *Alleluya V Assumpta est Maria*, the order of the texted voices is tenor-duplum-triplum. Note that the ordering of the voices, and the number of rondellus periods (two) in the *Alleluya V Assumpta est Maria* interlude is the same as Odington's example of *Ave mater domini* given above:

triplum	BC**A**	EF**D**
duplum	C**A**B	F**D**E
tenor	**A**BC	**D**EF

43   The tenor of the *Alleluya V Assumpta est Maria* is not extant. The triplum and duplum occupy seventeen staves, however, indicating that this alleluya setting was perhaps slightly longer than the setting of the *Alleluya V Dies sanctificatus*, whose three parts on the recto, according to my reconstruction of the fragments, occupied twenty-two staves.

The *Alleluya V Assumpta est Maria* interlude is also one of the few polytextual rondelli of the Rawlinson Fragments, with the duplum and triplum (and possibly the tenor, although this voice is not extant) set to different texts.[44] Although only portions of the duplum and tenor have survived, the *Alleluya V In conspectu angelorum*, which has the same order of voices as the *Alleluya V Assumpta est Maria*, also likely had different texts in each of its three voices, given that the extant duplum and tenor do carry different texts: these similarities might imply that at least these two rondelli were written by the same composer. Although I have classified this interlude as polytextual in Table 10.2, in fact the different texts for each voice in the *Alleluya V Assumpta est Maria* interlude are not sung simultaneously (see Appendix 1.2): when one voice begins its new text phrase the other voice has already switched to vocalising on the rhyming '-a' vowel with which their previous text phrase had ended.

In the *Alleluya V Dies sanctificatus* prelude, while the A music phrase is set to the same text phrase and passed through the voices in order, the effect here is polytextual, since the text phrase straddles the subsequent rondellus melodic phrase (phrase B). Two different texts are sung at the same time from L 11–15, 21–25, and 27–36 (marked with dashed boxes in Appendix 1.3). A consequence of this overlapping of the text phrase with the rondellus phrases is the necessity of a short 6 L coda (L 31–36) to conclude the rondellus (labelled in Appendix 1.3). The tenor voice's A melodic phrase ends at L 30, but its text continues for seven more syllables ('Christi natalitia'). While the tenor sings these seven text syllables to a musical phrase that is a variant on the B phrase, the upper two voices sing two new words ('cum letitia') that close the prelude, resulting in this 6 L coda phrase. A similar overlapping of the text and rondellus phrases may also have been a feature of the remaining rondellus preludes copied on the recto of the first rotulus; however, in each of these preludes the text only survives for a single voice, so it is impossible to state this with certainty (see the potential overlap of texts in Appendices 1.4, 1.5, and 1.6).[45]

Each of the freely composed sections listed in Table 10.2 (for which the music is extant) has a short coda.[46] Rather than a rhetorical exhortatory function with their

---

44 According to Sanders (1965, p. 20 n. 10), polytextuality is encountered rarely in *Stimmtausch* compositions. It is unclear here whether Sanders means to include rondelli under the umbrella of *Stimmtausch* compositions, although this observation is located within a discussion of rondellus. Lefferts (1986, p. 29) notes that most rondelli (and voice exchange passages), 'when not melismatic, bear a single text, in one voice at a time'.

45 The tenor voice is not extant for the *Alleluya V Assumpta est Maria*. In my reconstruction of its prelude, I have hypothesised that it would have continued its text with the expected 'mater regia' at L 38–45, creating polytextuality with the 'Ave pia Maria' of the two upper voices; however, it is possible that it also sang 'Ave pia Maria' monotextually with the upper voices (see Appendix 1.1).

46 This includes the two sections written with voice exchange on a *pes* (the prelude to the text booklet *Alleluya V Post partum virgo* and the postlude to the *Alleluya V Dies sanctificatus*), which have codas of 4 L and 8 L, respectively, even though they do not have the same sorts of textual overlap in their voice exchange periods that we find in the rondellus periods of the *Alleluya V Dies sanctificatus* prelude. In addition to their codas, three of the rondelli begin with an 8/5 sonority on D held for a single long before the rondellus proper commences (the *Alleluya V Assumpta est Maria* prelude and interlude and the *Alleluya V Hic est discipulus* prelude).

codas accommodating the sense and the length of the text phrases, as I have suggested here, Sanders proposed that the primary function of these freely composed sections and their codas, was to establish a 'key' for the setting.[47] And in cases where the respond begins on a pitch other than the plainchant final, Sanders held that the function of the preludes' codas was, to some degree, 'modulatory'.[48]

It is difficult to fully substantiate Sanders's claim based on an analysis of the Rawlinson alleluyas. The base plainchants for the first three alleluyas copied on the recto of the first rotulus begin on C and their final is on D: their preludes do indeed begin on a D sonority, affirming the plainchant final, and cadence on a C sonority in preparation for the first pitch of the respond (see the 'first & last sonority' and 'pc (plainchant) first note & final' columns of Table 10.2), supporting Sanders's assertion.[49] But no 'modulatory' function is necessary for the *Alleluya V Adorabo ad templum* prelude, the last alleluya copied on the recto of the first rotulus, since the base plainchant begins and ends on G, as does its prelude. The remaining two compositions for which the music of the freely composed sections survives – the *Alleluya V Post partum virgo* (the text booklet setting that has concordances with music elsewhere) and the *Alleluya V Assumpta est Maria* – have a plainchant final on E.[50] Both their preludes begin with a D sonority, and while the prelude of *Alleluya V Post partum virgo* ends on an E sonority (the same as the plainchant final), the first note of the respond is actually a C, so no 'modulatory' function appears to be in effect here. The prelude of *Alleluya V Assumpta est Maria* begins on a D sonority and does end with a C sonority, the same pitch that opens the respond; its freely composed interlude (sung between the respond and verse), however, ends on a D sonority, and the first pitch of the plainchant verse is F. In addition, while the last pitch of the plainchant respond incipit and the final pitch of the penultimate verse melisma is E (the standard place that the polyphonic setting should end), the composer of this setting has chosen to extend into the jubilus melisma by a few pitches so that the polyphonic setting of both the respond incipit and verse can end on a D sonority. In other words, in this polyphonic setting of the *Alleluya V Assumpta est Maria*, the

---

[47] Sanders (1965, p. 34 n. 71) did allow that the alleluya preludes also served as an introductory function similar to plainchant tropes.

[48] Sanders 1965, p. 34. Regarding the interludes of these alleluyas, Sanders (1963, p. 159) writes that in 'the Alleluia settings by William of Winchcomb the step from the tonic ending of the setting of a respond incipit to the supertonic beginning of a verse would have been negotiated in the "modulatory" third section'. This does not seem to actually be the case. It is not true of the *Alleluya V Assumpta est Maria* interlude, discussed in the main text above. Only two further interludes survive for the Rawlinson alleluyas. In the *Alleluya V Dies sanctificatus*, the first and last sonorities of the short interlude are on D, and the first note of the plainchant verse is D, so there is no bridging function here. Nor is one found in the text booklet *Alleluya V Post partum virgo*, where the short interlude begins and ends on D, even though the first pitch of the verse is F.

[49] The first three alleluyas on the recto of the first rotulus have the same plainchant melody.

[50] Sanders's (1963, p. 153 n. 80) claim that the first setting on the verso of the first rotulus is not a setting of the *Alleluya V Assumpta est Maria* but rather is part of the *Alleluya V Post partum virgo* must be incorrect: the verse text is clearly a prosulation of the *Assumpta est Maria* verse. These two alleluyas have the same plainchant melody.

sonority E is almost completely avoided as a hierarchically important sonority. The most obvious 'tonal' trend that can be observed in these alleluyas as a group, from this admittedly small sample size, seems to be their emphasis of D, and secondarily C, sonorities, regardless of the actual final pitch of the base plainchant.[51]

A Single Composer?

Can the Rawlinson alleluyas be specifically localised on the evidence of this musical analysis? Of the extant repertoire of insular prosulated polyphonic alleluyas, which numbers at least forty-six compositions, only the settings in the Rawlinson and Worcester Fragments have freely composed polyphonic preludes, interludes, and postludes.[52] Furthermore, only those in Rawlinson Fragments use rondellus technique.[53] The presence of freely composed rondellus sections in at least ten of the twelve Rawlinson alleluyas confirms their distinctly insular compositional style: Losseff has characterised the use of rondellus in the insular polyphonic conductus repertoire as indicative of what she terms the 'high insular style'. She has also confirmed that rondellus is only found in insular compositions.[54] The freely composed preludes, interludes, and postludes of the Rawlinson alleluyas have other similarities to the 'high insular style' as characterised by Losseff: specifically, in the 'drive and tension' created by irregular (and increasing) phrase lengths (in those settings with more than one period of voice exchange or rondellus) and the characteristic harmonic oscillation of neighbouring sonorities.

But beyond their distinctively insular musical style and structure, there is the evidence of the physical artefacts. Eleven of these twelve alleluyas are uniquely witnessed within a set of sources that have convincing connections to Reading Abbey and its dependent cell Leominster Abbey, and the remaining alleluya has concordances only in later sources. These Rawlinson Fragments are united by the presence of the same scribe in all three sources, with eight of the alleluyas copied by this scribe

---

[51]   This oscillation of two neighbouring sonorities is understood as a key aspect of insular polyphony. The most common final sonority of rondelli and *Stimmtausch* compositions, according to Sanders, is F. These F-based pieces emphasise tonic (F) and supertonic (G) sonorities. Pieces that centre on D tend to emphasise the subtonic (C) as a secondary sonority (Sanders 1965, p. 19). However, recently Catherine A. Bradley (2019, pp. 484–85) has shown that this harmonic oscillation around F and G is also characteristic of French polyphonic rondeaux and a group of French motets based on simple tenors that appear to have been chosen to support vernacular song idioms in their upper voices.

[52]   On the extent of the insular polyphonic prosulated repertoire, see Desmond 2020, pp. 688–97. One independent freely composed alleluya prelude is found in a source other than the Rawlinson and Worcester Fragments, the *Alleluya celica*, based on voice exchange, but not attached to a polyphonic setting of an alleluya plainchant (Princeton, UL, Garrett 119, frag. A).

[53]   Dittmer reconstructed the single voice fragment of the *Alleluya V Judicabunt sancti* prelude (WF 50) in Worcester Reconstruction II as a rondellus (Dittmer 1957, p. 81). Losseff, however, calls this reconstruction 'suspect' and suggests that this prelude was composed as voice exchange rather than as a rondellus, just as all the other Worcester preludes that also are composed with voice exchange (Losseff 1994, pp. 157–58).

[54]   Losseff 1994, pp. 100–101.

in two of the three sources. Were these eight settings also composed by this scribe, not merely copied by him, and what of the other four copied in another hand? Is it possible to attribute all twelve settings to the same creator or a small group of close collaborators working at Reading and Leominster, documenting a particular way of singing the alleluya polyphonically at these institutions?

Three of the Rawlinson alleluyas stand out in comparison to the rest, being more ambitious in scope, structure, and complexity of technique. Each of them was selected to commence distinct phases of the copying of the Rawlinson sources: (1) the first alleluya that opens the text booklet (*Alleluya V Post partum virgo*), copied by Scribe A, whom I have hypothesised was W. de Wicumbe, (2) the first alleluya on the recto of the first rotulus (*Alleluya V Dies sanctificatus*) copied by Scribe B, whom I have tentatively proposed was Hugo de Wicumbe, and (3) the first alleluya on the verso of the first rotulus (*Alleluya V Assumpta est Maria*), copied by Scribe A (Wicumbe). I would suggest that the balance of the evidence favours, for now, the acceptance of these hypotheses regarding the identity of these scribes. If not these actual individuals, then surely individuals very like them, with connections to Reading Abbey, likely charged with scribal and musical duties, composers of both the texts and music of plainchant and polyphony sung within their communities, who recorded these compositions in quotidian but functional manuscript formats.

The *Alleluya V Assumpta est Maria* was perhaps the lengthiest setting of all, with an interlude that has the longest and most ambitious rondellus. The *Alleluya V Post partum virgo* that follows this setting on the verso of the first rotulus might have used the *Alleluya V Assumpta est Maria* setting as a model, since both have the same plainchant melody. Further reconstruction and analysis of the chant-based portions of these two settings may confirm this hypothesis. Likewise, the extensive setting of the *Alleluya V Dies sanctificatus* copied on the recto of this same rotulus also served as the model for the two shorter settings that directly follow it, since the same melody is also used for the plainchants of the *Alleluya V Hic est discipulus* and *Alleluya V Vidimus stellam*. What is seen on both sides of the rotulus, then, is a composer using this spacious physical format to document (and perhaps even work out in writing) several settings of alleluyas that use the same plainchant melody.

Of the twelve alleluyas, the ambitious *Alleluya V Assumpta est Maria* was probably the first copied, if the hypothesis that Wicumbe copied the text booklet after the rotulus is accepted.[55] It may have been one of Wicumbe's first compositions. The *Alleluya V Dies sanctificatus* and the three compositions on the recto, whose structural components and deployment of rondellus are somewhat more regularised and homogenised (rondellus only in the preludes, the entry of texted voices regularised as triplum-duplum-tenor, the same text in all three voices, and the consistent deployment of the overlap of text with musical phrase, resulting in brief but regular moments of polytextuality), may be slightly later, and either composed by a collaborator (Hugo de Wicumbe?) in response to W. de Wicumbe's *Alleluya V Assumpta est Maria* or else also composed by W. de Wicumbe and copied by Hugo de Wicumbe. In addition to their shared structure and technique, some melodic motifs shared

---

[55] Desmond 2020, p. 697.

between the alleluyas copied on the recto and the verso of the rotulus might hint at a single composer for all six of the rotulus compositions (see Example 10.1); however, current understandings of the common figurations of mid-century insular melodic vocabulary are not advanced enough to make this claim with certainty.

The text booklet then might be understood to represent Wicumbe's first attempt to collect the alleluyas of his community into a larger codex copied in liturgical order.[56] This pair of bifolios begins with the third of the ambitious alleluya settings, the *Alleluya V Post partum virgo*, perhaps not composed by Wicumbe (since we have another setting of this plainchant on the verso of the first rotulus).[57] Or perhaps it was a second (and later) attempt at setting this same alleluya in which he experimented with a different compositional technique (voice exchange over a *pes*) in the prelude.[58] The remaining settings in the text booklet betray a variety of techniques and approaches: some settings shorter and more perfunctory (e.g., the *Alleluya V Hic Franciscus*), some, like the *Alleluya V Fit Leo fit Leonardus*, lengthier and more ambitious (with the second-longest prelude text of the text booklet settings, and the most extensive interlude); most with the standardised entry of texted voices as triplum-duplum-tenor but two with other orderings of the texted voices; one prelude apparently polytextual, the others monotextual, though possibly with the same overlapping of text phrase and rondellus phrase observed in the settings of the first rotulus.

That there are a variety of compositional approaches in the set of alleluyas collected in the text booklet is perhaps not surprising, since to assemble such a liturgically ordered collection, with alleluyas appropriate for the entire liturgical year, Wicumbe would have had to gather a group of compositions likely composed at different times and possibly produced by different creators. A rotulus, on the other hand, as I suggested in a previous study, as a more ephemeral or at least as a more forgiving format for experimentation (in its physical aspects and layout) could have been an ideal place to set down a composer's fair copy of a new work.[59] It is also quite likely that unicum compositions of the same genre found copied one after another on a rotulus at a specific point in time by one person might be stylistically more homogenous, especially if

---

[56] It should be noted, however, that the compositions on the rotulus are also copied in liturgical order. In a previous study, I wrote that 'the four Alleluyas copied on the recto of the first Rawlinson rotulus are probably in liturgical order, although it is difficult to be certain about this, since the tenors for the second and fourth alleluyas are unidentified' (Desmond 2020, p. 693). I have since identified the second and fourth alleluyas as *Alleluya V Hic est discipulus* and *Alleluya V Adorabo ad templum*, confirming that the four alleluyas on the recto are indeed copied in liturgical order. Further discussion of these identifications is in a forthcoming study (Desmond, 'W. de Wicumbe's Polyphonic Troper: From Roll to Codex').

[57] The two bifolia are contiguous, however, implying either that they were intended to be the central bifolios of a larger gathering, in which case the ambitious *Alleluya V Post partum virgo* would not have been as prominently placed, or that these alleluyas circulated here in a smaller standalone *libellus* of only two bifolios. This has yet to be resolved.

[58] Recall that voice exchange over a *pes* is found in the postlude to the *Alleluya V Dies sanctificatus* (recto, first rotulus).

[59] Desmond 2024. On the rotulus in the late medieval England, see the substantial discussion in Bent et al. 2021, pp. 299–334.

Example 10.1. Melodic similarities across the Rawlinson rondelli. (a) *Alleluya V Dies sanctificatus* prelude, L 1–4 (Scribe B); (b) *Alleluya V Vidimus stellam* prelude, L 1–4 (Scribe B); (c) *Alleluya V Dies sanctificatus* prelude, triplum, L 4–7 (Scribe B); (d) *Alleluya V Hic est discipulus* prelude, triplum, L 7–10 (e) *Alleluya V Assumpta est* prelude, triplum, L 7–10 (Scribe A).

the scribe was also the composer. The different formats are thus representative of different activities – one closer to composition and performance, one closer to assembly and organisation of pre-existing works.[60] What is witnessed in this rotulus is perhaps Wicumbe's compositional process in his working out polyphonic settings of alleluyas that have the same melody: on the verso, the two settings that share the *Alleluya V Assumpta est Maria* and *Alleluya V Post partum virgo* plainchant melody, and on the recto, three settings that share the *Alleluya V Dies sanctificatus* melody.

While the text booklet represents the remnants of a labour abandoned by Wicumbe for some as yet unknown reason, eventually perhaps he succeeded in his aim to produce a liturgical cycle of polyphonic alleluyas, as Dittmer and others proposed.[61] His contributions to the musical life of his community were still being referenced three decades after the copying of the Rawlinson Fragments, given that the list of compositions added at the back of the Reading manuscript Harley 978, which contains the reference to the compositions of 'W. de Wicb.' possibly dates to the 1270s, at this point perhaps being copied as 'classical' works.[62] Further study and reconstruction of the music on these fragments is needed, concentrating in particular on the ways in which the base plainchants were manipulated, using the composition I have suggested is most likely by Wicumbe, the *Alleluya V Assumpta est Maria*,

[60] See Anna Kathryn Grau's (2018, pp. 135–36) suggestion that a thematic cluster of compositions in the eighth fascicle of Mo may be representative of an exemplar that circulated in booklet format.

[61] Dittmer 1954, p. 37.

[62] The owner of the lost book of polyphony, W. de Wintonia (William of Winchester), is first documented at Leominster in 1276 (Taylor 2002, p. 110).

as a starting point for the analysis. In addition, identification of the institutional contexts for the base plainchants, and an explanation of the particular veneration of Saint Leonard attested to in the text booklet, given the ambitious nature of the polyphonic alleluya setting composed for him, will advance attempts to identify the creator(s) of these compositions and manuscripts.

Appendix 1:
Transcription and Reconstruction of the Rondelli in the Alleluya from Rotulus 1 (Oxford, Bod. Lib., Rawl. C.400*, fols. 5v–8r)[63]

Appendix 1.1: *Alleluya ℣ Assumpta est Maria*, prelude (rotulus 1, verso)

Appendix 1.2: *Alleluya V Assumpta est Maria*, interlude (rotulus 1, verso)

Appendix 1.3: *Alleluya V Dies sanctificatus*, prelude (rotulus 1, recto). The dashed boxes mark moments when two different texts are sung at the same time.

Appendix 1.4: *Alleluya V Hic est discipulus*, prelude (rotulus 1, recto)

Appendix 1.5: *Alleluya ℣ Vidimus stellam*, prelude (rotulus 1, recto)

Appendix 1.6: *Alleluya ℣ Adorabo ad templum*, prelude (rotulus 1, recto)

11

Rethinking Trouvère: Biographical and Historical Perspectives on Thirteenth-Century Musical Culture[1]

Brianne Dolce

For modern scholars, the term 'trouvère' functions fairly broadly as a marker of identity that is applied to the makers of songs and other literature in Old French dialects during the long thirteenth century. Whereas for musicologists trouvère typically means an individual associated with the crafting of songs (i.e., poetry with music), literary scholars tend to understand the term even more broadly, encompassing a wide range of literary practices in the Old French vernacular. In this way, trouvère could be said to have a wider remit than its southern counterpart, the troubadour, even while the two categories are often taken to be equivalents, albeit for French and Occitan writers, respectively. In the north, anyone from Chrétien de Troyes, known primarily for his epic rhyming poems and perhaps the first individual to whom we ascribe such an identity, to Adam de la Halle, a creator of songs, plays, and various polyphonic musical genres, falls under the category 'trouvère'. From opposite ends of trouvère chronology, these two individuals thus demonstrate the wide range of cultural activities with which scholars associate the term 'trouvère'.

The origins of this term are rather obscure, however, and the tendency to label any individual related to Old French culture as a trouvère is, it would seem, a rather modern inclination. Whereas troubadour has medieval precedents in historical documents, trouvère can, to my knowledge, only be located in literary texts of the Middle Ages.[2] For example, Frédéric Godefroy lists five instances of the use of

[1] I would like to thank the editors of this volume, Gaël Saint-Cricq and Anne-Zoé Rillon-Marne, for their incredibly helpful comments and generous support with this chapter. I would also like to thank Henry Parkes and the members of Yale's Medieval Song Lab, who read an early version of this chapter and offered useful feedback when it was presented in 2019. I extend a similar note of gratitude to the attendees of the conference *Compositeur(s) au Moyen Âge* in Rouen in May 2019; I benefitted greatly from the discussions that took place over the few days of the conference and am grateful to the many attendees for their feedback. More recently, Elizabeth Eva Leach read multiple versions of this piece and was, as ever, a kind and constructive interlocutor.

[2] Dictionaries by both Levy and Raynouard give historical contexts, such as monastic customaries, for the use of the term 'troubadour'. See Raynouard 1844, p. 429; Levy, cont. Appel 1924, p. 479.

the term 'trouvère' in the twelfth and thirteenth centuries to which a handful of other occurrences could be added.[3] In these contexts, the term's meaning is often anything but precise. Benoît de Saint-Maure's *Roman de Troie*, an epic poem about the Trojan War dating from the middle of the twelfth century, contains the earliest known example of the term's use. The emphasis in the *Roman de Troie*, however, is on a trouvère as a musician in the broadest sense – as a singer and on the aesthetic quality of their voice. The sense of the final line is somewhat ambiguous but suggests that in this context, 'trovere' should be associated with what modern scholars would call composition, or the 'finding' of sound: 'Mout ot en lui bon chanteor, / Mout aveit la voiz haute et clere / E de sonez ert bons trovere' (He was considered by many as a good singer, and had a voice both loud and clear, and in regard to sound, he was a good trouvère).[4] In the slightly later *Tristan menestrel* by Gerbert de Montreuil, thought to have been written around the second quarter of the thirteenth century, the term is used in such a way that reflects some kind of making or crafting: 'É il l'a or a feme prise, / Si com la matere descoevre / Gerbers, qui a reprise l'oevre, / Quant chascuns trouvere le laisse' (And he took her as his wife, as the story tells, I, Gerbers, who picks up the work, that other trouvères have left).[5] However, in this context, there is no implication of music: the emphasis is solely on words. Thus, while we can at least assert that there is medieval precedence for the use of trouvère, there appears to have been little precision in how it was used and whether it was aligned solely with the crafting of musical texts.[6]

What these early instances of the word 'trouvère' do suggest, though, is that the term was not used in the way that musicologists tend to use it today – namely, as a marker of musical identity. For medieval writers, the concept was broader, more fluid, and less defined and clearly not restricted to music making; by contrast, modern usage of the term often implies a cohesiveness of identity and sense of being – grounded in modern conceptions of the composer – rather than solely a cohesiveness in relation to a shared cultural practice. The tendency to affiliate trouvère with composer, I argue, does not represent contemporary, medieval understanding of the trouvère and thereby obscures the breadth of activities and cultural practices in which the so-called trouvères took part. Thus, in pigeon-holding trouvères into a singular type of cultural practice, modern scholarship attributes to the term a level

---

3   See 'Trouvère', in CNRTL, http://www.cnrtl.fr/definition/trouvere. See Godefroy 1891–99, vol. 8, p. 94 for the quotation and references of his five occurrences. Other instances include Rogier, *De saint Julien*; the *Roman d'Alexandre*; Adenet le Roi, *Les Enfances Ogier*; Huon de Mery, *Le Tournoiement Antechrist*; the *Roman d'Yder*; Gerbert de Montreuil's continuation of *Perceval*; and a *jeu-parti* by Richard de Fournival, *Amis Richart, j'eüsse bien mestier*. My thanks to the editors, Gaël Saint-Cricq and Anne-Zoé Rillon-Marne, for drawing these further examples to my attention.

4   Constans (ed.) 1904, lines 5190–92. I am grateful to David Murray for his suggestions with this translation as well as those in Old French that follow.

5   Weston and Bédier 1906, p. 498, translation my own.

6   For other surveys of the medieval terminology related to composition and composers, see the introduction to the current volume, chapters by Bent, Bradley, Everist, Desmond, and Parkes, and Doudet's essay for the composition of dramatic works.

of inherent stability that, as I show in this chapter, cannot be substantiated in the historical record.

Although Hendrik Van der Werf asked as early as 1965 whether trouvères were 'poets first and musicians second',[7] at least recognising the complication of isolating these two identities, recent musicological scholarship has tended to take the equation of trouvère with composer somewhat for granted.[8] But the alignment of trouvères with music making is, rather than the fault of recent scholarship, a long-standing association. In his 1581 *Recueil de l'origine de la langue et poésie françoise*, Claude Fauchet distinguished between those who composed (trouvères) and those who performed (jongleurs). In doing so, Fauchet inherently equated the figure of the trouvère with musical composition rather than the creation or making of text more generally.[9] Scholars of the nineteenth century, such as Arthur Dinaux, attempted briefly to expand the term, considering trouvères 'poets' in the broadest sense.[10] In the first modern scholarly monograph to treat trouvères exclusively, Mary O'Neill states that 'trouvères were poet-composers'.[11] The hybrid term 'poet-composer' now frequently graces the pages of musicological monographs, seeming to skirt around the issue of what precisely trouvères did. There has been considerably less ink shed on the trouvères than on the troubadours, but a recent surge in musicological scholarship is beginning to fill this gap.[12] But while this strand of scholarship tends to treat the trouvères through the repertory of the surviving songs in chansonniers, answering many questions about text-music relationships and the connection of trouvère song with other musical traditions, questions remain about how to critically understand the individuals that lie behind the works.

A close examination of the types of biographical and contextual information that can be known about individuals that we now call trouvères demonstrates the wide variety of backgrounds, experiences, and professions from which trouvères were drawn. In the wake of the French Revolution, new, large-scale biographies of the trouvères were undertaken, reflecting their increasing significant for a history of Old French culture and literature.[13] Early biographical studies were undertaken by

---

7 Van der Werf 1965, p. 61.

8 For reflections on the trouvères as composers of music and/or text in relation to manuscript ascriptions, see the chapter by Bent in this volume.

9 For more on the alignment of trouvères with composers, see Haines 2004, p. 52; Fauchet 1581, p. 72.

10 Dinaux 1837–63, vol. 1, pp. 1–2.

11 O'Neill 2006, p. 2.

12 Jennifer Saltzstein, for example, has studied the musical culture of the trouvères rather widely: see Saltzstein 2013; Saltztein (ed.) 2019. Recent work by Joseph W. Mason on the *jeu-parti* has shed extensive light on the genre from both analytical and historical angles: see, for example, Mason 2019, 2022. Elizabeth Eva Leach has recently considered the analysis of trouvère song in Leach 2019. Leach, Mason, and Thomson (eds.) 2022 considers a single trouvère chansonnier. Saint-Cricq explores the relationship between trouvère song and contemporary polyphonic repertories: see, for example, Saint-Cricq 2019.

13 See Haines 2004 and Ellis 2005.

Dinaux in his four-volume *Trouvères, jongleurs et ménestrels du nord de la France et du midi de la Belgique*, published between 1837 and 1863.[14] Dinaux's publications relied heavily on the literary works themselves and were divided geographically in an effort to identify more regionally specific groups. A few decades later, Adolphe Guesnon discussed documents pertaining to various trouvères operating in the city of Arras in a series of publications, linking aspects of their biographies to their literary and musical works.[15] Over half a century later, Roger Berger built on the archival discoveries of his predecessors and not only studied the historical records relevant to Arrageois trouvères but also various individuals named in their works.[16]

Drawing on similar methods to the scholars mentioned above, I will argue in this chapter that attention to the historical record and individual biographies allows for broader consideration of what fuelled musical and literary outputs in Old French during the long thirteenth century. I take the city of Arras as a case study on account of the high density of poets, manuscripts, and literary works that can be connected with the city but also because of the rich historical record that still survives. Two common themes emerge – moneylending and religious activity – that shed light on the individuals who took part in vernacular cultural life. By attending to the other aspects and facets of their lives, I show that not only were the activities associated with trouvère culture wide ranging and highly diversified but so, too, were the types of people who participated in it. Doing so, I suggest, pushes beyond questions of how to read or interpret the cultural outputs themselves and allows for consideration of points of commonality and difference amongst the individuals who contributed to this culture. What is more, this distinction allows us to recover the single aspect of homogeneity of the trouvères: that they were individuals who crafted Old French songs and literature. A more explicit acknowledgement of what precisely is meant by trouvère allows for the term's continued use without applying it wholesale in a way that limits our understanding of each trouvère's individuality. To understand the biographies of the participants in trouvère culture and how they related to one another, I use surviving records of the Confraternity of Jongleurs and Bourgeois as a way of consulting a population of individuals who shared a common trait: their participation in a particular form of religious life.

The Confraternity of Jongleurs and Bourgeois of Arras

The Confraternity of Jongleurs and Bourgeois of Arras, also known as the Carité Notre-Dame des Ardents, was a religious organisation founded in Arras sometime between the late eleventh and late twelfth centuries. Although nominally organised by jongleurs, or musicians, the confraternity welcomed the whole range of Arras's population, whether lay or cleric, man or woman, child or adult, rich or poor. The religious focus of the confraternity is evident from its founding miracle, which tells of two jongleurs, bitter rivals, who are sent to Arras by the Virgin Mary to help cure

---

[14] Dinaux, 1837–63.

[15] Guesnon 1895, 1902.

[16] Berger (ed.) 1981.

the city's inhabitants of a plague; when they succeed, the Virgin bestows upon them a candle, or the *sainte chandelle*, whose healing powers save the city and its people.[17]

The confraternity served as a central religious organisation for the Arrageois during its long history.[18] As scholars have argued, confraternities like that of the Confraternity of Jongleurs and Bourgeois served to build a sense of community, extend charity to its membership, and maintain religious activity and prayer.[19] Scholars have frequently connected the confraternity with Arrageois musical life, and the trouvères more specifically, for two primary reasons. The first is that the confraternity was founded by jongleurs, and musicians formed an integral part of the founding miracle; this link with musical life and the leading role that musicians play has turned the confraternity into the sight of serious interest to scholars of medieval musical culture. The second aspect of the confraternity that connects it with Arrageois musical life is its earliest surviving document, a register of members and collection of statutes dated between the late twelfth and mid-fourteenth centuries. Now Paris, BnF, fr. 8541 (fols. 3r–45r), this register contains the names of nearly eleven thousand individuals who belonged to the confraternity during the high to late medieval period. Amongst these names are those of many trouvères, and thus Paris, BnF, fr. 8541 is significant for the way that it helps locate certain trouvères within Arras, both geographically and temporally.[20]

Appendix 1 includes those individuals who were listed in Paris, BnF, fr. 8541 as members of the confraternity and who can broadly be considered musicians. By musician, I mean individuals who are ascribed as authors of vernacular literary works in surviving manuscripts, people who are named as cantors (liturgical musicians) in surviving religious records, or who are listed in the confraternity's manuscript with an identifier that suggests a musical trade or occupation, like a jongleur. In addition to the name (as it appears in the manuscript), I also include information about any works (both musical and literary) ascribed to these individuals in the last column. Some names, as is clear from double dates in the second column, were inscribed into the manuscript twice.

Many observations about the status of trouvères and their outputs can be gleaned from Appendix 1. Of the thirty-nine individuals who participated in song culture listed here (i.e., authors of at least one ascribed song), nineteen appear having

---

[17] For more information on the founding miracle, see Symes 2007, p. 85 n. 30. The miracle story survives in both Latin and vernacular versions. The Latin original hast been lost, but a version redacted in 1482, later copied by a seventeenth-century *maieur*, is extant and edited in Cavrois (ed.) 1876, pp. 91–103. The Latin and vernacular versions were most recently edited together by Berger (ed.) 1970, vol. 2, pp. 139–56. For another, more recent take on the miracle, see Vincent 2000.

[18] Like many such organisations, the Confraternity was suppressed during the French Revolution. However, during the 1860s and '70s, the Arrageois rebuilt the Confraternity and its religious significance for the city of Arras. On the post-Revolution Confraternity, see Brissy 1860, pp. 47–52 and Symes 2007, pp. 214–15.

[19] For an introduction to medieval confraternities, see Eisenbichler 2019, p. 1; Rosser 2015, pp. 7–9.

[20] For a study of this manuscript and what it offers for musicological study of Arrageois musical culture, see Dolce 2020a.

only been ascribed a single surviving song; of course, this may tell us less about the musical and literary activity of an individual and more about their renown (or lack thereof) in the period that the chansonniers were copied. Nevertheless, the vast majority of trouvères who were members of the confraternity seem to have been more occasional participants in the making of literature or song rather than individuals who regularly and expansively contributed to what we now consider trouvère culture. Others with more substantial literary and musical outputs, such as Jehan Bodel (entered at year 1209 in Appendix 1) and Jehan de Grieviler (1240), were still prominent members of the confraternity but were certainly not the norm. Moreover, authors of non-musical works – such as Jehan Bodel and Robert le Clerc (inscribed in 1272) – appear amongst the more traditional poet-musicians that we normally consider trouvères.[21] Finally, a number of cantors at Arras Cathedral and the Abbey of Saint Vaast can be identified amongst the confraternity's membership; their relationship to the creators of vernacular song will be discussed in detail below.

Although concrete biographical information cannot be found on each of the individuals in Appendix 1, there are certain connecting threads between those whose biographies can be at least partially reconstructed. First, the practice of money lending seems to have been somewhat common for individuals who partook in trouvère culture; from Audefrois Louchart (about whom more will be said below) to Nevelon Amions, trouvères in Arras seem to have earned often significant money through the practice of lending money at interest. The history of Arras in the Middle Ages would suggest that such an observation should be unsurprising: as economic historians have long acknowledged, the city was home to some of medieval Europe's most powerful, and unusually Christian, moneylenders from the latter half of the twelfth century.[22] Yet the fact that both prolific as well as occasional trouvères seem to have taken part in the practice indicates that cultural activity was inextricable from economics. On the other hand, many of the trouvères who are listed as members of the confraternity were deeply entwined with religious life, whether as clerics themselves or in less direct ways. Again, this observation is unsurprising; that these trouvères were members of an inherently religious organisation would suggest that they may have had ties with religious houses in Arras. Nonetheless, it points to a pervasive religious culture amongst vernacular literary and musical activity, consonant with observations made by other scholars of medieval Arras about the high literacy rates amongst the Arrageois and particularly those associated with musical or literary culture.[23]

Both of these activities – moneylending and economic activity on the one hand and religious life on the other hand – help to illuminate the types of people who participated in trouvère culture in Arras. By reading the details of the lives of some

[21] On the dramatic oeuvre of Jehan Bodel, see Doudet's chapter in this volume.

[22] See Bigwood 1924–25, part 1, p. 490. For other studies of the family, see Lestocquoy 1954.

[23] Berger estimated that approximately four hundred students could have been educated in Arras at any given time and that approximately one-quarter of the *bourgeois* population had received an education. Symes builds on this, positing that around half of the population, or sixteen thousand laymen, were functionally literate during the period. See Berger (ed.) 1981, p. 110; Symes 2007, pp. 178, 181.

of these individuals more closely and by putting them into dialogue with the other trouvères who were members of the confraternity, the highly varied nature of these individuals comes to the fore.

The Louchart Family and the Economics of Song

In thirteenth-century Arras, moneylending was a prosperous business. The Loucharts, whose name first appears in documents around 1170, was perhaps the most famous lending family in the city. Prominent members privately lent money to cities, ecclesiastical institutions, and major political figures, distinguishing their activities from those of their Lombard counterparts who formed societies for the sole purpose of credit.[24] The wealth of families like the Loucharts allowed them to hold great power in many of the city's ecclesiastical institutions, in many cases as clerics, and such families were frequently in possession of much of the city's property.

The Louchart family formed a distinguishable faction within the confraternity, with at least fifty individual members listed in the register of Paris, BnF, fr. 8541. Their family name first appears in 1194, the first year in which the document was copied. Audefrois Louchart, inscribed in the confraternity's record in 1273, is a familiar name to musicologists and literary scholars alike. Audefrois not only participated in but also judged *jeux-partis* (although, like with other *jeu-parti* judges' verdicts, his are not recorded), and his name featured in the songs of others as well.[25]

Alongside his involvement in trouvère culture, Audefrois was one of the family's most successful moneylenders. His accounts, as Georges Bigwood and later Berger recognised, were extensive and wide ranging, and he developed an increasingly powerful role in economic and political life in the region over the course of his lifetime. Like many moneylenders in Arras, Audefrois occasionally co-lent money. For example, in 1244, he lent 1,200 livres to the bishop of Liège with Ermenfroi Crespin; Ermenfroi was a member of another of Arras's famous lending families and was also a member of the confraternity.[26] This loan was paid back the following year, undoubtedly at a high rate of interest. By the 1260s, Audefrois was lending internationally. First, in 1262, he lent 2,000 livres to Prince Edward of England, future King Edward I.[27] In 1266, Audefrois lent an astounding sum, 10,000 livres, to Gui de Dampierre, the future count of Flanders; this loan was given in two separate installments.[28]

Although Audefrois's moneylending activities have been acknowledged in studies of Arras's medieval cultural milieu, the cultural prowess that his wealth afforded him and the long-term manifestations of it have rarely been connected with musical

---

[24] De Paermentier 2018.

[25] Audefrois is listed as the author of the *jeu-parti* RS 1850 but was also the possible judge of many others, including RS 101, 297, 664, 668, 669, 841, 862, 899, 940, 1026, 1034, 1092, 1121, 1584, 1672, and 1679. My sincere thanks to Joseph W. Mason for sharing his extensive research into the *jeu-parti* with me, including this information about Audefrois as a judge.

[26] See Berger (ed.) 1981, p. 376; Bormans and Schoolmeesters (eds.) 1893, pp. 466, 490, 517.

[27] Berger (ed.) 1981, p. 376, in reference to AdPC, série B, 858/1291–92.

[28] Berger (ed.) 1981, p. 376, in reference to GR, Charters of the Counts of Flanders, nos. 120–22.

life. Audefrois was married to a woman named Oede, likely the woman inscribed in Paris, BnF, fr. 8541 in 1272 ('feme Audefroi Oede'); based on marriage patterns amongst the Loucharts and other moneylending families, it seems possible, if not likely, that she was also from a lending family in the city, although this cannot be substantiated. Various scholars, most recently Jenna Philips, have posited that Oede Louchart may be the 'Demisele Oede' named as a judge of five *jeux-partis*, which can be dated to around the time she would have been alive.[29] Audefrois and Oede had at least four children (Jacques, Andrieu, Jean, and Mahieu) all of whom were inscribed in the confraternity's documents and all lent money at some point in their lives.

Audefrois and Oede's nuclear family also contains another musician, albeit one who is typically overlooked for his musical significance. In an obituary for Arras Cathedral, Jacques Louchart was inscribed as 'Dominus Jacobi Louchardi quondam cantoris et Canonicus nostri' (Master Jacques Louchard former cantor and canon).[30] From this obituary inscription, we glean that Jacques was cantor at Arras Cathedral, an office that not only required substantial musical ability but also the skills to write and organise the institution's liturgy. Although Jacques's career as a cleric might make us imagine that he left the world of moneylending behind, he nevertheless took on the family trade and continued to lend money well after he had become a canon. For example, in 1274, Jacques lent more than 200 livres to Margaret, countess of Flanders.[31] That Jacques continued to lend money despite his clerical career is indicative of the pervasiveness of lending activity in Arras and its connection to various other facets of life in the city during the long thirteenth century.

A more comprehensive view of Audefrois Louchart and his family thus demon-strates the importance of considering the identities of trouvères beyond their crafting of vernacular song. Looking at a single subset of the family reveals three individuals who were implicated in musical life in Arras but whose broader biogra-phies offer much beyond their musical activities. For Arras's moneylending families, high-interest lending is often considered to be a factor that connects generations, sometimes over a century and a half. But as the case of the Loucharts shows, partic-ipation in musical life transcended generations as well. As Eric Matheis and, more

---

[29] Doss-Quinby et al. (eds.) 2001, p. 33. Demisele Oede is listed as the judge of five *jeux-partis*: RS 8, 667=8, 1351, 1637, and 947=916. The authors suggest that scribes sought explicitly to pay tribute to Oede, given that the *jeux-partis* for which she is listed as judge in some manuscripts have male judges listed in other manuscripts. Moreover, some manuscripts transmit these songs with a different judge – namely, a certain 'Audefrois' – lending potential credence to the claims that this Oede is in fact Oede Louchart. On this issue, see Philips 2019.

[30] See Berger (ed.) 1981, pp. 379–82. See also Arras, MM 290, fol. 81v; Loisne (ed.) 1896, no. 124; Arras, MM 1088, fol. 27r; and Arras, Arch. Dép., 3 G, oblations. It should be noted that there are two individuals by the name of Jacques Louchart who lived around the same time. Bigwood was the first to acknowledge this, citing one as the son of Engelbert and the other as the son of Audefrois. Later, Berger showed that Audefrois's son was a canon at Arras Cathedral; although he did not identify Jacques as a cantor, this does confirm that this Jacques is the son of Audefrois, not Engelbert. See Bigwood 1924–25, part 1, p. 492; Berger (ed.) 1981, pp. 379–82.

[31] Berger (ed.) 1981, pp. 379, 382; Luykx 1961, no. 111.

recently, Eliza Zingesser have shown, references to the economic situation in Arras were frequent in contemporary Arrageois literature.[32] But starting from historical documentation, it is clear that economic activity also perpetuated musical cultures and opportunities, particularly for wealthy families like the Loucharts. Although Audefrois's moneylending practices are frequently acknowledged alongside his participation in the crafting and judging of songs, there remains little understanding of how, if at all, these two activities may have influenced each other. Moreover, a more comprehensive approach to Audefrois's biography allows for the acknowledgement that the musical impact of his family extended beyond trouvère culture, accounting for the wider musical contexts reflected in historical documents pertaining to Audefrois and his family.

Disentangling the Cleric-Trouvère

Members of religious life like Jacques Louchart were an important part of the confraternity's membership. In addition to monks from the Abbey of Saint Vaast and canons from Arras Cathedral, who made up a majority of the religious in the confraternity, female religious and clerics from institutions outside of the city were also prominent members.[33] On account of their presence in religious communities, where various forms of documentation mention each institution's religious by name, many of these individuals are easier to trace than their lay counterparts. While Jacques Louchart's connection to trouvère activity was through his father, his role as cantor at Arras Cathedral renders him as close to a fully focussed musician as we get in this period. But Jacques was not the only cathedral cantor who was a member of the confraternity. In the life of his predecessor, Guibert Kaukesel, who was active around the middle of the thirteenth century, the vernacular world of trouvère culture co-existed with liturgical music.

Guibert Kaukesel, inscribed in Paris, BnF, fr. 8541 in 1242, has four songs ascribed to him, all of which were copied in locally made manuscripts.[34] Whereas there is no further evidence for his vernacular musical activity, his presence as a canon at Arras Cathedral vibrantly depicts Guibert's religious career. Like Jacques, his cathedral obituary offers important information about his status in the community upon his death: 'Obit etiam Wibertus Caukesel scolasticus atrebatensis pro quo distribuntur xxix solidi per xxiii libris x solidi, iam habitis ex veneditione quorumdam librorum suorum et repositis in decima de Eikeborc' (And so died Guibert Kaukesel, *scholasticus* of Arras who gave 29 solidi through 23 livres and 10 solidi, now having sold certain of his books and placed them in the tithe of Eikeborc).[35] In addition to identifying him as the cathedral's 'scholasticus' (the person in charge of the education

---

[32] Matheis 2013; Zingesser 2019.

[33] For more on the women religious in the Confraternity, see Dolce 2020a, 2020b.

[34] These songs are RS 118, 811, 924, and 1785. Guibert's songs are transmitted in three prominent chansonniers from the area around Arras: R (Paris, BnF, fr. 1591), M (Paris, BnF, fr. 844), and T (Paris, BnF, fr. 12615).

[35] Arras, MM 424, fol. 83v.

of young boys in the cathedral's care), Guibert's obituary suggests that he sold personal books to pay for his cathedral obit and, as Berger noted, one of these books is still extant.[36] Now Boulogne-sur-Mer, BM 117, Guibert's surviving book is a copy of Gratian's *Decretum*, the primary medieval canon law text; the manuscript opens with an inscription indicating that, when Guibert obtained the manuscript, he was no longer the *scholasticus* at the cathedral.[37]

Papal documents from the 1260s offer further information about a later stage of Guibert's career. The most interesting is dated November 12, 1263, in which Guibert is identified as 'Cantori et magistro Wiberto, dicto Kaukesel, cappelano nostro, Canonicus Atrebatensis' (Cantor and Magister Guibert, called Kaukesel, our [papal] chaplain, and canon of Arras).[38] This identification of Guibert tells us that he was a cantor, and the contents of the other papal documents pertaining to him indicate that in his capacity as a chaplain to the pope, he had the power to create canonries and prebends. Although Guibert's position at the cathedral was already noted by Berger, the full extent of his duties and career have never been fully appreciated.[39]

In addition to Jacques and Guibert, many liturgical musicians were members of the confraternity and co-existed amongst its trouvères; their names appear in Appendix 1. From the Abbey of Saint Vaast in particular, a number of individuals prominent for other activities appear in records as musicians. Nicolas le Caudrelier, for example, first appears in Saint Vaast's records in 1270 as a *puer in scola*, or a boy in the monastery's choir.[40] His later career is easily reconstructed: he was first a *praepositus* at one of the abbey's priories, and eventually he became abbot, an office to which he was appointed in 1307.[41] Pieres de Harnez, one of the last individuals to be inscribed in Paris, BnF, fr. 8541 (at year 1350), held various offices at the abbey: first as *magister cantor* in 1330, then *sacrista* in 1334, and finally *thesaurarius* in 1345.[42] These offices, all interrelated, may have been held simultaneously: as cantor, Pieres would have been responsible for leading liturgical services, of course, but also for the maintenance and writing of liturgical books (a responsibility linked to that of the *thesaurarius*). And as sacristan, his responsibility for the maintenance of sacred objects directly related to the other of his two offices.

The liturgical musicians in the confraternity filled various roles in their communities, and their lives were never solely devoted to music making; and the same was true for the trouvères. Indeed, many trouvères held known connections to religious institutions within and beyond Arras, either as clerics themselves or in ways

---

[36] Berger (ed.) 1981, p. 321.

[37] The inscription reads, 'Decretum hoc fuit magistri Wiberti Caukesel quondam scolastici Attrebatensis' (This Decretum belonged to Magister Guibert Kaukesel, formerly the *scholasticus* of Arras).

[38] Guiraud (ed.) 1904, no. 2192.

[39] Berger (ed.) 1981, p. 321. It is puzzling that although Berger acknowledges that Guibert was listed as a canon and chaplain in the papal documents of the 1260s, he does not note that he was also named as a cantor in those same documents.

[40] Van Drival (ed.) 1878, p. 39.

[41] Van Drival (ed.) 1878, p. 39.

[42] Van Drival (ed.) 1878, p. 39.

that highlighted their own personal piety. Felipes de Verdieres, to whom a single *jeu-parti* is ascribed, was a canon and deacon at Arras Cathedral.[43] Sawalo Cosset, the documented author of one song, though not a cleric, paid for an obituary at Arras Cathedral, where he also funded a benefice for a chaplain.[44] Even Arras's most famous trouvères, whose corpora are extensive and suggest regular song-making activity, were connected with religious institutions: Jehan Bretel was the sergeant of the Abbey of Saint Vaast, a seemingly hereditary post that he held from at least 1256.[45] Mahius Tailliere, with whom Bretel shared a number of *jeux-partis*, offered a tithe to the abbey from 1254 along with his wife, Marie de Simencourt.[46]

The relationship that various trouvères held with the Church has been of increasing scholarly interest. Building on arguments made by Berger about the number of religious amongst the confraternity and the high level of clerical education amongst men in medieval Arras, Jennifer Saltzstein has coined the term 'cleric-trouvère' to describe a population of poet-composers who straddle the lay versus clerical and Latin versus vernacular divides.[47] In particular, in the genre of the *jeu-parti*, Saltzstein has demonstrated that Arrageois trouvères were familiar with Latin texts, referencing classical authors such as Ovid.[48] For Saltzstein, indications that trouvères were familiar with Latin literature prove that there was a depth to their clerical educations that has hitherto gone unrecognised.

'Cleric-trouvère' concisely creates a subsection of the trouvères and highlights a phenomenon – that is, a high degree of clerical education amongst vernacular poets – that appears to have been characteristic of Arras. But at the same time, it places emphasis on the concept of trouvère as one of identity, alongside 'cleric', as a type of religious identity. If anything, the temptation to qualify the term 'trouvère' itself with other identity markers seems only to suggest that our understanding of literary and song traditions in Old French that emerged c. 1200 has far surpassed the confines of a monolithic understanding.

Nevertheless, Saltzstein's coinage of the term 'cleric-trouvère' began to reveal currents that played a role in the cultivation of vernacular song and literary culture during the thirteenth century. Indeed, Guibert Kaukesel and Felipes de Verdieres are not the only 'cleric-trouvères' who were members of the confraternity (see Appendix 1). In addition to them, Tumas de Castel was also possibly a cleric at some point in his life, given that he was listed in a document in 1233 as celibate. Both Felipes and Tumas have a single surviving song ascribed to them. Thus, like Guibert, they appear more as occasional participants in the culture of vernacular song on the

---

[43] Loisne (ed.) 1896, no. 173; Berger (ed.) 1981, pp. 414–15.

[44] Cosset appears in the following cathedral obituaries: Arras, MM 290, fol. 79v; Brussels, KBR 21532–5, fol. 19v. For his funding of the chaplain, see Loisne (ed.) 1907, no. 124.

[45] Berger (ed.) 1981, p. 314. Charters concerning Bretel's career at the abbey can be found in Loisne 1899.

[46] Arras, MM 316, p. 144. See also Berger (ed.) 1981, p. 409. Other Arrageois trouvères were also involved in local ecclesiastical culture. For example, Gilles le Vinier was a canon in Lille and an ecclesiastical official in Arras. See Guesnon 1895, pp. 430–32.

[47] Berger (ed.) 1981, p. 110; Saltzstein 2012, 2013, particularly chap. 3.

[48] Saltzstein 2013, p. 110.

basis of the extant chansonniers. By considering the biographies of 'cleric-trouvères' more holistically, we may arrive at a more nuanced understanding of their clerical activities. These activities do more than simply allow us to elucidate different levels of complexity in their poetry; rather, they tell us about the broader social currents that gave rise to trouvère culture as well as types of individuals who participated in it.

The lives and careers of Audefrois Louchart and Guibert Kaukesel, particularly when set in relief amongst their contemporaries, exemplify the way that the designation of an individual as a trouvère can at best minimise and at worst erase other facets of their lives and significance. Consideration of their lives and how they appear in documentary sources demonstrates that there is great heterogeneity amongst the individuals we now call trouvères; they were drawn from a wide array of social and professional backgrounds, even in a context in which they gathered around the same purposes and activities, such as the confraternity in Arras. While the unification of these individuals under the umbrella of trouvère allows us to appreciate the shared cultural practice in which they engaged, I argue that we should use it with a bit of caution. Indeed, the biographies of the trouvères discussed in this chapter show that these individuals were active in the creation of culture in *many* different realms, rather than the singular realm of vernacular song making encompassed in our conception of the trouvère. The modern usage of the term 'trouvère' does not allow for this nuanced and complex understanding of these medieval musicians; indeed, such complexity is almost antithetical to the ways that we presently describe them. Our modern repertory- (rather than people-)focussed approach to trouvère culture accepts the inherent problems in considering trouvères as composers but has yet to fully disentangle the idea of trouvères from the distinctly modern premises and categories that underlie how we use the term today.

But much can be gained from re-centring people in our understanding of trouvère culture. As I have sought to demonstrate in this chapter, such an approach would need to fully account for the currents and impetuses – such as religious life and moneylending – that led to the flourishing of vernacular culture in the long thirteenth century. Active consideration of these contexts may not only help to understand the works of these individuals better but also to illuminate the kinds of circumstances that inspired vernacular culture and served as fodder for its creation. Emphasising the many aspects of individual lives and activities also reveals connections between different musical repertories and traditions, such as those of liturgical chant and vernacular song. Whether in the lives of individual people like Guibert Kaukesel or across generations of prominent Arrageois families like the Loucharts, it is clear that considerable overlap existed between different types of music making and the individuals who created and performed that music.[49]

---

[49] As previously mentioned, similar observations have recently been made in regards to the relationship between monophony and polyphony. I am thinking particularly of the study of the motets in Paris, BnF, fr. 12615 by Gaël Saint-Cricq in which he notes that the motets and triplum voices in this collection are largely secular and are either songs or drawing from a thematic repertory close to that of monophonic song. Moreover, he shows that several tenors of these compositions match perfectly with chants copied into the

Recently, Margot Fassler issued a similar plea for medieval musicologists to consider the lives of musicians more carefully. Referencing projects that take a prosopographic approach to the study of medieval people (i.e., a method of group biography that aims to elucidate shared traits of the individuals within the larger population), Fassler acknowledges that such documentary and archival work can reveal the names and identities of medieval musicians who are lost in the musico-historical record.[50] The contents provided in Appendix 1 are based on such prosopographic research, showing the possibilities that indeed exist with such a method; despite the prominence of trouvères, many of the other musicians listed would be otherwise unknown. I would contend, though, that the benefits of close attention to prosopography or other biographical research methods lie not solely in their abilities to reveal new musicians but also in the ways in which they help to throw into focus the non-musical aspects of individual's lives. As musicologists, there is a strong temptation to emphasise the details that make someone a musician, whether those details manifest in authorial ascriptions or in qualifying information in external documents that tell us about their musical activities. But a more comprehensive approach, which accounts both for the details of an individual's life and the broader context of the people with whom they were surrounded, ensures that we do not overextend the scope of their musical activities, or even weigh a single type of music making over others. In this way, such methodologies tell us something about people; rather than re-centre the musical repertory as such, it allows us to situate musical phenomena in much broader social contexts.

Such an appreciation of the people who participated in vernacular musical culture invites us to reflect anew on much of the literature composed in Arras during the period in which these creators were active. The opening stanza from an anonymous lyric, copied into a chansonnier in Arras sometime in the last quarter of the thirteenth century, betrays all of these overlapping themes:

> Arras is a school of all good understanding.
> When you take the worst thing from Arras,
> even that you can sell as the best elsewhere.
> Indeed, Arras's fame spreads far and wide.
> Yesterday, I saw the heavens open:
> God wants to learn Arras's motets.[51]

---

manuscripts of the Abbey of Saint Vaast, suggesting overlap between individuals crafting songs and motets and those familiar with local chant traditions. See Saint-Cricq with Doss-Quinby and Rosenberg (eds.) 2017, p. xviii. This work clearly builds on previous scholarship by Saint-Cricq and others that demonstrates the porousness between motets and monophonic song. See Bradley 2013; Thomson 2018; Saint-Cricq 2013, 2019.

[50] Fassler 2018, p. 177.

[51] 'Arras est escole de tous biens entendre. / Quant on veut d'Arras le plus caitiff prendre / En autre païs se puet por boin vendre. / On voit les honor d'Arras si estendre / Je vi l'autre jor le ciel lasus fendre: / Dex voloit d'Arras les motés aprendre' (edition from Berger (ed.) 1981, p. 120; translation my own).

According to this famous lyric, Arras was a school, the seat of a diocese, home to a thriving Benedictine monastic community, one of the leading cultural hubs of northern Europe. In light of the intersecting musical traditions to which Arras's medieval musicians attest, I would like to conclude by suggesting a new reading of the first line of this famous lyric. Taken as a double entendre, we could consider reading 'entendre' as 'to hear' as well as 'to understand'. Arras was a place where one could learn and hear all good things: chansons and *jeux-partis* but also motets, chant, civic music, possibly performed by the same individuals.

Appendix 1: Musicians Named in Paris, BnF, fr. 8541 and Their Attributed Works[52]

	Name	Year	Attributed works elsewhere
1194–1220	Warins Li Joglere	1203	
	Jehan Bodel	1209	Author: *Jeu de saint Nicolas*; *congés*; fabliaux; *pastourelles*; songs
	Henricus Amion	1210, 1241,?	Author: 2 *jeux-partis*; 1 song
	Jocosa	1216	
	Joculatrix	1218	
	Clamoator	1218	
	Abatia	1221	
	Cosset Sawalo	1215, 1247,1258	Author: 1 song. Founds chapel in cathedral of Arras with his wife. Listed in cathedral obituary[53]
1220–40	Castelains Hues	1226	Author: 1 song. Holds dîme to the chapter of Arras Cathedral. Wife listed in cathedral obituary[54]
	Fouchardus li Jogleres	1228	
	Li Bretels Jakemes	1229	Author: *Le Tournoi de Chauvency*. Owns two separate houses in Arras[55]
	Des Jongleurs Wis	1230	
	Histrionis Nicholes	1232	
	Jehan del Carpentier	1232	
	Cok Menestreus	1234	
	Major Vedasti Wibers	1236	
	Clamator Jehans	1238	
	De Grieviler Jehans	1240	Author: c. 50 songs and *jeux-partis*

[52] In addition to the musicians in the table, a 'Jehan Le Cuvelier' was inscribed in the manuscript in 1352; it is unclear whether this inscription refers to the individual to whom at least eight songs and a number of other *jeux-partis* are ascribed.

[53] Berger (ed.) 1981, pp. 328–29. On his activities at Arras Cathedral, see Paris, BnF, lat. 17737, fol. 64v and Loisne (ed.) 1907, no. 124. Further, Cosset is listed as an *éschevin* of Arras in *Diplomata Belgica: The Diplomatic Sources from the Medieval Southern Low Countries*, no. 15089 (www.diplomata-belgica.be<https://www.diplomata-belgica.be/charter_details_fr.php?dibe_id=15089).

[54] See Loisne (ed.) 1907, no. 34; Feuchère 1948, pp. 23–27.

[55] See Paris, BnF, lat. 10972, fol. 9v. It is not entirely clear whether this Jacques Bretel is the same as the one who composed the *Tournoi de Chauvency*. According to Delbouille, this is not the same individual, as he assumes that the date in Paris, BnF, fr. 8541 is one that

	Name	Year	Attributed works elsewhere
1241–60	Menestrella feme Henri	1241	
	Berta Joculatrix	1242	
	Kauque sel Wibers	1242	Author: 4 songs. Canon and *scholasticus* at Arras Cathedral. Chaplain to Pope Urban IV. Owner of manor at Harvain. Owner of books, including a copy of Gratian's *Decretum*
	Cantrix Liegars	1244	
	Viniers Willaumes	1245	Author: c. 27 songs, 12 *jeux-partis*, *pastourelles*
	Cantrix Agnes	1247	
	Simen Jehans	1247	Author: 1 *jeu-parti*
	Contredis Andrius	1248	Author: c. 20 songs, 1 *jeu-parti*, *pastourelles*
	Pro Nevelo Amions	1248, 1280, 1294	Author: 1 song. Money lender to the city of Troyes[56]
	Crieresse feme Jehan	1242	
	Felize Paons	1252	Author: 1 song
	Cousins li Jouglere	1252	
	Fontaine Jehans	1252, 1272	Author: 1 song
	Felipes de Verdieres	1253	Author: 1 *jeu-parti*. Canon and deacon at Arras Cathedral. Bequeaths his manuscripts to the Sorbonne
	Marc. Willaumes li Jouglere	1255	
	Del Vinier Jakemon	1256	Author: 7 songs
	Tailliere Mahius	1257	Author: 1 *jeu-parti*. Holds dîme at Saint Vaast with his wife. Provides financial relief to Guillaume de Bucquoy[57]
	Cauta Robers de le Piere	1257	Author: c. 9 songs, 5 *jeux-partis*. *Échevin*[58]
	Erardi Jehans	1258, 1259	Author: c. 27 songs
	Cri. Jehans li Crieres	1260	

indicates a death. See Delbouille (ed.) 1932, p. LVI. My thanks to Elizabeth Eva Leach for drawing this work to my attention.

[56] See Berger (ed.) 1981, p. 298 and PAn, J 195, no. 69.

[57] See Berger (ed.) 1981, p. 409; on his tithe to Saint Vaast, Arras, MM 316, p. 144; on rights to land near du Jardin, Guesnon (ed.) 1862, no. 33.

[58] On his career as an échevin, see AdPC, B 1593, no. 98.

	Name	Year	Attributed works elsewhere
1261–80	Gilebert le Vinier	1261	Author: 5 songs, 2 jeux-partis, 1 lai
	Feme Crieur Huon	1262	
	Tumas de Castel	1271	Author: 1 song. Listed in 1233 as celibate. Owns two houses in Arras[59]
	Jehan Bretiaus	1272	Author: c. 7 songs, jeux-partis. Moneylender to city of Troyes. Shares manor at Beaurains with his brother from 1261. Sergeant to the Abbey of Saint Vaast[60]
	Pro Fastoul Baude	1272, 1296	
	Gilet Croi	1272	Author: 1 song
	Au Clerc Robert	1272	Author: Les Vers de la mort; judge of 1 jeu-parti
	Audefrois Louchars	1273	Author: 2 songs?; judge of jeux-partis. Moneylender to bishop of Liège, to future Edward I of England, and to Gui de Dampierre. Property owner in Arras
	Sainte du Pré	1280	Author: 1 song
1281–1300	Rosel le Teilleur	1286	Author: 1 song
	Au Jougleur Hesselin	1293	
	D'Orguel Jehans	1297	Author: 2 songs
	Jehans Noevile	1297	Author: c. 12 songs
	Maistre Chopart	1297	Author: 1 jeu-parti; judge of 1 jeu-parti
	Menestreus Gherars	1299	
1301–20	Ferris Lambers	1302	Author: c. 4 songs; 26 jeux-partis
	De Castel Robert	1303, 1303	Author: c. 6 songs and jeux-partis. Land holder (property of Saint Vaast) near Bapaume[61]
	Au Sauvage le Trouvere	1305	Author: 1 song?
	A le Petite Jehane	1309	Author: 1 song
	Corbiaus Pieres	1309	Author: c. 7 songs; judge of 1 jeu-parti
	Louchars Jakemes canonnes	1310	Canon and cantor at Arras Cathedral. Son of Audefrois Louchart
	Jehan d'Escury	1318	Author: 1 song

[59] See Berger (ed.) 1981, p. 319; on his listing as a celibate man, see Arras, MM 316, p. 94; on the houses he owned, see Paris, BnF, lat. 10972, fols. 15r and 17v.

[60] See Berger (ed.) 1981, p. 314; on the manor in Beaurains, see Paris, BnF, lat. 10972, fol. 55v; on his role at the Abbey of Saint Vaast, see Loisne 1899, pp. 75–78.

[61] See Berger (ed.) 1981, p. 319; on his land holding, see AdPC, 1 H 1, fol. 276v; on the house he owned in Arras, see Paris, BnF, lat. 10972, fol. 35v.

	Name	Year	Attributed works elsewhere
1321–40	Simon d'Auchi	1321	Author: c.11 songs; 3 *jeux-partis*
	Douchet Andrieu	1322	Author: c. 2 songs; 1 *jeu-parti*. Money-lender to the city of Bruges[62]
	De Paris Andrieu	1323	Author: 1 song
	Le Jougleresse Catherine	1328	
	Legier Jehan	1329	Author: 1 *jeu-parti*
	De Lens Jougleur Jehan	1331	
	Ghillain Jougleur Mahieu	1331	
	Dant de Sainte Jemme Pieres	1332	Monk at Abbey of Saint Vaast. *Succentor*[63]
	Le Normant Jehan Dant. nient	1336	Monk at Abbey of Saint Vaast. *Magister puerorum*[64]
	Jouglete Marie	1336	
	Le Caudrelier Nicolas Dant	1337	Monk at Abbey of Saint Vaast. *Puer in scola Praepositus Hasprensis.* Abbot of Saint Vaast
	Crieur de vin Merllin	1337	
	Menestrel G. de Hachicourt	1337	
	De Harnez Dan Pieres	1350	Monk at Abbey of Saint Vaast. *Magister cantor. Sacrista. Thesaurarius*

---

[62] See Berger (ed.) 1981, p. 344.

[63] Van Drival (ed.) 1878, p. 40.

[64] Van Drival (ed.) 1878, p. 39.

12

Encounters of Poets, Composers, and Performers in *Ars nova* Song: The Case of Jaquet de Noyon, Minstrel, and the Ballade *Puis que je sui fumeux*[1]

Yolanda Plumley

Guillaume de Machaut is often described as the last of the trouvères for his equal prowess in the arts of poetry and music, especially as reflected in his many secular songs. The prevailing wisdom in our modern narratives of the development of late medieval French lyric poetry is that after Machaut, poets and composers became ever more specialised, and the two arts parted ways so as finally to emancipate lyric poetry from the yoke of music. The pronouncements in *L'Art de dictier* (1392), a manual on the art of composing lyric poetry by Eustache Deschamps, Machaut's self-professed poetic disciple, doubtless have encouraged this perspective; there, the poet advocates the independence of poetry, which he defines as 'natural' music as opposed to the 'artificial' kind represented by music per se.[2] Certainly, large collections of French lyrics in the so-called *formes fixes* survive from this period, including many by Deschamps himself and by others who we have no reason to believe possessed musical skills or conceived their poems with music in mind. And it is true that the contemporary anthologies of lyrics with musical settings feature a good many songs of a complexity that implies the input of specialist musicians.

How clear cut, though, is the case for a division of labour between wordsmiths and composers in French song writing in the late fourteenth century? We know that princes, courtiers, and city burghers alike were eager to learn the art of composing lyric poetry at that time, and treatises like Deschamps's were designed to guide them. But users of such manuals surely included, too, those church-trained musicians with whom we associate the *Ars nova* polyphonic song repertory. Indeed, the close relationship of text and music witnessed in certain songs invites us to suppose that in those cases, at least, poet and composer were likely to have been one and the

---

[1] Research for this essay was undertaken with the generous support of The Leverhulme Trust, the European Research Council, and the Netherlands Institute of Advanced Science.

[2] On Deschamps's conceptual dichotomy, see also Doudet's chapter in this volume.

same.[3] If musicians could learn to compose lyrics, might not some keen amateur poets likewise have sought to gain sufficient musical competence to produce simple polyphonic settings for fixed-form lyrics?[4] One princely amateur who certainly did was Johan, future king of Aragon; during the Christmas and New Year celebrations of 1379–80, he had one of the French chapel singers newly hired for his chapel teach him the skills to accomplish this. Johan was immensely proud of his achievement and wrote to his brother Martin informing him of his newfound skill and inviting Martin, or any courtier in his entourage, to send on to him French fixed-form lyrics they had composed so that he could furnish them with music of this kind: 'E si vós, ne altre alcú qui ab vós sia, vol fer viralay o rondell o ballada en ffrancès envi-ats-la·ns, quan feta sia, car nós la us trametrem notada ab son só novell' (And if you, or anyone else with you, wants to write a virelai, rondeau, or ballade in French, send it to me when it is done so that I can return it to you notated in the new style).[5] As we will see in this chapter, Johan was exceptionally passionate about music, but he was by no means alone amongst the elite aristocracy of the day to possess musical skills. Isabeau de Bavière, queen of King Charles VI of France, and her sister-in-law Valentina Visconti, for instance, both played the harp, and, as we will also see below, Deschamps himself informs us that in 1378 the young Pierre de Navarre was learning to play the chekker and the flute. Whether keen amateur musicians, albeit less exalted ones, composed any of the simpler *Ars nova* polyphonic songs that survive from this period is hard to say. But Johan of Aragon's example illustrates that some extant songs may be products of collaboration between poets and musicians, whether this entailed a composer providing music for an existing lyric at some temporal – or even geographic – remove, as in Johan's example, or whether it involved direct co-operation in real time.

Unfortunately, the manuscripts that preserve the *Ars nova* chanson repertory offer few clues regarding the compositional circumstances of works and their authors. Many French songs are presented anonymously, and even where ascriptions are present, ambiguities remain: should we understand these to identify the author of the lyric or of the music, or to name a single person who was responsible for both? And since song lyrics often travelled silently without their musical settings, we might ask the same question with respect to collections of unnotated lyrics. In this chapter, I take as a starting point one particular late fourteenth-century song that raises some interesting questions about authorship and, specifically, about the compositional and performance history of songs in the so-called *Ars subtilior* style.

---

[3]   For other reflections on the issue of collaboration between music composers and authors of texts in medieval musical works, see the chapters by Everist and Bent in this volume.

[4]   Despite Deschamps's assertion that music is a craft that can be learnt whereas poetry demands natural flair, only one of his own lyrics survives with music, and that was composed by someone other than himself; the same is true for lyric poets Christine de Pizan and Charles d'Orléans. Yet Jean de Le Mote demonstrates that Machaut was not an exception in mastering both arts; although today we credit him only as a poet, in his day he was ranked on a par with Machaut and Philippe de Vitry as a poet-composer. On Le Mote as author of an extant polyphonic song, see Plumley 2013, chap. 6. On Le Mote, see also Louviot's chapter in this volume.

[5]   Barcelona, ACA, Real Cancillería (herafter C), reg. 1658, fol. 108r.

The ballade *Puis que je sui fumeux* is a good example of this genre: it is a fascinating work, both in terms of its extravagant musical language and its idiosyncratic, whimsical text. But the sole manuscript copy to survive with music is intriguing, too, for what it suggests about creative encounters between various kinds of creative agent involved in the production and performance of such works: between poets and composers, on the one hand and, on the other hand, between the literate, church-trained singer-composer we more readily associate with these songs and the court minstrel, whom we attribute an oral rather than written tradition of music making. In what follows, I propose that this particular case lends important insights into such artistic exchanges and how they were facilitated by professional networks that operated across surprisingly wide geographical areas and by the geo-political relations of the powerful elites they served. As this case study suggests, by 1400, French song had become an international cultural commodity with the power not just to divert and entertain but also to build cultural capital for its listeners, patrons, and performers; its subtle charm brought together communities of songsters, performers, and listeners and well beyond France's borders.

The Song *Puis que je sui fumeux* and Its Curious Ascription in the Chantilly Codex

The song *Puis que je sui fumeux* can be dated on stylistic grounds to the end of the fourteenth century or the very early years of the fifteenth. It survives with its musical setting in just one of the key manuscript witnesses to song composition in the French late *Ars nova* style. The Chantilly codex (Chantilly, Bibl. Château 564, hereafter Chantilly), in which the song appears on fol. 34v, presents ninety-nine French-texted polyphonic songs, including many in the elaborate, so-called *Ars subtilior* style. It presents a significant number of ascriptions to lesser-known composers of the period about whom we possess few, if any, biographical details. Since the main scribe of Chantilly apparently was a southerner with poor French, the manuscript is believed to have originated in the south and, on the basis of various textual and biographical clues, its *Ars subtilior* contents connected to the courts of Avignon, Foix, Aragon, Navarre, and Milan. I have argued elsewhere that rather than representing an exclusively southern phenomenon, such songs were cultivated equally in the north and specifically at the Valois courts in Paris; I also connected a significant group to Jehan, duke of Berry, brother of King Charles V of France.[6] In our study of Chantilly, Anne Stone and I concluded that the manuscript itself was probably copied in the 1410s within the papal orbit in central Italy, where it was acquired by Francesco d'Altobianco degli Alberti, banker of Boniface IX, who later gave it to the daughters of Tommaso Spinelli, his former colleague and neighbour in Florence.[7]

Puis que je sui fumeux highlights the connection of the *Ars subtilior* song tradition with the milieu of the Parisian Valois courts. Its bizarre lyric on the vagaries of being *fumeux* – a strange, choleric, melancholic state – relates it directly to a number of

---

[6]   Plumley 2003a; Plumley and Stone (eds.) 2008, vol. 1; see also Stone 2002.

[7]   Plumley and Stone (eds.) 2008, vol. 1, pp. 173–82.

poems penned by poet-courtier Eustache Deschamps between the 1360s and early 1400s.[8] Several of the latter are parodies of legal documents in the voice of the poet, who, under the alias Jehan Fumee, emperor of the *Fumeux*, describes the unpredictable nature of his foolish, hot-headed subjects. The first, dated 1368, is the charter of the society, founded three years earlier, while a further three are satirical legal commissions:[9] one (1370) protects the privileges of some rampaging wolves, another (after 1382) orders punishment for a thieving dog and any subject who fails to beat it,[10] and the third (undated) sentences some drunken subjects to make amends by raising a glass or two together. The satirical tone of these eccentric poems is present, too, in Deschamps's ballade *Je doy estre chancelliers des Fumeux*, which again is in the voice of Eustache, now chancellor of the *Fumeux*; resigned to fill this role forever, he muses over the benefits of being *fumeux* and his own unstable character.[11] It is with this last poem that *Puis que je sui fumeux* chimes most clearly. Its lyric is also in ballade form but its idiom yet more extravagant: its play on words with the prefix 'fum-' is more extensive (highlighted in bold in Appendix 1), and in the notated version of Chantilly, the words are enhanced with music of a rhapsodic style; the jaunty melody and syncopated rhythms, in effect, translate the textual and notional *fumosité* into sound.[12]

Puis que je sui fumeux is one of two songs in Chantilly on the subject of the *fumeux*. The other, the rondeau *Fumeux fume par fumee*, is by Solage, the best represented composer in the manuscript whose identity remains shrouded in mystery. As I have proposed elsewhere, several of Solage's songs connect him with Jehan de Berry; this is most explicit in his virtuosic panegyric *S'aincy estoit*, which extols the prince's many virtues.[13] The bizarre text and music of *Fumeux fume par fumee* aligns it with *Puis que je sui fumeux*, but in the former the musical *fumosité* is manifested in a meandering tonality; the continually shifting tonal focus expresses in music the 'fumeuse speculacion' explored in the lyric.[14] Intriguingly, Deschamps mentions in his charter of the *Fumeux* society that musicians figured amongst the members, and it is tempting to imagine that the authors of the two *fumeux* songs belonged to this club or, at least, that they encountered Deschamps and his literary circle.

---

[8]   See Unruh 1983 and, most recently, Singer 2016.

[9]   Queux de Saint-Hilaire and Raynaud (eds.) 1878–1903, vol. 7, respectively, pp. 312–20, 336–42, 320–23, and 332–35.

[10]   On the dating of this poem to after September 1382, see Laurie 1998, pp. 11, 35 n. 16.

[11]   Queux de Saint-Hilaire and Raynaud (eds.) 1878–1903, vol. 4, pp. 331–32.

[12]   See Plumley and Stone (eds.) 2008, vol. 2, fol. 34v; for online images of the manuscript, see https://arca.irht.cnrs.fr/ark:/63955/md418k71np2v. The translation in Appendix 1 is my own. As Julie Singer (2016) has discussed in her stimulating study, the notion of being *fumeux* explored in this eccentric lyric, and in those by Deschamp, evokes the concept of bodily humours; the humours the narrator experiences cause his irascible and unstable mental state. *Fumee* also evokes smoke (from fire), but I have chosen to translate this as 'fumes' in Appendix 1 in order to embrace the metaphorical use of feeling *fumeux* to describe feeling angry, which today we sometimes describe as 'fuming'.

[13]   Plumley 2003a.

[14]   For an analysis of the tonal language of this song and an edition, see Lefferts 1998.

It seems possible that the lyric of *Puis que je sui fumeux* was penned by Deschamps himself. The text alone is transmitted along with many of his lyrics in Paris, BnF, n.a.f. 6221 (fol. 10r), a text manuscript copied c. 1430 from exemplars deriving from French royal court, and there is ascribed to 'le maistre fumeux'.[15] It features, too, in Cambridge, TCL, R.3.20 (pp. 92–93), a text manuscript copied by Chaucer scribe John Shirley, who served certain English lords in English-occupied Paris in the 1420s, and there carries a similarly worded rubric.[16] An unusual ascription in the notated version in Chantilly adds further complexity to the question of the work's authorship. Indeed, *Puis que je sui fumeux* is amongst several songs in the manuscript to present a double ascription, one given within the score and another – conflicting or confirmatory – at the top of the page. In this case, the main scribe placed his ascription after the text residuum, as he did in two other songs, but here it suggests the contribution of two creative agents: 'Jo. Simon de Haspre composuyt dictum .Ja. de Noyon'. The second scribe of Chantilly (who, at a later point in the manuscript's history added two picture songs to the front and three ascriptions in the main layer) wrote the name 'Hasprois' at the top of the page, which has led many to credit the music to the latter, not least because this name is associated with other songs from Chantilly and elsewhere.

In our study of Chantilly, Stone and I instead understood the Latin ascription to identify Hasprois as the creator of the lyric ('dictum') and, silently, to designate Jaquet composer of the music, as follows: 'Hasprois composed the text. Jaquet de Noyon [the music]'. We supported our hypothesis by demonstrating that in other songs in Chantilly with conflicting ascriptions, the name given within the score is confirmed in a second source or is strongly implied to be the author by the musical style, such as in the case of *En attendant, Esperance*, which is ascribed to Jacob de Senlechos (Senleches) in the score and to Galiot at the top of the folio (fol. 45r).[17] In *Puis que je sui fumeux*, though, two names rather than one are presented within the score, and both have been identified with musicians known from the historical record: Johannes Simonis de Haspre, a singer in the chapel of Benedict XIII, antipope between 1393 and 1403,[18] whose colleagues in papal Avignon included Jacob de Senlechos, Jehan Haucourt, and Matheus de Sancto Johanne, all known to us as

---

[15]   On Paris, BnF, n.a.f. 6221, see Connolly and Plumley 2006; for a detailed study of that same source, see also Delsaux 2014, part 1.

[16]   See Connolly and Plumley 2006.

[17]   Plumley and Stone (eds.) 2008, vol. 1, pp. 149–51. On *En attendant, Esperance*, see Plumley 1999. On the possible identifications of Galiot with reference to the ascription in Chantilly, see the chapter by Bent in this volume.

[18]   In a personal communication in 2004, Alejandro Planchart shared the following details he had discovered in his archival research: Hasprois, who died in 1417, was received as a small vicar in Cambrai on the fifty-first week of the fiscal year that went from the Friday before 11 June 1386 to 11 June 1387, which puts his entry in late May 1387 (and not 1384 as suggested by Ursula Günther); Lille, AdN, 4G 6787, fascicle of 1386–87, fol. 6r: 'li ebdomana x vicarii quod dominus Jo de Haspra fuit receptus vicarius, unus semi sex pueris et tres choris. vi lb viii s vi d o'.

composers in Chantilly; and Jaquet de Noyon, a minstrel named in the records of the royal courts of Aragon in the 1370s and 1390s.[19]

Because several *Ars subtilior* songs have been linked with church-trained musicians, Hasprois might indeed seem better to fit the profile as composer. In a paper I presented in 2019, I suggested that this assumption merits further appraisal.[20] I proposed that this particular case offers a rare glimpse into the artistic circles in which musicians of both stripes and lyric poets rubbed shoulders and had opportunity to collaborate.[21] Fresh reflection on the Latin ascription within the score led me to wonder whether it might indicate that the song was associated with, and thus named or known as, 'Ja. de Noyon' ('dictum Ja de Noyon'), and that Hasprois had adapted it into written form – that is, he had arranged or transcribed it ('Haspre composuyt'), so: 'Hasprois arranged/transcribed [the song] named Ja. de Noyon'. This suggests that the scribe of Chantilly identified the song with Jaquet de Noyon, whether as its composer or its performer, but credited Hasprois with the written version that was copied into the manuscript, which the second scribe also associated with Hasprois. If correct, one can imagine that Hasprois would have undertaken this task creatively and probably modified or embellished the existing song, which he perhaps encountered in aural rather than in written form. Jaquet de Noyon may not have been literate in mensural notation and, like Oswald von Wolkenstein, committed to memory French polyphonic songs or had them transcribed by an *amanuensis*.[22] Nevertheless, as Keith Polk has recently argued, minstrels like Jaquet who served in late fourteenth-century courts that employed instrumental ensembles, especially those of Aragon and the Valois princes that also sustained chapels of specialist singers, were well placed and probably able to perform *Ars nova* songs.[23] As a harpist and string player, Jaquet de Noyon might have accompanied himself or another singer in a performance of *Puis que je sui fumeux*, which is scored for a singing voice and an untexted tenor.

How exactly we should interpret the ascriptions in Chantilly and other sources, including lyric-only collections, is an important question but is not easy to answer.[24] As Stone and I have argued, the double ascriptions found in Chantilly may reflect the

---

[19]   Gómez-Muntané 1979, pp. 54–55.

[20]   Plumley 2019.

[21]   In an article published online several months after my presentation of the above paper, to which she refers, Lucia Marchi agreed with my premise that *Puis que je sui fumeux* bears witness to the involvement of minstrels in the cultivation of *Ars subtilior* songs. She argued, however, for an alternative interpretation of the Latin ascription to mine, proposing instead that the formula names Hasprois the composer and Jaquet the performer of the work. Marchi may be correct that the placement of the *puncta* has no bearing on the sense of the cryptic Latin as Stone and I proposed, but her interpretation of the Latin ascription does not entirely convince and she provides no new primary evidence from the period to support her argument. See Marchi 2019.

[22]   Busse Berger 2013, pp. 36–50.

[23]   Polk 2016.

[24]   For further reflections on manuscript ascriptions (including double and conflicting ones), see the chapter by Bent in this volume.

scribe's collation from two or more exemplars, including a small fascicle with *Puis que je sui fumeux* and the other songs with similarly presented ascriptions, including those by Senleches and Hasprois, whose story intersects with Jaquet's, as we will see. We may never know for certain whether Jaquet composed the music of this work, or wrote its lyric, or was simply the performer who made it famous. Perhaps more important is what we may infer from this case about the interaction of church-trained singers and composers, minstrel-instrumentalists and poets, and the role of court networks in bringing them together. In what follows, I weave together historical evidence drawn from newly discovered or overlooked primary sources with details already known to paint a picture that illustrates the contexts and mechanisms that facilitated such encounters, often across surprisingly wide geographic spans; by piecing together the biography of Jaquet de Noyon, I shall highlight how his path might have come to cross those of Deschamps and his cultural milieu at the Valois courts and Hasprois and other composers named in Chantilly.

The Minstrel Jaquet de Noyon in Aragon

Long ago, it was noted that two minstrels with names similar to those presented in the Latin ascription in *Puis que je sui fumeux* visited the royal courts of Aragon in the early 1370s, and it was assumed that these were one and the same musicians.[25] Although it is implausible that the minstrel Jehan Simon, a string player of Charles V of France who visited Aragon in 1370–71, is the composer Jehan Simon de Haspre/Hasprois – the latter is more likely the boy singer at Cambrai Cathedral in the 1380s who later joined the Avignon papal chapel – the case for matching the minstrel Jaquet de Noyon with the 'Ja. de Noyon' named in Chantilly invites further consideration. I have studied afresh the career of this particular minstrel by mining a large corpus of over six thousand archival documents relating to musical practice in royal medieval Aragon that is currently being edited by scholars at the University of Barcelona,[26] and further documents from the wider Aragon archive and from elsewhere. These have revealed new sightings of Jaquet de Noyon and new details that together now help deepen and refine our understanding of this musician's story. The insights that emerge lead me to conclude that despite the rather generic nature of the name, the match between the minstrel Jaquet de Noyon and the 'Ja. de Noyon' of Chantilly is quite compelling. As we will see, not only was the minstrel highly skilled in an exciting new musical style that was much prized by his Iberian

---

[25] Gómez-Muntané 1979, pp. 54–55. Reference to archival documents relating to the visits of these minstrels to the court of Aragon are provided below.

[26] The documents relating to musicians from the archives of royal Aragon cited in this essay are from the large corpus of documents currently being edited for the research project *Ioculator seu mimus* (MiMus): *Performing Music and Poetry in Medieval Iberia*, led by Professor Anna Alberni, University of Barcelona, and funded by the European Research Council (ERC-CoG-2017-772762), on which I have collaborated as senior research partner. The corpus now comprises over six thousand documents and a database with editions of a selection of these (see Alberni et al. (eds.) 2024). I extend my warm gratitude to Stefano Cingolani for his kind assistance with these and other archival documents from the royal Aragon archives consulted for this essay.

patron, but he had multiple opportunities to encounter Deschamps, Hasprois, and other *Ars subtilior* song composers with whose works *Puis que je sui fumeux* circulated, despite the time that he spent south of the Pyrenees and across the Alps. More generally, the details I present below shed tantalising light on the international careers of musicians of his kind and on the prestige associated with French music and musicians in late fourteenth-century courts, north and south.[27]

Until recently, the minstrel Jaquet de Noyon had been sighted in just a single document from one of the princely courts of Valois and a small handful from the royal courts of Aragon and Navarre. The earliest of these documents was noted in passing by Bernard and Henri Prost in their inventory of records from the court of Philippe II, duke of Burgundy: this is a payment made in 1374 to a minstrel of this name in the service of Louis I, duke of Anjou, brother of Philippe II 'the Bold' of Burgundy and also of Charles V of France and of Jehan, duke of Berry.[28] Some years ago, I inspected this document and noted its details: the payment, dated 28 October 1374 and made in Nîmes in southern France, specifies that the minstrel was paid sixty gold francs for his past and present services to the prince and for expenses incurred by his recent travel to the minstrel schools, including purchase of a harp.[29] The documents from the Aragon archives known until now pinpoint a string player of the same name who appears in the service of Prince Johan of Aragon, Duke of Girona, between December 1377 and July 1379, and again, briefly, in 1393.[30] Records from the courts of Charles II de Navarre and his son Charles III also show that a minstrel of this name was rewarded there four times in the 1380s and again in 1391; by then, Jaquet was in the service of Giangaleazzo Visconti, lord of Milan and brother-in-law of Charles V, Jehan de Berry, and Louis d'Anjou.[31] Intriguingly, a record from 1383 indicates he was paid on the same day as a harpist named Jaquemin de Sanleches, a name we know from several songs in Chantilly.

How, then, did Jaquet de Noyon, minstrel, come to transfer between these courts? My study of the corpus of documents relating to musicians in medieval Aragon and additional documents from the wider royal Aragon archive, has revealed some clues as to how he moved from the service of Louis d'Anjou to that of Prince Johan of Aragon. In a letter sent by the Aragonese prince in October 1376 to Louis's brother Jehan de Berry, Johan asked to borrow one of the French prince's two harpists, whom he had heard were excellent;[32] this intelligence was probably provided

---

[27] Such itinerancy between the Valois and southern courts was by no means limited to minstrels. The case of Jean d'Arras, the author of *Melusine ou la noble histoire de Lusignan*, who travelled to Aragon from the court of Robert de Bar, Johan's father-in-law, is discussed in Alberni 2021.

[28] Prost and Prost (eds.) 1902–4, pp. 240–41 n. 7.

[29] Paris, BnF, collection Clairambault 131, no. 134; see Plumley 1999, pp. 336–37 n. 63 and 2003a, 119.

[30] ACA, C, reg. 1745, fols. 22v and 58v; reg. 1684, fol. 110v; 1745, fol. 58v; 1744, fol. 133v; and RP, reg. 304, fols. 64v–65r. See Gómez-Muntané 1979, pp. 54–55.

[31] Anglès 1970, pp. 225, 289; Gómez 1987, pp. 114, 122.

[32] ACA, reg. 1743, C, fol. 137r. Gómez-Muntané 1979, document 165 suggests instead that the harpist in question was Thomas Guasc, but the latter only appears in the Aragonese

by Bernard de Villebon, a courtier of Jehan de Berry, who visited Aragon in August that year.[33] It is interesting to note that a minstrel named simply Jaquet is recorded in Berry's service between 1368 and 1374,[34] raising the possibility that before serving Louis d'Anjou, our minstrel was employed at Berry's court and that he resumed his role there before moving south to Aragon rather earlier than previously supposed.[35] An alternative possibility is that Jaquet was recruited directly from Louis d'Anjou's service in late 1377 on Johan of Aragon's orders. The presence at Johan's court of some of Jaquet's former colleagues from there may have supplied the conduit for our minstrel's transfer:[36] wind players Thomas de Chaumont and Thibaut de Varennes had served Louis between 1368 and 1370 and moved to the Aragonese court by January 1371, joining two other musicians there to form Johan's first instrumental ensemble. I have now ascertained that a third, Jehan de Saint-Leu (Johan de Sent Luch), who appears in Johan's service by May 1374, had also formerly served the duke of Anjou, in 1370–71.[37] I suspect that Johan's desire to acquire these French minstrels had initially been prompted by his ill-fated marriage in 1371 with Louis's aunt Jehanne, a prestigious match designed to cement Valois-Aragon relations. The bride's unfortunate death just before her arrival in Aragon did nothing to dampen Johan's enthusiasm to lure French musicians to his service, especially Louis's. Two documents from a few years later lend intriguing insight as to how he may have recruited Jaquet de Noyon. One reveals that shortly before 1 October 1377, the prince sent Thibaut de Varennes to Montpellier to recruit an unnamed minstrel,[38] which resulted in the unexpected arrival of two new minstrels at Johan's court: one was probably Jehan Estruman, a shawm player, the other an unnamed rota player who may have been Jaquet de Noyon, since soon after this musician's arrival, the prince tried to offload harpist Jehan Auber to his brother Martin.[39] A second document bearing the same date suggests that another Frenchman, Mathieu de Faucogney,

---

records a few years later (Guasc features in the records of Philippe of Burgundy in 1378 and after; see Wright 1979, p. 27).

[33] ACA, C, reg. 1722, fol. 7r.

[34] Wright 1979, p. 29 n. 53. The instrument of this musician is not specified.

[35] There is also a Jaquet who is described as the gittern player of Charles V in a record from March 1377; see Delisle (ed.) 1874, p. 820. Another candidate for the harpist loaned by Berry to Johan may be Jehan Auber, whose story, as we will see, is entangled with Jaquet's and who is also named in the court record of 1 December 1377 that first signals Jaquet's presence in Johan's court. However, Auber is probably the 'Johani', harpist, mentioned in the prince's service from the early 1370s: ACA, C, reg. 1745, fol. 22v. See also Gómez 1987, 111 n. 9. A safe conduct was issued by the court of Aragon on 3 December 1377 to a minstrel of Jehan de Berry named 'Huellequinus', whose instrument is unspecified; this man may have accompanied the French prince's harpist, whoever he was, to Aragon (ACA, C, reg. 1722, fol. 188r).

[36] Plumley 2003a, pp. 119–20.

[37] Prost and Prost (eds.) 1902–4, pp. 240–41; Lettenhove (ed.) 1875, p. 92.

[38] ACA, C, reg. 1744, fol. 69v.

[39] ACA, C, reg. 1744, fol. 101r.

was sent to Paris to engage a certain minstrel Johan had heard about.[40] Mathieu worked and travelled alongside both Jaquet de Noyon and Jehan Auber over the following years, and although he is generally described as a magician or actor (*tragitador*), he was apparently very knowledgeable about harps; this new record reveals that he was himself a guitar player.

For Johan, French musicians, especially those from the Valois courts, held great prestige, and it seems likely that the acquisition of Jaquet de Noyon to his service came about with the help of one of the minstrel's former colleagues from that princely milieu. The first document signalling Jaquet's presence in Aragon is dated 1 December 1377 and notes a substantial payment to him.[41] Two further new documents indicate that by early January 1378, Jaquet was already preparing a trip to the minstrel schools in Flanders during Lent, and they reflect the careful planning such journeys entailed. A letter from his new patron to Bureau de La Rivière, chamberlain of King Charles V, requests him to grant Jaquet safe passage in France; the other orders payment of forty gold florins to the minstrel for the purchase of a packhorse for the trip.[42] We know that Jaquet delayed setting off after hearing that his former patron Louis d'Anjou was in Béziers with his men and that the minstrel asked Johan to arrange for his passage by sea to avoid running into them.[43] His fears probably reflect the worsening political relations between the crown of Aragon and the Valois prince in the 1370s. Johan's hiring of Thomas de Chaumont, Thibaut de Varennes, and Jehan de Saint-Leu had likely come about as part of the diplomatic entente cordiale between the French and the Aragon crowns at the time of the prince's union with Jehanne de Valois, but Jaquet's move south may not have been sanctioned by Louis d'Anjou. Indeed, by 1374, relations between the Houses of Anjou and Aragon had become volatile after Louis inherited the rights to the kingdom of Majorca, as documents from the wider Aragon archive reflect. In 17 February 1374, Pere IV 'the Ceremonious', king of Aragon and Johan's father, wrote to Jehan de Berry beseeching him not support Anjou's planned invasion of Roussillon;[44] two years later, in a letter dated 21 April 1376, shortly before Jaquet's arrival in Aragon, Pere praised Johan's intention to lead a thousand men to resist Anjou's troops should they invade the Aragonese city of Perpignan.[45] In early 1378, as Jaquet was readying to leave Aragon, an ambassador of the cardinal of Thérouanne[46] visited Johan's court, bringing threatening letters from Anjou so venomous that the prince decided to spare

---

[40] ACA, C, reg. 1744, fol. 70r–v. Mathieu had performed *entremets*, with a colleague from the French royal court, at celebrations held in Perpignan to mark Johan's union with Jehanne de Valois in 1371: ACA, Real Patrimonio, MR, Serie E, reg. 34, fols. 42v–43r.

[41] ACA, C, reg. 1745, fol. 22v.

[42] ACA, C, reg. 1745, fol. 58v; ACA, C, reg. 1745, fol. 31v.

[43] ACA, C, reg. 1744, fols. 130v–131r.

[44] ACA, C, reg. 1240, fol. 146v.

[45] ACA, C, reg. 1251, fol. 123r–v; see Cingolani (ed.) 2019, p. 270, document 235.

[46] Gilles Aycelin de Montaigut, who had been appointed by the pope to mediate in the quarrel.

his father the details;[47] an unnamed minstrel of Louis d'Anjou, presumably one of Jaquet's former colleagues, who visited Johan's court in Zaragoza that February, may have borne these menacing letters.[48] Jaquet's fear of running into Louis d'Anjou in Béziers is thus understandable, but it also raises the suspicion that he may have quit the Angevin court without Louis's blessing.

Minstrels Abroad: From Aragon to the Minstrel Schools in Bruges

These and other archival documents thus shed fascinating light on the impact of fluctuating geo-political relationship on musicians' careers. But those relating to Jaquet de Noyon are valuable, too, for details they provide about the realities of minstrels' itinerancy in this period as well as about Jaquet himself. Due to the unforeseen delay to his departure from Aragon to Bruges, Jaquet had to be issued with a new safe conduct in mid-March 1378. This new letter asks for protection, within and beyond the Aragonese crown, to be given to the minstrel, who is here described as a harpist and said to be travelling with an unspecified number of horses and with money and luggage. We learn, too, that Jaquet was accompanied by his *familia*;[49] this probably refers to a valet, but new evidence discussed below raises the possibility that a family member had travelled with Jaquet to Aragon. A letter copied two days later sent from Zaragoza by Prince Johan to Berenguer de Magarola, his proctor in Roussillon then at court in Barcelona, reveals that the musician was travelling in the company of four other entertainers from Johan's household:[50] magician Mathieu de Faucogney and shawm players Jehan de Saint-Leu, Jehan Estruman, and Coecre. It also sheds fascinating light on their itinerary: from Perpignan, the Aragonese frontier city north of the Pyrenees, their route took them to Montpellier (and for that leg, Jaquet and his *familia* were to travel by boat from Canet to Aigues-Mortes to avoid the duke of Anjou in Béziers), and from there, they proceeded first to Montpellier, then on northward to Paris and thence to Bruges.

This letter sent by Prince Johan to Magarola in mid-March 1378 is interesting, too, for presenting the first evidence of Johan's anxiety about his minstrels' absence. In it, Johan asks his proctor to keep him briefed about his minstrels' precise whereabouts and activities and to inform him 'which day they'll have left Perpignan, and which Montpellier, and when they'll have left Paris to travel to Flanders, and on which [day] they enter Bruges. And the same for the return' (*qual dia seran partits de Perpenyà, et qual de Muntpesler, et qual de París per anar en Fflandres, et qual entraran en Bruges. E axí meteix del retornar*). The young prince was evidently very satisfied with his new musician recruits and, in particular, one of his two harpists whom I presume is Jaquet de Noyon, given that Johan had tried to move Auber to his brother Martin's service. In a letter dated 31 May, Johan comments to his usher Pere de

---

47 See Tasis 1959, p. 75.
48 ACA, C, reg. 1764, fols. 204v–205r, which records payment of ten Aragonese florins to Anjou's minstrel.
49 ACA, C, reg. 1723, fol. 76v.
50 ACA, C, reg. 1744, fol. 133v, dated 17 March 1377; discussed in Plumley 2003a.

Berga, who was in Avignon, that he no longer needs him to seek out a harpist there 'because I have one already who is certainly the best in the world' (*car nós n'avem ja I que és certament lo mellor del món*).[51] By 31 May, having heard nothing about the whereabouts of his minstrels and increasingly impatient for news, Johan wrote again to Magarola, who was now in Perpignan; two weeks later, still in the dark, he added a postscript in a further letter to this man that reflects his eagerness for this intelligence: 'vos manam que·ns certifiquets clarament ab vostra letra de tots ço que dels nostres ministrés, qui són anats, axí com sabets, a les escoles, hajats de novell' (we command you to confirm clearly all new information you have about our minstrels, who, as you know, have gone to the schools).[52] In late June, Johan wrote to Johan Janer, a trusted courtier, urging him to find out his minstrels' whereabouts from the hostelries – presumably those in Perpignan – or from Martin's minstrels, who had recently returned from the minstrel schools: 'sapiats per los hostals si·ls nostres ministrers seran venguts, et si no són venguts, et seran venguts los de l'infant, demanats-los si han vist los dits nostres ministrers, et on los jaquiren et quant deuen venir' (find out from the hostels if our minstrels have come, and if they have not and those of the infante [Martin] have, ask the latter if they have seen our said minstrels, and where they are and when they should come here).[53] The prince goes on to stipulate that they should be sent to him as soon as they arrive in Aragon, and it seems Jaquet de Noyon was especially the issue: on 19 July, Johan wrote again to Janer, thanking him for sending news of the minstrels and asking him to send his harpist Jaquet de Noyon to join him immediately in Zaragoza.[54]

Why this impatience? In a letter written to his brother Martin that same day, Johan complains that with his own minstrels away, he only has his wife's ones to entertain him, whom, he says, are unskilled in the 'mester novell' (new art).[55] To bridge the gap, he asks his brother to lend him one of his newly returned minstrels so that they can teach his wife's musicians some new repertory ('coses novelles' (new things)), and he asks that they should bring with them some of the new instruments they had purchased at the minstrel schools.[56] These comments suggest that Johan held his new French minstrels in particularly high esteem because of their ability to play in a new style not yet mastered by his longer standing local minstrels. Given his specific impatience to have Jaquet de Noyon back, I wonder whether this might relate to the *Ars subtilior* style that is so well showcased in *Puis que je sui fumeux*. Interestingly, just a few days later, Johan arranged for magician

---

[51] ACA, C, reg. 1745, fols. 92v–93r.

[52] ACA, C, reg. 1745, fol. 96v; ACA, C, reg. 1745, fol. 108v.

[53] ACA, C, reg. 1745, fol. 120v.

[54] ACA, C, reg. 1745, fol. 134r.

[55] ACA, C, reg. 1745, fol. 134r.

[56] ACA, C, reg. 1745, fol. 140v. We know from a letter from Johan to the marquis of Villena, a Catalan noble, that he, and other patrons like him, sent their minstrels to the northern schools to learn new repertory and to buy new instruments, novelties they could then share with other musicians once home; on 1 March 1378, Johan's minstrel Jehan de Saint-Leu taught Villena's minstrels six new songs (ACA, C, reg. 1744, fol. 128v; see Gómez Muntané 1979, document 39).

and guitar player Mathieu de Faucogney, who had evidently just returned, to travel straight to Valencia to purchase a double harp, which it is tempting to conclude was intended for Jaquet's use.[57] When Johan finally heard that his remaining minstrels had arrived in Montpellier in late August, he cancelled his request to borrow his brother's musicians.[58]

As Johan's exacting inquiries about his minstrels' whereabouts suggest, his musicians doubtless stopped off to perform at various courts as they made their way to and from the schools in Bruges. Such opportunities provided welcome staging posts but also served to supplement their monetary gains and to connect with former – and possible future – patrons and colleagues. Given that Prince Johan of Aragon had solicited Bureau de La Rivière to ensure Jaquet's safe passage in France, it seems highly probable that Jaquet entertained this important figure when he passed through Paris. He may well also have performed for Jehan de Berry and the French king, both of whom had fine residences close to that of Bureau, as we will see. Since Jaquet and his colleagues were travelling on to Flanders from Paris, they probably performed for other great nobles en route to or in Bruges itself, notably for Philip of Burgundy, youngest brother of Charles V, who had married the heiress of Flanders in 1369, although the Burgundian court records provide no confirmation. However, the records of the court of Holland in The Hague reveal that a shawm player (piper) of Johan of Aragon, together with one of his brother Martin's, was received and rewarded by the count of Holland on 13 May 1378.[59] Johan's shawm player was presumably one of Jaquet's travelling companions, Jehan de Saint-Leu, Jehan Estruman, or Coecre. Whether our harpist accompanied this musician on a jaunt to the court of Holland in Dordrecht – over 150 km northeast of Bruges – remains a mystery, but another overlooked document from the French royal court confirms that the minstrels' return journey took them back through Paris. Indeed, a record of payment issued at Vincennes on 12 June 1378 indicates that the French king had recently rewarded Johan's minstrels with fifty gold francs, a considerable sum that reflects the status of the prince of Aragon's musicians and suggests all five were present, each receiving 10 francs.[60]

---

[57] ACA, C, reg. 1745, fol. 138v.

[58] ACA, C, reg. 1745, fol. 150r.

[59] AGH 1234, fol. 90v. A fellowship at the Netherlands Institute of Advanced Study in 2019–20 gave me the opportunity to inspect the records of the court of Holland. I extend my gratitude to Jacques Boogaart for his kind assistance with this archival trip and his help reading these documents. The entry specifies a piper of the king of Aragon, and another one mentions payment to one of his brother's; since there is no record to indicate that any of the minstrels of King Pere travelled to the schools that year and we know that both Johan's and Martin's did so, I conclude this refers to their minstrels. On the accounts of the court of Holland, see also Janse 1986, p. 146.

[60] Paris, BnF, Orig. Clairambault, Sceaux, 216, p. 9701, cited in Léopold Delisle (ed.) 1874, p. 856, document 1742. For an analysis of the sums paid to musicians in this period, including as one-off rewards for visiting musicians at the French courts, see the discussion in Pocard 2018, vol. 1, chap. 10.

Jaquet de Noyon in Paris

When precisely Jaquet de Noyon returned to Aragon in the summer of 1378 after his trip to the north and, assuming he did, how long he stayed there, is unclear. The next sighting of him in the prince's records is in a letter dated 22 July 1379 in which prince Johan asks a merchant of Montpellier for news of certain of his minstrels, including Jaquet de Noyon, whom he was expecting back imminently.[61] Jaquet's absence from the Aragon records between the summers of 1378 and 1379 may suggest his temporary transfer to a nearby court, such as that of Castile or Navarre, to which his colleague Johan Auber moved for various spells.[62] But a distinct possibility is that he had remained in the north after his trip to the Bruges schools in the spring of 1378. Alternatively, if indeed he had returned to Aragon in the late summer of 1378, he might have ventured north again a few weeks later, perhaps in the company of an embassy sent by Johan to Charles V to negotiate the prince's marriage to Yolande de Bar, Charles V's niece, following the death of his wife, Marthe d'Armagnac, that September.[63]

In view of this fresh diplomacy between Johan and the Valois, I wonder whether Jaquet was given leave to remain in Paris and that he spent the months between December 1378 and the summer of 1379 plying his trade in the French capital – perhaps seconded to Jehan de Berry, who was actively supporting Johan's marriage bid – before rejoining his colleagues from Aragon when they passed through Paris on their way to the schools in June 1379.[64] This hypothesis is suggested by two recently reported documents from Paris that shed light on Jaquet de Noyon's activities in late 1378 and the spring of 1379: the first records his purchase of a property in the French capital on 11 December 1378 and the second its sale in May 1379. These documents offer fascinating insights into how minstrel networks operated well beyond the confines of individual courts, for Jaquet sold this house to fellow harpist Jehan Auber, his colleague from the Aragon court;[65] evidently, professional relationships served

---

[61] ACA, C, reg. 1657, fols. 92v–93r.

[62] Auber is mentioned as harpist of the king of Castile in a document dated 1 December 1380 but six months later is again described as Johan's minstrel (ACA, C, reg. 1660, fol. 59v; ACA, C, reg. 1664, fols. 89v–90r); he went on to serve Johan's brother Martin, then his father, King Pere.

[63] On these and other marriage negotiations involving the Aragonese court, see Juncosa Bonet 2021. It is worth noting that the minstrels of Charles V visited Aragon in the spring of 1379: ACA, C, reg. 1657, fol. 42r.

[64] Jaquet's name is absent from the various letters of safe conduct issued by Johan in the first half of 1379 for those of his minstrels who were setting off to the minstrel schools in the north. A letter dated 14 May 1379 mentions that the prince's harpist had recently returned to him (ACA, C, reg, 1657, fol. 30bisr–v), but this probably refers to Jehan Auber, who was expected back at that point, or to Thomas Guasc, whose appearance in Johan's service in early 1379 strengthens the suspicion that Jaquet was indeed absent from court.

[65] Chabannes 1999, Appendix V, pp. 221–22, 255, cited in Story 2007, p. 117, and Pocard 2018, vol. 2, p. 524. Pocard was unaware of minstrel Jaquet de Noyon's career in Aragon, Navarre, and Milan, nor of his likely identity with the poet/musician named in the Chantilly codex. Auber's name in this document is spelled 'Ober' or 'Oser'.

practical as well as artistic ends. From these documents, we also learn precious new details about Jaquet himself: that he played the fiddle as well as the harp and that he was married to a woman named Ayalette. It is possible that she had accompanied the minstrel to Aragon in the autumn or winter of 1377 when he joined Johan's team and that she was part of the *familia* mentioned in the safe conduct issued for Jaquet in March 1378;[66] alternatively, she might either have stayed in Paris, or the couple only met and married in the course of the spring of 1378, prompting Jaquet now to seek to establish a family base in the French capital. Since the sale document signals the minstrel's presence at the transaction, we now know that in May 1379, he indeed was in Paris.

Jaquet's purchase of a property in the city thus may have been designed to cover a temporary stay in Paris agreed with his Aragonese patron, but it might also signal the minstrel's desire to find long-term employment with another master. Either way, the minstrel's choice of neighbourhood for his new pied-à-terre was highly strategic (see Figure 12.1): his house (in black) was on the rue des Puits in the quarter of the Temple (Le Marais) (see Figure 12.2). This was in the thick of an area that was rapidly becoming populated by the high aristocracy and leading royal officers because of its proximity to Charles V's new palace of Saint-Pol. Among the more significant *hôtels* in the immediate neighbourhood (shown in light grey in Figure 12.1) were, a few metres to the northeast of Jaquet's street, the twin *hôtels* of Bureau de La Rivière, the influential chamberlain of Charles V whose help Johan of Aragon had solicited to safeguard Jaquet's travels in France, and the *hôtel* where Charles de Navarre (eldest son of Charles II 'the Bad') resided from 1378,[67] following his three-year stay at the court of Castile, which Johan's minstrels frequently visited. Next to those was that of Breton noble Olivier Clisson, which from 1392 was used by Charles de Navarre (by then King Charles III de Navarre). A few metres to the west was the *hôtel* of Bertrand du Guesclin, the celebrated constable of France, whose patronage of minstrels and connection with extant *Ars nova* songs I have recently considered elsewhere.[68] Just to the southwest of the rue des Puits were adjacent residences of Louis d'Anjou and Jehan de Berry, whom I have already noted as important patrons of musicians,[69] including Jaquet and others known to us from Chantilly; and beside those, was the house of Blanche de Navarre, dowager queen of their grandfather Philippe VI, king of France, and sister of Charles II de Navarre. Finally, Charles V's new palace of Saint-Pol was to the east; in short, the neighbourhood would have been a huge magnet for any international court minstrel passing through or seeking reward or employment.

---

[66] However, the Aragon documents usually specify when a wife travels with her minstrel husband, as in the example of Mathieu de Faucogney; my thanks to Stefano Cingolani for clarifying this point.

[67] Narbona Cárceles 2009. See also Mirot 1930.

[68] Plumley 2024.

[69] On these two patrons, see also Plumley 2003a and Plumley and Stone (eds.) 2008, vol. 1, pp. 129–42.

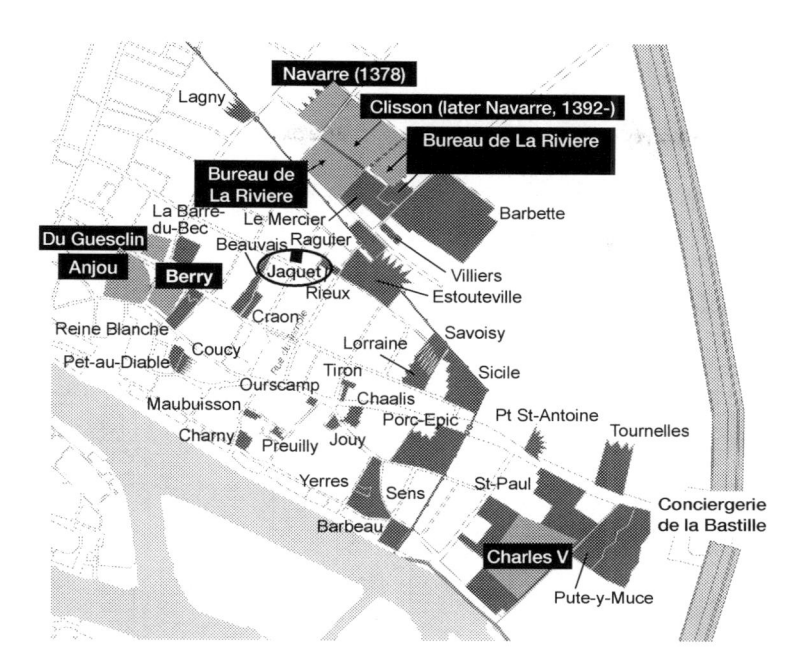

Figure 12.1. Jaquet de Noyon's neighbourhood (Temple) in Paris, 1378 (Jaquet's house, shown in black, in the rue des Puits is seen here to the north east of the residences of the dukes of Anjou and Berry; *hôtels* of these princes and other dignitaries connected with this minstrel are indicated in light grey). Map based on Bove 2013 (Creative Commons CC0).

Given Jaquet's former service to Louis d'Anjou, it is worth mentioning that the chapel of the latter's prestigious palace was completed by 1375,[70] and that among its impressive team of ten singers in November 1378 was Matheus de Sancto Johanne.[71] Matheus, who had been with Louis and the other French hostages in London in the 1360s, like Jaquet originated in Noyon, and he, too, is ascribed songs in Chantilly. Whether the two musicians met on this occasion is impossible to say, but it is hard to imagine that their paths did not cross at some point, given the cultural circles they shared. Matheus went on to serve Pope Clement VII in Avignon in the 1380s and died outside the curia before 1391, shortly before Hasprois appears in the papal chapel records. Matheus was certainly familiar with Jehan Haucourt, Hasprois's colleague there, to judge from the explicit intertextualities that link two of their songs presented side by side in Chantilly.[72] Matheus's case, and that of other clerk-singers mentioned below, illustrates how church musicians could be just as mobile as

---

[70] Weiss (ed.) 2012, pp. 20–21; Proust-Perrault 2009, pp. 47–69.

[71] Nádas 2004, p. 189.

[72] See Plumley 2003b, pp. 370–73.

Figure 12.2. Rue des Puits, now rue Aubriot, fourth arrondissement, Paris; photographed
by Eugène Atget (between 1885 and 1925). Musée Carnavalet, Histoire de Paris, PH16235.
CC0 Paris Musées/Musée Carnavalet – Histoire de Paris (black and white).

minstrels; there would have been ample occasions for him and Jaquet to meet,
whether in Paris or in Avignon.

In light of our knowledge concerning Jaquet's purchase of a house in the French
capital and the evidence for the circulation of the lyric of *Puis que je sui fumeux* with
Deschamps's poetic output, however, Paris seems a likely place of origin for this
particular work. Indeed, this hypothesis gains momentum with the knowledge that

Deschamps, too, by 1384, owned a house near to Jaquet's, on the rue du Temple just to the east of the rue des Puits (for the rue du Temple, see Figure 12.1).[73] By that time, the poet had entered royal service in the capital (he was by now sergeant at arms (*huissier d'armes*) of Charles V[74]) and one can well imagine their encountering one another in, or on the fringes of, the Valois courts in the capital. Interestingly, among Deschamps's collected poems is a humorous lyric letter dated February 1378 in the voice of the young prince Pierre de Navarre, another son of Charles II de Navarre and thus younger brother of the future Charles III de Navarre, whose residence in Paris was mentioned above. At that time, Pierre had been recently captured and was in the poet-courtier's custody. It mentions that among the young prince's coterie was a certain 'Platiau le musicien, / Qui jeue, quant je l'en requier, / De la harpe et de l'eschequier' (Platiau the musician, / who performs the harp and the chekker / when I request it).[75] It may be fanciful to imagine that this Platiau was Jaquet de Noyon himself, but this emphasises that the poet and his charge were associating with musicians of his kind, even outside the space of the courts. However, Jaquet's next career move to the service of Giangaleazzo Visconti of Milan-Pavia strengthens my suspicion that our minstrel knew Deschamps and his circle: the poet hailed from the county of Vertus, and in the first known reference to him, he is described in 1367–70 as administrator and juror of the count of Vertus,[76] which title Giangaleazzo Visconti had acquired through his marriage in 1360 to Isabelle de Valois, sister of Charles V. Perhaps Deschamps even facilitated the minstrel's transfer to Milan; it is very likely that they would have met again when the poet visited Milan as part of a French princely delegation in the 1380s.

Jaquet de Noyon in Milan and Last Sightings

Wherever Jaquet de Noyon was stationed over the winter of 1378 and spring of 1379 and whatever the reason, Johan's letter from July 1379 indicates that officially he was still in the prince of Aragon's service at that point.[77] But this is the last sighting of our musician in the Aragonese record for many years, and my suspicion is that Jaquet left Johan's service with little or no notice that summer. Indeed, by October 1379, after his recent intensive hiring of French musicians in anticipation of his wedding to Yolande de Bar, Johan decided to retain just five of his by then twenty-two minstrels, plus one harpist, and seven new singers recruited from Avignon for his chapel.[78] Intriguingly, in a letter to his chamberlain on this subject, the prince specifies that none of these singers should have served Louis d'Anjou: 'guardat-vos que no n'hi haja alcun qui haja

---

73 Laurie and Sinnreich-Levi (eds.), Curzon and Fiskin (trans.) 2003, p. 12.

74 Laurie and Sinnreich-Levi (eds.), Curzon and Fiskin (trans.) 2003, p. 10.

75 Queux de Saint-Hilaire and Raynaud (eds.) 1878–1903, vol. 8, p. 34. On the chekker, a stringed keyboard instrument that first emerged c. 1360, see Ripin 1975; Kinsela 1998.

76 Laurie and Sinnreich-Levi (eds.), Curzon and Fiskin (trans.) 2003, p. 7.

77 ACA, C, reg. 1657, fols. 92v–93r.

78 ACA, C, reg. 1658, fol. 25r–v.

servit al duch d'Anjou' (be sure that none of them has served the duke of Anjou).[79] Perhaps his fingers had been burned once too often by Louis's former musicians, and Jaquet's quitting was the final straw. Jaquet's motivation to sell his Parisian property in May 1379 thus may have been because by then, he had secured his new contract with Giangaleazzo Visconti and now planned to move to Italy.

We know of Jaquet's service to Visconti from payment records of the court of Navarre, which note his visits there in 1383, 1388 (twice, in April and December), and 1391[80] and describe him as minstrel of the count of Vertus. Curiously, as mentioned above, Jacob de Senleches, a harpist of Pedro de Luna, cardinal of Aragon, visited the court at the same time as Jaquet in 1383. This musician is surely the author of several songs in Chantilly and the person of that name who was awarded a canonicate at Saint-Martin's in Tour when Pedro was enthroned as Pope Benedict XIII in Avignon in 1394; by that date, Hasprois, too, had joined the papal chapel.[81] Senleches may have joined Pedro de Luna's service in 1382 after a spell in Spain serving Johan of Aragon's sister Eleanora, queen of Castile, whose death that year he laments in his song *Fuions de ci*; its lyric states that he must now seek his fortune in Aragon, France, or Brittany. Senleches and Jaquet probably frequented the same minstrel networks and might even have met multiple times, north and south of the Alps. Since both were harpists, it is an enticing idea that they shared repertory; indeed, it was recently suggested that Jaquet might have been the conduit for the transmission of the beautiful harp-shaped score of Senleches's *La Harpe de melodie* to Pavia, where it was appended to a compendium of music treatises copied there in 1391.[82]

That Jaquet spent time in person in Milan and/or Pavia is suggested by a hitherto overlooked record of payment, again dated 1383, from the court of Achaia in neighbouring Savoy, which enjoyed regular visits from Visconti's musicians (and his dwarf).[83] A recently discovered document from the Aragon archive confirms this: it records payment in June 1394 to Jaquet de Pavia,[84] who is evidently one and the same as the musician named Jaquet de Noyon and identified as 'minstrerio nostro' (our minstrel) in other documents from 1391 to 1393. These new sightings in the Aragonese records from the 1390s reveal that his stay in Aragon was considerably longer than previously supposed, stretching to at least three years. During that time, he would have encountered there a northern singer who joined the royal chapel and who, like Jacob de Senleches, served Benedict XIII, formerly cardinal of Aragon: this singer was Johannes Rogier de Wattignies, who served in the papal chapel in 1393 and 1403, alongside Hasprois and Haucourt, and also Eynart Le Fevre. Wattignies and Le Fevre had already sung together in Johan's chapel in 1384; between 1393 and 1403, they also sang in the household chapels of Jehan de Berry and Philippe

---

[79] ACA, C, reg. 1746, fol. 17v.

[80] Anglès 1970, pp. 289, 292; Gómez 1987, pp. 118, 122.

[81] Briegleb and Laret-Kayser (eds.) 1973, pp. 7–10.

[82] Chicago, Newberry Lib., Case 54.1, fol. 10r. See Pieragostino 2013.

[83] Saraceno (ed.) 1882, p. 261.

[84] ACA, Real Patrimonio, MR, reg. 395, fol. 140r.

of Burgundy as well as in the papal chapel, and soon after, they joined Haucourt as canons of Laon Cathedral.[85]

Once again, we see here evidence for the intersection at court of complementary networks of musicians, one populated by minstrels, the other by church singers. Such encounters enabled exchanges between musicians of different stripes and perhaps even facilitated compositional collaborations of the kind suggested by the dual ascription in Chantilly's copy of *Puis que je sui fumeux.* Some cleric-musicians, like Senleches and some of the singers Johan recruited to Avignon, were instrumentalists as well as singers, and some, like those and Matheus de Sancto Johanne, also enjoyed careers that were just as mobile as those of court minstrels. These two categories of musician thus had rather more in common than we might tend to assume, and it seems reasonable to imagine that they exchanged repertory and perhaps even performed and composed together. After all, we know that clerics, nobles, bourgeois, poets, and musicians interacted at the urban *puys*.[86] Certainly, as the case of *Puis que je sui fumeux* and Senleches's songs *Fuions de ci* and *La Harpe de melodie* suggest, musicians may have been responsible for devising the lyrics as well as the music of their songs. It is worth mentioning that Jehan Haucourt, elite singer and colleague of Hasprois and Matheus de Sancto Johanne in papal Avignon, is listed, as is Deschamps, in the ranks of the *cour amoureuse*, the prestigious poetry society founded by King Charles VI in Paris in 1400; the society's *prince*, Pierre de Hauteville, himself played musical instruments and frequented the society of minstrels.

The new evidence siting Jaquet de Noyon in Paris supports my long-held hypothesis that *Ars subtilior* was not just a southern phenomenon, as has often been assumed, but that it was practised at the courts of the Valois king and princes in the north as well as in southern centres. But as I have stressed previously, a north-south dichotomy is rather illusory, given that important patrons like the dukes of Berry and Anjou served as royal lieutenants of Languedoc and spent long periods south of the Loire, which doubtless facilitated the transfer of French minstrels like Jaquet to southern courts, including that of Aragon.[87] Nevertheless, Jaquet's sojourn in the French capital over the winter and spring of 1378–79, which I doubt was his first, must have afforded him multiple opportunities to connect or reconnect with former or future patrons and also with other musicians who, like himself and his colleague Jehan Auber, shuttled between the princely courts of the north and south. While in Paris, he very likely met Eustache Deschamps who, like him, was linked professionally to the Parisian royal courts and to that of Giangaleazzo Visconti of Milan. As we have seen, the lyric of *Puis que je sui*

---

[85] For Jehan Rogier de Wattignies as part of Johan's chapel in Aragon in 1394, see ACA, reg. 2018, fols. 55r–58r; for his and Le Fevre's presence there in 1384, see ACA reg. 1748, fol. 81r and MR, reg. 602, fol. 154r. On their careers more broadly and at Laon Cathedral, see Plumley 2002.

[86] See Plumley 2013, chap. 5. An example of such interactions in urban confraternities is the thirteenth-century Confraternity of Jongleurs and Bourgeois in Arras, which is at the core of the chapter by Dolce in this volume.

[87] Plumley 2003a.

fumeux is closely tied with that of Deschamps's *fumeux* lyrics, and its transmission history further connects it with this poet's output and with manuscripts originating in, or close to, the French royal courts. Recently, I discovered a further and hitherto overlooked copy of the song's lyric, which strengthens its connection with Deschamps's poetry and with the Parisian princely milieu in which it circulated. This new copy appears toward the end (fol. 57r) of a fifteenth-century manuscript that is now Carpentras, Bibl. inguimbertine 411. This manuscript, which was signed by a fifteenth-century (?) owner, Nicolas Huron, from Gonesse, near Paris (fol. 59v), transmits Renaud de Louhans's French translation of Boethius's *De consolatione philosophiae* from 1336, a fragment of which features in Bern, Burgerbibl., A 35 alongside Machaut's *Confort d'ami* and other late fourteenth-century items relating to Valois patronage.[88] One of the three other lyrics that follow our song text in Carpentras, Bibl. inguimbertine 411 is by Oton de Granson, the celebrated Savoyard knight-poet whose collected poems were in Queen Isabeau de Bavière's library; they appear in extant manuscripts from the Valois royal milieu, notably the Pennsylvania manuscript (Philadelphia, Univ. of Pennsylvania, Codex 902, c. 1390), which transmits song texts known from Chantilly alongside many by Machaut.[89]

Wherever the song *Puis que je sui fumeux* was composed, its lyric, at least, was apparently known in the Parisian courtly milieu by c. 1400, where it continued to circulate for decades to come. We may well wonder whether the readers of the various lyric anthologies that transmit it knew it as a song and who they believed was its author; as we have seen, the curious rubrics in manuscripts Paris, BnF, n.a.f. 6221 and Cambridge, TCL, R.3.20 suggest this was someone associated with Eustache Deschamps and his company of *fumeurs* in Paris. Interestingly, the reading of stanza II, line 3 of the lyric in the Carpentras manuscript aligns with that of Chantilly while those other two copies diverge (see Appendix 1, stanza II, line 3), suggesting that this new source may have derived from an exemplar of similar date and provenance to the one that served the Chantilly scribe.[90] To return to Chantilly, it is interesting to note that its reading of the lyric is surprisingly good, given the southern scribe's

---

[88] Written in the 1330s (fols. 1r–57v). For details of this source, see Archives de littérature du Moyen Âge (Arlima), https://www.arlima.net/mss/suisse/bern/burgerbibliothek/A_95.html#FJ1.

[89] The presence of the Granson lyrics and the two anonymous ones also in the Carpentras manuscript, but strangely not that of *Puis que je sui fumeux*, was noted in Grenier-Winther (ed.), 2010, p. 48. The Granson lyric is no. 24 in her edition. The reading of this in the Carpentras manuscript shares several variants with London, Westminster 21, which dates from the 1430s and like Cambridge, TCL, R.3.20 connects with English-occupied France; these two manuscripts are the only ones of the extant sources for Granson's *Ballade de saint Valentin double* to present just the first ballade of the two. It is also conceivable that during his time in Piedmont, Jaquet came across Granson on one of his visits to the county of Savoy, to which Granson was appointed lieutenant in 1386 (see Braddy 1938, p. 525).

[90] For some further thoughts concerning some of the French exemplars that served the Chantilly scribe and their relationship with text-only manuscripts including Paris, BnF, n.a.f. 6221, see Plumley and Stone 2023.

generally inexpert French; this version remains close to that of Paris, BnF, n.a.f. 6221, suggesting that the exemplar he used for this work perhaps had derived directly from French or Avignon circles.[91] As I mentioned at the start of this chapter, in Chantilly a second, French scribe added Hasprois's name to the top of the page at a later point. That same person added two further ascriptions in the manuscript: one to Jacob de Senleches, the other to Matheus de Sancto Johanne, whose histories I have shown here intersected closely with those of both Jaquet de Noyon and Jehan Hasprois. Perhaps this man was personally acquainted with those musicians; at the very least, it seems that he had sound knowledge of the professional networks to which they belonged.

Appendix 1: The Lyric of *Puis que je sui fumeux* in Chantilly, fol. 34v (A) with Textual Variants from Cambridge, TCL, R.3.20 (B), Carpentras, Bibl. inguimbertine 411 (C), and Paris, BnF, n.a.f. 6221(D)

Puis que je sui **fum**eux plains de **fum**ee,	Since I am fuming, full of fumes,
Fumer m'estuet, car se je ne **fum**oye,	Fume I must, for if I did not fume,
Ceulx qui dient que j'ay teste en**fum**ée,	Those who say that my head is enfumed,
Par **fum**ee je les desmentiroye.	I would contradict on a fumous whim.
Et nopourquant ja mais ne **fum**eroye 5	But nevertheless, I would never fume
De **fum**ee qui fust contre rayson:	With fumes that were against reason:
Se je **fum**e, c'est ma compleccion	If I fume, it's because my choleric
Quolerique qu'ainsi me fayt **fum**er;	Constitution makes me fume thus;
Je **fum**eray sanz personne graver,	I shall fume harming no-one,
C'est bien **fum**é; y n'i a point d'outrayge 10	That's well fumed; and there's nothing bad
Quant on **fum**e sans fayre autruy damage.	When one fumes causing others no harm.
Fumee n'est a nulli refusee,	Fumes are refused to no-one,
Fume qui veult, tenir ne m'en porroie:	Anyone may fume, I couldn't refrain:
J'ay en **fum**ant mainte chose fit rime;	I've composed many poems while fuming;
Encore sçay que mais n'i avenroye	I well know that I'd never manage this
Se per **fum**ee en **fum**ant n'i pensoye. 5	If I didn't think with fumes while fuming.
Fumee rent bien consolacion,	Fumes offer great comfort,
Aucune fois tolt tribulacion;	Sometimes soothing stress;
On se puet bien en **fum**ant deliter.	One can have fun while fuming.
Home **fum**eur peut en **fum**ant trover,	A fumer while fuming can find
Et si pluseurs profit et avantage, 10	Quite some profit and advantage,
Quant hom **fum**e sans fayre ab aulltrui damage.	When one fumes causing others no harm.

---

[91] The version in Cambridge, TCL, R.3.20, on the other hand, has significant variants with all three other sources, especially in the third stanza.

Se j'eusse le cervelle enpetree	Had I the learned brain
De Socrates, si com je le vodroye,	Of Socrates, as I'd wish I had,
J'euse bien la teste plus temperee,	I would possess a far calmer mind,
Car onques ne **fuma** par nulle voye.	For he never fumed at all.
Chascuns n'est pas çains de telle corroye, 5	Not everyone is influenced by such impulses
Car tel **fume** que peu s'en perçoyt on,	Because some fume, as one might observe,
Tant du cuer plus de confusion,	More from the heart than from confusion,
Quant il ne puet sa **fumee** monstrer,	When they can't express their fumosity,
Ou il n'ose pour paour d'enpirer.	Or don't dare for fear of making things worse;
Je ne tieng pas c'on ayt le cuer volage; 10	I don't agree that one has a flighty heart,
Quant on **fume** sans fayre aulltruy damage.	When one fumes causing others no harm.

I,2: ne]me (A) – I,3: Ceulx]Ceule (A) – I,4: desmentiroye]desenoye (B) – I,5: ja mais ne fumeroye]point fumer ne vouldroie (B) – I,6: fumee]fumer (A) – I,8: qu'ainsi me fayt fumer]qui mesmenent a fumer (B) – I,10: C'est bien fumé y]Fumee est bonne et (B) – I,11:on]home (B) – II,1: refuse]deneree (B) – II,3: rimee]dittes (B); rimee]rechinee (D) – II,4: Encore sçay que mais n'i avenroye]Et sy sçay bien que point ny avendroye (B); avenroye]venroye (A) – II,6:rent] donne (B); bien consolacion]grant consolacion (C) – II,7: tolt]tost (A); tolt]en (B) – II,8: On se puet bien en fumant deliter]On se puet en fumant bien delitter (B) – II,10: Et si]En lui (CD); Einsi pluseurs profit]Pluseurs honneurs proufiz (B); Einsi pluseurs profit]En lui pluseurs profit (D) – II,11: hom]on (BCD) – III,2: si com je le vodroye]ainsi que je vouldroye (C) – III,3: J'euse bien la teste plus temperee]J'eusse la test ung [peu?] plus attempree (C); plus temperee]plus attempree (D); plus temperee]mieulx trempee (B) – III,4: Car onques ne fuma par nulle voye]Et pense bien que plus ne fumeroye (B) – III,5: çains]clains (A) – III,6: Car]Mais (B) – III,7: Tant du cuer plus de confusion]Qu'il a en lui sens et discrecioun (B) – III,8: puet]veult (C) – III,9: Ou il n'ose pour paour d'enpirer]Aucoun foiz pour doubte d'empirer (B); ou]on (A); ou]car (C) – III,10: Je ne tieng pas c'on ayt le cuer volage]pour ce ne tiens pas un cuer a voulage (B); Je ne tieng pas]Je ne dy pas plus (C)

General Bibliography

Abramov-van Rijk, Elena, 2009. *Parlar Cantando: The Practice of Reciting Verses in Italy from 1300 to 1600* (Bern).

———, 2015. 'Who Was Francesco Landini's Antagonist in His Defense of Ockham?' *Philomusica On-line*, 14, 1–24, http://riviste.paviauniversitypress.it/index.php/phi/article/viewFile/1754/1836.

Akae, Yuichi, 2008. 'Between *Artes praedicandi* and Actual Sermons: Robert of Basevorn's *Forma praedicandi* and the Sermons of John Waldeby, OESA', in Roger Andersson (ed.), *Constructing the Medieval Sermon* (Turnhout), pp. 9–31.

Alberni, Anna, 2021. 'Mélusine à la cour d'Aragon: Jean d'Arras, 1380–1381', in Sylvie Lefèvre and Fabio Zinelli (eds.), *En français hors de France. Textes, livres, collections du Moyen Âge* (Strasbourg), pp. 219–41.

Alberni, Anna, Stefano Maria Cingolani, Anna Fernàndez-Clot, Simone Sari, and Carles Vela (eds.), 2024. *MiMus DB: Minstrels and Music in the Crown of Aragon* [online database], http://mimus.ub.edu/ca.

Alden, Jane, 2010. *Songs, Scribes and Society: The History and Reception of the Loire Valley Chansonniers* (Oxford and New York).

Alexander, Jonathan J. G., 1992. *Medieval Illuminators and their Methods of Work* (New Haven and London).

Aluas, Luminita Florea, 1996. 'The *Quatuor principalia musicae*: A Critical Edition and Translation, with Introduction and Commentary' (2 vols., Ph.D. dissertation, Indiana University).

Anderson, Gordon A., 1972–75. 'Notre Dame and Related Conductus: A Catalogue Raisonné', *Miscellanea Musicologica*, 6, 153–229 (part 1); 7, 1–81 (part 2).

Anderson, Gordon A. (ed.), 1979–. *Notre-Dame and Related Conductus: Opera omnia* (11 vols.), [Institute of Mediaeval Music] Collected Works 10 (Henryville, Ottawa and Binningen [vols. 7 and 11 never appeared]).

Andrieu, Michel (ed.), 1931–61. *Les Ordines Romani du haut Moyen Âge* (5 vols.), Spicilegium sacrum Lovaniense 11, 23, 24, 28, 29 (Leuven).

Anglès, Higinio, 1970. *Historia de la música medieval en Navarra* (Pamplona).

Apel, Willi, 1942. *The Notation of Polyphonic Music (900–1600)* (Cambridge, MA).

Apel, Willi, with Samuel N. Rosenberg (eds.), 1970–72. *French Secular Compositions of the Fourteenth Century* (3 vols.), Corpus Mensurabilis Musicae 53 [Rome].

Arlt, Wulf, 1998. 'Lescurel and the Function of Musical Language', in Margaret Bent and Andrew Wathey (eds.), *Fauvel Studies: Allegory, Chronicle, Music and Image in Paris, Bibliothèque Nationale de France, MS français 146* (Oxford), pp. 25–34.

Armstrong, Adrian, and Sarah Kay, 2011. *Knowing Poetry: Verse in Medieval France from the* Rose *to the* Rhétoriqueurs (Ithaca, NY).

Avril, François, 1981. 'Manuscrits', in Françoise Baron (ed.), *Les Fastes du Gothique. Le siècle de Charles V* [exhibition catalogue] (Paris), pp. 276–362.

———, 1998. 'Manuscrits', in Danielle Gaborit-Chopin (ed.), *L'Art au temps des rois maudits. Philippe le Bel et ses fils (1285–1328)* [exhibition catalogue] (Paris), pp. 256–334.

Axton, Richard, and John Stevens (comp. and trans.), 1971. *Medieval French Plays* (Oxford).

Babb, Warren (trans.), and Claude V. Palisca (ed.), 1978. *Hucbald, Guido, and John on Music: Three Medieval Treatises*, Music Theory Translation Series 3 (New Haven, CT).

Badel, Pierre-Yves (ed.), 1995. *Adam de la Halle. Œuvres complètes* (Paris).

Bain, Jennifer, 2015. *Hildegard of Bingen and Musical Reception: The Modern Revival of a Medieval Composer* (Cambridge).

——— (ed.), 2021. *The Cambridge Companion to Hildegard of Bingen* (Cambridge and New York).

———, 2021. 'Music, Liturgy, and Intertextuality in Hildegard of Bingen's Chant Repertory', in Jennifer Bain (ed.), *The Cambridge Companion to Hildegard of Bingen* (Cambridge), pp. 209–34.

Baltzell Kopp, Jane, 1971. 'Robert of Basevorn: *The Form of Preaching* (1322 A.D.)', in James J. Murphy (ed.), *Three Medieval Rhetorical Arts* (Berkeley and London), pp. 27–108.

Baltzer, Rebecca A., 1972. 'Thirteenth-Century Illuminated Miniatures and the Date of the Florence Manuscript', *Journal of the American Musicological Society*, 25:1, 1–18.

———, 2008. 'The Manuscript Makers of W_1: Further Evidence for an Early Date', in David B. Cannata, Gabriela I. Currie, Rena C. Mueller, and John L. Nádas (eds.), *Quomodo cantabimus canticum? Studies in Honor of Edward H. Roesner* (Middleton, WI), pp. 103–20.

———, 2018. 'The Decoration of Montpellier 8: Its Place in the Continuum of Parisian Manuscript Illumination', in Catherine A. Bradley and Karen Desmond (eds.), *The Montpellier Codex: The Final Fascicle: Contents, Contexts, Chronologies* (Woodbridge), pp. 78–89.

Bandur, Markus, 1996. 'Compositio/ Komposition', in Hans Heinrich Eggebrecht (ed.), *Handwörterbuch der musikalischen Terminologie*, Sonderband II, *Terminologie der musikalischen Komposition* (Stuttgart), pp. 1–34.

Barker-Benfield, Bruce, 1983. 'Notable Accessions: Western Manuscripts', *Bodleian Library Record*, 11, 114–18.

Baron, Françoise, 1968. 'Enlumineurs, peintres et sculpteurs parisiens des XIIIᵉ et XIVᵉ siècles d'après les rôles de la taille', *Bulletin archéologique du Comité des travaux historiques et scientifiques*, NS, 4, 37–121.

Barral i Altet, Xavier (ed.), 1986–90. *Artistes, artisans et production artistique au Moyen Âge. Colloque international, Centre National de la Recherche Scientifique, Université de Rennes II, Haute-Bretagne, 2–6 mai 1983* (3 vols., Paris).

Barthes, Roland, (1968) 1984. 'La mort de l'auteur', *Manteia*, 5, 12–17. Repr. in *Le bruissement de la langue. Essais critiques IV*, pp. 61–67 (Paris).

————, 1977. 'The Death of the Author', in Stephen Heath (comp. and trans.), *Roland Barthes: Image, Music, Text* (London), pp. 142–48.

Beer, Ellen J., 1959. *Beiträge zur oberrheinischen Buchmalerei in der ersten Hälfte des 14. Jahrhunderts, unter besonderer Berücksichtigung der Initialornamentik* (Basel and Stuttgart).

Bekker-Nielsen, Hans, 1968. 'The Victorines and Their Influence on Old Norse Literature', in Bjarni Niclasen (ed.), *The Fifth Viking Congress: Tórshavn, July 1965* (Tórshavn), pp. 32–36.

Bénichou-Samson, Édouard, 2014. 'Le rôle de l'Homme pécheur (BNF, manuscrits, NAF 6514). Édition critique' (Thèse de doctorat, École nationale des Chartes, Paris).

Bent, Margaret, (1981) 2002. 'Some Factors in the Control of Consonance and Sonority: Successive Composition and the Solus Tenor', in Daniel Heartz and Bonnie Wade (eds.), *International Musicological Society: Report of the Twelfth Congress, Berkeley 1977* (Kassel), pp. 625–34. Repr. in *Counterpoint, Composition, and Musica Ficta* (New York and London), pp. 241–54.

————, 1990. 'A Note on the Dating of the Trémoïlle Manuscript', in Bryan Gillingham and Paul Merkley (eds.), *Beyond the Moon: Festschrift Luther Dittmer* (Ottawa), pp. 217–42.

————, 1998a. 'Early Papal Motets', in Richard Sherr (ed.), *Papal Music and Musicians in Late Medieval and Renaissance Rome* (Oxford), pp. 5–43.

————, 1998b. 'Fauvel and Marigny: Which Came First?' in Margaret Bent and Andrew Wathey (eds.), *Fauvel Studies: Allegory, Chronicle, Music, and Image in Paris, Bibliothèque Nationale de France, MS français 146* (Oxford), pp. 35–52.

————, rev. Andrew Wathey, 2001. 'Vitry, Philippe de', *Grove Music Online*, https://doi.org/10.1093/gmo/9781561592630.article.29535.

————, 2004. 'The Musical Stanzas in Martin le Franc's Le Champion des dames', in John Haines and Randall Rosenfeld (eds.), *Music and Medieval Manuscripts: Paleography and Performance: Essays Dedicated to Andrew Hughes* (Aldershot), pp. 91–127.

———— (ed.), 2008. *Bologna Q15: The Making and Remaking of a Musical Manuscript: Introductory Study and Facsimile Edition* (2 vols.), Ars nova, nuova serie, 2 (Lucca).

————, 2013. 'The Trent 92 and Aosta Indexes in Context', in Danilo Curti-Feininger and Marco Gozzi (eds.), *I codici musicali trentini del quattrocento. Nuove scoperte, nuove edizioni e nuovi strumenti informatici* (Lucca), pp. 63–81.

————, 2014. '*Libri de cantu* in the Early Fifteenth-Century Veneto: Contents, Use and Ownership', in Alexander Rausch and Björn R. Tammen (eds.), *Musikalische Repertoires in Zentraleuropa (1420–1450): Prozesse & Praktiken* (Vienna), pp. 153–70.

————, 2015a. *Magister Jacobus de Ispania, Author of the* Speculum musicae (Farnham).

————, 2015b. 'Orfeo: *Dominus Presbiter Orpheus de Padua*', in Anna Zayaruznaya, Bonnie J. Blackburn, and Stanley Boorman (eds.), *'Qui musicam in se habet': Studies in Honor of Alejandro Enrique Planchart* (Middleton, WI), pp. 231–56.

————, 2016. 'Melchior or Marchion de Civilibus, prepositus brixiensis: New Documents', in Benjamin Brand and David J. Rothenberg (eds.), *Music and Culture in the Middle Ages and Beyond: Liturgy, Sources, Symbolism* (Cambridge), pp. 175–90.

————, 2022a. 'Artes Novae', *Music & Letters*, 103:4, 729–52.

————, 2022b. 'Washington, Library of Congress, M2.1 C6 1400 Case: A Neglected English Fragment', in Jared C. Hartt, Tamsyn Mahoney-Steel, and Benjamin Albritton (eds.), *Manuscripts, Music, Machaut: Essays in Honor of Lawrence Earp* (Turnhout), pp. 529–52.

————, 2023. *The Motet in the Late Middle Ages* (New York and Oxford).

Bent, Margaret, and Anne Hallmark (eds.), 1985. *The Works of Johannes Ciconia*, Polyphonic Music of the Fourteenth Century 24 (Monaco).

Bent, Margaret, Jared C. Hartt, and Peter M. Lefferts, 2021. *The Dorset Rotulus: Contextualizing and Reconstructing the Early English Motet* (Woodbridge).

Bent, Margaret, and Andrew Wathey (eds.), 2022. *Fragments of English Polyphonic Music c. 1390–1475*, Early English Church Music 62 (London).

Berger, Roger (ed.), 1970. *Le nécrologe de la confrérie des jongleurs et des bourgeois d'Arras (1194–1361)* (2 vols.), Mémoires de la commission départementale des monuments historiques du Pas-de-Calais 11/2 and 13/2 (Arras).

———— (ed.), 1981. *Littérature et société arrageoises au XIIIe siècle. Les chansons et dits artésiens*, Mémoires de la commission départementale des monuments historiques du Pas-de-Calais 21 (Arras).

Bergsagel, John, 1990. 'The Transmission of Notre-Dame Organa in Some Newly-Discovered "Magnus liber organi" Fragments in Copenhagen', in Angelo Pompilio et al. (eds.), *Atti del XIV Congresso della Società Internazionale di Musicologia: Trasmissione e recezione delle forme di cultura musicale* (3 vols., Turin), vol. 3, pp. 629–36.

Bernhard, Michael (ed.), 1992–2006. *Lexicon Musicum Latinum Medii Aevi. Munich: Verlag der Bayerischen Akademie der Wissenschaften*, https://www.woerterbuch-netz.de/LmL.

Berschin, Walter, 1972. *Bonizo von Sutri: Leben und Werk*, Beiträge zur Geschichte und Quellenkunde des Mittelalters 2 (Berlin).

————, 2010. 'Rufillus von Weißenau (um 1200) in seiner Buchmalerwerkstatt', in Walter Berschin (ed.), *Mittellateinische Studien II* (Heidelberg), pp. 353–56.

Berthier, Jacques, 1970. *50 pièces d'orgue pour l'office d'aujourd'hui, préludes, postludes et versets* (Paris).

Besseler, Heinrich, 1927. 'Studien zur Musik des Mittelalters, II, Die Motette von Franko von Köln bis Philipp von Vitry', *Archiv für Musikwissenschaft*, 8:2, 137–258.

———— (ed.), 1954. *Guillaume de Machaut: Musikalische Werke*, Vierter Band, *Messe und Lais* (Leipzig).

———— (ed.), rev. David Fallows, 1995. *Guillelmi Dufay, Opera omnia*, vol. 7, *Cantiones*, Corpus Mensurabilis Musicae 1/6 [Rome].

Bevilacqua, Gregorio, 2016. 'The Earliest Source of Notre-Dame Polyphony? A New Conductus Fragment from the Early Thirteenth Century', *Music & Letters*, 97:1, 1–41.

Biet, Christian, 2009. 'Towards a Dramaturgy of Appearance: An Aesthetic and Political Understanding of the Theatrical Event as Session', *Performance Research*, 14:3, 102–109.

Bigwood, Georges, 1924–25. 'Les financiers d'Arras. Contribution à l'étude des origines du capitalisme moderne', *Revue belge de philologie et d'histoire*, 3:3, 465–508 (part 1); 3:4, 769–819 (part 2); 4:1, 109–19 (part 3); 4:2–3, 379–421 (part 4).

Billanovich, Giuseppe, 1996. *Petrarca e il primo umanesimo*, Studi sul Petrarca 25 (Padova).

Blackburn, Bonnie J., 1997. 'For Whom Do the Singers Sing?', *Early Music*, 25:4, 593–609.

Blum, Rudolf, 1948. 'Maître Honoré und das Brevier Philipps des Schönen', *Zentralblatt für Bibliothekswesen*, 62, 225–30.

Boogaart, Jacques, 2018. 'A Prism of Its Time: Social Functions of the Motet in Fourteenth-Century France', in Jared C. Hartt (ed.), *A Critical Companion to Medieval Motets* (Woodbridge), pp. 155–74.

Booth, William Stone, 1909. *Some Acrostic Signatures of Francis Bacon* (Boston and New York).

Boretius, Alfred, and Viktor Krause (eds.), 1897. *Walahfridi Strabonis, Libellus de exordiis et incrementis quarundam in observationibus ecclesiasticis rerum*, MGH Capitularia Regum Francorum 2 (Hanover), pp. 473–516.

Bormans, Stanislas, and Emile Schoolmeesters (eds.), 1893. *Cartulaire de l'église Saint-Lambert de Liège*, Collection des chroniques belges inédites 26, vol. 1 (Brussels).

Born, Georgina, and Andrew Barry, 2018. 'Music, Mediation Theories and Actor-Network Theory', *Contemporary Music Review*, 37:5–6, 443–87.

Bouhaïk-Gironès, Marie, 2003. 'Le procès des farceurs de Dijon (1447)', *European Medieval Drama*, 7, 117–34.

———, 2007. *Les Clercs de la Basoche et le théâtre comique (Paris, 1420–1550)* (Paris).

———, 2012. 'À qui profite l'auteur? Théâtre, responsabilité de la parole et fonction-auteur à la fin du Moyen Âge', *Parlement(s)*, 8, 27–37.

———, 2023. *Le mystère de Romans (1509). Une cité en spectacle* (Paris).

Bouhaïk-Gironès, Marie, and Estelle Doudet, 2014. 'L'auteur comme praxis. Un dialogue disciplinaire sur la fabrique du théâtre aux XVᵉ et XVIᵉ siècles', *Perspectives médiévales*, 35, https://doi.org/10.4000/peme.4142.

———, 2024. 'The Performing Arts in Fifteenth- and Sixteenth-Century France. The Making of Theater', in Clare Finburgh Delijani and Christian Biet (eds.), *A New History of French Theater* (Cambridge), pp. 39–54.

Bourgain, Pascale, 2001. 'Les verbes en rapport avec le concept d'auteur', in Michel Zimmermann (ed.), *Auctor et auctoritas. Invention et conformisme dans l'écriture médiévale. Actes du colloque tenu à l'Université de Versailles-Saint-Quentin-en-Yvelines (14–16 juin 1999)* (Paris), pp. 361–74.

Bove, Boris, 2013. 'Les hôtels à Paris vers 1400', in Hélène Noizet, Boris Bove, and Laurent Costa (eds.), *Paris de parcelles en pixels* (Vincennes), p. 264, https://alpage.huma-num.fr/documents/Illustration_colloque/BOVE_Hotels1400_p264.pdf (Creative Commons CC0).

Boynton, Susan, 2004. 'From the Lament of Rachel to the Lament of Mary: A Transformation in the History of Drama and Spirituality', in Nils H. Petersen, Claus Clüver, and Nicolas Bell (eds.), *Signs of Change: Transformations of Christian Traditions and Their Representation in the Arts (1000–2000)* (Amsterdam and New York), pp. 319–40.

Braddy, Haldeen, 1938. 'Messire Oton de Graunson, Chaucer's Savoyard Friend', *Studies in Philology*, 35:4, 515–31.

Bradley, Catherine A., 2013. 'Contrafacta and Transcribed Motets: Vernacular Influences on Latin Motets and Clausulae in the Florence Manuscript', *Early Music History*, 32, 1–70.

———, 2019. 'Choosing a Thirteenth-Century Motet Tenor: From the *Magnus liber organi* to Adam de la Halle', *Journal of the American Musicological Society*, 72:2, 431–92.

———, 2022a. *Authorship and Identity in Late Thirteenth-Century Motets* (Abingdon and New York).

———, 2022b. 'Polyphony from and for Refrains in Dance-Song Motets', in Jared C. Hartt, Tamsyn Mahoney-Steel, and Benjamin L. Albritton (eds.), *Manuscripts, Music, Machaut: Essays in Honor of Lawrence Earp* (Turnhout), pp. 413–39.

———, 2023. 'Perspectives for Lost Polyphony and Red Notation around 1300: Medieval Motet and Organum Fragments in Stockholm', *Early Music History*, 41: 1–92.

Bradley, Catherine A., and Karen Desmond (eds.), 2018. *The Montpellier Codex: The Final Fascicle: Contents, Contexts, Chronologies* (Woodbridge).

Bradley, Robert John, 1992. 'Musical Life and Culture at Savoy (1420–1450)' (2 vols., Ph.D. dissertation, City University of New York).

Bragard, Roger (ed.), 1955–73. *Jacobi Leodiensis, Speculum musicae* (7 vols.), Corpus scriptorum de musica 3 [Rome].

Branca, Vittore (ed.), 1974. *Tutte le opere di Giovanni Boccaccio*, vol. 3, *Amorosa visione. Ninfale fiesolano. Trattatello in laude di Dante* (Milan).

Brandmüller, Théo, 1979. *Elegia: Für Schlagzeug und Orgel* (Wiesbaden and Berlin).

Branner, Robert, 1972. 'The Johannes Grusch Atelier and the Continental Origins of the William of Devon Painter', *The Art Bulletin*, 54:1, 24–30.

Brayer, Édith, and Anne-Françoise Leurquin-Labie (eds.), 2008. *La Somme le Roi par frère Laurent* (Paris and Abbeville).

Brewer, Charles E., 2012. 'The Web of Sources for *Planctus ante nescia*', in Robert Klugseder (ed.), *Cantus Planus: Papers Read at the 16th Meeting. Vienna, Austria 2011* (Vienna), pp. 72–77.

———, 2020. 'Locating the Codex Buranus: Notational Contexts', in Tristan E. Franklinos and Henry Hope (eds.), *Revisiting the Codex Buranus: Contexts, Contents, Concepts* (Woodbridge), pp. 283–315.

[Brial, Michel-Jean-Joseph (Dom)], 1820. 'Geofroi, Sous-prieur de Sainte-Barbe, et Godefroi, Chanoine régulier de Saint-Victor de Paris', in *Histoire Littéraire de la France*, vol. 15, pp. 69–85.

Briegleb, Pervenche, and Arlette Laret-Kayser (eds.), 1973. *Documents relatifs au grand schisme*, vol. 6, *Suppliques de Benoît XIII (1394–1422)*, Analecta Vaticano-Belgica 26 (Brussels).

Briscoe, Marianne G., and Barbara H. Jaye, 1992. *Artes praedicandi. Artes orandi* (Turnhout).

Brissy, Alphonse, 1860. *Notice sur la sainte chandelle d'Arras* (Arras).

Brown, Cynthia J. (ed.), 1989. *André de La Vigne, La Ressource de Chrestienté. Édition critique*, Inedita et rara 5 (Montreal).

——— (ed.), 2005. *Pierre Gringore, Les Entrées royales à Paris de Marie d'Angleterre (1514) et Claude de France (1517)*, Textes littéraires français 577 (Geneva).

Brusegan, Rosanna, 2004. 'Encore sur le *Jeu du Pèlerin*: autoportrait d'Adam de la Halle?' in Maria Colombo Timelli and Claudio Galderisi (eds.), *'Pour acquerir honneur et pris'. Mélanges de moyen français offerts à Giuseppe Di Stefano* (Montreal), pp. 359–65.

Buckley, Ann, 2003. 'Abelard's *planctus* and Old French *Lais*: Melodic Style and Formal Structure', in Marc Stewart and David Wulstan (eds.), *The Poetic and Musical Legacy of Heloise and Abelard: An Anthology of Essays by Various Authors* (Ottawa), pp. 49–59.

Bugyis, Katie Ann-Marie, A. B. Kraebel, and Margot E. Fassler (eds.), 2017. *Medieval Cantors and Their Craft: Music, Liturgy and the Shaping of History (800–1500)* (York).

Bukofzer, Manfred, 1953. 'Interrelations between Conductus and Clausula', *Annales musicologiques*, 1, 65–103.

Buron, Emmanuel, Olivier Halévy, and Jean-Claude Mühlethaler (eds.), 2015. *L'Infortuné, Instructif de la seconde rhétorique*, in Jean-Charles Monferran (ed.), *La Muse et le Compas. Poétiques à l'aube de l'âge moderne. Anthologie* (Paris), pp. 66–138.

Busby, Keith, 2002. *Codex and Context: Reading Old French Verse Narrative in Manuscript* (2 vols., Amsterdam).

Busse Berger, Anna Maria, 2005. *Medieval Music and the Art of Memory* (Berkeley and London).

———, 2013. 'Orality, Literacy and Quotation in Medieval Polyphony', in Giuliano Di Bacco and Yolanda Plumley (eds.), *Citation, Intertextuality and Memory in the Middle Ages and Renaissance*, vol. 2, *Cross-Disciplinary Perspectives on Medieval Culture* (Liverpool), pp. 30–50.

Butterfield, Ardis, 2003. '*Enté*: a Survey and Reassessment of the Term in Thirteenth- and Fourteenth-Century Music and Poetry', *Early Music History*, 22, 67–101.

Büttner, Fred, 1990. *Klang und Konstruktion in der englischen Mehrstimmigkeit des 13. Jahrhunderts: Ein Beitrag zur Erforschung der Stimmtauschkompositionen in den Worcester-Fragmenten* (Tutzing).

Campbell, Gordon (ed.), 2009. 'Bedford Master [Master of the Bedford Hours; Master of the Breviary of the Duke of Bedford]', in *The Grove Encyclopedia of Northern Renaissance Art*, https://www.oxfordreference.com/view/10.1093/acref/9780195334661.001.0001/acref-9780195334661-e-149.

Caraci Vela, Maria, 1997. 'Una nuova attribuzione a Zacara da un trattato musicale del primo Quattrocento', *Acta Musicologica*, 69:2, 182–85.

Carey, Richard J. (ed.), 1972. *Jean de Le Mote, Le Parfait du paon*, University of North Carolina Studies in the Romance Languages and Literatures 118 (Chapel Hill).

Carlevaris, Angela (ed.), 1995. *Hildegardis Bingensis, Liber vitae meritorum*, Corpus Christianorum. Continuatio Mediaevalis 90 (Turnhout).

Cassagnes-Brouquet, Sophie, 2014. 'Les ateliers d'artistes au Moyen Âge: entre théorie et pratiques', *Perspective*, 1, http://journals.openedition.org/perspective/4391.

Catalunya, David, 2017. 'Nuns, Polyphony, and a Liégeois Cantor: New Light on the Las Huelgas "Solmization Song"', *Journal of the Alamire Foundation*, 9:1, 89–133.

———, 2018. 'Insights into the Chronology and Reception of Philippe de Vitry's Ars Nova Theory: Revisiting the Mensural Treatise of Barcelona Cathedral', *Early Music*, 46:3, 417–38.

Caullet, Gustave, 1907–8. 'Les manuscrits de Gilles Le Muisit et l'art de la miniature au XIVe siècle. Le relieur tournaisien Janvier', *Bulletin du Cercle historique et archéologique de Courtrai*, 5, 200–25.

Cavrois, Louis (ed.), 1876. *Cartulaire de Notre-Dame-des-Ardents à Arras* (Arras).

Cerquiglini, Bernard, 1989. *Éloge de la variante. Histoire critique de la philologie* (Paris).

———, 1999. *In Praise of the Variant: A Critical History of Philology*, trans. Betsy Wing (Baltimore).

Chabannes, Claire, 1999. 'Les ménétriers à Paris à la fin du Moyen Âge' (Mémoire de maîtrise, Université Paris VII Denis Diderot, Paris).

Chailley, Jacques (ed.), 1942. *Adam de la Halle (1240?–1288?). Rondeaux à 3 voix égales* (Paris).

——— (ed.), 1948. *Guillaume de Machaut (1300–1377). Messe Notre-Dame dite du sacre de Charles V (1364) à 4 voix égales* (Paris).

Chaouche, Sabine, Estelle Doudet, and Olivier Spina, 2017. 'Introduction', in Sabine Chaouche, Estelle Doudet, and Olivier Spina (eds.), 'Écrire pour la scène (XVe–XVIIIe siècle)', *European Drama and Performance Studies*, 9:2, 9–44.

Charland, Thomas-Marie, 1936. *Artes praedicandi. Contribution à l'histoire de la rhétorique au Moyen Âge* (Paris and Ottawa).

Charma, Antoine (ed.), 1868. *Fons philosophie, Poème inédit du XIIe siècle* (Caen).

Chartier, Roger, 2014. *L'Œuvre, l'Atelier et la Scène. Trois études de mobilité textuelle* (Paris).

Chenu, Marie-Dominique, 1927. 'Auctor, Actor, Autor', *Archivum Latinitatis Medii Aevi*, 3, 81–86.

Chevalier, Ulysse, 1889–1920. *Repertorium hymnologicum. Catalogue des chants, hymnes, proses, séquences, tropes en usage dans l'Église latine depuis les origines jusqu'à nos jours* (6 vols., Leuven and Brussels).

Cingolani, Stefano M. (ed.), 2019. *Pere III el Ceremoniós, Epistolari* (Barcelona).

Clark, Robert L. A., 1994. 'The *Miracles de Nostre Dame par personnages* of the Cangé Manuscript and the Sociocultural Function of Confraternity Drama' (Ph.D. dissertation, Indiana University).

Clark, Suzannah, 2007. '"S'en dirai chançonete": Hearing Text and Music in a Medieval Motet', *Plainsong and Medieval Music*, 16:1, 31–59.

Clément, Gisèle, Isabelle Fabre, Gilles Polizzi, and Fañch Thoraval (eds.), 2021. *Poésie et musique à l'âge de l'Ars subtilior. Autour du manuscrit Torino, BNU, J.II.9* (Turnhout).

Coates, Alan, 1999. *English Medieval Books: The Reading Abbey Collections from Foundation to Dispersal* (Oxford).

Cohen, David, 2002. 'Notes, Scales, and Modes in the Earlier Middle Ages', in Thomas Christiansen (ed.), *The Cambridge History of Western Music Theory* (Cambridge), pp. 307–63.

Colette, Marie-Noël, 2009. 'A Witness to Poetic and Musical Invention in the Twelfth Century: The Troper-Proser of Nevers (BnF n.a. lat. 3126)', in Gunilla Iversen and Nicolas Bell (eds.), *Sapientia et Eloquentia: Meaning and Function in Liturgical Poetry, Music, Drama, and Biblical Commentary in the Middle Ages* (Turnhout), pp. 259–300.

Colgrave, Bertram (ed. and trans.), (1968) 1985. *The Earliest Life of Gregory the Great by an Anonymous Monk of Whitby* ([Lawrence, KS]; repr. Cambridge).

Colton, Lisa, 2017. 'Music, Text and Structure in 14th-Century English Polyphony: The Case of *Ave miles celestis curie*', *Early Music*, 45:1, 27–40.

Connolly, Margaret, and Yolanda Plumley, 2006. 'Crossing the Channel: John Shirley and the Circulation of French Lyric Poetry in England in the Early Fifteenth Century', in Godfried Croenen and Peter Ainsworth (eds.), *Patrons, Authors and Workshops: Books and Book Production in Paris around 1400* (Leuven), pp. 311–32.

Constans, Léopold (ed.), 1904. *Le Roman de Troie, par Benoît de Sainte-Maure, publié d'après tous les manuscrits connus*, vol. 1 (Paris).

Coste, Florent, 2021. 'La littérature médiévale est-elle bien un atelier d'écriture?' *COnTEXTES*, 31, https://doi.org/10.4000/contextes.10334.

Courtenay, William J., 2011. 'Theological Bachelors at Paris on the Eve of the Papal Schism: The Academic Environment of Peter of Candia', in Kent Emery Jr., Russell L. Friedman, and Andreas Speer (eds.), *Philosophy and Theology in the Long Middle Ages: A Tribute to Stephen F. Brown* (Leiden), pp. 921–52.

Courtenay, William J., and Eric D. Goddard (eds.), 2013. *Rotuli Parisienses: Supplications to the Pope from the University of Paris*, vol. 3/1, 1378–1394, Education and Society in the Middle Ages and Renaissance 44 (Leiden).

Coussemaker, Charles Edmond Henri de, 1852. *Histoire de l'harmonie au Moyen Âge* (Paris).

——— (ed.), (1864–76) 1963. *Scriptorum de musica medii aevi nova series a Gerbertina altera* (4 vols., [Paris]; repr. Hildesheim).

———, 1865. *L'art harmonique aux XIIe et XIIIe siècles* (Paris).

——— (ed.), 1872. *Œuvres complètes du trouvère Adam de la Halle. Poésies et musique* (Paris).

Couturier, Marcel, and Graham Runnalls (eds.), 1991. *Le Compte du Mystère de la Passion (Châteaudun, 1510)* (Chartres).

Coxe, Henricus O., 1852. *Catalogus codicum mss. qui in collegiis aulisque Oxoniensibus hodie adservantur* (2 vols., Oxford).

Crocker, Richard, 1990. 'French Polyphony of the Thirteenth Century', in David Hiley and Richard Crocker (eds.), *The New Oxford History of Music*, vol. 2, *The Early Middle Ages to 1300*, 2nd ed. (New York and Oxford), pp. 636–78.

Curran, Sean, 2013. 'Vernacular Book Production, Vernacular Polyphony, and the Motets of the "La Clayette" Manuscript (Paris, Bibliothèque nationale de

France, Nouvelles acquisitions françaises 13521)' (Ph.D. dissertation, University of California, Berkeley).

⸺, 2018. 'A Palaeographical Analysis of the Verbal Text in Montpellier 8: Problems, Implications, Opportunities', in Catherine A. Bradley and Karen Desmond (eds.), *The Montpellier Codex: The Final Fascicle: Contents, Contexts, Chronologies* (Woodbridge), pp. 32–65.

Cuthbert, Michael Scott, 2006. 'Trecento Fragments and Polyphony beyond the Codex' (Ph.D. dissertation, Harvard University).

⸺, 2009a. 'Palimpsests, Sketches, and Extracts: The Organization and Compositions of Seville 5-2-25', in Francesco Zimei (ed.), *L'Ars nova italiana del Trecento*, vol. 7, *'Dolci e nuove note'* (Lucca), pp. 57–78.

⸺, 2009b. 'Tipping the Iceberg: Missing Italian Polyphony from the Age of Schism', *Musica Disciplina*, 54, 39–74.

⸺, 2017. 'Trecento Theory in Italian and Italian Theorists as Composers', paper presented at the Medieval and Renaissance Music Conference, Prague.

Damon, Phillip, 1960. 'The Preconium Augustini of Godfrey of St. Victor', *Mediaeval Studies*, 22, 92–107.

Dauphant, Clotilde (ed. and trans.), 2014. *Eustache Deschamps. Anthologie* (Paris).

Davis, Shelley, 1967. 'The Solus Tenor in the 14th and 15th Centuries', *Acta Musicologica*, 39:1–2, 44–64.

Davison, Archibald T., and Willi Apel (eds.), 1947. *Historical Anthology of Music: Oriental, Medieval and Renaissance Music* (Cambridge, MA).

Davril, Anselme, and Timothy M. Thibodeau (eds.), 1995–2000. *Guillelmi Duranti, Rationale divinorum officiorum* (3 vols.), Corpus Christianorum. Continuatio Mediaevalis 140 (Turnhout).

Debiais, Vincent, 2009. *Messages de pierre. La lecture des inscriptions dans la communication médiévale (XIIIe–XIVe siècle)* (Turnhout).

Deeming, Helen (ed.), 2013. *Songs in British Sources c. 1150–1300* (London).

⸺, 2015a. 'An English Monastic Miscellany: The Reading Manuscript of *Sumer is icumen in*', in Helen Deeming and Elizabeth Eva Leach (eds.), *Manuscripts and Medieval Song: Inscription, Performance, Context* (Cambridge), pp. 116–40.

⸺, 2015b. 'Multilingual Networks in Twelfth- and Thirteenth-Century Song', in Mary Carruthers (ed.), *Language in Medieval Britain: Networks and Exchanges* (Donington), pp. 127–43.

Dehaisnes, Chrétien, 1886. *Documents et extraits divers concernant l'histoire de l'art dans la Flandre, l'Artois et le Hainaut avant le XVe siècle* (2 vols., Lille).

Delbouille, Maurice (ed.), 1932. *Jacques Bretel, Le Tournoi de Chauvency* (Paris).

Delcourt, Thierry (ed.), 2009. *La Légende du roi Arthur* (Paris).

Delhaye, Philippe, 1951. *Le Microcosmus de Godefroy de Saint-Victor. Étude théologique* (Lille).

Delisle, Léopold (ed.), 1874. *Mandements et actes divers de Charles V (1364–1380)* (Paris).

⸺, 1885a. 'Discours', *Annuaire-bulletin de la Société de l'Histoire de France*, 22:1, 82–139.

⸺ (ed.), 1885b. 'Testament de Blanche de Navarre, reine de France', *Mémoires de la Société de l'histoire de Paris et de l'Île-de-France*, 12, 1–64.

De Looze, Laurence N., 1991. 'Signing off in the Middle Ages: Medieval Textuality and Strategies of Authorial Self-Naming', in Alger N. Doane and Carol Braun Pasternack (eds.), *Vox Intexta: Orality and Textuality in the Middle Ages* (Madison), pp. 162–78.

Delsaux, Olivier, 2014. 'L'humaniste Simon de Plumetot et sa copie des poésies d'Eustache Deschamps. Une édition génétique au début du XVe siècle?' *Revue d'histoire des textes*, 9, 273–349 (part 1); 10, 141–95 (part 2).

Denifle, Heinrich, and Emile Chatelain (eds.), (1894) 2014. *Chartularium Universitatis Parisiensis*, vol. 3 ([Paris]; repr. Cambridge).

De Paermentier, Els, 2018. '"A no grant besoing, en boine mounoie et bien contee": The XIIIth-Century Flemish Counts' Appeal for Funds to Moneylenders from Arras', in Cristina Mantegna and Olivier Poncet (eds.), *Les documents du commerce et des marchands entre Moyen Âge et époque moderne (XIIe–XVIIe siècle)* (Rome), pp. 153–68.

Derolez, Albert, and Peter Dronke (eds.), 1996. *Hildegardis Bingensis, Liber divinorum operum*, Corpus Christianorum. Continuatio Mediaevalis 92 (Turnhout).

De Smet, Joseph-Jean (ed.), 1841. *Recueil des chroniques de Flandre (Corpus chronicorum Flandriae)*, vol. 2 (Brussels).

Desmond, Karen, 2000. 'New Light on Jacobus, Author of *Speculum musicae*', *Plainsong and Medieval Music*, 9:1, 19–40.

———, 2018a. *Music and the Moderni (1300–1350): The ars nova in Theory and Practice* (Cambridge).

———, 2018b. '"One is the loneliest number … ": The Semibreve Stands Alone', *Early Music*, 46:3, 403–16.

———, 2018c. 'Texture, Rhythm, and Stylistic Groupings in Montpellier 8 Motets', in Catherine A. Bradley and Karen Desmond (eds.), *The Montpellier Codex: The Final Fascicle: Contents, Contexts, Chronologies* (Woodbridge), pp. 139–60.

———, 2020. 'W. de Wicumbe's Rolls and Singing the Alleluya ca. 1250', *Journal of the American Musicological Society*, 73:3, 639–709.

———, 2023. 'The Indicative Mood: A Response to Margaret Bent', *Music & Letters*, 104:1, 114–22.

———, 2024. 'Medieval Music Rolls, Scribes and Performance: The Extant Rolls of Thirteenth-Century English Polyphony', in Antonella Brita, Janina Karolewski, Matthieu Husson, Laure Miolo, and Hanna Wimmer (eds.), *Manuscripts and Performances in Religions, Arts, and Sciences* (Berlin and Boston), pp. 189–210, https://doi.org/10.1515/9783111343556-007.

De Van, Guillaume (ed.), 1949. *Guglielmi de Mascaudio: Opera I, la Messe de Nostre Dame*, Corpus Mensurabilis Musicae 2 [Rome].

D'Haenens, Albert, 1959a. 'Gilles Li Muisis historien', *Revue bénédictine*, 69:3–4, 258–86.

——— (ed.), 1959b. 'Le *Tractatus de consuetudinibus* de Gilles Li Muisis (1347)', *Bulletin de la Commission royale d'histoire*, 124, 143–96.

Di Bacco, Giuliano, and John L. Nádas, 1994. 'Verso uno "stile internazionale" della musica nelle cappelle papali e cardinalizie durante il Grande Scisma (1378–1417): Il caso di Johannes Ciconia da Liège', in Adalbert Roth (ed.), *Collectanea I* (Vatican City), pp. 7–74.

Dinaux, Arthur, 1837–63. *Trouvères, jongleurs et ménestrel du nord de la France et du midi de la Belgique* (4 vols., Paris).

Dittmer, Luther A., 1954. 'An English Discantuum Volumen', *Musica Disciplina*, 8, 19–58.

———, 1957. *The Worcester Fragments: A Catalogue Raisonné and Transcription* [Rome].

Dobson, Eric J., and Frank Ll. Harrison (eds.), 1979. *Medieval English Songs* (New York and London).

Dobszay, László, 1988. 'As ómagyar Mária-siralom zenei vonatkozásai', *Zenetudományi dolgozátok*, 9–20.

Dolce, Brianne, 2020a. 'Making Music and Community in Thirteenth-Century Arras: A Study of the Confraternity of Jongleurs and Bourgeois' (Ph.D. dissertation, Yale University).

———, 2020b. '"Soit hom u feme": New Evidence for Women Musicians and the Search for the "Women Trouvères"', *Revue de musicologie*, 106:2, 301–27.

Dominguez, Véronique, 2008. 'Prologues, rimes, personnages dans le *Jeu de saint Nicolas* de Jean Bodel, *Le Jeu de la feuillée* et *Le Jeu de Robin et Marion* d'Adam de la Halle', in Christelle Reggiani, Claire Stolz, and Laurent Susini (eds.), *Styles, genres, auteurs (Jean Bodel, Adam de la Halle, Des Périers, Viau, Voltaire, Hugo, Bernanos)* (Paris), pp. 11–32.

Doss-Quinby, Eglal, Joan Tasker Grimbert, Wendy Pfeffer, and Elizabeth Aubrey (eds.), 2001. *Songs of the Women Trouvères* (New Haven).

Doudet, Estelle, 2008. '*Par le non conuist an l'ome*. Désignations et signatures de l'auteur, du XIIe au XVIe siècle', in Pierre Chiron and Francis Claudon (eds.), *Constitution du champ littéraire. Limites, intersections, déplacements* (Paris), pp. 105–24.

——— (ed.), 2012. 'Le Jeu de Pèlerinage [de vie] humaine', in Jonathan Beck, Estelle Doudet, and Alan Hindley (eds.), *Recueil général de moralités d'expression française*, vol. 1, Bibliothèque du théâtre français 9 (Paris), pp. 525–650.

———, 2018. *Moralités et jeux moraux. Le théâtre allégorique en français (XVe–XVIe s.)* (Paris).

——— (ed.), 2019. 'La Moralité du jour saint Antoine', in Jonathan Beck, Estelle Doudet, and Alan Hindley (eds.), *Recueil général de moralités d'expression française*, vol. 2, Bibliothèque du théâtre français 53 (Paris), pp. 15–130.

———, 2020. 'Hantologies médiévales: Les écritures du spectacle face à l'archéologie des média', *Tropics*, 9, https://tropics.univ-reunion.fr/1577.

Doudet, Estelle, and Shanshan Lu, 2020. 'Pierre Gringore et les orateurs. Statut d'auteur et pratiques théâtrales au XVIe siècle', *Cahiers de recherches médiévales et humanistes*, 40:2, 323–41.

Douteil, Herbert (ed.), 1976. *Johannis Beleth, Summa de ecclesiasticis officiis* (2 vols.), Corpus Christianorum. Continuatio Mediaevalis 41 (Turnhout).

Dreves, Guido Maria (ed.), 1895. *Cantiones et Muteti, Lieder und Moteten des Mittelalters. Erster Folge: Cantiones natalitiae, partheniae*, Analecta Hymnica Medii Aevi 20 (Leipzig).

——— (ed.), 1905. *Pia Dictamina: Reimgebete und Leselieder des Mittelalters*, vol. 7, Analecta Hymnica Medii Aevi 46 (Leipzig).

Dreves, Guido Maria, and Clemens Blume (eds.), 1909. *Ein Jahrtausend Lateinischer Hymnendichtung: Eine Blütenlese aus den Analecta Hymnica mit literarhistorischen Erläuterungen* (2 vols., Leipzig).

Dronke, Peter, 1984. *Women Writers of the Middle Ages: A Critical Study of Texts from Perpetua (†203) to Marguerite Porete (†1310)* (Cambridge).

———, 1992. 'Laments of the Maries: From the Beginnings to the Mystery Plays', in Peter Dronke (ed.), *Intellectuals and Poets in Medieval Europe* (Rome), pp. 457–89.

——— (ed. and trans.), 1994. *Nine Medieval Latin Plays*, Cambridge Medieval Classics 1 (Cambridge).

Dronke, Peter, and Giovanni Orlandi, 2005. 'New Works by Abelard and Heloise?' *Filologia mediolatina*, 12, 123–77.

Du Cange, Charles D. F. sieur, 1883–87. *Glossarium Mediæ et Infimæ Latinitatis* (10 vols., Niort, orig. 1678).

Duchesne, Louis (ed.), (1886–92) 1955–57. *Le Liber pontificalis* (2 vols., [Paris]; repr. Paris).

Du Méril, Édélestand, 1843. *Poésies populaires latines antérieures au douzième siècle* (Paris).

Duplat, André (ed.), 1979. *André de La Vigne, Le Mystère de saint Martin (1496)*, Textes littéraires français 277 (Geneva).

Dupré, Marcel (ed. and arr.), 1942. *Pérotin, Deux Points d'orgue en triple*, Anthologie des maîtres classiques de l'orgue 27 (Paris).

Durand, Georges, 1910. *Inventaire sommaire des archives départementales antérieures à 1790*, vol. 5 (Amiens).

Dyer, Joseph, 1984. 'Latin Psalters, Old Roman and Gregorian Chants', *Kirchenmusikalisches Jahrbuch*, 68, 11–30.

———, 2012. 'The Bible in the Medieval Liturgy c. 600–1300', in Richard Marsden and E. Ann Matter (eds.), *The New Cambridge History of the Bible*, vol. 2, *From 600 to 1450* (Cambridge), pp. 659–79.

———, 2019. 'Didactic Images in a Thirteenth-Century French Music Theory Treatise: The *Scientia artis musice* of Hélie Salomon', *Plainsong and Medieval Music*, 28:1, 1–27.

Earp, Lawrence, 1989. 'Machaut's Role in the Production of Manuscripts of His Works', *Journal of the American Musicological Society*, 42:3, 461–503.

———, 1995. *Guillaume de Machaut: A Guide to Research* (New York and London).

———, 2011. 'Reception', in Mark Everist (ed.), *The Cambridge Companion to Medieval Music* (Cambridge), pp. 335–70.

———, 2021. 'Introduction', in Lawrence Earp and Jared C. Hartt (eds.), *Poetry, Art, and Music in Guillaume de Machaut's Earliest Manuscript (BnF fr. 1586)* (Turnhout), pp. 21–55.

Earp, Lawrence, and Jared C. Hartt (eds.), 2021. *Poetry, Art, and Music in Guillaume de Machaut's Earliest Manuscript (BnF fr. 1586)* (Turnhout).

Earp, Lawrence, Domenic Leo, and Carla Shapreau (eds.), 2014. *The Ferrell-Vogüé Machaut Manuscript* (2 vols.), DIAMM Facsimiles 5 (Oxford).

Edmunds, Sheila, 1990. 'Catalogue des manuscrits savoyards', in Agostino Paravicini Bagliani (ed.), *Les manuscrits enluminés des comtes et ducs de Savoie* (Turin), pp. 193–230.

Egbert of York. *De institutione catholica dialogus*, PL 89. 435–442.

Eisenbichler, Konrad, 2019. 'Introduction: A World of Confraternities', in Konrad Eisenbichler (ed.), *A Companion to Medieval and Early Modern Confraternities* (Leiden), pp. 1–19.

Eisenstein, Elizabeth L., 1983. *The Printing Revolution in Early Modern Europe* (Cambridge).

Ellis, Katharine, 2005. *Interpreting the Musical Past: Early Music in Nineteenth-Century France* (Oxford and New York).

Ellsworth, Oliver B. (ed. and trans.), 1984. *The Berkeley Manuscript: University of California Music Library, Ms. 744 (olim Phillipps 4450)*, Greek and Latin music theory 2 (Lincoln, NE).

Everist, Mark, 1990. 'From Paris to St. Andrews: The Origins of *W1*', *Journal of the American Musicological Society*, 43:1, 1–42.

———, 1996. 'The Polyphonic *Rondeau* c. 1300: Repertory and Context', *Early Music History*, 15, 59–96.

———, 2007. 'Motets, French Tenors, and the Polyphonic Chanson ca. 1300', *The Journal of Musicology*, 24:3, 365–406.

———, 2017. 'Anonymous IV and the *Conductus*', paper presented at the Medieval and Renaissance Music Conference, Prague, and at the Annual Meeting of the American Musicological Society, Rochester.

———, 2018a. *Discovering Medieval Song: Latin Poetry and Music in the Conductus* (Cambridge).

———, 2018b. 'Le conduit à nombre de voix variable (1150–1250)', in Christelle Cazaux-Kowalski, Christelle Chaillou-Amadieu, Anne-Zoé Rillon-Marne, and Fabio Zinelli (eds.), *Les noces de philologie et musicologie. Texte et musique au Moyen Âge* (Paris), pp. 329–44.

———, 2018c. 'Montpellier 8: Anatomy of … ', in Catherine A. Bradley and Karen Desmond (eds.), *The Montpellier Codex: The Final Fascicle: Contents, Contexts, Chronologies* (Woodbridge), pp. 13–31.

———, 2019. 'Friends and Foals: The Polyphonic Music of Adam de la Halle', in Jennifer Saltzstein (ed.), *Musical Culture in the World of Adam de la Halle* (Leiden and Boston), pp. 311–51.

———, 2020. 'The Variable-Voice Conductus', in Tess Knighton and David Skinner (eds.), *Music and Instruments of the Middle Ages: Essays in Honour of Christopher Page* (Woodbridge), pp. 195–219.

———, 2023. 'Rhythm and Reception in the Age of Dante', in Albert Rizzuti and Daniele Sabaino (eds.), *Musica e letteratura al tempo di Dante*, special issue of *Philomusica on-line*, 22, 97–120, http://riviste.paviauniversitypress.it/index.php/phi/article/view/2259.

Falck, Robert, 1972. '*Rondellus*, Canon, and Related Types before 1300', *Journal of the American Musicological Society*, 25:1, 38–57.

———, 1981. *The Notre Dame Conductus: A Study of the Repertory* (Henryville, Ottawa and Binningen).

————, 2001. 'Adam de la Halle', *Grove Music Online*, https://doi.org/10.1093/gmo/9781561592630.article.00163.

Fallows, David, 1998. 'Jean Molinet and the Lost Burgundian Court Chansonniers of the 1470s', in Martin Staehelin (ed.), *Gestalt und Entstehung musikalischer Quellen im 15. und 16. Jahrhundert* (Wiesbaden), pp. 35–42.

————, 1999. *A Catalogue of Polyphonic Songs 1415–1480* (Oxford).

————, 2018. *Henry V and the Earliest English Carols (1413–1440)* (Abingdon).

Fassler, Margot E., 1985. 'The Office of the Cantor in Early Western Monastic Rules and Customaries: A Preliminary Investigation', *Early Music History*, 5, 29–51.

————, 1993. *Gothic Song: Victorine Sequences and Augustinian Reform in Twelfth-Century Paris* (Cambridge).

————, 1998. 'Composer and Dramatist: "Melodious Singing and the Freshness of Remorse"', in Barbara Newman (ed.), *Voice of the Living Light: Hildegard of Bingen and Her World* (Berkeley), pp. 149–75.

————, 2018. 'Music and Prosopography', in Mark Everist and Thomas Forrest Kelly (eds.), *The Cambridge History of Medieval Music*, vol. 1 (Cambridge), pp. 176–209.

Fauchet, Claude, 1581. *Recueil de l'origine de la langue et poesie françoise, ryme et romans. Plus les noms et sommaire des œuvres de CXXVII poetes François, vivans auant l'an M. CCC.* (Paris).

Fawtier, Robert (ed.), 1930. *Comptes du trésor (1296, 1316, 1384, 1477)*, Recueil des historiens de France. Documents financiers 2 (Paris).

Fenzi, Enrico, with Luciano Formisano and Francesco Montuori (eds.), 2012. *Nuova Edizione Commentata delle Opere di Dante*, vol. 3, *De Vulgari Eloquentia* (Rome).

Ferreira, Manuel Pedro, 2008. 'Compositional Calculation in Philippe de Vitry', *Studi Musicali*, 37:1, 13–36.

Fétis, François-Joseph, 1827. 'Découverte de plusieurs manuscrits intéressans pour l'histoire de la musique', *Revue Musicale*, 1, 3–11.

————, 1837. *Biographie universelle des musiciens et bibliographie générale de la musique*, vol. 1 (Bruxelles).

Feuchère, Pierre, 1948. *De l'épée à la plume. Les châtelains d'Arras* (Arras).

Fischer, Kurt von, and F. Alberto Gallo (eds.), 1976. *Italian Sacred Music*, Polyphonic Music of the Fourteenth Century 12 (Monaco).

———— (eds.), 1987. *Italian Sacred and Ceremonial Music*, Polyphonic Music of the Fourteenth Century 13 (Monaco).

Flotzinger, Rudolf, 2007. *Von Leonin zu Perotin: Der musikalische Paradigmenwechsel in Paris um 1210* (Bern).

Foucault, Michel, (1969) 2001. 'Qu'est-ce qu'un auteur?', *Bulletin de la Société française de philosophie*, 63:3, 73–104. Repr. in Daniel Defert and François Ewald (eds.), *Michel Foucault, dits et écrits I (1954–1975)* (Paris), pp. 819–39.

————, 1977, 'What is an Author?' in Donald F. Bouchard (comp. and ed.), *Michel Foucault, Language, Counter-Memory, Practice: Selected Essays and Interviews*, trans. Donald F. Bouchard and Sherry Simon (Ithaca, NY), pp. 113–137.

Frere, Walter Howard, 1934. *Studies in Early Roman Liturgy*, vol. 2, *The Roman Gospel-Lectionary* (London).

Friedlein, Gottfried (ed.), 1867. *Anicii Manlii Torquati Severini Boetii De institutione arithmetica libri duo, De institutione musica libri quinque. Accedit Geometria quae fertur Boetii* (Leipzig).

Führkötter, Adelgundis, and Angela Carlevaris (eds.), 1978. *Hildegardis Bingensis, Scivias*, vol. 1, Pars I–II, Corpus Christianorum. Continuatio Mediaevalis 43 (Turnhout).

Fuller, Sarah, 1985. 'A Phantom Treatise of the Fourteenth Century? The Ars nova', *Journal of Musicology*, 4:1, 23–50.

Gaffurio, Franchino, 1520. *Apologia Franchini Gaffurii musici adversus Ioannem spatarium complices musicos Bononienses* (Turin).

Gallo, F. Alberto (ed.), 1966. *Prosdocimi de Beldemandis, Opera*, vol. 1, *Expositiones tractatus pratice cantus mensurabilis magistri Johannis de Muris* (Bologna).

———, 1974. 'Marchettus in Padua und die "franco-venetische" Musik des frühen Trecento', *Archiv für Musikwissenschaft*, 31:1, 42–56.

Gameson, Richard, 2001. 'Hugo Pictor, enlumineur normand', *Cahiers de civilisation médiévale*, 174, 121–38.

———, 2005. 'A Scribe's Confession and the Making of the Anchin Hrabanus (Douai, Bibliothèque Municipale, ms. 340)', in Brigitte Dekeyzer and Jan Van der Stock (eds.), *Manuscripts in Transition: Recycling Manuscripts, Texts and Images* (Leuven), pp. 65–79.

Gancarczyk, Paweł, 2006. 'Petrus Wilhelmi De Grudencz (b. 1392) – A Central European Composer', *De musica disserenda*, 2:1, 103–12.

Gaposchkin, M. Cecilia, 2008. *The Making of Saint Louis: Kingship, Sanctity, and Crusade in the Later Middle Ages* (Ithaca, NY, and London).

Gardner, Julian, 2015. 'The Cardinals' Music: Musical Interests at the Papal Curia c. 1200–1304', *Early Music History*, 34, 97–132.

Garnier, Jacques, 1850. 'Inventaires du trésor de la cathédrale d'Amiens, publiés d'après les manuscrits', *Mémoires de la Société des Antiquaires de Picardie*, 10, 229–389.

Gasparri, Françoise, 1982. 'Observations paléographiques sur deux manuscrits partiellement autographes de Godefroid de Saint-Victor', *Scriptorium*, 36:1, 43–50.

———, 1985. 'Godefroid de Saint-Victor. Une personnalité peu connue du monde intellectuel et artistique parisien au XIIe siècle', *Scriptorium*, 39:1, 57–69.

Gastoué, Amédée, 1922. *Les Primitifs de la musique française* (Paris).

——— (ed. and arr.), 1939. *Pérotin, 2 Points d'orgue en triple sur un alleluia du VIIe ton* (Paris).

Gennrich, Friedrich, 1949–51. 'Adam de la Halle', in *Die Musik in Geschichte und Gegenwart*, vol. 1 (Kassel), pp. 78–79.

——— (ed.), 1955. *Perotinus Magnus: Das Organum, Alleluja Nativitas gloriose virginis Marie und seine Sippe*, Musikwissenschaftliche Studienbibliothek 12 (Darmstadt).

———, 1957. *Bibliographie der ältesten französischen und lateinischen Motetten* (Darmstadt).

——— (ed.), 1962. *Le jeu de Robin et de Marion. Li rondel Adam*, Musikwissenschaftliche Studien-Bibliothek 20 (Langen bei Frankfurt).

————— (ed.), 1966. *Florilegium motetorum: Ein Querschnitt durch das Mottetenschaffen des 13. Jahrhunderts*, Summa musicae medii aevi 17 (Langen bei Frankfurt).

Gerbert, Martin, 1774. *De cantu et musica sacra a prima ecclesiae aetate usque ad praesens tempus* (2 vols., St Blasien).

—————, 1784. *Scriptores ecclesiastici de musica sacra potissimum* (3 vols., St Blasien).

Gérold, Théodore, 1936. *Histoire de la musique des origines à la fin du XIVe siècle* (Paris).

Glorieux, Palémon, 1972. 'Alain de Lille, le moine et l'abbaye du Bec', *Recherches de théologie ancienne et médiévale*, 39:1, 51–62.

Gneuss, Helmut, 1985. 'Liturgical Books in Anglo-Saxon England and Their Old English Terminology', in Michael Lapidge and Helmut Gneuss (eds.), *Learning and Literature in Anglo-Saxon England: Studies Presented to Peter Clemoes on the Occasion of His Sixty-Fifth Birthday* (Cambridge), pp. 91–141.

Godefroy, Frédéric, 1891–99. *Dictionnaire de l'ancienne langue française et de tous ses dialectes, du IXe au XVe siècle* (10 vols., Paris).

Gómez-Muntané, Maria del Carmen, 1979. *La música en la Casa Real catalano-aragonesa (1336–1442)*, vol. 1, *Historia y Documentos* (Barcelona).

—————, 1985. 'Une version à cinq voix du motet *Apollinis Eclipsatur/Zodiacum Signis* dans le manuscrit E-BCEN 853', *Musica Disciplina*, 39, 5–44.

—————, 1987. 'La musique à la maison royale de Navarre à la fin du Moyen-Âge et le chantre Johan Robert', *Musica Disciplina*, 41, 109–51.

Gorochov, Nathalie, 1997. *Le Collège de Navarre de sa fondation (1305) au début du XVe siècle (1418). Histoire de l'institution, de sa vie intellectuelle et de son recrutement* (Paris).

Grau, Anna Kathryn, 2010. 'Representation and Resistance: Female Vocality in Thirteenth-Century France' (Ph.D. dissertation, University of Pennsylvania).

—————, 2018. 'Thematic Clusters and Compilational Strategies in Montpellier 8', in Catherine A. Bradley and Karen Desmond (eds.), *The Montpellier Codex: The Final Fascicle: Contents, Contexts, Chronologies* (Woodbridge), pp. 121–36.

Grenier-Winther, Joan (ed.), 2010. *Oton de Granson, Poésies*, Les classiques français du Moyen Âge 162 (Paris).

Grier, James, 1995. 'Roger de Chabannes (d. 1025), Cantor of St Martial, Limoges', *Early Music History*, 14, 53–119.

—————, 2003. 'Adémar de Chabannes, Carolingian Musical Practices, and *Nota Romana*', *Journal of the American Musicological Society*, 56:1, 43–98.

Gros, Gérard, 1988. 'Étude sur les rondels des *Miracles de Nostre Dame par personnages*', *Romania*, 109:2–3, 303–53.

Gross, Guillaume, 2007. *Chanter en polyphonie à Notre-Dame de Paris aux 12e et 13e siècles* (Turnhout).

Guesnon, Adolphe (ed.), 1862. *Inventaire chronologique des chartes de la ville d'Arras: documents* (Arras).

—————, 1895. *Recherches biographiques sur les trouvères artésiens* (Paris).

—————, 1902. 'Nouvelles recherches biographiques sur les trouvères artésiens', *Le Moyen Âge*, 15, 137–73.

Guiraud, Jean (ed.), 1904. *Les registres d'Urbain IV (1261–1263). Recueil des bulles de ce pape publiées ou analysées d'après les manuscrits originaux du Vatican*, vol. 3, *Registre ordinaire, tome II* (Paris).

Günther, Ursula, 1966. 'Die "anonymen" Kompositionen des Manuskripts Paris, B.N., fonds it. 568 (Pit)', *Archiv für Musikwissenschaft*, 23:2, 73–92.

Gushee, Lawrence (ed.), 1975. *Aureliani Reomensis, Musica Disciplina*, Corpus scriptorum de musica 21 [Rome].

Haacke, Hrabanus (ed.), 1967. *Ruperti Tuitiensis, Liber de divinis officiis*, Corpus Christianorum. Continuatio Mediaevalis 7 (Turnhout).

Haggh, Barbara H., 1990. 'The Celebration of the "Recollectio Festorum Beatae Mariae Virginis" (1457–1987)', *Studia Musicologica Academiae Scientiarum Hungaricae*, 30:1, 361–73. Repr. in Angelo Pompilio et al. (eds.), *Atti del XIV Congresso della Società Internazionale di Musicologia: Trasmissione e recezione delle forme di cultura musicale* (3 vols., Turin), vol. 3, pp. 559–74.

——— (ed.), 1995. *Two Offices for St Elizabeth of Hungary: Gaudeat Hungaria and Letare Germania*, Musicological Studies 65/1 (Ottawa).

Haines, John, 2004. *Eight Centuries of Troubadours and Trouvères: The Changing Identity of Medieval Music* (Cambridge).

———, 2010a. *Medieval Song in Romance Languages* (Cambridge).

———, 2010b. *Satire in the Songs of* Renart le Nouvel (Geneva).

———, 2019. 'Aristocratic Patronage and the Cosmopolitan Vernacular Songbook: The *Chansonnier du Roi* (*M-trouv.*) and the French Mediterranean', in Jennifer Saltzstein (ed.), *Musical Culture in the World of Adam de la Halle* (Leiden and Boston), pp. 95–120.

Hammond, Frederick F. (ed.), 1970. *Walter Odington, Summa de speculatione musicae*, Corpus scriptorum de musica 14 [Rome].

Handschin, Jacques, 1949–51. 'The Summer Canon and Its Background', *Musica Disciplina*, 3:2–4, 55–94 (part 1); 5, 65–113 (part 2).

Hanly, Michael, 1997. 'Courtiers and Poets: An International Network of Literary Exchange in Late Fourteenth-Century Italy, France, and England', *Viator*, 28, 305–32.

Hanssens, Jean Michel (ed.), 1948–50. *Amalarii episcopi, Opera liturgica omnia* (3 vols.), Studi e testi 138–40 (Vatican City).

Harbinson, Denis (ed.), 1975. *Willehelmi Hirsaugiensis, Musica*, Corpus scriptorum de musica 23 [Rome].

——— (ed.), 1976. *Petrus de Cruce Ambianensi, Tractatus de Tonis*, Corpus scriptorum de musica 29 [Rome].

Harrison, Frank Ll., 1959–60. 'Rota and Rondellus in English Medieval Music', *Proceedings of the Royal Musical Association*, 86, 98–107.

——— (ed.), 1968. *Motets of French Provenance*, Polyphonic Music of the Fourteenth Century 5 (Monaco).

——— (ed.), 1980. *Motets of English Provenance*, Polyphonic Music of the Fourteenth Century 15 (Monaco).

——— (ed.), 1986. '*Musicorum Collegio': Six Fourteenth-Century Musicians' Motets* (Monaco).

Hart, Columba, and Jane Bishop (trans.), 1990. *Hildegard of Bingen, Scivias* (New York).

Haug, Andreas, 2018. 'Tropes', in Mark Everist and Thomas Forrest Kelly (eds.), *The Cambridge History of Medieval Music* (Cambridge), vol. 1, pp. 263–99.

Haug, Hélène, 2013. '*Maistre Pierre de Hurion agille imitateur*. Bilan sur les auteurs actifs à la cour de René d'Anjou (1434–1480)', *Romania*, 131:1–2, 130–51.

Hauréau, Barthélemy, 1890–93. *Notices et extraits de quelques manuscrits latins de la Bibliothèque Nationale* (6 vols., Paris).

Hayez, Michel, and Anne-Marie Hayez (eds.), 1979. *Urbain V (1362–1370). Lettres communes analysées d'après les registres dits d'Avignon et du Vatican*, vol. 5, 1365–1366 (Paris).

Hennig, Ursula, 1992. 'Die lateinische Sequenz "Planctus ante nescia" und die deutschen Marienklagen', in Nikolaus Henkel and Nigel F. Palmer (eds.), *Latein und Volkssprache im deutschen Mittelalter (1100–1500): Regensburger Colloquium 1988* (Tübigen), pp. 164–77.

Henry, Albert (ed.), 1981. *Jehan Bodel, Le Jeu de saint Nicolas*, Textes littéraires français 290 (Geneva).

Higgins, Paula M., 1991. 'Parisian Nobles, a Scottish Princess, and the Woman's Voice in Late Medieval Song', *Early Music History*, 10, 145–200.

———, 1999. 'Celebrating Transgression and Excess: Busnoys and the Boundaries of Late Medieval Musical Culture', in Paula Higgins (ed.), *Antoine Busnoys: Method, Meaning, and Context in Late Medieval Music* (Oxford), pp. 1–20.

Hiley, David, 1993. *Western Plainchant: A Handbook* (Oxford).

———, 2006. '"Cantate Domino canticum novum": Old and New in Medieval Chant and the Status of St Gregory', *Musica e Storia*, 14:1, 127–41.

Hindley, Alan (ed.), 2000. *Pierre Gringore, Le Jeu du Prince des Sotz et de Mere Sotte*, Renaissance française 9 (Paris).

——— (ed.), 2019. '*Le Jeu d'Argent*', in Jonathan Beck, Estelle Doudet, and Alan Hindley (eds.), *Recueil général de moralités d'expression française*, vol. 2 (Paris), pp. 380–487.

Hœpffner, Ernest, 1906. 'Anagramme und Rätselgedichte bei Guillaume de Machaut', *Zeitschrift für romanische Philologie*, 30:4, 401–13.

Hohler, Christopher, 1978. 'Reflections on Some Manuscripts Containing 13th-Century Polyphony', *Journal of the Plainsong and Mediaeval Music Society*, 1, 2–38.

Holford-Strevens, Leofranc, 1997. 'Du Fay the Poet? Problems in the Texts of His Motets', *Early Music History*, 16, 97–165.

———, 2015. 'The Latin Poetry of Johannes Ciconia and "Guilhermus"', in Anna Zayaruznaya, Bonnie J. Blackburn, and Stanley Boorman (eds.), *'Qui musicam in se habet': Studies in Honor of Alejandro Enrique Planchart* (Middleton, WI), pp. 437–69.

Honorius of Autun. *Gemma animae*, PL 172. 541–738.

Hoppin, Richard H., 1957. 'The Cypriot-French Repertory of the Manuscript Torino, Biblioteca Nazionale, J. II. 9', *Musica Disciplina*, 11, 79–125.

Hübsch, Hanns (ed.), 1953. *Guillaume de Machault. La Messe de Nostre Dame* (Heidelberg).

Hucbald. *De harmonica institutione*, PL 132. 905–29.

Hucke, Helmut, 1955. 'Die Entstehung der Überlieferung von einer musikalischen Tätigkeit Gregors des Großen', *Die Musikforschung*, 8:2–3, 259–64.

Hudry, Françoise (ed.), 2003. *Alain de Lille (?), Lettres familières (1167–1170)*, Études et Rencontres de l'École des Chartes 14 (Paris).

Hudson, John (ed. and trans.), 2002–7. *Historia ecclesie Abbendonensis/The History of the Church of Abingdon* (2 vols., Oxford).

Huglo, Michel, 2001. 'Guy de Saint-Denis', *Grove Music Online*, https://doi.org/10.1093/gmo/9781561592630.article.12067.

Husmann, Heinrich (ed.), 1940. *Die drei- und vierstimmigen Notre-Dame-Organa: Kritische Gesamtausgabe mit Einleitung*, Publikationen älterer Musik 11 (Leipzig).

———— (ed.), 1955. *Die mittelalterliche Mehrstimmigkeit: Eine Beispielsammlung zur Musikgeschichte*, Das Musikwerke 8 (Köln).

Huot, Sylvia, 1985. 'Poetic Ambiguity and Reader Response in Boccaccio's *Amorosa Visione*', *Modern Philology*, 83:2, 109–22.

————, 1987. *From Song to Book: The Poetics of Writing in Old French Lyric and Lyrical Narrative Poetry* (Ithaca, NY, and London).

Ibos-Augé, Anne, 2018a. 'Adam de la Halle et les "jeux". Les premiers exemples de théâtre profane chanté à Arras à la fin du XIIIe siècle', in Marie-Françoise Alamichel (ed.), *Les villes au Moyen Âge en Europe occidentale (ou comment demain peut apprendre d'hier)* [Champs-sur-Marne], pp. 229–63.

————, 2018b. '… *Que ne dit "cief bien seans"*: Quoting Motets in Montpellier 8', in Catherine A. Bradley and Karen Desmond (eds.), *The Montpellier Codex: The Final Fascicle: Contents, Contexts, Chronologies* (Woodbridge), pp. 211–30.

————, 2019. 'Refrain Quotations in Adam's *Rondeaux*, Motets and Plays', in Jennifer Saltzstein (ed.), *Musical Culture in the World of Adam de la Halle* (Leiden and Boston), pp. 249–81.

Ingrand-Varenne, Estelle, Elisa Pallotini, and Janneke Raaijmakers (eds.), 2023. *Writing Names in Medieval Sacred Spaces: Inscriptions in the West, from Late Antiquity to the Early Middle Ages* (Turnhout).

Iogna-Prat, Dominique, 2005. 'Introduction générale: La question de l'individu à l'épreuve du Moyen Âge', in Brigitte Miriam Bedos-Rezak and Dominique Iogna-Prat (eds.), *L'individu au Moyen Âge* (Paris), pp. 7–29.

Isidore of Seville. *De musica*, PL 82. 163–69.

Iversen, Gunilla, 2009. 'From *Jubilus* to Learned Exegesis: New Liturgical Poetry in Twelfth-Century Nevers', in Gunilla Iversen and Nicolas Bell (eds.), *Sapientia et Eloquentia: Meaning and Function in Liturgical Poetry, Music, Drama, and Biblical Commentary in the Middle Ages* (Turnhout), pp. 203–58.

Jacob, Walter (ed.), 1952. *Cassiodori-Epiphanii Historia ecclesiastica tripartita*, Corpus Scriptorum Ecclesiasticorum Latinorum 71 (Vienna).

James, M. R. (ed.), 1933. *The Romance of Alexander: A Collotype Facsimile of MS. Bodley 264* (Oxford).

Janse, Antheunis, 1986. 'Het muziekleven aan het hof van Albrecht van Beieren (1358–1404) in Den Haag', *Tijdschrift van de Vereniging voor Nederlandse Muziekgeschiedenis*, 36, 136–57.

Jeffery, Peter, 1984. 'The Introduction of Psalmody into the Roman Mass by Pope Celestine I (422–432): Reinterpreting a Passage in the "Liber Pontificalis"', *Archiv für Liturgiewissenschaft*, 26, 147–65.

Jennings, Lauren McGuire, 2014. *Senza Vestimenta: The Literary Tradition of Trecento Song* (Farnham).

John the Deacon. *Vita sancti Gregorii*, PL 75. 59–242.

Johnson, Glenn Pierr, 1991. 'Aspects of Late Medieval Music at the Cathedral of Amiens' (2 vols., Ph.D. dissertation, Yale University).

Juncosa Bonet, Eduard, 2021. 'En busca de princesa. La diplomacia matrimonial (official y "rebelde") en la Corona de Aragón a fines del trescientos', in José Manuel Nieto Soria and Óscar Villarroel González (eds.), *Diplomacia y cultura política en la península ibérica (siglos XI al XV)* (Madrid), pp. 109–28.

Kájoni, János, (1676) 1719. *Cantionale Catholicum* (Csíksomlyó).

Kearney, Eileen F., 2014. 'Peter Abelard's *Planctus* "*Dolorum solatium*": A New Song for David', in Babette S. Hellemans (ed.), *Rethinking Abelard: A Collection of Critical Essays* (Leiden), pp. 253–81.

Kehrein, Joseph (ed.), 1873. *Lateinische Sequenzen des Mittelalters aus Handschriften und Drucken* (Mainz).

Kelly, Thomas Forrest, 2006. 'Medieval Composers of Liturgical Chant', *Musica e Storia*, 14:1, 95–125.

Kessler, Herbert L., 2019. *Experiencing Medieval Art* (Toronto).

Khan-ad-Din, Felinah M. H., 2003. 'Old Age, Height and Nutrition: Common Misconceptions about Medieval England', http://sirguillaume.com/wp-content/uploads/2012/01/Old_Age-Height-Nutrition.pdf.

Kinsela, David, 1998. 'The Capture of the Chekker', *The Galpin Society Journal*, 51, 64–85.

Kirkham, Victoria, 2001. *Fabulous Vernacular: Boccaccio's* Filocolo *and the Art of Medieval Fiction* (Ann Arbor).

Klaes, Monika (ed.), 1993. *Vita sanctae Hildegardis*, Corpus Christianorum. Continuatio Mediaevalis 126 (Turnhout).

Klinck, Anne L., 2003. 'Poetic Markers of Gender in Medieval "Woman's Song": Was Anonymous a Woman?' *Neophilologus*, 87:3, 339–59.

Klundert, Sieglinde van de (ed.), 1998. *Guido von Saint-Denis, Tractatus de tonis: Edition und Studien* (2 vols., Bubenreuth).

Knight, Alan (ed.), 2001–11. *Les Mystères de la procession de Lille* (5 vols.), Textes littéraires français 535, 554, 569, 588, 607 (Geneva).

Knox, Ronald (trans.), 1954. *The Holy Bible: A Translation from the Latin Vulgate in the Light of the Hebrew and Greek Originals* (New York).

Kügle, Karl, 1997. *The Manuscript Ivrea, Biblioteca Capitolare 115: Studies in the Transmission and Composition of Ars Nova Polyphony* (Ottawa).

———, 2008. 'Two Abbots and a Rotulus: New Light on Brussels 19606', in David B. Cannata, Gabriela I. Currie, Rena C. Mueller, and John L. Nádas (eds.), *Quomodo cantabimus canticum? Studies in Honor of Edward H. Roesner* (Middleton, WI), pp. 145–85.

———, 2012. 'Glorious Sounds for a Holy Warrior: New Light on Codex Turin J.II.9', *Journal to the American Musicological Society*, 65:3, 637–90.

Langlois, Ernest (ed.), 1902. *Recueil d'arts de seconde rhétorique* (Paris).

——— (ed.), (1924) 1958. *Adam le Bossu, trouvère artésien du XIIIe siècle. Le Jeu de Robin et Marion suivi du Jeu du Pèlerin*, Les classiques français du Moyen Âge 36 ([Paris]; repr. Paris).

Latour, Bruno, 2005. *Reassembling the Social: An Introduction to Actor-Network Theory* (Oxford and New York).

Laurens, Pierre (ed.), Alain-Philippe Segonds, Franck La Brasca, and André Longpré (trans.), 2003. *Pétrarque, Lettres familières*, vol. 3 (Paris).

Laurie, Ian S., 1998. 'Biography', in Deborah M. Sinnreich-Levi (ed.), *Eustache Deschamps, French Courtier-Poet: His Work and His World* (New York), pp. 1–72.

Laurie, Ian S., and Deborah M. Sinnreich-Levi (eds.), David Curzon and Jeffrey Fiskin (trans.), 2003. *Eustache Deschamps: Selected Poems* (New York and London).

Leach, Elizabeth Eva, 2011. *Guillaume de Machaut: Secretary, Poet, Musician* (Ithaca, NY).

———, 2019. 'Do Trouvère Melodies Mean Anything?' *Music Analysis*, 38:1–2, 3–46.

Leach, Elizabeth Eva, Joseph W. Mason, and Matthew P. Thomson (eds.), 2022. *A Medieval Songbook: Trouvère MS C* (Woodbridge).

Lebedev, Sergej (ed.), 2000. *Cuiusdam Cartusiensis monachi, Tractatus de musica plana*, Musica mediaevalis Europae Occidentalis 3 (Tutzing).

Leclercq, Jean (ed.), 1953. 'Les lettres familières d'un moine du Bec', *Analecta monastica*, 2nd ser., Studia Anselmiana 31, pp. 141–73 (Rome).

Lecoy, Félix (ed.), 1979. *Jean Renart, Le roman de la Rose ou de Guillaume de Dole*, Les classiques français du Moyen Âge 91 (Paris).

Leech-Wilkinson, Daniel, 1982–83. 'Related Motets from Fourteenth-Century France', *Proceedings of the Royal Musical Association*, 109, 1–22.

———, 1984. 'Machaut's *Rose, Lis* and the Problem of Early Music Analysis', *Music Analysis*, 3:1, 9–28.

———, 1995. 'The Emergence of *Ars nova*', *The Journal of Musicology*, 13:3, 285–317.

Lefferts, Peter M., 1986. *The Motet in England in the Fourteenth Century* (Ann Arbor).

——— (ed. and trans.), 1991. *Robertus de Handlo, 'The Rules', and Johannes Hanboys, 'The Summa'*, Greek and Latin Music Theory 7 (Lincoln, NE).

———, 1998. '*Subtilitas* in the Tonal Language of *Fumeux Fume*', *Early Music*, 16:2, 176–83.

Lehmann, Hans-Thies, 2006. *Postdramatic Theatre*, trans. Karen Jürs-Munby (London and New York).

Leitmeir, Christian Thomas, 2005. 'Types and Transmissions of Musical Examples in Franco's *Ars cantus mensurabilis musicae*', in Suzannah Clark and Elizabeth Eva Leach (eds.), *Citation and Authority in Medieval and Renaissance Musical Culture: Learning from the Learned* (Woodbridge), pp. 29–44.

Lelong, Chloé, 2011. *L'œuvre de Nicolas de Vérone. Intertextualité et création dans la littérature épique franco-italienne du XIVe siècle* (Paris).

Lemaître, Henri (ed.), 1906. *Chronique et Annales de Gilles Le Muisit, abbé de Saint-Martin de Tournai (1272–1352)* (Paris).

Leo, Domenic, 2013. *Images, Texts and Marginalia in a 'Vows of the Peacock' Manuscript (New York, Pierpont Morgan Library MS G24)* (Leiden and Boston).

LeRoux, Mary Protase, 1965. 'The "De Harmonica Institutione" and "Tonarius" of Regino of Prüm' (Ph.D. dissertation, Catholic University of America).

Lestocquoy, Jean, 1954. 'Deux familles de financiers d'Arras. Louchard et Wagon', *Revue belge de philologie et d'histoire*, 32:1, 51–76.

Lettenhove, Kervyn de (ed.), 1875. *Œuvres de Froissart. Chroniques*, vol. 20, *Table analytique des noms historiques* (Brussels).

Levy, Emil, cont. Carl Appel, 1924. *Provenzalisches Supplement-Wörterbuch: Berichtigungen und Ergänzungen zu Raynouards Lexique Roman*, vol. 8 (Leipzig).

Levy, John F., 2013. 'Acrostics as Copyright Protection in the Franco-Italian Epic: Implications for Memory Theory', in Elma Brenner, Meredith Cohen, and Mary Franklin-Brown (eds.), *Memory and Commemoration in Medieval Culture* (Farnham), pp. 195–220.

Lipton, Sara, 2005. '"The Sweet Lean of His Head": Writing about Looking at the Crucifix in the High Middle Ages', *Speculum*, 80:4, 1172–1208.

Loisne, Auguste de (ed.), 1896. *Le cartulaire du chapitre d'Arras* (Arras).

———, 1899. 'Anciennes chartes inédites en langue vulgaire reposant en original aux Archives du Pas-de-Calais (1221–1258)', in *Bulletin historique et philologique*, pp. 65–78.

——— (ed.), 1907. *Le cartulaire des chapellenies d'Arras. Manuscrit de 1282, avec additions des XIVe et XVe siècles* (Arras).

Losseff, Nicky, 1994. *The Best Concords: Polyphonic Music in Thirteenth-Century Britain* (New York and London).

———, 2004. 'Wycombe, W. of (fl. c. 1275), Music Copyist and Benedictine Monk', *Oxford Dictionary of National Biography*, https://doi-org.may.idm.oclc.org/10.1093/ref:odnb/60119.

Louviot, Manon, 2021. 'Uncovering the Douai Fragment: Composing Polyphony and Encoding a Composer in the Late Fourteenth Century', *Early Music History*, 40, 85–166.

Ludwig, Friedrich, (1910) 1978. *Repertorium organorum recentioris et motetorum vetustissimi stili*. Vol. 1: *Catalogue raisonné der Quellen* (Part 1: *Handschriften in Quadrat-Notation* (Halle), 1910. 2nd ed. Luther Dittmer (Hildesheim and New York), 1964. Part 2: *Handschriften in Mensural-Notation*, Friedrich Gennrich (ed.) (Frankfurt), 1961. Rev. ed. Luther Dittmer (Assen), 1978). Vol. 2: *Musikalisches Anfangs-Verzeichnis des nach Tenores geordneten Repertorium*, Friedrich Gennrich (ed.) (Frankfurt), 1962. Repr., Luther Dittmer (ed.) (Hildesheim and New York), 1972.

——— (ed.), 1926–29. *Guillaume de Machaut: Musikalische Werke*, vols. 1–3 (Leipzig).

Luykx, Theo, 1961. *De grafelijke financiële bestuursinstellingen en het grafelijk patrimonium in Vlaanderen tijdens de regering van Margareta van Constantinopel (1244–1278)* (Brussels).

Machabey, Armand (ed.), 1948. *Messe Notre Dame à quatre voix de Guillaume de Machault* (Paris).

———, 1955. *Guillaume de Machault (130?–1377). La vie et l'œuvre musical* (2 vols., Paris).

Madan, Falconer, 1924. 'The Literary Work of a Benedictine Monk at Leominster in the Thirteenth Century', *Bodleian Quarterly Record*, 4, 168–70.

Maddox, Donald, and Sara Sturm-Maddox (eds.), 2008. *Parisian Confraternity Drama of the Fourteenth Century. The Miracles de Nostre Dame par personnages* (Turnhout).

Maillard, François (ed.), 1961. *Comptes royaux (1314–1328)* (2 vols.), Recueil des historiens de France. Documents financiers 4 (Paris).

Manitius, Max, 1931. *Geschichte der lateinischen Literatur des Mittelalters*, vol. 3 (Munich).

Mann, Nicholas, 1987. 'In margine alla quarta egloga: piccoli problemi di esegesi petrarchesca', *Studi Petrarcheschi*, NS, 4, 17–32.

Marbach, Karl, 1907. *Carmina scripturarum scilicet Antiphonas et Responsoria* (Strasbourg).

Marchi, Lucia, 2019. 'Traces of Performance in Early Fifteenth-Century Musical Attributions', *Philomusica On-line*, 18:1, 1–22, http://riviste.paviauniversitypress. it/index.php/phi/article/view/2015.

Marcusson, Olof (ed.), 1976. *Prosules de la messe*, vol. 1, *Tropes de l'alleluia*, Corpus troporum 2 (Stockholm).

———, 1979. 'Comment a-t-on chanté les prosules? Observations sur la technique des tropes de l'*alleluia*', *Revue de musicologie*, 65:2, 119–59.

Mariaux, Pierre Alain, 2015. 'Women in the Making: Early Medieval Signatures and Artists' Portraits (9th–12th c.)', in Therese Martin (ed.), *Reassessing the Roles of Women as 'Makers' of Medieval Art and Architecture* (Leiden), pp. 393–427.

Martin, Henri, 1909. 'Un caricaturiste du temps du roi Jean: Pierart dou Thielt', *Gazette des Beaux-Arts*, 2nd ser., 51, 89–102.

Maschke, Eva, 2020. 'On Westphalian Woodworms and Rhenish Missionaries: The Soest Conductus Fragments and Their Afterlife', *Music & Letters*, 101:2, 189–237.

Mason, Joseph W., 2019. 'Structure and Process in the Old French *Jeu-parti*', *Music Analysis*, 38:1–2, 47–79.

———, 2021. '*Trouver et partir*: The Meaning of Structure in the Old French *Jeu-parti*', *Early Music History*, 40, 207–51.

———, 2022. 'Oral and Written Transmission in the Early *Jeu-parti*', *Music & Letters*, 103:3, 399–429.

Matheis, Eric, 2013. 'Capital, Value, and Exchange in the Old Occitan and Old French *Tenson* (Including the *Partimen* and the *Jeu-parti*)' (Ph.D. dissertation, Columbia University).

Maw, David, 2018. '*Je le temoin en mon chant*: The Art of Diminution in the Petronian Triplum', in Catherine A. Bradley and Karen Desmond (eds.), *The Montpellier Codex: The Final Fascicle: Contents, Contexts, Chronologies* (Woodbridge), pp. 161–83.

McCarthy, T. J. H. (ed.), 2015. *Aribo, De musica and Sententiae* (Kalamazoo).

McGrade, Michael, 1996. 'Gottschalk of Aachen, the Investiture Controversy, and Music for the Feast of the *Divisio apostolorum*', *Journal of the American Musicological Society*, 49:3, 351–408.

McGrady, Deborah, and Jennifer Bain (eds.), 2012. *A Companion to Guillaume de Machaut* (Leiden and Boston).

McGurk, Patrick (ed. and trans.), 1998. *The Chronicle of John of Worcester*, vol. 3, *The Annals from 1067 to 1140 with the Gloucester Interpolations and the Continuation to 1141* (Oxford).

McKinnon, James, 2000. *The Advent Project: The Later Seventh-Century Creation of the Roman Mass Proper* (Berkeley and London).

——, 2001. 'Gregorius presul composuit hunc libellum musicae artis', in Thomas F. Heffernan and E. Ann Matter (eds.), *The Liturgy of the Medieval Church* (Kalamazoo), pp. 673–93.

McLaughlin, Mary Martin, and Bonnie Wheeler (eds. and trans.), 2009. *The Letters of Heloise and Abelard: A Translation of their Collected Correspondence and Related Writings* (New York).

Meconi, Honey, 2018. *Hildegard of Bingen* (Urbana).

Meech, Sanford B., 1935. 'Three Musical Treatises in English from a Fifteenth-Century Manuscript', *Speculum*, 10:3, 235–69.

Mehler, Ulrich, 1997. *Marienklagen in spätmittelalterlichen und frühneuzeitlichen Deutschland: Textversikel und Melodietypen*, vol. 2, *Materialteil* (Amsterdam).

Meindl, Robert J., 2017. 'The Latin Works', in Ana Sáez-Hidalgo, Brian Gastle, and R. F. Yeager (eds.), *The Routledge Research Companion to John Gower* (Oxford and New York), pp. 341–54.

Meiss, Millard, 1974. *French Painting in the Time of Jean de Berry*, part 3, *The Limbourgs and Their Contemporaries* (2 vols., London and New York).

Menegaldo, Silvère, 2010. 'Les jongleurs et le théâtre en France au XIIIe siècle. Leurs activités et leurs répertoires', *Romania*, 128:1–2, 46–91.

——, 2015. *Le Dernier Ménestrel? Jean de Le Mote, une poétique en transition (autour de 1340)* (Geneva).

Meneghetti, Maria Luisa, 1984. *Il pubblico dei trovatori: Ricezione e riuso dei testi lirici cortesi fino al XIV secolo* (Modena).

Mercer, Frank (ed.), 1957. *Charles Burney, a General History of Music: From the Earliest Ages to the Present Period (1789)* (2 vols., New York).

Mews, Constant J., 2011. 'Gregory the Great, the Rule of Benedict and Roman Liturgy: The Evolution of a Legend', *Journal of Medieval History*, 37:2, 125–44.

Mews, Constant J., John N. Crossley, Catherine Jeffreys, Leigh McKinnon, and Carol J. Williams (eds. and trans.), 2011. *Johannes de Grocheio, Ars musice* (Kalamazoo).

Mews, Constant J., Carol J. Williams, John N. Crossley, and Catherine Jeffreys (eds. and trans.), 2017. *Guy of Saint-Denis, Tractatus de tonis* (Kalamazoo).

Meyer, Christian (ed.), 1998. *Musica plana Johannis de Garlandia*, Collection d'études musicologiques 91 (Baden-Baden and Bouxviller).

—— (ed. and trans.), 2000. *Jean de Murs, Écrits sur la musique* [Paris].

——, 2016. 'Versus de musica. Les versifications du Corpus hollandrinien', in Michael Bernhard and Elżbieta Witkowska-Zaremba (eds.), *Traditio Iohannis Hollandrini*, vol. 7 (Munich), pp. 71–141.

Meyer, Christian (ed.), and Karen Desmond (trans.), 2015. *The 'Ars musica' Attributed to Magister Lambertus/Aristoteles* (Farnham and Burlington).

Meyer, Paul, and Gaston Raynaud (eds.), 1892. *Le chansonnier français de Saint-Germain-des-Prés (Bibl. Nat. Fr. 20050)* (2 vols. [vol. 2 never appeared], Paris).

Michaud-Quantin, Pierre (ed.), 1956. *Godefroy de Saint-Victor, Fons Philosophiae*, Analecta mediaevalia Namurcensia 8 (Namur).

Michels, Ulrich (ed.), 1970. *Die Musiktraktate des Johannes de Muris. Quellenkritik und Besprechungen*, Beihefte zum Archiv für Musikwissenschaft 8 (Wiesbaden).

Michon, Solange, 1987. 'Un moine enlumineur du XIIe siècle: Frère Rufillus de Weissenau', *Zeitschrift für schweizerische Archäologie und Kunstgeschichte*, 44:1, 1–8.

Migot, Georges, 1979. *2d Livre d'orgue. 24 pièces non mesurées sur les touches blanches, en hommage à Léonin et Pérotin* (Strasbourg and Paris).

Millar, Eric G., 1959. *The Parisian Miniaturist Honoré* (London).

Mills, Léonard R. (ed.), 1965. *Le Mystère de saint Sébastien*, Textes littéraires français 114 (Geneva).

Minnis, Alastair, 1988. *Medieval Theory of Authorship: Scholastic Literary Attitudes in the Later Middle Ages*, 2nd ed. (London).

Mirot, Léon, 1930. 'Communication sur l'histoire de l'ancien hôtel de Navarre, rue Braque n° 2 et rue des Archives n° 49', *Procès-verbaux de la Commission municipale du Vieux-Paris* (année 1925), 51–54.

Misset, Eugène, and Pierre Aubry (eds.), 1900. *Les Proses d'Adam de Saint-Victor. Texte et musique* (Paris).

Mone, Franz Joseph, 1852. *Schauspiele des Mittelalters*, vol. 2, 2nd ed. (Mannheim).

Monks of Solesmes (eds.), 1889. *Le Codex 339 de la Bibliothèque de Saint-Gall*, Paléographie musicale 1 (Solesmes).

——— (eds.), 1961. *The Liber Usualis with Introduction and Rubrics in English* (New York).

Muckle, Joseph T., 1953. 'The Personal Letters between Abelard and Heloise: Introduction, Authenticity, and Text', *Mediaeval Studies*, 15, 47–94.

Nádas, John, 1998. 'A Cautious Reading of Simone Prodenzani's "Il Saporetto"', *Recercare*, 10, 23–38.

———, 2004. 'Secular Courts during the Period of the Great Schism: Documentation in the Archivio Segreto Vaticano', in Bianca Maria Antolini, Teresa M. Gialdroni, and Annunziato Pugliese (eds.), *'Et facciam dolçi canti': Studi in onore di Agostino Ziino in occasione del suo 65° compleanno* (Lucca), pp. 184–206.

Narbona Cárceles, María, 2009. 'Las residencias de Carlos III el Noble en París a comienzos del siglo XV: el *Hôtel de Clisson* y el *Hôtel de Navarre*', in Georges Martin and Françoise Lainé (eds.), *L'itinérance des cours (fin XIIe siècle–milieu du XVe siècle). Un modèle ibérique?* special issue of *e-Spania*, 8, http://e-spania.revues.org/18699.

Nicholson, Peter, 2017. 'The French Works: The Ballades', in Ana Sáez-Hidalgo, Brian Gastle, and R. F. Yeager (eds.), *The Routledge Research Companion to John Gower* (Oxford and New York), pp. 312–20.

Nordenfalk, Carl, 1964. 'Maître Honoré and Maître Pucelle', *Apollo*, 79, 356–64.

Obst, Wolfgang, 1983. '*Sumer is icumen in* – A Contrafactum?' *Music & Letters*, 64:3–4, 151–61.

Ó Cuív, Brian, 1992. 'St. Gregory and St. Dunstan in a Middle-Irish Poem on the Origins of Liturgical Chant', in Nigel Ramsay, Margaret Sparks, and Tim W. T.

Tatton-Brown (eds.), *St Dunstan: His Life, Times and Cult* (Woodbridge), pp. 273–97.

Odelman, Eva (ed.), 1986. *Prosules de la messe*, vol. 2, *Les prosules limousines de Wolfenbüttel. Édition critique des prosules d'alleluia du manuscrit Wolfenbüttel, Herzog August Bibliothek Cod. Guelf. 79 Gud. lat.*, Corpus troporum 6 (Stockholm).

O'Neill, Mary. 2006. *Courtly Love Songs of Medieval France: Transmission and Style in the Trouvère Repertoire* (Oxford).

Oudin, Casimir, 1722. *Commentarius de scriptoribus ecclesiæ antiquis*, vol. 2 (Leipzig).

Page, Christopher, 1976. 'A Catalogue and Bibliography of English Song from Its Beginnings to c. 1300', *Royal Musical Association Research Chronicle*, 13, 67–83.

————, 1989. *The Owl and the Nightingale: Musical Life and Ideas in France 1100–1300* (London).

————, 1998. 'Tradition and Innovation in BN fr. 146: The Background to the Ballades', in Margaret Bent and Andrew Wathey (eds.), *Fauvel Studies: Allegory, Chronicle, Music, and Image in Paris, Bibliothèque nationale de France, MS français 146* (Oxford), pp. 353–94.

————, 2010. *The Christian West and Its Singers: The First Thousand Years* (New Haven).

Palazzo, Éric, 2016. *Peindre c'est prier. Anthropologie de la prière chrétienne* (Paris).

Palmer, Barton R. (ed. and trans.), with Uri Smilansky (music ed.) and Domenic Leo (art history com.), 2019. *Guillaume de Machaut: The Complete Poetry and Music*, vol. 2, *The Boethian Poems* (Kalamazoo).

Palmquist, Mary, with John Kulas (eds.), James McGrath, and Adelgundis Führkötter (trans.), 1995. *The Life of the Holy Hildegard by the Monks Gottfried and Theoderic* (Collegeville).

Panayotova, Stella (ed.), 2016. *Colour: The Art & Science of Illuminated Manuscripts* [exhibition catalogue] (London).

Panayotova, Stella, and Paola Ricciardi (eds.), 2017–18. *Art & Science* (2 vols., Turnhout).

Paris, Gaston, and Ulysse Robert (eds.), 1876–93. *Miracles de Nostre Dame par personnages* (8 vols., Paris).

Parkes, Henry, 2017. 'Wild Strawberries from Reichenau: Ruminations on Authority and Difference in Eleventh-Century "Gregorian" Chant', *Journal of the American Musicological Society*, 70:1, 1–60.

———— (ed.), 2019. *Berno Augiensis, Tractatus liturgici*, Corpus Christianorum. Continuatio Mediaevalis 297 (Turnhout).

Paulinus of Milan. *Vita sancti Ambrosii*, PL 14. 27–46.

Payne, Thomas B., 1986. '*Associa tecum in patria*: A Newly Identified Organum Trope by Philip the Chancellor', *Journal of the American Musicological Society*, 39:2, 233–54.

————, 1991. 'Poetry, Politics, and Polyphony: Philip the Chancellor's Contribution to the Music of the Notre Dame School' (2 vols., Ph.D. dissertation, University of Chicago).

————, 2001. 'Datable "Notre Dame" Conductus: New Historical Observations on Style and Technique', *Current Musicology*, 64, 104–51.

————— (ed.), 2011. *Philip the Chancellor, Motets and Prosulas*, Recent Researches in the Music of the Middle Ages and Early Renaissance 41 (Middleton, WI).

—————, 2017. 'Chancellor *versus* Bishop: The Conflict between Philip the Chancellor and Guillaume d'Auvergne in Poetry and Music', in Gilbert Dahan and Anne-Zoé Rillon-Marne (eds.), *Philippe le Chancelier. Prédicateur, théologien et poète parisien du début du XIIIe siècle* (Turnhout), pp. 265–306.

Pérez-Simon, Maud, and Alison Stones (eds.), 2019. *D. J. A. Ross, Illustrated Medieval Alexander-Books in French Verse* (Turnhout).

Perkins, Leeman L., 1999. 'Conflicting Attributions and Anonymous Chansons in the "Busnoys" Sources of the Fifteenth Century', in Paula Higgins (ed.), *Antoine Busnoys: Method, Meaning, and Context in Late Medieval Music* (Oxford), pp. 317–58.

Pesce, Dolores (ed. and trans.), 1999. *Guido d'Arezzo's Regule rithmice, Prologus in antiphonarium, and Epistola ad Michahelem, Musicological Studies 73* (Ottawa).

Peter Abelard. *Sermones*, PL 178. 379–610.

Philippot, Michel P. (ed. and arr.), 1983. *Alléluia Nativitas pour la fête de la Nativité de la Vierge* [Givors].

Philips, Jenna, 2019. 'Singers without Borders: A Performer's *Rotulus* and the Transmission of *Jeux-partis*', *Journal of Medieval History*, 45:1, 55–79.

Piekut, Benjamin, 2014. 'Actor-Networks in Music History: Clarifications and Critiques', *Twentieth-Century Music*, 11:2, 191–215.

Pieragostini, Renata, 2013. 'Augustinian Networks and the Chicago Music Theory Manuscript', *Plainsong and Medieval Music*, 22:1, 65–85.

Planchart, Alejandro E. (ed.), 1994. *Beneventanum Troporum Corpus I: Tropes of the Proper of the Mass, A.D. 1000–1250* (2 vols.), Middle Ages and Early Renaissance M016–18 (Madison).

—————, 2018. *Guillaume Du Fay: The Life and Works* (Cambridge).

Plumley, Yolanda, 1999. 'Citation and Allusion in the Late *Ars nova*: The Case of *Esperance* and the *En attendant* Songs', *Early Music History*, 18, 287–363.

—————, 2002. 'Musicians at Laon Cathedral in the Early Fifteenth Century', *Urban History*, 29:1, 19–34.

—————, 2003a. 'An "Episode in the South"? *Ars subtilior* and the Patronage of French Princes', *Early Music History*, 22, 103–68.

—————, 2003b. 'Intertextuality in the Fourteenth-Century Chanson', *Music & Letters*, 84:3, 355–77.

—————, 2013. *The Art of Grafted Song: Citation and Allusion in the Age of Machaut* (New York and Oxford).

—————, 2019. 'Virtuoso Musicians, Itinerancy, and the Market for Modern French Music, ca. 1400', paper presented at the MALMECC project conference, University of Oxford.

—————, 2024. 'Music, Heraldry and Material Culture in the Late Middle Ages: Ars Nova Songs for Louis I of Anjou and Bertrand du Guesclin', in Vincenzo Borghetti and Alèxandros Maria Hatzikiriakos (eds.), *The Media of Secular Music in the Medieval and Early Modern Period (1100–1650)* (New York and Milton Park).

Plumley, Yolanda, Giuliano Di Bacco, and Stefano Jossa (eds.), 2011. *Citation, Intertextuality, and Memory in the Middle Ages and Renaissance*, vol. 1, *Image, Music and Text, from Machaut to Ariosto* (Exeter).

Plumley, Yolanda, and Anne Stone (eds.), 2008. *Codex Chantilly, Bibliothèque du Château de Chantilly, Ms. 564: Introduction, Fac-simile* (2 vols., Turnhout).

Plumley, Yolanda, and Anne Stone, 2023. 'Machaut on the Loose in Italy: Two Case Studies', in Jared C. Hartt, Tamsyn Mahoney-Steel, and Benjamin L. Albritton (eds.), *Manuscripts, Music, Machaut: Essays in Honor of Lawrence Earp* (Turnhout), pp. 335–68.

Pocard, Pierre, 2018. '"Pour leur peine et salaire d'avoir joué ensemble de leurs instruments". Organisation et reconnaissance du métier de musicien instrumentiste dans la société urbaine de la fin du Moyen Âge (XIVe–XVIe siècle)' (2 vols., Thèse de doctorat, École nationale des Chartes, Paris).

Poe, Elizabeth W., 1995. 'The *Vidas* and *Razos*' in F. R. P. Akehurst and Judith M. Davis (eds.), *A Handbook of the Troubadours* (Berkeley), pp. 185–98.

Polk, Keith, 2016. 'Tradition and Innovation in Fourteenth-Century Instrumental Music: Evidence from Archival and Musical Sources', in Benjamin Brand and David J. Rothenberg (eds.), *Music and Culture in the Middle Ages and Beyond: Liturgy, Sources, Symbolism* (Cambridge), pp. 158–74.

Powell, Morgan, 2020. *Gender, Reading, and Truth in the Twelfth Century: The Woman in the Mirror* (Leeds).

Prost, Bernard, and Henri Prost (eds.), 1902–4. *Inventaires mobiliers et extraits des comptes des ducs de Bourgogne de la maison de Valois (1363–1477)*, vol. 1, *Philippe le Hardi (1363–1377)* (Paris).

Proust-Perrault, Josette, 2009. 'Une résidence princière parisienne: l'hôtel d'Anjou (XIVe–XIVe siècles)', *Bulletin de la Société de l'histoire de Paris et de l'Île-de-France*, 134–135 (années 2007 et 2008), 47–69.

Queux de Saint-Hilaire, Antoine, and Gaston Raynaud (eds.), 1878–1903. *Œuvres complètes d'Eustache Deschamps* (11 vols., Paris).

Quicherat, Jules (ed.), 1856. *Les vers de maître Henri Baude, poète du XVe siècle* (Paris).

Ragnard, Isabelle, 2019. 'The Songs of Adam de la Halle', in Jennifer Saltzstein (ed.), *Musical Culture in the World of Adam de la Halle* (Leiden and Boston), pp. 189–228.

Raynouard, François-Juste-Marie, 1844. *Lexique roman ou dictionnaire de la langue des troubadours comparée avec les autres langues de l'Europe latine*, vol. 5 (Paris).

Reaney, Gilbert (ed.), 1982. *Anonymus,* De valere notularum tam veteris quam novae artis *(Ms. Paris, Bibl. Nat., lat. 15128)*. *Anonymus,* Compendium musicae mensurabilis tam veteris quam novae artis *(Ms. Paris, Bibl. Nat., lat. 15128)*. *Anonymus,* De diversis maneriebus in musica mensurabili *(Ms. Saint-Dié, Bibl. Municipale 42)*, Corpus scriptorum de musica 30 [Rome].

Reaney, Gilbert, and André Gilles (eds.), 1974. *Franconis de Colonia, Ars cantus mensurabilis*, Corpus scriptorum de musica 18 [Rome].

Reckow, Fritz (ed.), 1967. *Der Musiktraktat des Anonymus 4* (2 vols.), Beihefte zum Archiv für Musikwissenschaft 4–5 (Wiesbaden).

————, 1972–2006. 'Rondellus/rondeau, rota', in Hans Heinrich Eggebrecht (ed.), *Handwörterbuch der musikalischen Terminologie*, vol. 5 (Stuttgart).

Reimer, Erich (ed.), 1972. *Johannes de Garlandia, De mensurabili musica: Kritische Edition mit Kommentar und Interpretation der Notationslehre* (2 vols.), Beihefte zum Archiv für Musikwissenschaft 10–11 (Wiesbaden).

Riemann, Hugo, 1884. *Musik-Lexikon*, 2nd ed. (Leipzig).

Rillon-Marne, Anne-Zoé, 2017. 'Les sources de la lyrique de Philippe le Chancelier: une approche pragmatique des collections liées au corpus', in Gilbert Dahan and Anne-Zoé Rillon-Marne (eds.), *Philippe le Chancelier, prédicateur, théologien et poète parisien du début du XIIIe siècle* (Turnhout), pp. 229–63.

Ripin, Edwin M., 1975. 'Towards an Identification of the Chekker', *The Galpin Society Journal*, 28, 11–25.

Robertson, Anne Walters, 1988. '*Benedicamus domino*: The Unwritten Tradition', *Journal of the American Musicological Society*, 41:1, 1–62.

————, 1995. 'Remembering the Annunciation in Medieval Polyphony', *Speculum*, 70:2, 275–304.

————, 2002. *Guillaume de Machaut and Reims: Context and Meaning in His Musical Works* (Cambridge).

————, 2012. 'The Seven Deadly Sins in Medieval Music', in Richard G. Newhauser and Susan J. Ridyard (eds.), *Sin in Medieval and Early Modern Culture: The Tradition of the Seven Deadly Sins* (York), pp. 191–222.

————, 2024. 'Two French Secular Motets in the Cyprus Codex and a New Composer from Cyprus', in Barale, Elisabetta, Alberto Rizzuti, and Angelica Staltari (eds.), *Il codice cipriota (I-Tn, J.II.19): Origini, storie, contesto culturale* (Venice), pp. 163–85.

Rockstro, William Smith, 1879–90. 'Modes, the Ecclesiastical', in George Grove (ed.), *A Dictionary of Music and Musicians (A.D. 1450–1880)* (London), vol. 2, pp. 340–43.

Roesner, Edward H., François Avril, and Nancy Freeman Regalado (eds.), 1990. *Le Roman de Fauvel in the Edition of Mesire Chaillou de Pesstain: A Reproduction in Facsimile of the Complete Manuscript, Paris, Bibliothèque Nationale, Fonds Français 146* (New York).

Rogers, Everett, 1962. *Diffusion of Innovations* (New York).

Rokseth, Yvonne, 1936. *Polyphonies du XIIIe siècle. Le manuscrit H 196 de la Faculté de médecine de Montpellier*, vol. 3 (Paris).

Roques, Mario (ed.), 1957. *L'Estoire de Griseldis en rimes et par personnages (1395)*, Textes littéraires français 74 (Geneva).

Rose-Steel, Tamsyn, 2011. 'French Ars Nova Motets and their Manuscripts: Citational Play and Material Context' (Ph.D. dissertation, University of Exeter).

Rosser, Gervase, 2015. *The Art of Solidarity in the Middle Ages: Guilds in England (1250–1550)* (Oxford).

Rossi, Carla, 2009. 'Autour d'Alain de Lille: nouvelles propositions', *Cahiers de civilisation médiévale*, 52, 415–26.

————, 2017. 'L'auteur des "Lettres familières d'un moine du Bec" attribuées à Alain de Lille', *Theory and Criticism of Literature and Arts*, 2:1, 27–44.

Rouse, Mary A., and Richard H. House, 1997. 'The Goldsmith and the Peacocks: Jean de le Mote in the Household of Simon de Lille, 1340', *Viator*, 28, 281–304.

Rouse, Richard H., and Mary A. Rouse, 2000. *Manuscripts and Their Makers: Commercial Book Producers in Medieval Paris (1200–1500)* (2 vols., Turnhout).

Rozier, Charles C., 2017. 'Symeon of Durham as Cantor and Historian at Durham Cathedral (c. 1090–1129)', in Katie Ann-Marie Bugyis, A. B. Kraebel, and Margot E. Fassler (eds.), *Medieval Cantors and Their Craft: Music, Liturgy and the Shaping of History (800–1500)* (York), pp. 190–206.

Runnalls, Graham A., 1981. 'René d'Anjou et le théâtre', *Annales de Bretagne et des pays de l'Ouest*, 88:2, 157–80.

———, 2002. 'La Passion de Mons (1501). Étude sur le texte et sur ses rapports avec la Passion d'Amiens (1500)', *Revue belge de philologie et d'histoire*, 80:4, 1143–88.

Ruys, Juanita Feros, 2014. *The Repentant Abelard: Family, Gender, and Ethics in Peter Abelard's* Carmen ad Astralabium *and* Planctus (New York).

Ryan, William Granger (ed. and trans.), 2012. *Jacobus de Voragine, The Golden Legend: Readings on the Saints* (Princeton).

Sachs, Klaus-Jürgen, 1990. 'Musikalische Elementarlehre im Mittelalter', in Frieder Zaminer (ed.), *Geschichte der Musiktheorie*, vol. 3, *Rezeption des antiken Fachs im Mittelalter* (Darmstadt), pp. 105–61.

Sáez-Hidalgo, Ana, Brian Gastle, and R. F. Yeager (eds.), 2017. *The Routledge Research Companion to John Gower* (Oxford and New York).

Saint-Cricq, Gaël, 2010. 'Formes types dans le motet du XIIIe siècle: étude d'un processus répétitif' (2 vols., Ph.D. dissertation, University of Southampton).

———, 2013. 'A New Link between the Motet and the Trouvère Chanson: The Pedes-Cum-Cauda Motet', *Early Music History*, 32, 179–223.

———, 2019. 'Genre, Attribution and Authorship in the Thirteenth Century: Robert de Reims vs "Robert de Rains"', *Early Music History*, 38, 141–213.

Saint-Cricq, Gaël, with Eglal Doss-Quinby and Samuel N. Rosenberg (eds.), 2017. *Motets from the Chansonnier de Noailles*, Middle Ages and Early Renaissance M042 (Middleton, WI).

Saltzstein, Jennifer, 2012. 'Cleric-trouvères and the Jeux-partis of Medieval Arras', *Viator*, 43:2, 147–63.

———, 2013. *The Refrain and the Rise of the Vernacular in Medieval French Music and Poetry* (Cambridge).

——— (ed.), 2019. *Musical Culture in the World of Adam de la Halle* (Leiden and Boston).

———, 2019. 'Adam de la Halle's Fourteenth-Century Musical and Poetic Legacies', in Jennifer Saltzstein (ed.), *Musical Culture in the World of Adam de la Halle* (Leiden and Boston), pp. 352–63.

Sanders, Ernest H., 1963. 'Medieval English Polyphony and Its Significance for the Continent' (Ph.D. dissertation, Columbia University).

———, 1965. 'Tonal Aspects of 13th-Century English Polyphony', *Acta Musicologica*, 37:1–2, 19–34.

———, 1967. 'The Question of Perotin's Oeuvre and Dates', in Ludwig Finscher and Christoph-Hellmut Mahling (eds.), *Festschrift für Walter Wiora* (Kassel), pp. 241–49.

————, 1975. 'The Early Motets of Philippe de Vitry', *Journal of the American Musicological Society*, 28:1, 24–45.

————, 1978. [Letter from Ernest H. Sanders], *Journal of the American Musicological Society*, 31:1, 168–73.

————, 1984. 'Style and Technique in Datable Polyphonic Notre-Dame Conductus', in Luther Dittmer (ed.), *Gordon Athol Anderson (1929–1981): In memoriam von seinen Studenten, Freunden und Kollegen* (2 vols., Henryville, Ottawa and Binningen), vol. 2, pp. 505–30.

————, 2001. 'Wycombe [Wicumbe, Whichbury, Winchecumbe], W. de.', *Grove Music Online*, https://doi.org/10.1093/gmo/9781561592630.article.30632.

Sanders, Ernest H., rev. Peter M. Lefferts, 2001. 'Petrus de Cruce', *Grove Music Online*, https://doi.org/10.1093/gmo/9781561592630.article.21491.

Saraceno, Filippo (ed.), 1882. 'Regesto dei principi di casa d'Acaja (1295–1418). Tratto dai conti di Tesoreria', in *Miscellanea di storia italiana* 20 (Turin), pp. 97–287.

Sarbak, Gábor, and Lorenz Weinrich (eds.), 2008. *Sicardi Cremonensis episcopi, Mitralis de officiis*, Corpus Christianorum. Continuatio Mediaevalis 228 (Turnhout).

Schering, Arnold (ed.), 1931. *Geschichte der Musik in Beispielen* (Leipzig).

Schmitt, Jean-Claude, (1989) 2001. 'La "découverte" de l'individu: une fiction historiographique?' in Paul Mengal and Françoise Parot (eds.), *La fabrique, la figure et la feinte. Fictions et statut des fictions en psychologie* (Paris), pp. 213–36. Repr. in *Le corps, les rites, les rêves, le temps. Essais d'anthropologie médiévale* (Paris), pp. 241–62.

Schofield, Bertram, 1948. 'The Provenance and Date of "Sumer is icumen in"', *Music Review*, 9, 81–86.

Scholes, Percy A., rev. John Owen Ward (ed.), 1970. *The Oxford Companion to Music*, 10th ed. (Oxford).

Schönbach, Anton Emanuel, 1874. *Über die Marienklagen: Ein Beitrag zur Geschichte der geistlichen Dichtungen in Deutschland* (Graz).

Schottmann, Hans, 2013. *Kleine Schriften* (Münster).

Schrade, Leo, 1956. 'Philippe de Vitry: Some New Discoveries', *The Musical Quarterly*, 42:3, 330–54.

———— (ed.), 1956. *The Works of Guillaume de Machaut*, vol. 2, Polyphonic Music of the Fourteenth Century 3 (Monaco).

Schumann, Otto, and Bernhard Bischoff (eds.), 1970. *Carmina Burana*, vol. 1, part 3, *Die Trink- und Spielerlieder, Die geistlichen Dramen* (Heidelberg).

Seay, Albert (ed.), 1975–78. *Johannes Tinctoris, Opera theoretica* (2 vols.), Corpus scriptorum de musica 22 [Rome].

Servet, Pierre (ed.), 1993. *Le Mystère de la Résurrection (Angers, 1456)* (2 vols.), Textes littéraires français 435 (Geneva).

———— (ed.), 2006. *Maistre Chevalet, la vie de sainct Christofle*, Textes littéraires français 579 (Geneva).

Shahar, Shulamith, 1993. 'Who Were Old in the Middle Ages?' *Social History of Medicine*, 6:3, 313–41.

Sharpe, R., J. P. Carley, R. M. Thomson, and A. G. Watson (eds.), 1996. *English Benedictine Libraries: The Shorter Catalogues*, Corpus of British Medieval Library Catalogues 4 (London).

Showerman, Grant (trans.), (1914) 1947. *Ovid, Heroides and Amores* ([Cambridge]; repr. London and New York).

Sigebert of Gembloux. *Chronica*, PL 160. 57–240.

Silvas, Anna (trans. and intr.), 1999. *Jutta and Hildegard: The Biographical Sources* (University Park).

Singer, Julie, 2016. 'Lyrical Humor(s) in the "Fumeur" Songs', in Blake Howe, Stephanie Jensen-Moulton, Neil Lerner, and Joseph Straus (eds.), *The Oxford Handbook of Music and Disability Studies* (Oxford), pp. 497–516.

Smits van Waesberghe, Joseph (ed.), 1950. *Johannes Affligemensis, De musica cum tonario*, Corpus scriptorum de musica 1 [Rome].

——— (ed.), 1955. *Guidonis Aretini, Micrologus*, Corpus scriptorum de musica 4 [Rome].

Smits van Waesberghe, Joseph, and Eduard Vetter (eds.), 1985. *Guidonis Aretini, Regulae rhythmicae*, Divitiae musicae artis A.IV (Buren).

Sowa, Heinrich, 1935. *Quellen zur Transformation der Antiphonen: Tonar- und Rhythmusstudien* (Kassel).

Spanke, Hans, 1955. *G. Raynauds Bibliographie des altfranzösischen Liedes*, vol. 1 (Leiden).

Stäblein, Bruno, 1968. '"Gregorius Praesul", der Prolog zum römischen Antiphonale', in Richard Baum and Wolfgang Rehm (eds.), *Musik und Verlag: Karl Vötterle zum 65. Geburtstag am 12. April 1968* (Kassel), pp. 537–61.

Steiner, Ruth, 1969. 'The Prosulae of the MS Paris, Bibliothèque Nationale, f. lat. 1118', *Journal of the American Musicological Society*, 22:3, 367–93.

Šter, Katarina, 2014. 'Resacralization of the Sacred: Carthusian Liturgical Plainchant and (Re)biblicization of Its Texts', *Muzikološki zbornik*, 50:2, 157–80.

Stevens, John, 1986. *Words and Music in the Middle Ages* (Cambridge).

Stoessel, Jason, 2012. 'A New Composition by Denis Le Grant', https://jjstoessel. blog/2012/01/11/a-new-composition-by-denis-le-grant/.

Stone, Anne, 2002. 'The Ars subtilior in Paris', *Musica e storia*, 10:2, 373–404.

Stones, Alison, 1990. 'Prolegomena to a Corpus of Vincent of Beauvais Illustrations', in Serge Lusignan, Monique Paulmier-Foucart, and Alain Nadeau (eds.), *Vincent de Beauvais. Intentions et réceptions d'une œuvre encyclopédique au Moyen-Âge* (Montreal and Paris), pp. 301–44.

———, 1993. 'The Illustrated Chrétien Manuscripts and Their Artistic Context', in Keith Busby, Terry Nixon, Alison Stones, and Lori Walters (eds.), *Les manuscrits de Chrétien de Troyes* (2 vols., Amsterdam and Atlanta), vol. 1, pp. 227–322.

———, 1998. 'The Artistic Context of the *Roman de Fauvel* with a Note on *Fauvain*', in Margaret Bent and Andrew Wathey (eds.), *Fauvel Studies: Allegory, Chronicle, Music, and Image in Paris, Bibliothèque Nationale de France, MS Français 146* (Oxford), pp. 529–67.

———, 2009. 'Honoré d'Amiens (1288)', in Andreas Beyer, Bénédicte Savoy, and Wolf Tegethoff (eds.), *Allgemeines Künstlerlexikon Online*, https://www. degruyter.com/database/AKL/entry/_00143330/html.

———, 2013–14. *Gothic Manuscripts (1260–1320)* (4 vols., London and Turnhout).

———, 2018. 'Style and Iconography of Montpellier folio 350r', in Catherine A. Bradley and Karen Desmond (eds.), *The Montpellier Codex: The Final Fascicle: Contents, Contexts, Chronologies* (Woodbridge), pp. 66–77.

———, 2020. 'Pen-Flourished Decoration', in Frank T. Coulson and Robert G. Babcock (eds.), *The Oxford Handbook of Latin Palaeography* (Oxford), pp. 674–90.

———, forthcoming. 'Notes on a Little-Known French Thirteenth-Century Psalter-Hours: Texts, Decoration, and Illustration', *Rivista di Storia de la Miniatura*.

Story, Christina Maria Nest, 2007. 'Music and Musicians in the Court and City of Paris during the Reign of Charles VI (1380–1420)' (Ph.D. dissertation, Royal Holloway, University of London).

Suckale, Robert, 2006. 'Stilgeschichte zu Beginn des 21. Jahrhunderts: Probleme und Möglichkeiten', in Bruno Klein and Bruno Boerner (eds.), *Stilfragen zur Kunst des Mittelalters: Eine Einführung* (Berlin), pp. 271–81.

Sullivan, Thomas, 2004. *Parisian Licentiates in Theology, A.D. 1373–1500: A Biographical Register*, vol. 1, *The Religious Orders* (Leiden).

Sweeney, Cecily, and André Gilles (eds.), 1971. *Anonymous, De musica mensurabili. Anonymous, De semibrevis caudatis*, Corpus scriptorum de musica 13 [Rome].

Symes, Carol, 2007. *A Common Stage: Theater and Public Life in Medieval Arras* (Ithaca, NY).

———, 2019. 'The "School of Arras" and the Career of Adam', in Jennifer Saltzstein (ed.), *Musical Culture in the World of Adam de la Halle* (Leiden and Boston), pp. 21–50.

Symons, Thomas (ed. and trans.), 1953. *The Monastic Agreement of the Monks and Nuns of the English Nation* (London).

Szövérffy, Josef (ed.), 1965. *Die Annalen der lateinischen Hymnendichtung: Ein Handbuch*, vol. 2 (Berlin).

Tackels, Bruno, 2015. *Les écritures de plateau. État des lieux* (Paris).

Taruskin, Richard, 2010. *Music from the Earliest Notations to the Sixteenth Century* (New York).

Tasis, Rafael, 1959. *Joan I, el rei caçador i músic* (Barcelona).

Taucci, Raffaele, 1934–35. 'Fra Andrea dei Servi: Organista e compositore del trecento', *Studi storici sull'Ordine dei Servi di Maria*, 2:2, 73–108.

Taylor, Andrew, 2002. *Textual Situations: Three Medieval Manuscripts and Their Readers* (Philadelphia).

Theodericus Epternacensis. *Vita sanctae Hildegardis virginis*, PL 197. 91–130.

Thibodeau, Timothy M. (ed. and trans.), 2015. *William Durand, Rationale V: Commentary on the Divine Office*, Corpus Christianorum in Translation 23 (Turnhout).

Thomasseau, Jean-Marie, 2010. 'Pour une génétique du théâtre non contemporain. Traces, objets, méthodes', in Almuth Grésillon, Marie-Madeleine Mervant-Roux, and Dominique Budor (eds.), *Genèses théâtrales* (Paris), pp. 233–48.

Thomson, Matthew, 2018. 'Building a Motet around Quoted Material: Textual and Musical Structure in Motets Based on Monophonic Songs', in Jared C. Hartt (ed.), *A Critical Companion to Medieval Motets* (Woodbridge), pp. 243–60.

Thoraval, Fañch, 2021. 'Dévotion, liturgie, performativité. "Religion royale" et "géographie religieuse" dans les motets du manuscrit Turin J.II.9 et les offices du Saint-Sépulcre', in Gisèle Clément, Isabelle Fabre, Gilles Polizzi, and Fañch Thoraval (eds.), *Poésie et musique à l'âge de l'Ars subtilior. Autour du manuscrit Torino, BNU, J.II.9* (Turnhout), pp. 145–66.

Thurston, Ethel (ed.), 1970. *The Works of Perotin* (New York).

Tischler, Hans (ed.), 1978–85. *The Montpellier Codex* (4 vols.; vol. 4 trans. Susan Stakel and Joel C. Relihan), Recent Researches in the Music of the Middle Ages and Early Renaissance 2–8 (Madison).

——— (ed.), 2005. *The Earliest Polyphonic Art Music: The 150 Two-Part Conductus in the Notre-Dame Manuscripts* (2 vols.), [Institute of Medieval Music] Collected works 24 (Ottawa).

Tissier, André (ed.), 1997. *Recueil de farces (1450–1550)*, vol. 9 (Genève).

Traill, David A., 2003. 'Philip the Chancellor and F10: Expanding the Canon', *Filologia mediolatina*, 10, 219–48.

———, 2006a. 'A Cluster of Poems by Philip the Chancellor in *Carmina Burana* 21–36', *Studi medievali*, 3rd ser., 47, 267–85.

———, 2006b. 'More Poems by Philip the Chancellor', *The Journal of Medieval Latin*, 16, 164–81.

——— (ed. and trans.), 2013. *Walter of Châtillon, The Shorter Poems: Christmas Hymns, Love Lyrics and Moral-Satirical Verse* (Oxford).

——— (ed. and trans.), 2018. *Carmina Burana* (2 vols.), Dumbarton Oaks Medieval Library 48–49 (Cambridge, MA).

Trapp, Damasus, 1956. 'Augustinian Theology of the 14th Century: Notes on Editions, Marginalia, Opinions and Book-Lore', *Augustiniana*, 6, 146–274.

Treitler, Leo, 1974. 'Homer and Gregory: The Transmission of Epic Poetry and Plainchant', *Musical Quarterly*, 60:3, 333–72.

——— (ed.), 1998. *Strunk's Source Readings in Music History*, rev. ed. (7 vols., New York).

Trovato, Paolo, 2014. *Everything You Always Wanted to Know about Lachmann's Method: A Non-Standard Handbook of Genealogical Textual Criticism in the Age of Post-Structuralism, Cladistics, and Copy-Text* (Padova).

Trowell, Brian, 1957. 'A Fourteenth-Century Ceremonial Motet and Its Composer', *Acta Musicologica*, 29:2–3, 65–75.

Unger, Carl Richard (ed.), 1871. *Mariu Saga: Legender om Jomfru Maria og Hendes Jertegn*, vol. 2 (Christiana).

Unruh, Patricia, 1983. '"Fumeur" Poetry and Music of the Chantilly Codex: A Study of Its Meaning and Background' (MA dissertation, University of British Columbia).

Valois, Jean de (ed. and arr.), 1957. *Pérotin 'le Grand', E Semine rosa. Reconstitution modale d'après le ms. Ed. IV. 6 de Bamberg* (Paris).

Van Acker, Lieven (ed.),1993. *Hildegardis Bingensis, Epistolarium II*, Corpus Christianorum. Continuatio Mediaevalis 91A (Turnhout).

Van der Werf, Hendrik, 1965. 'The Trouvère Chansons as Creations of a Notionless Musical Culture', *Current Musicology*, 1, 61–68.

————, 1972. *The Chansons of the Troubadours and Trouvères: A Study of the Melodies and Their Relation to the Poems* (Utrecht).

———— (ed.), 1977–79. *Trouvères – Melodien* (2 vols.), Monumenta monodica medii aevi 11–12 (Kassel, Basel, and Tours).

————, 1992. 'Anonymous IV as Chronicler', *Musicology Australia*, 15:1, 3–13.

Van Drival, Eugène (ed.), 1878. *Nécrologe de l'Abbaye de Saint-Vaast d'Arras publié pour la première fois au nom de l'académie d'Arras* (Arras).

Vidier, Alexandre, 1901. 'Notes et documents sur le personnel, les biens et l'administration de la Sainte-Chapelle du XIIIe au XVe siècle', *Mémoires de la Société de l'histoire de Paris et de l'Île-de-France*, 28, 213–383.

Vincent, Catherine, 2000. 'Fraternité rêvée et lien social fortifié. La confrérie Notre-Dame des Ardents à Arras (début du XIIIe siècle–XVe siècle)', *Revue du Nord*, 82:337, 659–79.

Vivell, P. Cölestin (ed.), 1919. *Frutolfi Breviarium de musica et Tonarium*, Philosophisch-historische Klasse. Sitzungsberichte 188/2 (Vienna).

Vizkelety, András, 1985. 'Der Löwener Kodex: Bilanz der Forschung – neue Ergebnisse – weitere Aufgaben', *Hungarian Studies*, 1:1, 19–29.

————, 1986a. 'Die Altungarische Marienklage und die mit ihr überlieferte Texte', *Acta Litteraria*, 28, 3–27.

————, 1986b. *Világ világa, virágnak virága …'* [Ómagyar Mária-Siralom] (Budapest).

Waddell, Chrysogonus, 1970. 'The Origin and Early Evolution of the Cistercian Antiphonary: Reflections on Two Cistercian Chant Reforms', in M. Basil Pennington (ed.), *The Cistercian Spirit: A Symposium in Memory of Thomas Merton* (Spencer, MA), pp. 190–223.

Wahlgren-Smith, Lena, 2006. Review of 'Françoise Hudry (ed.), *Alain de Lille (?). Lettres familières (1167–1170)'*, *Speculum*, 81:2, 536–37.

Waite, William G., 1961. 'The Abbreviation of the "Magnus liber"', *Journal of the American Musicological Society*, 14:2, 147–58.

Walters, Lori J., 1996. 'Wonders and Illuminations: Pierart dou Thielt and the *Queste del saint Graal*', in Keith Busby (ed.), *Word and Image in Arthurian Literature* (New York), pp. 339–80.

Wathey, Andrew, 1988. 'Lost Books of Polyphony in England: A List to 1500', *Royal Musical Association Research Chronicle*, 21, 1–19.

————, 1993a. *Manuscripts of Polyphonic Music: Supplement to RISM B/IV, 1–2: The British Isles (1100–1400)* (Munich).

————, 1993b. 'The Motets of Philippe de Vitry and the Fourteenth-Century Renaissance', *Early Music History*, 12, 119–50.

————, 1994. 'The Motet Texts of Philippe de Vitry in German Humanist Manuscripts of the Fifteenth Century', in John Kmetz (ed.), *Music in the German Renaissance: Sources, Styles, and Contexts* (Cambridge), pp. 195–201.

Webber, Teresa, 2017. 'Cantor, Sacrist or Prior? The Provision of Books in Anglo-Norman England', in Katie Ann-Marie Bugyis, A. B. Kraebel, and Margot E. Fassler (eds.), *Medieval Cantors and Their Craft: Music, Liturgy and the Shaping of History (800–1500)* (York), pp. 172–89.

Wegman, Rob C., 1996. 'From Maker to Composer: Improvisation and Musical Authorship in the Low Countries (1450–1500)', *Journal of the American Musicological Society*, 49:3, 409–79.

——, 2003. 'New Music for a World Grown Old: Martin Le Franc and the "Contenance Angloise"', *Acta Musicologica*, 75:2, 201–41.

——, 2016. 'Jacobus de Ispania and Liège', *Journal of the Alamire Foundation*, 8:2, 253–74.

—— (trans.), 2017. *Jacobus de Ispania, The Mirror of Music: Book the Seventh* (Lexington, KY).

Weinrich, Lorenz, 1969. 'Peter Abaelard as Musician', *Musical Quarterly*, 55:3, 295–312 (part 1); 55:4, 464–86 (part 2).

Weiss, Valentine (ed.), 2012. *La demeure médiévale à Paris. Répertoire sélectif des principaux hôtels* (Paris).

Wenzel, Siegfried, 2015. *Medieval 'Artes Praedicandi': A Synthesis of Scholastic Sermon Structure* (Toronto).

Weston, Jessie L., and Joseph Bédier, 1906. 'Tristan ménestrel, extrait de la continuation de Perceval par Gerbert', *Romania*, 35, 497–530.

Wibberley, Roger, 1976. 'English Polyphonic Music of the Late Thirteenth and Early Fourteenth Centuries: A Reconstruction, Transcription, and Commentary' (D.Phil. thesis, Oxford University).

Wilken, Ernst Heinrich, 1872. *Geschichte der geistlichen Spiele in Deutschland* (Göttingen).

Wilkins, Ernest H., 1951. 'Maria ... Prete', *Italica*, 28:2, 101–3.

Wilkins, Nigel (ed.), 1967. *The Lyric Works of Adam de la Hale (Chansons, Jeux-partis, Rondeaux, Motets)*, Corpus Mensurabilis Musicae 44 [Rome].

——, 1974. 'Music in the Fourteenth Century *Miracles de Nostre Dame*', *Musica Disciplina*, 28, 39–75.

Williamson, Amy, 2016. 'Genre, Taxonomy and Repertory in Insular Polyphony of the "Long Thirteenth Century" (c. 1150–c. 1350)' (Ph.D. dissertation, University of Southampton).

Wilmart, André, 1937. 'Poèmes de Gautier de Châtillon dans un manuscrit de Charleville', *Revue bénédictine*, 49, 121–69 (part 1); 322–65 (part 2).

Wilton, Peter, 1998. 'The Transmission of the Alleluia Prosula: Stability, Variation and Change' (Ph.D. dissertation, Royal Holloway, University of London).

Winiarski, M. Victoria Rodríguez, 2017. '*Vidas* and *razos*', http://www.trob-eu.net/en/vidas-and-razos.html.

Wittekind, Susanne, 2008. 'Die mittelalterliche Verwendung spätantiker Elfenbeine', in Dietrich Boschung and Susanne Wittekind (eds.), *Persistenz und Rezeption: Weiterverwendung, Wiederverwendung und Neuinterpretation antiker Werke im Mittelalter* (Wiesbaden), pp. 285–317.

Wolf, Johannes, 1914. 'Ein Beitrag zur Diskantlehre des 14. Jahrhunderts', *Sammelbände der Internationalen Musikgesellschaft*, 15:3, 505–34.

Wolinski, Mary E., 1992. 'The Compilation of the Montpellier Codex', *Early Music History*, 11, 263–301.

———, 2018. 'How Rhythmically Innovative Is Montpellier 8?', in Catherine A. Bradley and Karen Desmond (eds.), *The Montpellier Codex: The Final Fascicle: Contents, Contexts, Chronologies* (Woodbridge), pp. 184–96.

Wright, Craig, 1979. *Music at the Court of Burgundy (1364–1419): A Documentary History* (Henryville, Ottawa and Binningen).

Yearley, Janthia, 1981. 'A Bibliography of Planctus', *Journal of the Plainsong and Mediaeval Music Society*, 4, 12–52.

———, 1983. 'The Medieval Latin Planctus as a Genre' (3 vols., Ph.D. dissertation, University of York).

Young, Karl, 1933. *The Drama of the Medieval Church* (2 vols., Oxford).

Yudkin, Jeremy (ed. and trans.), 1990. *De musica mensurata: The Anonymous of St Emmeram, Complete Critical Edition, Translation and Commentary* (Bloomington, IN).

Yver, Jean, 1990. '"Vavassor". Note sur les premiers emplois du terme', *Annales de Normandie*, 40:1, 31–48.

Zanovello, Giovanni, 2014. '"In the Church and in the Chapel": Music and Devotional Spaces in the Florentine Church of Santissima Annunziata', *Journal of the American Musicological Society*, 67:2, 379–428.

Zayaruznaya, Anna, 2018. 'New Voices for Vitry', *Early Music*, 46:3, 375–92.

———, 2020. 'Old, New, and Newer Still in Book 7 of the *Speculum musice*', *Journal of the American Musicological Society*, 73:1, 95–148.

———, forthcoming. *The Making of Philippe de Vitry*.

Zazulia, Emily, 2018. 'A Motet Ahead of Its Time? The Curious Case of *Portio nature/Ida capillorum*', in Jared C. Hartt (ed.), *A Critical Companion to Medieval Motets* (Woodbridge), pp. 341–54.

Zimei, Francesco, 2018. 'Un elenco veneto di composizioni del Trecento con inedite attribuzioni a Marchetto da Padova e altre novità', *Recercare*, 30:1–2, 5–14.

Zingesser, Eliza, 2019. 'The Poets of the North: Economies of Literature and Love', in Jennifer Saltzstein (ed.), *Musical Culture in the World of Adam de la Halle* (Leiden and Boston), pp. 51–75.

Zink, Michel (ed. and trans.), 2001. *Rutebeuf. Œuvres complètes*, rev. ed. (Paris).

Ziolkowski, Jan M., 2004. 'Women's Lament and the Neuming of the Classics', in John Haines and Randall Rosenfeld (eds.), *Music and Medieval Manuscripts: Paleography and Performance: Essays Dedicated to Andrew Hughes* (Aldershot), pp. 128–50.

Index of Sources

Index of Proper Nouns and Places

Index of Works

Studies in Medieval and Renaissance Music

Volumes already published

Machaut's Music: New Interpretations
edited by Elizabeth Eva Leach

The Church Music of Fifteenth-Century Spain
Kenneth Kreitner

The Royal Chapel in the time of the Habsburgs:
Music and Court Ceremony in Early Modern Europe
edited by Juan José Carreras and Bernardo García García

Citation and Authority in Medieval and Renaissance Musical Culture:
Learning from the Learned. Essays in Honour of Margaret Bent
edited by Suzannah Clark and Elizabeth Eva Leach

European Music, 1520–1640
edited by James Haar

Cristóbal de Morales:
Sources, Influences, Reception
edited by Owen Rees and Bernadette Nelson

Young Choristers, 650–1700
edited by Susan Boynton and Eric Rice

Hermann Pötzlinger's Music Book:
The St Emmeram Codex and its Contexts
Ian Rumbold with Peter Wright

Medieval Liturgical Chant and Patristic Exegesis:
Words and Music in the Second-Mode Tracts
Emma Hornby

Juan Esquivel: A Master of Sacred Music during the Spanish Golden Age
Clive Walkley

Essays on Renaissance Music in Honour of David Fallows:
Bon jour, bon mois et bonne estrenne
edited by Fabrice Fitch and Jacobijn Kiel

Music and Ceremony at the Court of Charles V:
The *Capilla Flamenca* and the Art of Political Promotion
Mary Tiffany Ferer

Music and Meaning in Old Hispanic Lenten Chants:
Psalmi, Threni and the Easter Vigil Canticles
Emma Hornby and Rebecca Maloy

Music in Elizabethan Court Politics
Katherine Butler

Verse and Voice in Byrd's Song Collections of 1588 and 1589
Jeremy L. Smith

The Montpellier Codex: The Final Fascicle. Contents, Contexts, Chronologies
edited by Catherine A. Bradley and Karen Desmond

A Critical Companion to Medieval Motets
edited by Jared C. Hartt

Piety and Polyphony in Sixteenth-Century Holland:
The Choirbooks of St Peter's Church, Leiden
Eric Jas

Music, Myth and Story in Medieval and Early Modern Culture
edited by Katherine Butler and Samantha Bassler

The Segovia Manuscript: A European Musical Repertory in Spain, c.1500
edited by Wolfgang Fuhrmann and Cristina Urchueguía

Revisiting the Codex Buranus: Contents, Contexts, Composition
edited by Tristan E. Franklinos and Henry Hope

Music and Instruments of the Middle Ages
edited by Tess Knighton and David Skinner

The Dorse Rotulus: Contextualizing and Reconstructing the Early English Motet
Margaret Bent, Jared C. Hartt and Peter M. Lefferts

A Medieval Songbook: Trouvère MS C
edited by Elizabeth Eva Leach, Joseph W. Mason and Matthew P. Thomson

Printed in the United States
by Baker & Taylor Publisher Services